Accession no.
01_____

D0486906

Virtual Society?

'This book shows the essential contribution of social sciences to the understanding of the network society, our society. Based on scholarly research, it provides a rigorous account of the diverse effects of information and communication technologies on the social fabric of our lives. It is a great antidote to the mythologies and media hype on this critical subject matter.'

Manuel Castells, Professor of Sociology, University of California at Berkeley

'This stunning volume is obligatory reading for all those studying "cyberspace" and its contents and discontents. It is one of the first deep empirical studies of this scope analyzing the changes occasioned by the widespread development of networked information technologies. A subtle, intertwined scholarly effort, this book is a landmark achievement, marking the maturity of social studies of computing and IT.'

Susan Leigh Star, Professor of Communication,
University of California at San Diego

'From Woolgar's "five rules of virtuality" to Pollner's delightful account of his adventures as a dot com investor, this challenging collection will be essential reading for all of those interested in the social relations of the new information technologies.'

Donald MacKenzie, Professor of Sociology, Edinburgh University;
Author of Inventing Accuracy

'This work shows social scientists seriously getting to grips with the complexities of the social implications of electronic technologies. It should also be read widely beyond this community, stimulating dialogue with others working in the area, such as industry practitioners, government planners, and academics from other disciplines and societies.'

Geoff Walsham, Professor of Management Studies, Judge Institute,
University of Cambridge

Virtual Society?

Technology, Cyberbole, Reality

STEVE WOOLGAR

LIBRARY		
ACC. No. 01139063	DEPT. pSS	3 wk
CLASS No. 303.4833		WOO
UNIVERSITY COLLEGE CHESTER WARRINGTON CAMPUS		

OXFORD
UNIVERSITY PRESS

OXFORD
UNIVERSITY PRESS

Great Clarendon Street, Oxford OX2 6DP

Oxford University Press is a department of the University of Oxford.
It furthers the University's objective of excellence in research, scholarship,
and education by publishing worldwide in

Oxford New York

Auckland Bangkok Buenos Aires Cape Town Chennai
Dar es Salaam Delhi Hong Kong Istanbul Karachi Kolkata
Kuala Lumpur Madrid Melbourne Mexico City Mumbai Nairobi
São Paulo Shanghai Taipei Tokyo Toronto

Oxford is a registered trade mark of Oxford University Press
in the UK and in certain other countries

Published in the United States
by Oxford University Press Inc., New York

© The Various Contributors, 2002

The moral rights of the authors have been asserted
Database right Oxford University Press (maker)

First published 2002

All rights reserved. No part of this publication may be reproduced,
stored in a retrieval system, or transmitted, in any form or by any means,
without the prior permission in writing of Oxford University Press,
or as expressly permitted by law, or under terms agreed with the appropriate
reprographics rights organization. Enquiries concerning reproduction
outside the scope of the above should be sent to the Rights Department,
Oxford University Press, at the address above

You must not circulate this book in any other binding or cover
and you must impose this same condition on any acquirer

British Library Cataloguing in Publication Data

Data available

Library of Congress Cataloging in Publication Data

Virtual society? get real! : the social science of electronic technologies / [edited by]
Steve Woolgar.
 p. cm.
Includes bibliographical references and index.
1. Information technology—Social aspects. 2. Internet—Social aspects.
I. Woolgar, Steve.
HM851 V58 2002   303.48'33—dc21   2002074289
ISBN 0-19-924875-3 (hbk.)
ISBN 0-19-924876-1 (pbk.)

10 9 8 7 6 5 4 3 2

Typeset by Newgen Imaging Systems (P) Ltd., Chennai, India
Printed in Great Britain
on acid-free paper by
Biddles Ltd., Guildford and King's Lynn

PREFACE

The chapters in this collection (with exceptions, below) result from research carried out under the auspices of the ESRC funded research programme—*Virtual Society? the social science of electronic technologies*. This Programme was a £3m research investment running from 1997–2001, comprising 22 interrelated research projects and 76 researchers working at 25 universities in Britain (and at 4 universities overseas). The Programme was directed initially from CRICT (Centre for Research into Innovation, Culture and Technology) at Brunel University and subsequently from the Saïd Business School at the University of Oxford. A key strategic objective of the Programme was to establish a UK research sector in the area of social impacts of electronic technologies. This effort is widely regarded as pre-eminent in academic circles throughout the world. The emerging results have also proved influential in business, industry, and government.

The Programme organization enabled an unusually high degree of synthesis and cross collaboration between projects with otherwise distinct disciplinary origins, and this is reflected in the present collection. Throughout the Programme, research project teams met, presented and, discussed their work with each other at six-monthly Synthesis Meetings attended by all Programme researchers. In addition, groups of projects organized and conducted a separate series of 'academic topic meetings' around common themes and findings. For this volume, project leaders were given the brief to write a chapter which reports and discusses some of the most significant findings to emerge from their research, and to organize their discussion around the question of the relation between the virtual and the real. Earlier versions of all the chapters were presented and discussed as part of an international conference held at Ashridge in May 2000, entitled *Virtual Society? Get Real!* (which was also the title originally proposed for this volume). The conference brought together 150 national and international researchers working both in and beyond the Virtual Society? Programme. Keynote speakers were invited on the basis that they would respond to some of the central concerns and findings emerging from the research. Three chapters by non-Programme members (Geoff Cooper and colleagues, Mel Pollner, and Marilyn Strathern) are included because they especially fit the central themes of the collection. Much credit for this volume goes to the army of anonymous referees, both internal and external to the programme, as well as to the publisher's anonymous readers and reviewers, who offered detailed comment and advice on the chapters as they were being developed.

The collection offers a flavour of some of the research resulting from Virtual Society? auspices. Inevitably, however, space restrictions necessitated difficult decisions about inclusion in this volume; less than two thirds of the programme projects are represented here. So it should be emphasized that this particular selection does scant justice to the full range of activities, contributions, and outputs of programme members, nor to their considerable energy and commitment to the cause. This collection presents some significant outcomes, but certainly does not stand as a complete account of all the research, let alone a comprehensive overview. A fuller record of the publications, activities and outputs can be found at the programme website: www.virtualsociety.org.uk

At Brunel University, CRICT provided an enormously supportive intellectual base from which to pursue a national programme. My thanks go especially to Christine Hine, Richard Hull, Alan Irwin, Janet Low, Mike Lynch, Ruth McNally, David Oswell, Julian Petley, Dick Pels, Frederic Vandenberghe, Janet Vaux, Andrea Buchholz, Marike van Harskamp, Daniel Neyland, and Andrea Whittle. As Programme Director I was privileged to be able to act as spokesperson on behalf of a considerable, widely dispersed research effort, and I am enormously grateful as much for the widespread 'good citizenship' among my colleagues as for their stimulating and persistent intelligence in helping move forward the research agenda in this important domain. I especially value their support in addressing the intellectual challenge which increasingly characterizes contemporary scholarship, the project of outreach and relevance to 'users', of making the value of top-class academic Social-Science evident to 'unsuspecting captains of industry'. Many of the latter also proved to be an invaluable resource in engaging with, and assisting the definition and development of the research. My special thanks go to Geoff Robinson for his wise and sympathetic counsel and to the other members of a lively Advisory Committee: John Leighfield, Sonia Livingstone, Geoff McMullen, Elizabeth Mills, and Paul Williams. I was fortunate to work with three outstanding Programme Administrators: my thanks for their excellent support to Donna Page, Caroline Ingram and, especially for her tireless assistance in compiling this volume, to Sara Ward.

Finally, I thank Otto Imken for stimulating the neologism in the subtitle. Cyberbole (pronounced saɪ·bə·ɹbŏlɪ) is borrowed with a slightly adapted spelling from Imken (1999: 102) and denotes the exaggerated depiction (hyperbole) of the capacities of virtual (cyber) technologies.

SWW
Wolvercote
June 2001

CONTENTS

LIST OF FIGURES AND BOXES

Figures

Boxes

ABBREVIATIONS

3GM	third-generation mobile
AOL	America Online
ARPANET	Advanced Research Projects Agency Network
B2B	business to business
B2C	business to consumer
CAD	computer-aided design
CB	Citizens' Band
CCTV	closed circuit television
CEC	Commission of the European Communities
CER	Centre for Employment Research
CFS	Chronic Fatigue Syndrome
CIIR	Catholic Institute for International Relations
CITU	Central Information Technology Unit
CMC	computer-mediated communication
DfEE	Department for Education and Employment
DCMS	Department for Culture, Media, and Sport
DoE	Department of the Environment
DTI	Department of Trade and Industry
DVLA	Driver and Vehicle Licensing Authority
EC	European Commission
G-MING	Greater Manchester Information Network Group
HE	higher education
HEFCE	Higher Education Funding Council for England
HIT	Human Interface Technology
HRM	human resource management
ICQ	'I seek you' (communications software)
ICT	information and communications technology
IEE	Institution of Electrical Engineers
I/I	investment/internet
IP	internet protocol
IPO	Initial Public Offering
IPPR	Institute for Public Policy Research

IRC   internet relay chat (rooms)
ISDN   Integrated Services Digital Network
ISP   Internet Service Provider
ITC   Independent Television Commission
ITV   Independent Television
MAN   Manchester Area Network
MC   market capitalization
MCIN   Manchester Communities Information Network
MLM   Managing Local Markets
MMU   Manchester Metropolitan University
MSIM   Museum of Science and Industry in Manchester
MUD   multi-user domain
NOP   National Opinion Poll
NTIA   National Telecommunications and Information Administration
OECD   Organization for Economic Cooperation and Development
OMG   Operations Management Group
QAA   Quality Assurance Agency
RAE   Research Assessment Exercise
SIDE   Social Identity Model of Depersonalization Effects
SME   small to medium-sized enterprise
SNU   Safe Neighbourhoods Unit
SRHE   Society for Research into Higher Education
TQA   Teaching Quality Assessment
UMIST   University of Manchester Institute of Science and Technology
UNDP   United Nations Development Program
VR   virtual reality
WEVH   Women's Electronic Village Hall

NOTES ON CONTRIBUTORS

Jon Agar, University of London   Jon is an honorary Visiting Research Fellow at the Department of Science and Technology Studies, University College, London. Recent books include *Turing and the Universal Machine* (Icon) and *Science and Spectacle* (Harwood Academic). Before moving to London, he was Lecturer in History of Technology and Director of the National Archive for the History of Computing at the Centre for History of Science, Technology and Medicine, University of Manchester.

Steven Brown, Loughborough University   Steve is Lecturer in Psychology at Loughborough University. His research interests are around the social shaping of new technologies, the cultural performance of stress and emotion, and poststructuralism and social theory. He is co-author of two books, *Psychology without Foundations* and *Social Remembering* (both forthcoming from Sage in 2003).

Roger Burrows, University of York   Roger is a Reader in Social Policy and Co-Director of the Centre for Housing Policy at the University of York. He has carried out research and published on issues in housing, health, and social aspects of ICTs.

Graham Button, XRCE, Cambridge   Graham's research interests are within ethnomethodology and conversational analysis, and generally concern the specification of order in the workings of commonplace action, interaction, and society. He joined the Xerox Research Centre Europe's Cambridge Laboratory in September 1992 and is now the Director.

Sally Coates, University of Plymouth   Sally worked as Research Assistant on the Virtual Society? project at Plymouth University until September 2000. Previously she completed her Social Science Degree and Masters in Sociology at Manchester Metropolitan University.

Geoff Cooper, University of Surrey   Geoff is a Senior Lecturer in the Department of Sociology at the University of Surrey. His research interests are in science and technology studies, and in theoretical issues in social science. He is currently doing research on the shaping of mobile telecommunications, and on theoretical and deconstructive approaches to knowledge transformation.

Charles Crook, Loughborough University   Charles did doctoral research at the Cambridge Psychological Laboratory and has since held positions relating to developmental psychology at Brown, Strathclyde, and Durham universities. Currently he is Reader in Psychology at Loughborough. Lately his research has concerned use of new technology by young people in both recreational and educational settings. The goal of this work has been to contribute to building a more cultural version of psychology.

Nicola Green, University of Surrey   Nicola is a Lecturer in New Media and New Technologies in the Department of Sociology at the University of Surrey. Her research interests are in the intersections of technology, culture, gender, embodiment, and design. Her recent publications include *Wireless World*, with B. Brown and R. Harper (Springer Verlag), and a number of articles on mobile technologies and virtual reality technologies.

Sarah Green, University of Manchester   Sarah obtained her Ph.D. in Social Anthropology at the University of Cambridge. She is now a Lecturer at the University of Manchester. Her ongoing research interests include issues of sexuality and gender, the changing conditions in which people are negotiating their conception of themselves, particularly the asserted 'globalizing' effects of the Internet.

Richard Harper, University of Surrey   Richard is Director of the Digital World Research Centre, University of Surrey. Throughout the past ten years, he has researched the use of sociological and interdisciplinary techniques for specifying user requirements for new technologies in organizational, mobile, and domestic life. His most recent books include *The Myth of the Paperless Office* with A. J. Sellen (MIT Press), and *Wireless World*, with B. Brown and N. Green (Springer Verlag).

Penelope Harvey, University of Manchester   Penny is Professor in Social Anthropology at the University of Manchester. Her ethnographic study of the social and cultural dynamics of technological innovation in Manchester reflects her long-term interest in the objectification of relationships and skills, on how people attribute meaning to things, and on the social and political understandings that are implied in such practice.

John A. Hughes, Lancaster University   John is based in the Department of Sociology at Lancaster University. His main interests are in ethnomethodology and, for the last decade or so, he has been involved in a number of research projects working with computer scientists in trying to relate fieldwork to system design.

David Knights, Keele University David is Professor of Organizational Analysis and Head of the School of Management at Keele University. He has published widely on Information Technology Management. Recent works include *The Re-engineering Revolution?: Critical Studies of Corporate Change* (edited, with H. Willmott, Sage, 1999) and *Management Lives! Power and Identity in Work Organizations* (with H. Willmott, Sage, 1999).

Gloria Lankshear, University of Plymouth Gloria is Senior Research Fellow in the Department of Sociology at the University of Plymouth. She is currently working on an ESRC-funded programme, Innovative Health Technologies, studying the technological management of childbirth. Previous interests have included barriers to the implementation of technology in the NHS.

Scott Lash, Goldsmiths College, University of London Scott is Director of the Centre for Cultural Studies and Professor of Sociology at Goldsmiths College, University of London. His research interests are information society, global media, continental philosophy, technology and culture, and the problem of 'flows'. He has published widely and his work has been translated into ten languages.

Martin Lea, University of Manchester Martin is a Research Fellow in Psychology at the University of Manchester. He has written about computer-mediated communication and the internet in social psychology, communication, organization science, and human computer interaction journals and books.

Sonia Liff, Warwick Business School Sonia is a Reader in Industrial Relations and Organization Behaviour at the Warwick Business School, Warwick University. She was the principal investigator on a Virtual Society? project researching cybercafés and community technology provision as non-traditional sites for public access to the internet. She has also researched and written more broadly on social inclusion/exclusion and ICTs, and on workplace equality issues.

Paul Light, King Alfred's College, Winchester Paul has held a Chair in Education at the Open University and a Chair in Psychology at Southampton University, whence he moved to be Pro-Vice-Chancellor at Bournemouth University before taking up his present post, as Principal of King Alfred's College, in 2000.

Geoffrey Lightfoot, Keele University Before joining Keele as a Lecturer in Management Information Systems/Accounting, Geoffrey held a number of posts in the Civil Service, including spells at the Enterprise and Deregulation Unit at the DTI and the Financial Management Division at Customs and Excise. His research interests and publications centre on smaller and family businesses, financial markets, and the virtual organization.

Brian D. Loader, University of Teesside Brian is Reader in Sociology and Director of the Community Informatics Research and Applications Unit (www.cira.org.uk) based at the University of Teesside. He is also General Editor of the international journal *Information, Communication and Society* (www.infosoc.co.uk)

Celia Lury, Goldsmiths College, University of London Celia is a Lecturer in Sociology at Goldsmiths College. She is especially interested in the changing relationship between the image and the object as part of her ongoing interests in visual culture and the commodity character of contemporary culture. Particular interests are the importance of time, memory, and duration for perceptions of the object.

David Mason, University of Plymouth David is Head of the Department of Sociology, and Associate Dean for Research in the Faculty of Human Sciences, at the University of Plymouth. His longstanding research interests have been in the sociology of race and ethnicity, and he is well known for his work on labour market issues and equal opportunities. In recent years he has extended his interests in the social organization of work and employment to include the impact of electronic technologies. He is also engaged in research under the Innovative Health Technologies programme examining the technological management of childbirth.

Brian McGrail, University of the Highlands and Islands; Open University Brian is an Associate Lecturer for both the University of the Highlands and Islands project and the Open University, teaching social science and area studies. He previously gained a Ph.D. in the Department of Building at Heriot-Watt University and worked as a Research Fellow at the Open University on two ESRC-funded projects, including one under the Virtual Society? programme.

Steven Muncer, University of Durham Steven is a Lecturer in the Department of Psychology at the University of Durham. His original research was in psycholinguistics and dealt with such areas as phrase structure, non-human language, sign language, and also reading. His more recent research has been in the general area of social psychology, with specific interests in aggression, social development, network analysis, and social representations.

Ged Murtagh, Digital World Research Centre, University of Surrey Ged is a Research Fellow at the Digital World Research Centre, University of Surrey. He is currently investigating the everyday use of digital and mobile technologies and their implications for everyday communication and interaction. His research interests include ethnography, ethnomethodology, conversation analysis, methodology in the social sciences, and theoretical constructions of human action.

Sarah Nettleton, University of York Sarah is a Senior Lecturer in the Department of Social Policy and Social Work at the University of York. She has researched and published on various aspects of the sociology of health and illness.

Faith Noble, University of Nottingham, recently retired Faith has an MA in Sociology from the University of California at Berkeley, and came to Britain in 1964, where she lectured and tutored in sociology and management for many years and gained an MBA and a Ph.D. in Management from British universities. From 1987 to 2000 she was involved in a series of research projects on information technology and organizations, the most recent being the ESRC Virtual Society? project, and published a number of articles on that theme. Since retiring from the University of Nottingham, she has been a freelance research consultant, and is currently working on consumer education in personal finance.

Nicholas Pleace, University of York Nicholas is a Research Fellow in the Department of Social Policy and Social Work at the University of York. His background is as a social policy researcher, largely working on applied policy research. His main areas of interest are in research related to homelessness, housing and community care, and social housing management.

Melvin Pollner, UCLA, Los Angeles Mel is Professor of Sociology at the University of California at Los Angeles. His research examines tacit assumptions and practices in legal, mental health and everyday settings.

Mark Rouncefield, Lancaster University Mark is a Research Officer in the Department of Sociology at Lancaster, carrying out a number of ethnomethodologically informed ethnographic studies of computer supported cooperative work. These include an EPSRC project 'Evolving Legacy Systems to Intranet-based Architectures' using ethnographic methods to study the impact of legacy systems on business processes within a large multinational bank, in collaboration with the Computing Department at Lancaster.

Russell Spears, University of Amsterdam Russell is Professor of Experimental Social Psychology in the Department of Psychology, University of Amsterdam. His main research interests are in intergroup relations, social identity, and social psychological aspects of computer-mediated communication.

Fred Steward, Aston Business School, Aston University Fred is Reader in Innovation and Director of the Innovation Research Centre at Aston Business School. He has conducted a range of research projects on innovation and social change. He is a member of the editorial board of the *International Journal of Innovation Management* and of the journal *Technology Analysis and Strategic Management* and has been Chair of the ESRC postgraduate subject area panel on Science, Technology and Innovation Studies. He lectures MBA and other students on innovation and entrepreneurship.

Marilyn Strathern, University of Cambridge Dame Marilyn is the William Wyse Professor of Social Anthropology and Mistress of Girton College, University of Cambridge. She is an anthropologist well known for her work on such issues as gender, kinship, new reproductive technologies, and intellectual property rights.

G. M. Peter Swann, Manchester Business School   Peter is Professor of Economics and Management of Innovation at Manchester Business School, in the University of Manchester. He previously worked at London Business School and Brunel University. Most of his research is concerned with innovation.

Tiziana Terranova, University of Essex   Tiziana is a Lecturer in the Sociology of Media, Culture and Film at the University of Essex. She is the author of *Network Culture: The Cultural Politics of Cybernetic Communications* (Pluto Press, forthcoming) and several essays on cyberculture and digital media.

Graham Thomas, University of East London   Graham is a Senior Lecturer in the School of Cultural and Innovation Studies at the University of East London. His main interests concern issues of innovation and governance in the area of information and communications technologies and services.

Pete Tolmie, XRCE, Cambridge   Pete is a Research Scientist at Xerox Research Centre Europe's Cambridge Laboratory. He was previously a Research Assistant at Lancaster University, working as an ethnographer on several ESRC-funded projects. His current role is as an ethnographer within XRCE's Work Practice Studies Competency, working as a member of multidisciplinary design teams engaged in technological innovation.

Theodore Vurdubakis, Manchester School of Management, UMIST   Theo is a Senior Lecturer in Management Information Systems and Technology Management at the University of Manchester Institute of Science and Technology. His main research interests are the social study of science and technology, with particular reference to information systems in organizations and the relationship between financial practices and liberal forms of government.

Susan Watt, Cardiff University   Sue is a Lecturer at Cardiff University, School of Social Sciences. She is a social psychologist with research interests in group behaviour.

Peter Watts, Canterbury Christ Church University College   Peter is a Lecturer at Canterbury Christ Church University College. His background is in sociology and he completed his Ph.D. at Brunel University. His thesis research explored the effects on the governance of the self of self-help literatures published in relation to HIV/AIDS. His general academic interests lie in the area of discourse analytic approaches to public understandings of scientific knowledge.

Tim Watts, Aston Business School, Aston University   Tim is a Teaching Fellow in Innovation Management at Aston Business School. He previously undertook a full-time research post at Manchester Business School, where he participated in a number of research contracts in the area of technology and innovation management. His principal research interest lies in exploring the role of virtual reality technology in business. He has helped to produce a number of case studies for the DTI and ESRC investigating the business benefits of VR technology and has conducted numerous workshops on this topic.

Hugh Willmott, Judge Institute of Management Studies, University of Cambridge Hugh is Diageo Professor of Management Studies at the Judge Institute of Management Studies, University of Cambridge. His research focuses on the theme of the changing organization and management of work.

Andreas Wittel, Nottingham Trent University Andreas is Lecturer in the Department of English and Media Studies, Nottingham Trent University. He has worked in Tübingen, Bochum, and London. He has published on industrial sociology, anthropology of work, and ethnographic methods. His research interests concern contemporary transformations of culture and the social, particularly in the relation between culture and economy. He has a special interest in new media, the culture of late capitalism, and new culture industries.

Steve Woolgar, Saïd Business School, University of Oxford Steve is Professor of Marketing at the University of Oxford, having previously been Professor of Sociology, Head of the Department of Human Sciences and Director of CRICT (Centre for Research into Innovation, Culture and Technology) at Brunel University. His research is in various aspects of social studies of science and technology, with particular reference to its implications for social theory and for organization analysis and management.

Sally Wyatt, University of Amsterdam Sally teaches in the Department of Communication Studies, University of Amsterdam. She is also the President of EASST (European Association for Studies in Science and Technology). Together with Flis Henwood, Nod Miller, and Peter Senker, she edited *Technology and In/equality: Questioning the Information Society* (Routledge, 2000). She is currently researching the role of the internet in the ways in which people construct risks associated with health problems and treatments. She has no intention of ever owning or using a car, but continues to use the internet.

1

Five Rules of Virtuality

Steve Woolgar

WHY STUDY THE SOCIAL DIMENSIONS OF ELECTRONIC TECHNOLOGIES?

We are continuing to witness the burgeoning growth of new electronic information and communications technologies (ICTs). These include interactive and
multimedia communications, Internet and World Wide Web, video conferencing, virtual realities, computer-aided design, the information superhighway,
and the technologies of electronic surveillance and consumer profiling. These
new electronic technologies have been widely regarded as the impetus for
radical changes. All these technologies are set to modify the nature and
experience of interpersonal relations and communications across a vast range
of human activities. Education, politics, medicine, arts, the law, music, entertainment, government, and business are just some of the many areas of life that
may be affected, if not wholly transformed, by these technologies. Unsurprisingly, then, the development of new ICTs is central to emerging industries and
regulatory policies throughout the world, based on the recognition that they are
the key to future vitality. Accordingly, government agencies have deliberated on
the appropriate regulatory and policy measures—for example, by way of UK
and European White Papers on Growth and Competitiveness—and users in
industry have in turn identified the social context in which technologies are
actually used as a vital area for understanding.

All aspects of social, cultural, economic, and political life thus stand to be
affected by the continued massive growth in electronic technologies. Given
their potential radically to transform many fundamental and wide-ranging
aspects of society, these new technologies require us to rethink the very basis of

Thanks to Christine Hine, Daniel Neyland, and Sara Ward for comments on an earlier version of
this chapter.

the ways in which we relate to one another. If there are radical transformations in the structures of information and data flow, what will be the nature of the 'social glue' that holds societies together in the future? It follows from the enormity of such questions that the genesis and impacts of new electronic technologies need careful scrutiny. Are fundamental shifts taking place in how people behave, organize themselves, and interact as a result of the new technologies? Are electronic technologies bringing about significant changes in the nature and experience of interpersonal relations, in communications, social control, participation, inclusion and exclusion, social cohesion, trust, and identity? In short, are these new technologies actually making a significant difference? The answers to these questions are increasingly central to the policy agenda and will have a crucial bearing on commercial and business success, on the quality of life, and on the future of society.

In this book, discussion of the social consequences of new electronic technologies is organized around one contentious summary claim about the likely effects of new electronic technologies: the idea that the transformative effects of these technologies amount to our transition to a virtual society. What is connoted by a 'virtual society'? As Peter Swann and Tim Watt (this volume) recall, the idea of the virtual is most famously associated with the novels of Gibson (1984) and Stephenson (1993) (cf. Burrows 1997). In this vision, electronic technologies can enable communication via computers (and other electronic technologies) that replaces face-to-face interaction. With the onset of virtuality it was envisaged that people would spend as much, if not more time in an imaginary virtual world as in their real world. Among many other profound consequences, this will herald the much vaunted death of distance (Cairncross 1998). In this situation, social and psychological interaction, economic transactions, and political relations may proceed unimpeded by the need for physical proximity.

Although the particular idea of 'virtual society' has enjoyed a relatively sparse popularity in the social-science literature, the term 'virtual' has been the focus of diverse discussion across a wide range of areas. The literature ranges from Pierre Levy's enthusiastic popularization (1997, 1998) of theories of cyberspace, in which he champions the 'virtual' as a concept that provides the natural precondition for an inevitable technological future (cf. Day 2001: ch. 4), to the recent growing attention to the methodological problems and possibilities for social-scientific use of 'virtual' technologies (e.g. Lyman and Wakeford 1999; Hine 2000; Hine and Woolgar 2000; Wakeford 2000). The term has enjoyed particular popularity in the numerous debates and discussions of 'virtual community'. An early enthusiasm for the transforming effects of electronic technologies shifted previous attention from the use of computer-mediated communication (CMC) in work processes and organizations to the possibility of achieving a form of electronically mediated social relationships built around enhanced community values (Baym 1998). The utopian pioneering spirit that characterizes many of the early discussions is captured in the subtitle of Rheingold's well-known treatment (1993) of the topic: building a virtual community was tantamount to 'homesteading on the electronic frontier'.

'Unbounded sociability was the promise' (Castells 2001: 119). But the evidence for the success of these ventures is mixed (Watson 1997; Jones 1998; Kolko and Reid 1998; Du Val Smith 1999; K. Ward 2000). In particular, the early enthusiasm has given way to a realization that discussions about virtual community often embodied confused ideals about what 'community' entails (Smith and Kollock 1999). The sociological literature reveals enormous discrepancies as to what might count as 'community', long before the possibility of its virtual counterpart emerged (Bell and Newby 1971; Wellman *et al*. 1988; Wellman and Gulia 1999).

Of course, 'virtual society' is just one summary term used to describe the upshot of the new technologies. It is just one vision of the world transformed by technology, which sits alongside, for example, information society, network society, and global society. In particular, it is worth noting that 'virtual society' is one of a class of what we might call 'epithetized phenomena' (Woolgar 2000a), descriptions used to conjure a future consequent upon the effects of electronic technologies. In this usage, 'virtual', like 'interactive', 'information', 'global', 'remote', 'distance', 'digital', 'electronic' (or 'e-'), 'cyber-', 'network', 'tele-', and so on, appears as an epithet applied to various existing activities and social institutions. Examples of epithetized activities are learning, working, mail, shopping, commuting, banking, governance, medicine, and sex. Examples of epithetized social institutions include education, community, society, organization, medicine, government, university, reality, media, and social science. We thus observe the emergence of (discussions about) 'electronic shopping', 'information society', 'e-government', 'remote learning', 'global governance', 'digital banking', 'tele-working', and many more. While it is often unclear from these labels exactly how the application of the epithet actually modifies the activity/institution in question, a claim to novelty is usually central, especially at the hands of those promoting the new entity. The implication is that something new, different, and (usually) better is happening. Indeed, 'new' is itself a candidate member of the class of epithets, appearing as it does, for example, in discussions of 'new media'. In the same way, the coupling of 'virtual' and 'society' can be understood as a claim that some new set of activities and arrangements contrasts with 'ordinary' or 'real' (non-virtual?) society and, perhaps more controversially, improves upon it.

In this collection, then, the idea of 'virtual society' stands on behalf of a wide range of concurrently emerging epithetized visions about technologically transformed futures. They all suggest a major and profound change. The particular virtue (if we might say that) of using and interrogating the term 'virtual society' is that it connotes an especially marked contrast with the existing state of affairs; the virtual is so different and so transformative that it stands in polar opposition to the real. This, in turn, has the advantage of asking us to rethink what we have been taking for granted about the non-changed entity. What have we been assuming about the nature of 'real' society, against which its 'virtual' counterpart constitutes a significant change?

It is now recognized that much initial research on the social impacts of electronic technologies was characterized by a polarization between narrow suspicion and uncritical enthusiasm (see Kitchin 1998; Gauntlett 2000; Silver 2000). While the positive assessments of the new technologies were vital in drawing public and academic attention to the phenomena, we can now see that this phase depended on the largely uninterrogated adoption of technological attributes. Negative assessments similarly tended to consider that limiting and unfavourable social consequences would flow directly from the capacities of the technologies. Both sets of views tended to assume that the effects of these technologies would be predictable and universal. It was as if academic social scientists had largely imbibed one or other extreme position on the benefits or ills of ICTs.

Are we now beyond the hype? Shields (2000: 11) goes as far as to suggest that 'the 1990s appear to have seen societies in retreat from the liminoid qualities at first celebrated in visions of cyberspace and virtual society'. But Castells (2001: 117) warns that the key questions 'are still couched in simplistic, ideological dichotomies that make an understanding of the new patterns of social inter-action difficult'. Undoubtedly part of the answer is more informed careful empirical study. In this view, the more widespread usage of Internet techno-logies makes possible a more considered approach, whereby we can accumulate detailed information to make more reliable assessments of the nature and extent of impact (Castells 2001). However, this in itself may be insufficient. Arguably, our tendency to accept uncritically the claimed effects of technology has resulted in theories of the information society that tend to depend on synoptic, top-down (and often unexplicated) depictions of technical capacity and effect. The best of them have served us well, but, especially in the light of their limited capacity for projecting future developments, they perhaps now require revision. It is also clear that the first tranche of studies tended to treat cyberphenomena in rather general terms and, most notably, with little reference to the actual circumstances and experiences of use. The current need is for theoretical general-ization informed by close scrutiny of the widely varying actual experiences of the design and use (and misuse) of the technologies on the ground. It follows that we need to develop and maintain a more sceptical awareness, both of our implicit reliance on notions of technical effect and of the parameters within which the debates about social impact of technology have been established. In the next section, I develop this point by reconsidering some of the features of the rationale for this kind of research with which we began.

THE RATIONALE RECONSIDERED

Let us look again at the two paragraphs with which this chapter began.

We are continuing to witness the burgeoning growth of new electronic information and communications technologies (ICTs). These include interactive and multimedia communications, Internet and World Wide Web, video conferencing, virtual realities, computer-aided design, the information superhighway, and the technologies of electronic surveillance and consumer profiling. These new electronic technologies have been widely regarded as the impetus for radical changes. All these technologies are set to modify the nature and experience of interpersonal relations and communications across a vast range of human activities. Education, politics, medicine, arts, the law, music, entertainment, government, and business are just some of the many areas of life that may be affected, if not wholly transformed, by these technologies. Unsurprisingly, then, the development of new ICTs is central to emerging industries and regulatory policies throughout the world, based on the recognition that they are the key to future vitality. Accordingly, government agencies have deliberated on the appropriate regulatory and policy measures—for example, by way of UK and European White Papers on Growth and Competitiveness—and users in industry have in turn identified the social context in which technologies are actually used as a vital area for understanding.

All aspects of social, cultural, economic, and political life thus stand to be affected by the continued massive growth in electronic technologies. Given their potential radically to transform many fundamental and wide-ranging aspects of society, these new technologies require us to rethink the very basis of the ways in which we relate to one another. If there are radical transformations in the structures of information and data flow, what will be the nature of the 'social glue' that holds societies together in the future? It follows from the enormity of such questions that the genesis and impacts of new electronic technologies need careful scrutiny. Are fundamental shifts taking place in how people behave, organize themselves, and interact as a result of the new technologies? Are electronic technologies bringing about significant changes in the nature and experience of interpersonal relations, in communications, social control, participation, inclusion and exclusion, social cohesion, trust, and identity? In short, are these new technologies actually making a significant difference? The answers to these questions are increasingly central to the policy agenda and will have a crucial bearing on commercial and business success, on the quality of life, and on the future of society.

This kind of rationale[1] for a social science of electronic technologies is by now familiar, not to say pervasive. Many introductions to a large, diverse, and growing body of research have conveyed broadly similar sentiments. At one level, the main thrust of the rationale seems reasonable enough: it provides the grounds for asking what in fact are the impacts of the Internet, CMC, mobile telecommunications, and so on. And yet it can be argued that our research on these topics has now reached the stage where we should no longer take this kind of rationale at face value. This is not to say the rationale is without value. It has been and continues to be the organizing principle behind considerable bodies of high-quality research. It appeals to many kinds of diverse audience. And it supplies the motivation for research support and funding. But I want to suggest that we also need to look carefully and critically at the constituent

---

[1] The above paragraphs are taken, with little adaptation, from the initial documents issued in 1997 to announce the research of the 'Virtual Society?' programme. It is consistent with the evolution of the 'analytic scepticism' of the programme that this early formulation of the aims and objectives of the programme is now returning to haunt its propagator (namely, the Programme Director). Several contributors to this volume (e.g. Strathern, Knights *et al.*) point gently to the nature of the implicit assumptions in these statements.

components that make up this justification. We now need to understand the manner and extent to which our efforts at researching the social dimensions of electronic technologies are already constrained by the ways we pose the research questions in the first place. In order to do this, we need to dissect these terms of reference, the frame being used and the underlying assumptions of this kind of research rationale.

The *first* and perhaps most striking characteristic of the above rationale is its sweeping grandiloquence. The effect arises in part from the ambition of its questions: to seek synoptic answers to very general issues organized around summary invocations of 'the new technologies'. If the immodesty of this enterprise has a familiar ring, it is hardly surprising. This is the synoptic talk of enthusiastic journalism, supply-side marketing, and overly simplified policy vision with which academic social science is in dialogue. Nor is this feature the exclusive preserve of the optimists. The doomsayers are similarly adept at this kind of summarizing talk.

The full extent of the tendency to synopsis, summarizing description, and totalizing depiction—we can subsume these under the summary term 'clumping'—becomes evident when we begin to dissect the terms of the rationale above. Consider the following examples. The initial premiss—that we are continuing to witness the burgeoning growth of new electronic ICTs—enlists a form of royal 'we'. But who exactly is the 'we' referred to here? In relation to questions about social inclusion and exclusion, it is especially appropriate to ask who exactly is doing the witnessing. More importantly, for whom exactly does burgeoning growth matter and for whom does it matter most? The phrase 'new electronic technologies have been widely regarded as the impetus for radical changes' similarly connotes the performance of particular audiences and constituencies. By exactly whom and which groups and agencies have these technologies been regarded as the impetus for radical changes? Fairly evidently, these formulations presume and promote a uniformity of opinion and effect. 'Are fundamental shifts taking place in how people behave...?' On reflection, it is easy to see that such phrases are crying out for disaggregation. We need to ask: which people? 'In short, are these new technologies actually making a significant difference?' We need to ask: a difference to whom and in what ways?

A *second* related feature of these calls for understanding new technologies is the assumption that the experience of these new technologies is related unproblematically to general overarching macro-level trends. Summarizing talk tends to encourage synopsis in terms of analysis: for example, shifts in socio-economic conditions are assumed to bear upon the use and deployment of the technologies on the ground. Or, to put it differently, attention at the macro-level gives rather little clue as to how these technologies are actually used and experienced in every day practice. Arguably, the very formulation of the problem in macro-analytic terms adopts the clumping tendencies of the proclamations we need to assess more critically. Responsibility for this form of overenthusiastic clumping must lie with certain trends and styles of social-science analysis. 'All aspects of social, cultural, economic, and political life thus stand to be affected by the continued massive growth...' We have now reached the point in the evolution of the field where we need to disaggregate the phenomenon, to focus much more on bottom-up experiences, on the nitty-gritty of actually making the damn modem work. We need to ask critically whether, to what extent, and how such everyday experiences relate, for example, to shifting patterns of employment, to the development of wider social networks, and to global society.

The *third* feature of the above rationale, an important and recurrent feature of discussions about new technology, is their infusion with confident declarations of effect. It is, of course, unremarkable that discussion about technologies should involve talk about their effects. After all, 'technology talk', as we might call it, is quintessentially about effects, outcomes, impacts, changes that may or may not result from the development, adoption, and use of new technology. More notable, I suggest, at the current stage in the development of our understanding of new technologies, is the marked confidence of these descriptions, their peculiar expression as definitive accounts of effects, or of impact or outcome. This feature deserves consideration in detail.

The definitive character of descriptions of technology, normally unremarked upon, becomes most apparent when things go wrong, or when technology operates against expectation, or when its effects contrast markedly with what has been claimed for it. Consider the following example, frequently discussed in a variety of forums. The advent of Internet shopping, it is said, is set to revolutionize the practices and experience of shopping (cf. Knights *et al.*, this volume). To a degree never imagined by home shopping via television, or through mail-order catalogues, the possibility of shopping online means that more and more people can opt for the convenience of ordering their groceries via the Internet. Instead of enduring the weekly grind of slogging to the supermarket, filling large trolleys, queuing and processing it all through the check-out, transferring bags to the car, driving home and unloading, it is now possible to order via your PC and have the weekly shop delivered to your door.

However, this attractive scenario has a drawback. As this means of shopping becomes more and more popular, so more and more delivery vans are deployed in transporting the goods. As numbers grow, the traffic becomes increasingly congested. Roads begin to clog up. To prevent total seizure of the road system someone suggests a way of rationalizing the delivery procedure. Instead of delivering to individual households it is decided to combine deliveries to specific localities by depositing composite orders to local depots. Individual shoppers can then collect their orders from the depots. This not only reduces the delivery traffic, it also solves the emerging problem that many Internet shoppers are not actually home to receive the deliveries when they arrive. Now they can collect them from the depot at their own convenience. The further idea arises that these depots could try diversifying their business by offering various sidelines, items that Internet shoppers might not have thought to order when online, newspapers, a lottery ticket, shoe laces, a box of matches. Someone comes up with a yet further brilliant idea: these depots could be called 'shops'!

The appeal of this kind of story, for me at least, lies in the inversion of the claimed effects—specifically, the manner and degree to which the envisaged displacement of an existing system by new technology turns out to be misjudged. Something very like the old existing system re-emerges once the hype has died down. The definitive character of the original claims heightens the appeal of the story. The inversion would be very much less marked if the original claims had been more moderate and cautious.

What is the source of the confidence associated with accounts of definitive effects of technology? On the whole, it emanates from a wide range of quite specific constituencies: supply-side electronic industries and suppliers of electronic goods in general; the advertisers who emphasize the beneficial effects; the media accounts that tend both to dramatize and to polarize potential outcomes; commentators and analysts (some social scientists included) who wish to draw attention to specific kinds of impact; the legion of experts and consultants who offer certainty in the midst of uncertainty; and participants in policy debates and policy processes, not least politicians and various government agencies. The persistence of this confidence, even in the face of setbacks to the envisioned scale of growth and development, might be explained in part by the ways in which these separate constituencies interrelate and support one another. The social science of electronic technologies requires not just that we recognize the extent to which talk of definitive effects—the discourse of the definite—pervades rationales for the analysis of technology. It also requires us to understand the constituencies and networks within which such discourse takes hold and flourishes.[2]

All this suggests the need for a rather more sophisticated approach to the problem than is perhaps characteristic of previous analyses. We cannot simply take at face value the terms of the agenda set out in the kinds of rationale interrogated above. Our recognition that they depend on the kinds of features just pointed out—clumping aggregations, top-down synoptic causation, and presumed definitive outcomes—asks us to treat these formulations with caution. At the same time, the very fact that they work, make sense to, and mobilize an array of different social constituencies means that it would be unwise simply to dismiss them. Their constitutive function makes them part of the phenomenon to be understood. A complete disregard for these terms of the debate would quickly alienate many potential audiences for social-science research. So we

---

[2] Marilyn Strathern (this volume) offers the suggestive argument that there are resonances between the practices of decontextualization as they occur in different arenas within contemporary modern society. Her example is the resonance between claims about ICTs and the practice of audit in higher education and research. The analysis here points in a slightly different direction. It suggests that the drive to choose is itself at the heart of the modernistic malaise.

need instead to find a way of both retaining the central terms and assumptions of the problem as commonly formulated, and at the same time interrogating them as we proceed with our research. We need, so to speak, to run with both standard and italicized versions of the research rationale.

THE VIRTUAL AND THE REAL: A GENEALOGY OF THE QUESTION MARK

The main guiding principle that arises from our dissection of the terms of reference for this debate—beware clumping!—applies equally to our treatment of the polar contrast between virtual and real. As we have said, the current state of our understanding of the new electronic technologies requires our attention to the form of the debate around claimed technological impacts. In particular, it is not enough, certainly misses the point, and is perhaps even wrong-headed to attempt a straightforward evaluation of these claims. To set out to assess whether or not a virtual society is possible is already to accept the terms of reference of the debate. As Cooper *et al.* (this volume) put it, we need some mutual contamination of the categories that make up the real/virtual opposition. We should proceed by neither endorsing nor debunking the concept of virtual society. Nettleton *et al.* (this volume) similarly indicate that alignment with either extreme is inappropriate; they quote Wellman and Gulia's observation (1999: 167) that 'statements of enthusiasm or criticism leave little room for moderate, mixed situations that may be the reality'.[3]

As indicated above, the challenge is to find a way of interrogating the terms of the debate without disengaging from them altogether. This is an important aim both academically and strategically. The terms of the debate are themselves motivated, by which I mean they are deeply imbued with relations, meanings, implied connections, and performed communities of associations. These terms of reference thereby involve, give rise to, and sustain a form of social ordering. So, to undertake a straightforward evaluation of the claims is to align oneself with one or other constituency or version of (a particular) social order. On the other hand, the lofty disdain traditionally associated with an academic perspective is tantamount to the loss of engagement with these constituencies.

How then to give space to moderate assessments of the situation to be sustained alongside, and on an equal footing with, the cyberbole?[4] At an early stage

---

[3] Elsewhere (Woolgar and Cooper 1999) it is argued that there may be advantages to the position of ambivalence, as an alternative to the reasonable middle ground that is appealed to here.

[4] A neologism borrowed (with a slightly adapted spelling) from Imken (1999: 102): 'It is easy to make long-term predictions and spew cyperbole [sic] that has no relation to reality, whether virtual or actual'. In the current chapter 'cyberbole' denotes the exaggerated depiction (hyperbole) of the capacities of cyber-technologies.

of this research venture I was presented with the draft specification for the programme. The opening rationale for the research programme closely followed the paragraphs already interrogated above. My immediate reaction was that the stated rationale both vastly exaggerated the likely effects of the new technologies and bought into an unsophisticated form of technological determinism: '... all these technologies are set to modify the nature and experience of interpersonal relations and communications ...'. And my first instinct was to set about redrafting the text so as to introduce large doses of academic caution: '... *we might anticipate that perhaps some* electronic technologies *might* have *some* impact on *some* aspects of interpersonal relations ...'. The dramatic effect of this introduction of modalities was to downgrade the confident facticity of declarations about technological impact (cf. Latour and Woolgar 1986: 75–88). This, in turn, gave rise to my feeling, as the redraft became replete with modifiers and hedges, that the central urgency of the research was becoming lost. I recalled Greg Myers's excellent socio-linguistic analysis (1991, 1993) of the texts of calls for research proposals. Myers points out how the production of such texts involves the input from, and attention to, many different (and often competing) interests and views. The end result is a compromise, or better a composite, of elements designed for different constituencies. So a recurrent mistake of those who respond to calls for research proposals is to imagine that there is a single straightforward objective and audience in mind. I realized that my attempt at redrafting was effectively an attempt to redefine the audience, to reorient the programme towards a singular implied reader, captured perhaps in the persona of the cautious academic. The effect was to diminish the urgency, edge, and provocation of the original draft, clearly oriented to a variety of other audiences, not least those who might be sufficiently impressed by the drama of potential technological impacts to support the allocation of funding for research into the actual effects of these technologies.

At this point, my dilemma—how to make the draft more friendly to the cautious academic while retaining the pragmatic value of its cyberbolic overtones— was effectively finessed by the ESRC. I was advised that extensive redrafting was not possible because the draft had by then already been approved by the appropriate committee. In other words, the text already carried some measure of institutional approval of the reader constituencies that it performed. The solution was to retain (in large part) the given form of words, but to inject a question mark in the title. From that moment the 'Virtual Society' research programme became the 'Virtual Society?' research programme. The question mark signals the spirit of analytic scepticism (cf. Woolgar 1999) that needs to run in concert with balder depictions of technological impact. It signals, for example, that the very notion of 'impact' needs critical attention, not least because it implies a separation of technology and the contexts that constitute them. This very separation should instead be brought into scrutiny as part and parcel—perhaps even as the crucial central focus—of the phenomenon to be explained (cf. Agar *et al.*, this volume).

Of course, no one could expect that the simple insinuation of a punctuation mark would by itself achieve the subtle and difficult goal of bringing audiences of diverse expectations into easy coexistence. The question mark acquired a seen but unnoticed quality. It became apparent that some people close to the programme only first noticed the question mark in the title after several months of dealing with its papers and committees. Frequently the title of the programme was transcribed without the question mark into public written statements such as announcements of conferences and public lectures, acknowledgements in academic publications (e.g. Castells 2001: p. xi) and seminar reports. The question mark was either overlooked altogether or it was assumed to be a typographical error in the information supplied to the publisher. Perhaps most telling of all, it turned out that the protocol for web-site addresses does not allow the inclusion of a question mark. We had to make do with www.virtualsociety.org.uk not www.virtualsociety?.org.uk. Such observations are indicative of the extent of the challenge of sustaining analytic scepticism in a context characterized predominantly by definitive versions of the capacity and effect of new technologies. The extent of the challenge can be understood as the degree of effort required simultaneously to satisfy audiences with quite diverse expectations.

THE ORGANIZATION OF THE ARGUMENT AND THE ORGANIZATION OF THE TECHNOLOGY

The present volume comprises an interdisciplinary collection of research reports that, through their greater or lesser responses to the principle of analytic scepticism, help contribute to the new social science of electronic technologies. However, it follows from our insistence on a critical attitude to the discourses that enframe discussions of these new technologies that the very presentation or ordering of these reports can benefit from due reflexive attention to the ordering assumptions involved. Just as technologies tie things (and people) together, so we need to be aware of how the typologies used to present them embody and encourage certain presumptions about our analytic aspirations.

The experience of working in a major research programme highlights the difficulty of synthesizing research findings across a very broad area of social-scientific investigations of ICTs. Throughout the programme, researchers received a constant stream of requests for specific information about particular areas and topics. For example, how do mobile phones change ways of working in office environments? How quickly do primary school children assimilate new computer skills? Are protest organizations using the most effective means of electronic communications? What is the extent of adoption and take-up amongst particular ethnic minorities? The diversity of areas of enquiry underscores the phenomenon at hand: there is barely any aspect of modern society potentially untouched by the effect of new electronic technologies. For the simple practical reason that we cannot hope to cover every conceivable topical area or subject, it behoves us to distil generic messages, principles of sufficient generality that they might usefully be 'applied to'—or, more sensibly, worked through in relation to—quite diverse particular instances of implementation and use. The answer to questions about the implications of technologies outside the scope of the research should not be 'sorry, we don't have any research on that problem'; it should instead be 'here are the general principles/guidelines that will help you work out the likely effects in any particular case'.

One way to organize a diverse set of discussions about the impacts of new technology is by substantive focus: we could look in turn at the impacts on education, on work, on medicine, and so on. Many recent publications in the area are organized along these lines. Similarly, many recent publications are organized around a particular social and/or political theme. For example, governance and digital democracy (Loader 1997; Hague and Loader 1999; Ludlow 2001); the cyberspace/digital divide (Loader 1998); crime and security (Thomas and Wyatt 2000); power and politics (Toulouse and Luke 1998; Dutton 1999; Jordan 1999); communities (Smith and Kollock 1999); capitalism (Schiller 2000). One drawback of these otherwise intriguing contributions is that their organization in terms of substantive focus or social-scientific theme can detract attention from the general analytic messages that arise. Quite apart from the redundancy involved in having to repeat (perhaps rework) the same set of general arguments and basic principles in relation to each new substantive area, this approach carries the danger of suggesting that appropriate insights are wholly unique to the substantive domain under consideration.

An alternative is to organize by a typology of different kinds of electronic technology. This would generate separate sections on each of, say, Internet technologies, mobile phones, video imaging, and so on. The difficulty here is that this typology gives too much weight to the notion of the technology itself. By contrast, the whole thrust of the present volume is to emphasize the importance of circumstances that surround, sustain, and make sense of the 'technology itself'. Furthermore, it is important to take into account that conceptions of the technology are themselves changing. Watt *et al.* (this volume) make the important point that, just as the Internet itself is changing, so too are our views of what the Internet is and what it is capable of. In a small way, this collection and the research reported herein itself contributes to this process. Our gradually increasing familiarity with 'the Internet' and its various ramifications is signalled in this volume (as elsewhere[5]) by its description henceforth as 'the internet' (lower case).[6] The processes of familiarization, and of changing conceptions of

---

[5] For example, the texts of contributions to the recent collection by Gauntlett (2000) tend to use 'internet', although the titles of some its individual chapters and sections use 'Internet'. The contributions to the Crang *et al.* (1999) collection use 'Internet' throughout.

[6] By analogy with the earlier discussion of attempts to establish the question mark in 'Virtual Society?', such simple declarations of change are in tension with prevailing conventions. Thus,

technology more generally, have a special significance, for example, in the context of (especially some government) claims that within a short time everyone will have 'access to the internet'. This could turn out to be true, to the extent that 'internet' comes to denote a rather different set of applications from those we have previously associated with the 'internet'.[7]

To what extent can the insights of research reported here be applied to other, newer kinds of electronic technology? A widespread concern, among both academic researchers and commentators and analysts outside the research community, is the extent to which sustained research, necessarily spread over several years, is unable to provide insight into the uptake and use of the very latest technologies. The perceived limitation of publicly funded research, necessarily commissioned through an exhaustive process of peer review and evaluation, and typically designed as carefully focused studies of specific technological applications, is that it will tend to provide only old news. Research reports eventually appearing in collections that have undergone the long process of a publisher's evaluation and production will surely be out of date? Although claims about the obsolescence of technologies under academic focus are exaggerated, it is undeniable that the longevity of a careful social-scientific research project will probably exceed the period when the technology under study is deemed cutting edge. Against this, it should be remembered that technology is only ever cutting edge for certain specific groups—for example, the supply side of the electronics industry and some (self-styled) sophisticated users. Thus, for example, the telephone is still out of reach to large proportions of the population of the world as a whole.[8] But this does not invalidate the study of its adoption and effects. There may be important lessons to be learned about the situations and circumstances that enabled and/or constrained take-up.

FIVE RULES OF VIRTUALITY

In the light of the above considerations, the contributions to this volume are organized under five broad analytic themes, each of which can be said to correspond to a 'rule' for apprehending or making sense of the prospects for a virtual society. That is, in the face of determinative claims about the effects and impacts of any new technology that comes on stream, each of these rules

for example, the copy editor for this volume commented: 'I see that halfway through the Introduction you introduce the spelling "internet", with an initial lower case. The usual OUP style is for Internet, with an initial upper case. Is the use of lower case vital to your argument, or may we use the usual style?'

[7] For example, the idea that WAP phones 'provide access to the internet' implicates a set of different usages from users accessing the internet via a PC.

[8] '...Between a third and a half of the world's population still lives more than two hours away from the nearest telephone' (Bingham 1999: 255).

provides a rule of thumb or slogan for evaluating these claims. Two points should be emphasized. First, as should be evident from their discussion below, the status of these 'rules' is intended as advisory rather than determinate. They should be taken not as prescriptions or indicators but instead, to borrow the suggestive phrase attributed to Harold Garfinkel, as 'aids to the sluggish imagination'. Secondly, although these rules provide the organizing principle for presenting the research outcomes, the ensuing allocation of individual chapters to particular rules is fairly arbitrary. There is considerable overlap in the rough-and-ready typology below, so that chapters listed below as exemplifying one rule often also illustrate another.

Rule 1: The uptake and use of the new technologies depend crucially on local social context

The chapters under this rubric explore different aspects of 'context' that bear upon the reception and deployment of electronic technologies. The importance of these 'non-technical' circumstances is that they explain, for example, why the current rate of straightforward rapid expansion may not continue.

Against the simple expectation that the take-up of new electronic technologies is characterized by an unstoppable bandwagon of growth, Sally Wyatt and colleagues (Chapter 2) review some of the surprisingly counter-intuitive evidence of extensive non- and former use of the internet.[9] They identify the various social and contextual factors that affect individual and collective patterns of use. In particular, they urge a rehabilitation of the concept of non-use. By analogy with the non-use of automobiles, they argue that we need to develop a much more sophisticated appreciation of the relations between online and offline, between users and non-users, and of the influence of non-users on the development of the internet.

Peter Swann and Tim Watts (Chapter 3) examine the problem of take-up with reference to virtual reality (VR). They identify as crucial those aspects of 'social context' that bear upon the coordination of expectations and visions between diverse technology developers and diverse users. They argue that the current pre-paradigmatic state of VR, with a slow to develop market, sharply falling share prices following initial optimism, and a general loss of nerve, provides a powerful demonstration of the importance of developing a coherent vision for take-up. While Wyatt *et al.* caution against 'universalistic' depictions of the impact of technology, Swann and Watts show in detail how a specific technology

---

[9] As this volume goes to press, further evidence of saturation in the use of internet technologies is provided by an OFTEL survey (Office of Telecommunications 2001) that shows a small fall (between May and August 2001) in the percentage of UK households with internet access.

can fall victim to the 'paradox of ubiquity': the very diversity of expectations and potential makes it especially difficult to develop coherent relations between developers and users.

Is the internet making us less social? Susan Watt and colleagues (Chapter 4) bring a social psychological perspective to the central question of how the use of the internet, in their case specifically computer-mediated communication (CMC), compares with face-to-face communication. They challenge the wide-spread notion—prevalent both within and beyond social psychology—that, because of the limited bandwidth and reduced social cues, internet commun-ications tend to undermine socially normative behaviour. They advance a novel model of the Social Identity of Depersonalization Effects (SIDE) to explain how reduced bandwidth and increased anonymity can actually accentuate feelings of group belongingness and identification. By thus taking specific senses of con-text into account, Watt *et al.* let us glimpse the basis for an accentuated, perhaps even novel, form of sociality arising from the use of internet communications.

What kinds of context encourage or inhibit use of the internet technologies? Chapter 5 by Sonia Liff and colleagues looks specifically at the social and phys-ical contexts of internet access and use, through a study of the different kinds of 'e-gateway' that promise access to and participation in the virtual world. The analysis of these new kinds of social institution underscores the importance of the social dimensions of access and in particular the importance of social networks as we move beyond the simple assumption that technical access will suffice. Liff *et al.* stress the need for a grounded look at the actual use of techno-logies in particular social settings. UK e-gateway users were found to be more representative of the population at large—both in terms of age profile and gender distribution—than are home internet users; and users were predominantly local people. The findings suggest that 'third-place' characteristics of local social context—a social setting separate from both domestic and economic spheres—provide a key to the successful integration of the real and the virtual.

Rule 2: The fears and risks associated with new technologies are unevenly socially distributed

Whereas the first rule emphasizes the importance of social context for use, the second explores a corollary of this—namely, that views about new technology, the anticipations, concerns, enthusiasm, and so on are unevenly socially distributed.

David Knights and colleagues (Chapter 6) offer a way of understanding this phenomenon in terms of technology stories, narratives that enable the enact-ment of 'the virtual'. They examine how particular ideas, stories, and versions about the virtual affect the ways in which organizations, especially financial services organizations, engage with new technologies. They identify and detail two diametrically opposed visions of the virtual: future-shock stories and emperor's-new-clothes stories. Drawing on recent controversies about the socially constructed character of technological characteristics, they argue that the success of technology narratives depends on the strength of the actor network through which a technology is enacted. We thus see the transformative power of expectations about, and performances of, technological artefacts in social action.

The uneven distribution of views about new technology comes into sharp focus in Brian McGrail's study (Chapter 7) of the use and reception of closed circuit television (CCTV) and related surveillance technologies in high-rise housing. The capabilities of CCTV turn out to be far from simply given. Instead, views about surveillance technologies are bound up in communication, inter-action, contestation, and justification, and these views are continuingly being promoted and recanted. McGrail draws upon a recognitive theory of power to show that the technology is constantly 'at stake'. Of particular note are the unexpected alternative forms of resistance and opposition that can arise, in some cases ironically from those it is designed to protect or from those charged with its implementation.

David Mason and colleagues (Chapter 8) switch the substantive focus from high-rise housing to the impact of surveillance-capable technologies on social relations at work. Against expectation, their respondents accorded a markedly low priority to the question of privacy at work. Mason *et al.* use this finding as the basis for challenging some common assumptions about the privacy impacts of new technologies at work, especially in those literatures influenced by the labour-process tradition. Instead of starting with the assumption that relations between management and employees are intrinsically oppositional, Mason *et al.* stress the importance of examining the actual usage and experience of new technologies in complex social situations, and reveal a variety of counter-intuitive usages of technology that are not easily classifiable as either conformity or resistance to surveillance-capable technologies.

Rule 3: Virtual technologies supplement rather than substitute for real activities

Research shows that new technologies tend to supplement rather than sub-stitute for existing practices and forms of organization. The virtual thus sits alongside the real that, in much popular imagination, it is usually supposed to supplant. The iconic example is the much-vaunted 'paperless office'. Against expectation, the computerization and automation of office practices did not make obsolete the use of paper communication. Instead, the new forms of electron-ically mediated communication sit alongside the continued use of memos, notes, and so on. This gives rise to interesting new forms of interrelationship between the virtual and the real, and the modification of both modes of communication. In the office situation this is iconically captured in novel conversational exchanges that take place in the corridor: 'I've just sent you an e-mail'!

Charles Crook and Paul Light (Chapter 9) critically examine the prospects for 'virtual learning' (one part of the vision of 'virtual universities'). They stress the importance of context (rule 1) and argue that the mistake of many virtual learning projects is to decouple learning from its (especially) cultural context, which includes artefacts, technologies, symbol systems, institutional structures, and other cultural paraphernalia. Crook and Light reflect on the imagery associated with the practice of study in the promotional literature of educational institutions and undertake a detailed examination of undergraduates' self-reports of study activity. They find that the mere ability of students to access ICT failed to re-mediate the communal dimensions of learning. For some purposes, the success of new ('virtual') communication tools depends crucially on the extent to which these incorporate existing informal practices of exchange. At the same time, it is clear that successful implementation of new communicative modes of study may require the recovery of formal characteristics of conversations. All this underpins the observation that new virtual technologies cannot and do not simply substitute for old ones.

Sarah Nettleton and colleagues (Chapter 10) consider the increasing mediation of changing patterns of social support by various forms of ICT. Using qualitative data from a range of different sources, they report largely positive accounts of the experience of different types of social support. Participants benefited from gaining information and advice but importantly also experienced the medium as providing companionship and esteem. They found, in particular, that they could enjoy a far more strategic, precise, and focused type of support than is available offline. Online support seems also to have contributed to a sense of ontological security. Importantly, the indications are that virtual social life provides a further dimension to a person's real social life, not a substitution for it. The sources of virtual support via the internet were used together with other resources and became enmeshed into people's social lives, in some cases thereby transcending the boundaries of real and virtual life.

Rule 4: The more virtual the more real

This rule is an extension of the previous one. Not only do new virtual activities sit alongside existing 'real' activities, but the introduction and use of new 'virtual' technologies can actually stimulate more of the corresponding 'real' activity. The chapters under this heading document this phenomenon, about which there has already been some largely speculative discussion across several substantive areas. For example, it was found that one unanticipated outcome of teleworking is that teleworkers end up travelling more than they had done previously (cited in Woolgar 1998). Why did this happen? Electronic communication enabled the teleworkers rapidly and efficiently to make many more contacts with prospective clients. But the accepted mode of then relating to these new clients was to meet and deal with them face to face. Hence increased physical travel on the part of the teleworkers. In a similar way there has been speculation that the very large increases in (especially intercontinental) business air travel over recent years owe much to the increased use of e-mail between businesses. Or that the increase in the numbers of museums online has lead to an increase in the number of people (physically) visiting museums (which we should now properly designate 'offline museums'). Or that virtual or e-banking, far from making the high-street branch redundant, has in some cases lead to the opening of new (physical) offices. Or that televising football leads to an increase, not a decline, in the numbers actually attending football games.

The precise nature and extent of these kinds of 'rule 4' crossover effect are not yet well known. Suffice it to say that the effects may be widespread and applicable to unexpected domains. For example, it prompts the thought that the researchers' own use of virtual technologies (Hine 2000) may perhaps stimulate more ways of using real research methods and/or a reappraisal of the concepts and assumptions that inform 'real'—that is, non electronically mediated research methods (see Hine and Woolgar 2000). Again it is worth emphasizing that many chapters other than those listed under this heading also exemplify this rule. For example, Nettleton *et al.* (Chapter 10) include evidence that a person's use of CMC leads to further or increased use of more traditional communicative media. In their study, mailing list participation can be seen to lead to an increase in phone conversations and letter writing. The general point here in turn raises key questions about the implications for the realignment of work and leisure activities, and about new forms of interrelation between social organization, social relations, and citizenship (Putnam 2000).

Andreas Wittel, Celia Lury, and Scott Lash (Chapter 11) discuss the interplay of real and virtual connectivity in the new media sector in London ('Silicon Alley'). Basing their research on ethnographic studies, they find that connectivity is an increasingly prevalent mode of organization that characterizes production based on networks and products rather than hierarchies and markets. In the new media sector in particular, these products are typically virtual objects that connect client firms to consumers, users, and audiences through both real and virtual connectivity; the products of the new media can themselves be understood as packets of connectivity. New forms of organization are increasingly associated with the production of new media: they are described as heterarchic, open, non-linear, self-governing, and reflexive. But Wittel *et al.*'s case studies remind us of the extent to which the non-linearity and connectivity of virtual culture have their roots in the real economy.

Steven Brown and Geoffrey Lightfoot (Chapter 12) critically examine the promise of information systems for changes in business practice, specifically the claim that networking computing can fundamentally change the nature and management of organizational memory. Their analysis of e-mail usage in two organizations supports the view that e-mail sits alongside rather than replaces existing activities such as sending memos but further illustrates how e-mail actually stimulates or encourages more of such activity. Against the view that e-mails facilitate more open informal communication, Brown and Lightfoot observe the genesis of strategies for managing e-mail exchanges such that e-mail is experienced as a highly formal space of interaction where issues of personal accountability are constant and pressing.

Melvin Pollner (Chapter 13) reports his participant observer experiences as an investor and member of a stock market electronic discussion forum. He explores in particular the operation of this highly reflexive communication medium; the quintessential feature of the Motley Fools discussion board is its capacity to effect that to which it points (cf. Strathern, this volume). At one level, Pollner's account is an intriguing and salutory tale of how he started out making both money and ethnographic observations, and ended up losing financially. But perhaps the real value of his account is in illuminating the processes by which it is possible also to 'lose' the ethnography. In effect, Pollner here articulates an intriguing version of the slogan: the more virtual the more real. He shows how a whole series of concepts—such as social network, social life as text, the narrative constitution of self and reality, self-fulfilling prophecy—lose their ironic analytic edge when transposed to the arena of reflexive social life that comprises cyberspace. Pollner suggests how the deflation of the stock market bubble neatly presages a parallel deflation of the social scientist's conceptual bubble, and the consequent need for quite new ways of thinking about the virtual society.

Rule 5: The more global the more local

Virtual technologies are famously implicated in the much-discussed phenomenon of globalization. In one (of many possible) interpretations of the term, globalization comprises the rapid movement and spread of symbolic and financial capital. Electronic technologies facilitate the rapid traffic in communication, the instantiation of activities and institutions at widespread locales, and the insinuation of standardized identities and imagery (especially brands) in multiple locations. Globalization is quintessentially about the death of distance. Against this, our final rule encompasses those findings that show how instantiations of global communication and identity depend critically on attention to the local setting. The claim here differs from our first rule. It is not just that local context affects uptake and use. Instead, the very effort to escape local context, to promote one's transcendent global (and/or virtual) identity, actually depends on specifically local ways of managing the technology.

John Hughes and colleagues (Chapter 14) investigate how new forms of 'virtual organization' are implemented and adopted in their study of a major retail bank. They find that the realization of the ideal of a 'virtual organization' was set aside in favour of more trusted business solutions—especially through the rhetoric of standardization—to the organizational problems of coordination. Commonly held expectations about virtual organizations proclaim the need for radically new skills and working practices, but Hughes *et al.*'s close analysis of working interactions shows that participants strive to preserve the normality of existing relations. Their efforts are directed primarily at making the technology at home within existing work practices. In so doing, it is local relevancies that are crucial rather than global ones.

Jon Agar, Sarah Green, and Penny Harvey (Chapter 15) deploy an especially discursive and reflexive sense of context to illuminate the development and use of new electronic technologies in 'virtual Manchester'. Whereas the central promise of these new technologies is freedom from location—they are 'space defying, boundary crossing, ubiquitously linking'—Agar *et al.* reveal the processes whereby various histories and culturally derived ideas, notably that of Manchester itself, are created and reconstituted in a way that achieves the relocation of technologies. In Manchester at least, the use of ICTs reiterated spatial divisions and distinctiveness rather than helping to ameliorate them. A significant lesson of the work is that, like that of Pollner, it suggests the need for a significant reassessment of our use of core social-science concepts for making sense of virtuality. Important as it is to view ICT developments 'in context' (rule 1), here we are shown the crucial importance of understanding that 'context', whether social or spatial or both, is itself actively fashioned and constituted.

Geoff Cooper and colleagues (Chapter 16) recount their studies of the everyday use of mobile telecommunications as the basis for considering how the simultaneous demands of distant and co-present communications are managed in public and private spaces. They demonstrate how devices apparently designed to render location insignificant are in fact always used within, and with reference to, a particular local context. They note some of the myriad ways in which posture, gaze, and gesture are used to negotiate the boundaries between the private and public, and consider the argument that mobile usages are part of a contemporary reconfiguration of space and time. Their careful assessment of various competing propositions about the determinative effects of mobile technologies leads them to urge caution in adopting summary views of the impacts of mobile technologies upon society.

Finally, Marilyn Strathern's comment (Chapter 17) rounds off the collection by highlighting some analytic resonances between 'Virtual Society?' research and other extant concerns. In particular, she invites us to reconsider the issue of 'context' (the brave buttress of our first rule). If the social science of electronic technologies is fundamentally the effort to reinsert context into decontextualized descriptions of those technologies, it is important to see how decontextualization similarly characterizes other contemporary phenomena. She commends the comparative perspective of social anthropology—itself resonant with the notion

of analytic scepticism—to highlight parallels with decontextualization processes in the audit of higher education and research. Her examples articulate
the ethnographic sensibility that both underlies much of the research of this
volume and is signalled in the question mark of the programme title.

ON COUNTER-INTUITIVE FINDINGS

The above synopsis of some of this volume's central research findings embodies the claim (sometimes made explicit) that they are counter-intuitive. In other
words, the outcomes run against expectation. In short, the new technologies are
not being used to the extent we imagined, by the people anticipated, nor in the
ways we expected. But, in line with our initial concerns about the tendency to
'clumping', these summary claims can themselves benefit from disaggregation.
It is instructive to ask: 'counter-intuitive for whom (and under what circumstances, how and why)?' Whose expectations do these findings confound and
why? The possibility that for some people these outcomes are not in fact
counter-intuitive prompts an intriguing alternative question. If these findings
only appear counter-intuitive, we might need to ask what (on earth) has happened to our intuitions over the past few years![10] How (by whom and what)
have our expectations been so shaped that, for example, the discovery of
widespread non-use of the internet appears striking? Many contributors to this
volume allude to the disaggregated reception of these findings. Thus, for
example, Mason et al. (this volume) note that, although strikingly counter-
intuitive when set against much press commentary and discussion of certain
institutions, their findings appear unexceptional from the perspective of many
of the participants/respondents themselves. It is also important to note that
'counter-intuitive' does not necessarily refer to effects that are unexpectedly
negative. It simply means against expectation, whether that expectation connotes a positive or a negative outcome. As, for example, Knights et al. (this
volume) note (citing Cochrane 2001), claims about the counter-intuitive effects
of new technology can also work as a claim about its unexpectedly beneficial
outcomes.

CONCLUSION

It is perhaps no coincidence that the deflation (if not the actual bursting) of the
dot.com bubble comes at a time of a more gradual appreciation of the

---

[10] I owe this point to Richard Sykes. It was he whose memorable contribution to a UK
Government Foresight seminar on Future Scenarios, by stark contrast with the usual accounts
of labour-saving gizmos, offered a (utopian?) view of a future characterized by a widespread
sophisticated analytic appreciation of the social effects and reception of new technologies.

importance of the human and social dimensions of the new electronic technologies. Although examples are still common,[11] we are perhaps now nearing
the end of the current cycle of extreme forms of hype about the impact of the
new technologies. The research of programmes like 'Virtual Society?' can claim
some credit for this, by helping temper cyberbole through its attempts to
establish the question mark as a central enduring feature of our attitudes to
new technologies. The outstanding issue is then how to set the agenda for the
future. The contributions of this volume explicate the social basis of the much
vaunted 'impacts'. They underscore the importance of discerning the relation
between the technical and the social dimensions of ICTs. The analyses also
suggest ways in which we might move from mere 'access' to meaningful use of
ICTs. But a crucial overriding theme is the recognition that careful research into
actual experiences of ICT usage is just one half of the major intellectual challenge of understanding the social implications of new electronic technologies.
The other half is to convey the importance of the necessary sceptical attitude to
those in a position to make key decisions about the genesis and implementation of these new technologies.

In sum, the distinctive contribution of this collection is twofold. First, it starts
to address the need to get under the skin of synoptic visions of technological
impacts. It offers a series of accounts of the complex and varied experience of
internet and other electronic technologies that challenge the totalizing tendencies of pronouncements about 'impacts'. Second, by recommending a focus
upon implications rather than just on impacts, the contributions here encourage a consideration of the ways in which new technologies challenge the nature
and scope of existing social-scientific concepts.[12]

---

[11] The following example of enduring cyberbole is taken from the announcement for a
conference (The Third World Symposium of Information Technologies) held in April 2001: 'The
Internet... is a revolution at the world level. ...Information technologies modify in depth our
way of thinking, speaking, working, entertaining, or buying and selling, our relations with the
others... We live under the sign of speed and adaptation to a permanent change. It is necessary
for us to try to follow, to understand. We are coming into a new civilization.'

[12] It is striking that, with relatively few exceptions, existing research has thus far done little to
exploit the opportunities provided by ICTs for novel forms of research into ICTs. The transformation of sociality and the attendant changes in the nature of ICT-mediated communication raises a whole series of opportunities and questions about the appropriate unit of analysis,
relationships between researchers and their subjects, the whereabouts of field sites, the ethics
of participation online, and so on. Future research may benefit by developing approaches and
methods that are adaptive to the new forms of sociality under study.

2

They Came, They Surfed, They Went Back to the Beach: Conceptualizing Use and Non-Use of the Internet

Sally Wyatt, Graham Thomas, and Tiziana Terranova

INTRODUCTION

This chapter reports research that draws on insights and approaches from cultural studies, and science and technology studies, in order to explore how the internet has been and continues to be socially produced. Many 'information-society' enthusiasts claim that the internet will improve access to information and entertainment and lead to greater social justice. Dissident voices suggest it will exacerbate social inequalities through the creation of information haves and have-nots and result in greater social control through the growth of electronic surveillance. Technological determinism can be detected on both sides. We reject technological determinism and instead highlight the complexity and dynamism of the internet, and contribute to the development of a sceptical critique of the 'information society'. As an example of this complexity and dynamism, we focus on access by users, the emergence of new intermediaries, and control by producers, in order to explore the relationship between consumption and production, and the relationship between technological change and social and economic inequality. We treat the internet as a complex, socio-technical system that has both symbolic and practical significance. In this introductory section we summarize the key findings of the project before exploring more fully the results that support what Woolgar (this volume) calls the first rule of virtuality: given its crucial dependence on local social context, the current rate of straightforward expansion (of the internet) may not continue.

We are grateful to Steve Woolgar, Sara Ward, and anonymous referees, who provided us with very useful comments for redrafting this chapter.

First, our analysis of the history of the internet confirms the view that it is socially shaped. Its current configuration was not inevitable: there were alternative mechanisms for distributing digital data in the 1970s and 1980s that have faded away. Similarly, the future of the internet cannot be presumed. The reasons for the massive growth of the internet in the 1990s can be traced to the influence of a 'public-service culture' in earlier decades. The current dominance of commercial operations challenges and weakens that culture, whilst also complicating the relationship between the larger population and the internet. This becomes apparent in the way users seem to have acquired a contradictory and varied relationship to the internet. The internet will continue to grow, but it may lose some of the features central to its original success. This has immense practical significance but it also has theoretical importance for understanding the development of large technical systems and the concept of closure (Thomas and Wyatt 1999).

Second, we explored the relationship between producers and users of the internet. Despite the growing concentration of resources in a small number of global companies, internet micro-businesses remain important sources of innovation on the internet, often testing and introducing new ideas and actively capitalizing on forms of users' participation that were already part of the history of the internet (mailing lists, discussion groups, content in general). The pioneering world of the early 'dot.coms' has had to readjust itself to the demands of business, and the whole field is undergoing an uneven professionalization. Many of the people who entered this new industry did so out of a desire to escape traditional working environments, yet they have found themselves working extremely long hours, with little or no financial reward. A gendered separation between soft and hard skills has also re-established a division of labour that early internet apologists rejected (Terranova 2000).

The third main finding relates to the role of users in providing content. Interactivity and user participation are still the main strategies for the generation of content on the internet. In spite of the increasing professionalization of the web industry, large amounts of content are generated by users. User-generated content is not only responsible for a substantial part of internet content through home pages, but is also actively relied on by corporate sites. Writing reviews, participating in mailing lists, hosting chat lines, uploading music and videos, writing open-source software, and keeping virtual communities active are some of the main ways through which users' labour is used to sustain the economic development of the internet (Terranova 2000).

We have concentrated on the material and economic complexity of the internet. However, our fourth point relates to the discourse surrounding the internet. Metaphors are a valuable source of information regarding the perceptions and expectations of the actors involved in shaping the internet and can play a key part in the processes by which actors not only define their own interests but also attempt to embed these definitions into the perceptions of potential allies, decision-makers, and the public. Our analysis illustrates that

THEY CAME, SURFED, AND WENT BACK TO THE BEACH   25

there are contradictions inherent in attempting to hold biological and market metaphors simultaneously, as internet enthusiasts often do. Our work on patterns of access (see below) challenges the universalist claims implicit in those metaphors (Wyatt 2000).

This challenge to universalism is central to our final claim. Analysis of secondary data reveals that access to the internet remains unequal, with the typical user being a young, educated, white man, although this pattern varies across countries with high levels of internet usage. In addition, our review of internet usage data suggests that some people do not intend to use the internet and that some choose to stop using the internet. This challenges the conventional industrial and political wisdom that everyone is a potential user and thus casts doubt on the widespread view that the main policy challenge is to remove barriers to access (Thomas and Wyatt 2000).

In this chapter, we focus in particular on the last of these findings and explore some of the issues associated with the use of the internet and (more interestingly from our perspective) its non-use. The internet as it is now (2000) is potentially available to all. The idea that everyone can or should be connected is central to much policy discussion. Access to the internet is seen as necessarily good. Making access cheaper and providing more education and training are thus amongst the obvious solutions. It is assumed that, once these barriers to use are overcome, people will embrace the technology wholeheartedly. From the perspective of politicians, the hope is that people will then use this knowledge to create wealth and employment, but maybe they will use it to look at pornography, play games, or trace long-lost friends and relatives. In a discussion of a US survey of internet use, Langdon Winner (2000) reports that the most common uses are for news, entertainment, and health information, with shopping and financial transactions trailing far behind. Maybe some people will not use it at all and—hard though it might be to accept—maybe its lack does not have to be a source of inequality and disadvantage.

The role of users was increasingly addressed during the 1990s within the technology studies literature (Silverstone and Hirsch 1992; Lie and Sørenson 1996). In part, this reflects the recognition that users are not simply the passive recipients of technology but that they are active and important actors in shaping and negotiating its meanings. In part, the inclusion of users is an attempt to overcome the problems associated with those approaches that emphasize the powerful actors in producing technologies such as scientists, engineers, politicians, financiers, and marketers. But by focusing only on use to the neglect of non-use, we are in danger of uncritically accepting the promises of technology. Defining people only as producers or as users of technologies confirms the technocratic vision of the centrality and normativity of technology. Users of technology also need to be seen in relation to another, even less visible group—namely, non-users. In the remainder of this chapter, we explore use and non-use of the internet. The next section reviews data about the profile of typical internet users. In the next two sections, we examine the available data about people who do not use the internet, and explore possible reasons for non-use. We then present a taxonomy of non-use and examine the implications of the phenomenon of non-use for policy making. In conclusion, partly through an analogy with car use and non-use, we explore what this phenomenon might mean for technology studies.

WHO USES THE INTERNET?

The dramatic increase in the number of internet hosts since the development of the World Wide Web tempts many commentators to conclude that this rate of growth will continue, or even accelerate. It is assumed the internet is following a path taken by many other successful technologies before it. Economists refer to this path as 'trickle down'—the process whereby technologies that are initially expensive to use become cheaper over time, simultaneously providing more people with the benefits of the technology and enlarging the market. In the case of the internet, the early users were a small number of academics who used computers paid for largely from university budgets or defence contracts. Academics are now in the minority, as firms, governments, administrative bodies, political parties, voluntary groups, and individuals at home all use the internet for a huge variety of applications and purposes.

According to the trickle-down view, there may be inequalities of access and use during the early stages of a technology, but it is assumed these disappear, or are at least much reduced, as the technology becomes more widely diffused. Internet enthusiasts often claim that connection is a global process, albeit an uneven one. This is not unique to the internet. Similar claims can be found in much literature and in policy statements about industrialization and modernization more generally. Individuals, regions, and nations will 'catch up'; those who are not connected now, will or should be soon. This is tantamount to the wholesale annihilation of space by time: the assumption that the entire world shares a single timeline of development, in which some groups are further ahead than others along this shared path.

These views of trickling down or catching up contain several fallacies, two of which will be discussed here. The first is that growth is evenly distributed, whereas most of the available data suggest that it is not. The second fallacy relates to the assumption that growth will indeed continue.

First, the evidence for the catching-up assumption and thus a more even distribution of access is furnished—at least within so-called advanced industrial societies—by time series of statistics relating to ownership of consumer goods such as motor vehicles, televisions, and refrigerators, all of which were once owned by very small percentages of households but are now much more widely diffused. Globally, however, the catching-up effect would seem to be less obvious, and measurement of ownership of consumer goods *per se* says nothing about inequalities in the type and quality of goods possessed.

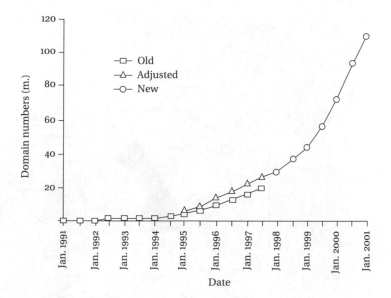

Fig. 2.1. Internet host count.

Source: Internet Software Consortium (www.isc.org).

A word of caution about what follows: collecting and interpreting data about internet use is not straightforward. Defining a host, ascertaining its location, identifying users and their demographic characteristics are all fraught with difficulty. Jordan (2001) demonstrates how estimates of the size and growth of the internet are often motivated by commercial needs and are not well informed by reliable sampling methods. Despite our critical approach to the data, we present some of them below, both because such data have had practical significance in policy discussions and because, despite the limitations, some patterns can be discerned.

Fig. 2.1 shows the broadly exponential growth of the number of internet hosts (computers with internet addresses) since 1991. Such figures, with numbers of hosts, connections, or users along the vertical axis, often illustrate news reports and policy documents about the growth of the internet that forecast exponential growth, even though the rate of growth has been quite stable over a long period. Despite the growth, differences between countries remain stark. The 1999 report from the United Nations Development Program (UNDP) illustrates this (see Fig. 2.2). In mid-1998, industrialized countries—with less than 15 per cent of the world's population—accounted for more than 88 per cent of internet users. The USA, with less than 5 per cent of the world's people, had more than a quarter of the world's internet users.

The stereotypical user remains a young, white, university-educated man. However, closer examination of the available data indicates some weakening of this stereotype. Gender differences have shown the most dramatic reduction

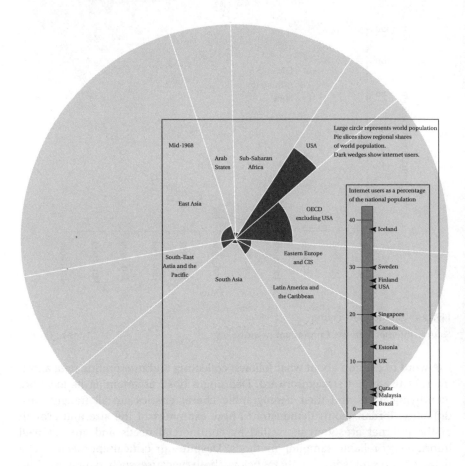

Fig. 2.2. Global inequalities in internet access.
Source: UNDP (1999).

since the development of the World Wide Web. Georgia Technical University (1999) has been conducting online surveys of internet users approximately every six months since January 1994. In the first survey, only 5 per cent of users were women. By October 1998 (the last such survey placed in the public realm), women represented just over one-third of users worldwide. The Pew Internet Project (2001) claims that indeed half of US internet users are women.

Differences based on race and income remain very marked. The first national survey in the USA to collect data on ethnicity and internet use was conducted during December 1996–January 1997, based on nearly 6,000 respondents. Hoffman and Novak (1998) analyse these data and conclude that race continues to matter. Whites are more likely to own home computers and to have used the internet than African Americans, even allowing for differences in education. The most startling result occurs amongst high school and college students who do not have access to a home computer. Of these, the white students (nearly 38 per cent) are more likely than African American students (16 per cent) to find some alternative means of accessing the internet. This may reflect different patterns of access within schools, or—the explanation favoured by Hoffman and Novak—different schools may have variable levels of internet-related resources.

Within Europe, we often look to the USA to see what the future with the internet will look like. The UK data indicate a picture that is not dissimilar to that of the USA. The 1997 British Household Panel Survey provides data about the distribution of internet access from the home. Burrows *et al.* (2000) analyse these data and confirm that the typical British user is again a young man, either a student or in employment, more likely to be living in London or the south of England. Not surprisingly, individuals with higher incomes and higher social classes are also more likely to be wired. But they do find some more intriguing results, very different from those found for the USA. The most notable is that people from ethnic minorities were more likely to have home internet access than those who identified themselves as 'white'. Households inhabited by couples and children are more likely than other household types to have internet access.

The contours of the divide may vary between countries, reflecting national traditions of difference and exclusion, but it is becoming clear that social divisions in internet access continue to exist. The US Census Bureau conducted large-scale surveys (of approximately 48,000 households) on behalf of the National Telecommunications and Information Administration (NTIA) in 1995, 1998, 1999, and 2000. The analysis of these surveys highlights what the authors call a 'persisting digital divide'. They note substantial increases in internet access, but go on to state:

Nonetheless, a digital divide remains or has expanded slightly in some cases, even while internet access and computer ownership are rising rapidly for almost all groups. For example, the August 2000 data show that noticeable divides still exist between those with different levels of income and education, different racial and ethnic groups, old and young, single and dual-parent families, and those with and without disabilities.   (NTIA 2000; emphasis in original)

A second fallacy implicit in the trickle-down assumption about continued growth is precisely that growth will indeed continue. The NOP Research Group (1999) has conducted regular large-scale surveys (of approximately 10,000 respondents) of aggregate internet use since the end of 1995. Between mid-1998 and mid-1999, they find that the number of internet users increased from almost 19 per cent of the population to 27.5 per cent, an increase of 46 per cent. They predict the internet will continue to attract over 11,000 new users a day. But will this continue at the same rate until everyone is connected? Why should this be the case? Extrapolation is a notoriously unreliable forecasting technique, but one frequently used with respect to the internet. Recognition that the

'S curve' of market-driven internet diffusion might flatten before universal access is achieved is provided in the UK Communications White Paper published in December 2000 in which the UK government committed itself to the aim of providing universal internet access by 2005 (without, however, saying how this was to be achieved) and prudently kept open the possibility of including high-bandwidth internet access within the scope of the Universal Service Obligation in telecommunications (DTI and DCMS 2000: ch. 3).

Interestingly, the hopes for market expansion often expressed by the promoters of new devices for accessing the internet—interactive televisions, palmtops, mobile phones, and so on-are accompanied by the recognition that there is a point, short of universality, at which demand for internet use via personal computers will be saturated. The prospects for these other devices, however, are also uncertain. In 2001, the UK government was expressing concern about the slow rate of adoption of digital TV (which offers a limited form of internet access), and industry commentators were voicing worries about the economic viability of third-generation mobile phone services (whose chief selling point is access to high-speed data services).

WHO DOES NOT USE THE INTERNET?

The surveys referred to in the preceding section are all concerned to demonstrate growth, and, of course, growth has been impressive according to all available indicators, including numbers of hosts, domain names, and users. Much of the academic and policy literature focuses on how to increase the number of users, and nearly all takes the additional step of assuming that, once a user, always a user. For example, the conclusions of Hoffman and Novak (1998: 9) are to 'ensure access and use will follow [and] access translates into usage'. Moreover, they conclude, 'programs that encourage home computer ownership...and the adoption of inexpensive devices that enable internet access over the television should be aggressively pursued, especially for African Americans' (Hoffman and Novak 1998: 9).

We shall leave aside for the moment the question of indirect use of the internet (for example, people making a query in a shop or agency where an employee uses the internet to provide the information needed). Recent empirical work suggests that providing access may not be the sure, simple solution it appears.[1] Cyber Dialogue (2000), an internet research consultancy based in the

---

[1] A literature search on various combinations of internet, computers, information technology, technology, on the one hand, and rejection, drop-out, non-use, barriers, have-nots, on the other, yielded very little. 'Barriers' yielded most, but much of that was about national level adoption or education. 'Drop-outs' also provided quite a few, including some interesting material about young people who dropped out of school or university as a result of doing too much internet surfing.

USA, has found evidence of a slowdown in internet growth, based on interviews with 1,000 users and 1,000 non-users. They claim that the rate of growth is slowing down overall and that there is evidence of an absolute decline in the number of users aged 18 to 29. In part, they attribute non-use to cost: some people cannot afford a computer and online access. They also claim that approximately a third of all US adults simply do not believe they need the internet and what it offers.[2] Even more significant is the growth in the number of adults who have tried the internet and then stopped using it—only a third of whom expected they might use it again at some point in the future. In early 1997, Cyber Dialogue estimated there were 9.4 million former users; by September 1999, they calculated that there were as many as 27.7 million former users. In 2001, the US Pew Internet Project (2001) found that half of all adults in the USA did not have internet access and 57 per cent of those non-users were not interested in getting online. A survey conducted in the UK in 2000 found that a third of British adults has no intention of ever using the internet (M. Ward 2000).

Based on two national, random telephone surveys, Katz and Aspden (1998) suggest there are patterns to non-use. Their analysis of 'internet drop-outs' was a side effect of some research about barriers to internet use in the USA. They candidly admit they included the category of 'former user' in their surveys only for logical completeness. They were surprised to discover in October 1995 that ex-users and current users each accounted for about 8 per cent of the sample. They did another survey in November 1996, by which time the proportion of current users had more than doubled to 19 per cent of the sample. Interestingly, the proportion of ex-users had also increased, but by less, to 11 per cent. People who stop using the internet are poorer and less well educated. People who are introduced to the internet via family and friends are more likely to drop out than those who are self-taught or who receive formal training at work or school. Teenagers are more likely to give up than people over 20, and the reasons for dropping out varied by age. Older people are more likely to complain about costs and difficulties of usage, whereas younger people are more likely to quit because of loss of access or lack of interest. Many ex-users have computers at home that they continue to use for other purposes, but not for internet access.[3]

The Cyber Dialogue data and the results of Katz and Aspden need to be treated with caution, as former users can of course become active users again at a later date. They are interesting because they call into question the assumption of never-ending growth. They also suggest that public access provision, quality of information, and training remain important policy issues. If the results about

---

[2] Winner (2000) discusses a survey of over 1,500 adults and 600 children, conducted on behalf of National Public Radio, the Kaiser Family Foundation, and the Kennedy School of Government during November and December 1999. Winner does not provide the details but he claims that 'a small but not insignificant minority' do not have a computer or any plans to acquire one. Three-quarters of this unspecified minority do not feel this as a lack.

[3] This further complicates internet usage data, because it is likely many of these people will remain in the global statistics about ever-increasing numbers of users.

teenagers are replicated elsewhere on a large scale, certain assumptions about the rate of exponential growth have to be re-examined. Turkle (1996) draws on Erikson's theories of adolescent identity development to explain some of her observations of young people's behaviour on multi-user domains (MUDs).[4] She suggests that MUDs provide a safe environment in which adolescents and young adults can experiment with different forms of interaction and relationships. Maybe the internet is one of many things with which teenagers experiment only to abandon or use in moderation as they become older.

Other new technologies provide some pointers to patterns of use and non-use. For example, mobile phones have a longer history than the internet as a consumer technology. Leung and Wei (1999) identify the factors important in determining the take-up of mobile telephony in Hong Kong. Age, income, gender, and education all work in expected ways. However, age dominates—if you are older (unspecified), having more money and more education does not make much difference. Income levels are declining in significance, thus providing some support for the effectiveness of 'trickle down'. Intensity of use of mass media is not significant, but belonging to social groups that use mobile phones is. Equally unsurprising is the finding that non-users perceive the technology to be unnecessary because they have an alternative or because they find mobile phones either complex to choose and use or intrusive. Leung and Wei's results confirm a growing gap between communication rich and poor, with mobile phone users more likely to possess a range of alternative and complementary forms of telecommunication—pagers, answering machines, and so on—whereas non-users simply had one reasonable alternative. Leung and Wei accept the premiss that having multiple communication devices is intrinsically good, whereas having only one adequate communication device is a sign of deprivation.

Leung and Wei's results are not very surprising: people do not use mobile phones if they have alternatives or find them intrusive and/or expensive. By extension, maybe some people do not use the internet because they have alternative sources of information and forms of communication that are appropriate to their needs, or because they think it is cumbersome and expensive.

PATTERNS OF USAGE AND REASONS FOR NON-USE

The internet has changed significantly over the course of its existence, from an experimental network (during its ARPANET years), via academic resource (the USENET years), to a general communication and transaction medium (for a fuller treatment of these changes, see Thomas and Wyatt 1999). These changes

---

[4] Multi-user domains (MUDs)—a generic term for the huge variety of online, usually text-based role-playing games. Much early internet research, of which Turkle's is perhaps the best known, focused on text-based applications such as these.

have not stopped since the commercial 'take-off' of the internet in the mid-1990s, as providers have developed and refined their services and strategies. How users perceive the internet, which to some extent determines how they use it, varies according to the date they first came into contact with it and the length of time they have been using it. It is possible that some of the explanation for why people might stop using the internet could lie in the difference between the time when the value of the internet was generally recognized—before or around the time of the 'take-off'—and the somewhat later time when the majority of today's users obtained access to it.

This could be expressed as a potential gap between heightened expectations and the reality of the 'internet experience'. Internet hype can imply that the net is an easy way to access a cornucopia of exciting information, to communicate instantly and at low cost with people around the globe, and to buy a great variety of goods and services cheaply and conveniently. It can indeed be all these things, but often is—or is perceived to be—something less wonderful. Since the commercial expansion of the internet, users have consistently expressed disappointment and worry over problems of finding desired information, navigating through the Web, receiving unwanted information, and keeping their personal details secure.

We can imagine a cycle of cynicism and despair that new users may experience. At first, instead of the promised cheap and easy access to untold treasures, they receive more junk e-mail than useful mail in their inbox and become frustrated with the waste of time (and often money) while trying to access the information they require. They may become annoyed by the time taken up with the forced downloading of unwanted 'pop-up' advertisements and with responding to inducements to click on links that promise more than they deliver. They may become bogged down in newsgroups where discussion of the notional topic is obscured by irrelevant and offensive contributions, or where the same topic is covered in multiple groups. They might also receive unwanted or inappropriate goods/services that were purchased online; and then receive even more junk e-mail as a result of information passed on to organizations as a by-product of some of the previous activities. Under such circumstances the attractiveness of the 'internet experience' for new users is likely to be severely diminished.

To what extent can such disappointing experiences be put down to the internet's temporary 'growing pains'? The prognosis is mixed. Navigation tools are becoming more sophisticated, but so are marketing tactics designed to lure users towards information they may not have originally wanted. In any case, the growth of the net has been outstripping the ability of search engines and other navigational tools to cope. Much information, therefore, is either badly indexed or not indexed at all. One way in which the complexity and chaos of the internet is being tackled is by guiding users towards a particular subset of 'approved' content. This is the strategy of large-scale access providers, who design 'portals' intended to provide 'one-stop' access to facilities (with the emphasis being on facilities that can make money for the portal operators). In some cases, guidance is replaced by coercion, where users are restricted to accessing only a subsection of the internet approved by the access provider (and from which other users are excluded—the term 'walled gardens' has been coined to describe such restricted access to closed networks). While this may be an effective strategy for reducing complexity, it also reduces variety and choice. At the start of the twenty first century, this is not a major issue for most internet users, as— in most advanced countries at least—people have a wide choice of provider and can avoid such restrictions if they wish. It will become a much more important issue to the extent that reduction in the number of access providers (and hence of access provider strategies) restricts such choice.

The projected proliferation of access devices (PCs, interactive TVs, palmtops, mobile phones, and so on) is likely to lead to even further fragmentation of the internet. The link between means of access and provision of content may well become stronger as device-specific content is developed—at the time of writing (2001), very few web pages can be successfully accessed from a WAP-enabled mobile phone, for instance. Indeed, the proliferation of devices is likely to legitimize the tying of access to content in a way that was not possible when computers acted as universal access devices. TV-based access, for example, is being developed by organizations that have made their entire living from restricting access to (paid-for) content, and that are comfortable with guiding users into specific 'channels'.

The other factor that helps to legitimate the tie-in of access (and access devices) to content is the trend for 'free' internet access. When users are paying for access services, they may well feel they have a right to demand access to the widest possible range of services and content; where access is 'given away', they may feel they have less justification for such demands. At the moment, competition means that even most of the 'free' access providers are not unduly restrictive, but mergers, takeovers, and economies of scale are reducing the number of access providers: again, the consequences of this process of concentration are likely to become more of an issue in coming years.

With regard to unwanted e-mail, a range of tools, agreements, and policies can be implemented to mitigate the problem (filtering software for individual users and ISP gateways, contractual stipulations for service providers, inter-ISP agreements to ban offenders, and so on). However, there is no sign that the hunger of service providers for information about their customers is abating: 'cookies' that can personalize a user's experience of a site can just as easily provide information to site-owners; registration requirements also give information to providers, although this is at least done in a way that requires the user's active collaboration; addresses are routinely taken from trawls through newsgroup archives, and so on. If anything, the current emphasis on the internet as a tool for e-commerce has exacerbated the tendencies for service providers to gather and process information about users. Laws designed to regulate and limit such information gathering become ineffective as soon as information and services cross legal (usually national, though wider in the case of the EU) boundaries, falling prey to the disparity between national legal systems and the global reach of the internet.

Whether disappointment with the 'internet experience' leads to abandonment of internet use in part or in whole depends on a variety of factors such as: how much time and money have been invested in hardware and software purchases and in learning to use the net; how available are alternative means of accessing goods/services equivalent to those distributed over the internet (something that is likely to be an increasing problem as providers close down other distribution channels on cost grounds); and how far the user is embedded in social circles that value and promote internet use. Such circles might not necessarily reproduce the stereotype of the white, young, male professional. A recent study by Miller and Slater (2000), for example, has highlighted the importance of the internet for diasporic communities, such as the Trinidadians, who regularly use e-mail and ICQ to keep in touch with relatives who have emigrated abroad.

Further factors that might influence the decision to stop using the internet include the declining amount of 'positional goods' and social prestige that can be gained from being an internet user as a result of the expansion of access (although some might say that the 'geek' image of the internet devotee cancelled out most of the social cachet that might have been available in earlier times) and the image of the internet promoted and reinforced by advertisements and by commentaries on the 'e-commerce revolution'. As noted elsewhere (Wyatt 2000), the metaphors used to describe and 'sell' the internet have an impact on the way the net is perceived, and hence on usage patterns. Reports of the internet as being primarily a vast reservoir of pornography led many people to delay internet access within a family setting. Similarly, if the internet is primarily 'sold' as an e-commerce infrastructure ('the online shopping mall'), then it is likely to attract different usage patterns from an internet that is sold as a universal information and communication resource.

TAXONOMY OF NON-USE AND IMPLICATIONS FOR POLICY MAKING

The question of drop-outs may be a transient issue only if all drop-outs eventually return to the internet, perhaps when their income rises or through their use of one of the new access devices. Alternatively, the internet may follow the model of Citizens' Band (CB) radio,[5] the model of explosive growth followed

---

[5] For one of the very few scholarly analyses of Citizens' Band (CB) radio, see Griset (2001). In France, there were 15,000 CB users in 1979 and over 600,000 in 1984. This extraordinary episode, replicated in many other countries, in the history of mobile communication has been remarkably under-studied.

by collapse (admittedly unlikely, but a possibility). In any event, in the USA alone, there are literally millions of former users about whom very little is known. They may be a source of important information for subsequent developments. Kline and Pinch (1996) vividly demonstrate the important role played by anti-car farmers in the USA early in the twentieth century. Some rural inhabitants opposed the use of motor cars, and, even after accepting its presence, used the car for a variety of agricultural purposes, including grinding grain, ploughing fields, and transporting produce. Kline and Pinch demonstrate the significance of this for subsequent designs of motor cars and roads. In a similar way, non-users might have something to contribute to design processes of the internet.

Even within the rhetoric of increasing access, it is important for internet promoters to know why some people stop using the internet and what could be done to lure them back. Rather than denying the possibility of their existence,[6] internet service and content providers as well as policy-makers potentially have much to learn from this group.

There are different categories of non-use. As Bauer (1995: 14–15) points out, there is a difference between passive 'avoidance behaviour' and active resistance. Also, care should be taken to distinguish between non-use of a technological system (such as the internet) as a whole and non-use of specific aspects of it (Miles and Thomas 1995: 256–7). In a preliminary taxonomy of non-use we identify four types of non-user. The first group includes the 'resisters', those people who have never used the internet because they do not want to. We label the second group 'rejectors', those who have stopped using the internet voluntarily, perhaps because they find it boring or expensive, or because they have perfectly adequate alternative sources of information and communication. The third group is those people who have never used the internet because they cannot get access for a variety of reasons; and can thus be considered as socially and technically 'excluded'. The final group have effectively been 'expelled' from the internet; they have stopped using it involuntarily either because of cost or because of the loss of institutional access.

The policy implications are different for the different groups. For the resisters and rejectors, it might be appropriate to develop new services in order to attract them. If internet access is seen as inherently desirable, this might be accompanied by the provision of measures to ease the transition from alternatives, as the French government has been doing in order to encourage a switch from Minitel to the internet (OECD 1998: 25). Another possibility is to accept that some people will never use the internet. This could lead either to a focus on existing users or—moving away from the perspective of the suppliers and promoters who see non-use only as a deficiency that needs to be remedied—to policies that would ensure that alternatives to the internet were available to

---

[6] Steve Woolgar tells us that, when he first told one industrialist about these data regarding the existence of former users, the response was that this must be 'completely bonkers'.

people who want or need them. Access issues related to cost, skill, and location are more relevant for the third and fourth groups, the excluded and the expelled who would like access.

Once one has made the step of including 'former user', as well as 'current user' and 'never a user', it is not too much more of a leap to begin to take apart the notion of 'user'. What exactly does it mean to be a user? How is it defined? The NOP survey (NOP Research Group 1999) mentioned above suggests that 26 per cent of users did not access the internet at all in the week preceding the survey, and a further 20 per cent accessed it only once or twice. Their estimates for total numbers of users are based on answers to the question, 'have you personally used the internet in the last twelve months?' This allows for an enormous range in frequency of use. The notion of internet usage needs to be treated in a rather more nuanced way, distinguishing between complete 'surfies', active participants who subscribe to mailing lists and are also likely to have their own web page, and those people who do not like to get their hair wet and only venture into the water occasionally to find very specific information. The internet 'user', then, needs to be conceptualized along a continuum, with different degrees and forms of participation that can change over time. Different modalities of use need to be understood in terms of different types of users, but also in relation to different temporal and social trajectories. The latter include changes in lifestyle determined by processes such as ageing, changing jobs, educational history, geographical mobility, and so on. Internet use, then, needs to encompass not only a structural table of different types of use, but also the possibility of reversals and changes of direction in the individual and collective patterns of use.

CONCLUSION

In this chapter, we offer some evidence to support the first rule of virtuality. We question the universalizing claims made not only by people trying to sell internet-related products and services but also by policy-makers. We argue that there is indeed evidence to suggest that the rates of internet growth witnessed in the late 1990s may not continue and we have examined the policy implications of this. Here we consider the implications of consideration of non-use for technology studies.

Some of our reflection on this topic was prompted by examining our own relationships to one of the most important socio-technical innovations of the twentieth century—namely, the automobile. None of us owns one. Our reasons are varied but include lack of skill and money as well as an awareness of the environmental and personal risks. The production of cars is often presented as an indicator of a nation's economic well-being. Equally, individual ownership of cars is regarded as a sign of economic and social inclusion in our automotive world. Yet, as university employees with relatively secure jobs, we are not amongst the socially and economically excluded. At the very least, the existence of people like us means we have to be careful about how we interpret data about non-ownership and non-use of particular technologies.

Thinking about cars also highlights the connections between the online world and the offline world. We simultaneously inhabit the same world as car drivers and a different one. Our lives are affected by cars—as pedestrian, cyclist, or scooter rider, we have to be wary of them; as bus users, we are slowed down by them. Cars pollute the air we need as organisms that need oxygen. There is also a parallel universe that we visit only occasionally—an alien world of out-of-town shopping malls, inner-city 'rat runs', petrol stations, car dealers, repair centres, motorway services, drive-on ferries, and so on. Just as there are different maps of the physical world, so there are of the internet (a good selection can be found at http://www.cybergeography.org).

Cars, highways, and roadkill[7] have been part of the discourse of widening access to the internet, in its 'information superhighway' phase in the mid-1990s. The image of the roadkill on the information superhighway vividly represented the danger of non-access, obsolescence, and social exclusion (almost death) implicit in non-use. However, Al Gore's superhighway metaphor, which projected the internet into public consciousness in 1994, was almost immediately rejected by many internet users. For instance, *A Magna Carta for the Knowledge Age*, the response of Esther Dyson, Alvin Toffler, George Gilder, and George Keyworth (Dyson *et al.* 1994), dismissed the information superhighway as the worst possible description for the new economy ushered in by the internet age, largely because the engineering image of highways suggested a technology that was amenable to government control. By contrast, Dyson *et al.* were keen to promote the image of an evolving, organic system.

Will the cyberworld come to dominate the real world to anything like the same extent that the automobile system does? Is it possible to turn off the machine? Or, will everyone's choices come to be shaped by the net? For example, just as the shift of retail outlets from town centres to out-of-town shopping centres makes life more difficult for non-drivers, will the disappearance of other information sources limit some people's ability to participate in economic and public life? For instance, the growth of telephone and internet banking has been accompanied by a dramatic reduction of bank branches in areas of lower population density. To conclude, we briefly discuss three areas where motor vehicles and the internet may be compared and for which the study of non-use has implications. Each of the three areas—surveillance capabilities, cultural significance, and systemic nature—highlights the presumption of universalism made by proponents of these technologies.

---

[7] 'Roadkill' is the term used, largely in Canada and the USA, to describe the animals that meet their deaths under the wheels of a car.

In most countries, one needs a licence to drive a car, though this was not the case during its early days.[8] In some parts of the world, including Canada, the UK, and the USA, which do not have compulsory identity cards, a driver's licence serves as official identification. In the UK, one is legally obliged to inform the Driver and Vehicle Licensing Authority (DVLA) of a change of address. Many people are not aware of it, but this effectively serves as a population register, and is used as such by the police. These days, much car use is subject to enormous levels of surveillance through the spread of closed circuit television (CCTV). In the Netherlands, there is serious discussion about introducing electronic tracking of all cars in order to implement road pricing. The internet, however, is itself a recording device, and, therefore, potentially a technology of direct surveillance. Many of us choose to ignore the surveillance capacities of the internet in our daily practices, hoping that the sheer volume of traffic will serve to protect our privacy, but all of our activities on the internet are pretty transparent.[9] If you wish to escape the surveillance capabilities of modern societies, avoid modern technologies (see also McGrail, this volume).

All technologies are imbued with cultural significance. This is especially true of the car, which became a paradigmatic symbol of modernity in the twentieth century. To many people cars reflect wealth, power, virility, and freedom. The internet promises many of the same attributes, on an even larger scale, with its promise of global reach. While this simply might not be appropriate for many individuals and organizations for whom time is not short and for whom geographical distance between self and significant others is not great, the symbolic importance remains profound. The symbolic value of having internet access is mainly perceived as a sign of inclusion in an unspecified, high-tech future. It is, in a sense, a way to declare one's stake in the accelerating digital economy of knowledge work. In this context, internet non-use can be taken to imply a refusal of the intimidating pace of technological and social innovation. Such a pace demands from citizens and workers a higher level of active involvement in keeping up with technology. Its rejection might then also signal disillusionment with the promises of information economy hype—an attitude that has in any case become more common following the bursting of the dot.com investment bubble in the year 2000.

Another marker of the cultural significance of both the car and the internet is the central role both have played in social-science research. In the 1970s and throughout part of the 1980s, the car and its industry were the site of much empirical research. Moreover, the auto worker was taken to be the prototypical industrial worker. To what extent, then, does the internet supply defining images for today's social-science research? Is the prototypical worker now the

---

[8] In Belgium they became compulsory only on 1 January 1967; anyone over 18 on that date received a licence automatically.

[9] Internet communications have become even more transparent since regulatory measures such as the UK's Regulation of Investigatory Powers bill became law (see http://www.homeoffice.gov.uk/oicd/ripbill.htm for details).

code slave, the call centre operator, the supercool multimedia designer, or a mixture of all three? For better or worse, the car industry became the symbol of industrial society, and much effort was expended in understanding the dynamics of that industry. There were problems with this, including the promulgation of the idea of the skilled male worker as the norm, and the generalization of a set of industrial relations and working practices to other sectors. Social theory focused on questions of alienation and massification, extending them, not always appropriately, to other areas of social life.

Cars are not simply wheels, engines, and steel: they include test centres for drivers and vehicles, motorways, garages, petro-chemical industry, drive-in movies, out-of-town shopping centres. The more people use cars, the greater the infrastructure to support them, and the lessening of car-free space. Similarly, the internet is not just web content. It includes many other applications as well as computers, telecommunication links, routers, servers, educators, trainers, and cybercafés. The more people use it, the more pressure there is to develop user-friendly interfaces and provide more access equipment, greater bandwidth, and faster switching and routing. But there is a paradox here: as the network expands and becomes more useful, it may also become more difficult to create well-working communities. It is thus important to analyse the internet not only along a single dimension or characteristic but as a large technical system (Mayntz and Hughes 1988; Summerton 1994; Coutard 1999). In this chapter, we have argued that not only is it important to understand the changing relationships between system builders and users but also that it is essential to consider the role of non-users in the development of large technical systems such as the internet.

3

Visualization Needs Vision: The Pre-Paradigmatic Character of Virtual Reality

G. M. Peter Swann and Tim P. Watts

> The eye which is the window of the soul is the chief organ whereby the understanding can have the most complete and magnificent view of the infinite works of nature.
>
> (Leonardo da Vinci, *Trattato della Pittura*)[1]

> Virtual Reality is not a technology; it is a destination.
>
> (Biocca *et al.* 1995: 4)

INTRODUCTION

Many have been captivated by the potential of *virtual reality* (VR)—or interactive 3D visualization as it is sometimes called. The rationale seems compelling. Moore's law[2] offers the prospect of unlimited computing power if only we can solve the interface problem. But that cannot happen if we continue to use primitive forms of human–computer interface. Enter virtual reality, where the

We are especially indebted to Bob Stone for many enlightening discussions about VR, and also to: Roger Frampton, Alan Pearson, Garth Shepherd, Paul Windrum, members of the UK VR-Forum Steering Group, and participants in seminars at Université Paris Dauphine, University of Maastricht, and a North-West VR SIG meeting at Manchester Business School. The editor and two referees made very helpful comments on an earlier draft and several suggestions for improvement. The usual disclaimer applies.

[1] Quoted from Richter (1952: 110).

[2] Moore's Law, first proposed in 1964 by Gordon Moore, one of the founders of Intel Corporation, asserts that the number of components per semiconductor chip doubles every eighteen months. This prediction has been remarkably accurate, even into the twenty-first century, and vividly describes the extraordinary potential offered by semiconductor technology.

user is immersed in multidimensional databases, is consequently much better placed to envisage them, and has many more degrees of freedom through which to input data. Roberts and Warwick (1993) put it boldly: 'virtual reality is the science of integrating man with information'.

The potential seems huge, and indeed VR pioneers have developed pilot applications in a very wide variety of fields. But the market has been slow to develop, share prices of some VR vendors have fallen sharply after initial optimism, and at the time of writing some companies are losing their nerve and deciding that they are no longer 'VR companies', but something else. What's new? Is this not just another sad story of a technology that has been 'hyped' out of all proportion and that cannot hope to live up to the 'hype'? No, the current state of VR is a powerful illustration of an often-overlooked reason why markets for new technologies do not materialize.

It is not an issue of technological failure or lack of potential demand. Rather it is because of a lack of coordination of expectations and vision between diverse technology developers and diverse users. Even if VR has the potential to meet real user needs, vendors and users do not manage to focus on the same paradigm for VR. At present VR remains in a pre-paradigmatic stage and until that stage is passed diffusion will remain slow. VR lacks a coherent vision and is, in a sense, a victim of its own ubiquitous potential.

The structure of this chapter is as follows. The next section explains the proposition that, when technologies and markets are in a pre-paradigmatic state, the market will be slow to take off. The following section then assesses the position of VR, the extent to which it is still pre-paradigmatic in character, and the extent to which that is holding back the market. In conclusion, the final section discusses the implications of our findings for the five rules of virtuality.

THE PROPOSITION

The proposition as developed here has its origins in the economics of path dependence (David 1985, 1997). In what follows, we develop the argument in relation to VR, though the argument is general and could apply to a wide range of technologies. But in the next section we shall argue that the particular character of the VR industry makes this argument especially relevant to VR.

To keep the exposition as simple as possible, we shall refer throughout to the Venn diagram in Fig. 3.1. Suppose that the potential of VR can be described by one set and the scope of users to exploit that potential can be described by another (overlapping) set. These spaces are *technological* spaces. In principle, VR could take any form in the left-hand set, or indeed take several forms. As such, the functionality of VR is incompletely determined. Equally, the configuration of the user and the application is incompletely determined. Users could

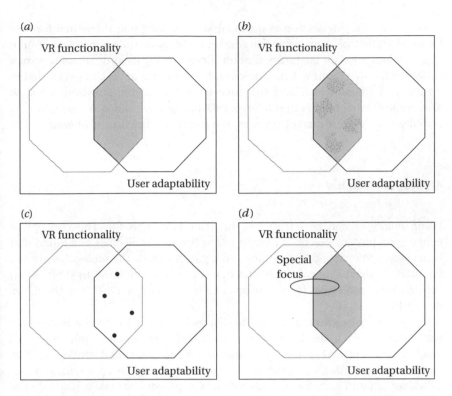

Fig. 3.1. Technological potential and user adaptability (*a*) A 'thin mist' in the intersection (*b*) Clusters of users and vendors start to emerge (*c*) Coherent foci emerge (*d*) The purist's definition as a focusing device.

in principle adapt themselves to use any technological form or combination of characteristics in the right-hand set.

Any vendor may, at a particular time, be seeking to configure VR in a way that could be represented by a single point in the left-hand set. In principle, that vendor could reposition anywhere else in the left-hand set. In some circumstances, however, the vendor may become 'locked in' to a particular point in the space (David 1985) and finds it hard to reposition because there are heavy costs of 'switching' (Klemperer 1987). Equally, any given user, at a particular time, may be configured to look for a particular technological form and application. Again, in principle and in the absence of lock-in, that user can reposition anywhere in the right-hand set.

The intersection of these two sets defines those technological forms that are also user compatible. Indeed, because these sets intersect, there is potential for a growing market in VR applications. The issue is whether, and how quickly, a market will actually emerge in that intersection.

As drawn, this intersection is quite large, indicating that the actual form or forms of VR that will succeed in the market is still quite wide open. At first sight this may look good for the future market success of VR: users do actually want a variety of feasible forms of VR. Moreover, it indicates that VR can get started in a variety of different ways and still succeed in the market. However, we shall also argue in what follows that a large and diffuse intersection of this sort may actually work against market success. We call this a *paradox of ubiquity*.

A Physical Metaphor

Using analogies can be hazardous, but this one is useful. The concept of cohesion in physics describes the attraction between molecules of a liquid that is necessary to enable drops to form. In a gas, however, the molecules are too far apart for significant cohesion, and hence drops do not form. In short, when the density of molecules is high, drops can form, but when it is low, the drops do not form.

In the same way, we argue that coherent foci (or paradigms) for a technology will emerge only if the intersection has a sufficiently dense population of vendors and users. When these foci start to emerge, users and vendors start to be attracted towards these 'leading designs' and this builds up a *critical mass*[3] of activity around each focus. Only when that process has taken place do the conventional models of technology diffusion start to operate. Fig. 3.1 (*a–c*) illustrate the transition from a thin mist to the emergence of coherent foci. To move from this 'thin mist' to some coherent foci it is necessary to increase the density of users and vendors in (some parts of) this intersection. We shall discuss below how that may be done in practice.

By contrast, if the intersection is too sparsely populated, then the interactions required to achieve coherent *foci* or 'leading designs' do not happen. If no 'drops' or coherent *foci* exist, then there is nothing to attract a critical mass of users and vendors. Conventional diffusion models cannot start to operate because there is nothing coherent to diffuse.

So far, this physical metaphor offers a timeless story. So long as density is low in the intersection, then 'drops' will not emerge. But even after an indefinite wait, it would in principle be possible to increase density to a point at which 'drops' emerge.

Market opportunities are not so patient. The reason for this is twofold. First, vendors and users are liable to get locked in. Because of economies of scale, vendors cannot supply VR applications all the way across these sets. They have

---

[3] Critical mass in physics defines the weight of radioactive material required to sustain a chain reaction. In the economics of path dependence, the term is used to describe the size a consumption or production cluster must reach before its growth becomes self-sustaining.

to select a particular region and concentrate on that. Expertise developed in a particular area of the set is imperfectly portable to another part of the set. Hence, when vendors focus on a particular part of this set for a long time, they tend to get stuck there. Equally, users are not continuously adaptable. *Ex ante*, users may be able to adapt to any point within these sets, but once they have started to focus in one area, it becomes difficult to relocate. In short, while users and vendors may be mobile at an early stage, they are less mobile at a later stage.

Second, to increase the density of vendors and users in a market requires an influx of entrants—vendors and users. An initial burst of 'hype' can serve to trigger such an influx—and indeed did so in the VR industry in the early 1990s. But, if this 'hype' is exaggerated and if those attracted to enter are disappointed about their subsequent experiences, then they will be more sceptical about subsequent bursts of 'hype' and cautious about investing in the technology (Stone and Swann 2001). After that, it becomes harder to engineer an increase in density. For these reasons, markets may give a limited window of opportunity in which coherent *foci* can emerge.

In summary, referring to Fig. 3.1, we can see a variety of circumstances in which cohesion may not take place:

- many vendors are (unwittingly) concentrating their activities outside the intersection;
- those vendors within the intersection are too diffuse;
- some users are currently configured to operate outside the intersection;
- those users within the intersection are too diffuse.

All these conceptual possibilities translate into economic realities and are indeed highly relevant in the context of VR, as we discuss in the next section.

Now we need to move beyond physical metaphor and into economic explanation. First, we need to understand why the emergence of a focus (or paradigm) is so important to the growth of the market. Second, we need to understand in more concrete economic terms why low vendor and user density in the intersection mean that no foci (or paradigms) emerge.

The Role of Paradigms

In the literature on innovation, the 'drop' or focus described in the last section is most commonly described as the foundation of a paradigm. Kuhn (1962: 23) put the paradigm at the centre of what he calls *normal science*: 'Paradigms gain their status because they are more successful than their competitors in solving a few problems that the group of practitioners has come to recognize as acute. To be more successful is not, however, to be either completely successful with a

single problem or notably successful with any large number.' Some are sceptical about applying the Kuhnian analysis to social sciences. Nevertheless, Dosi
(1982) has shown how the concept can be applied in the field of technological
change. Since then, some commentators have read deterministic overtones in
the discussion of paradigms, but there need be nothing inherently deterministic
about them. The paradigm is a socially constructed model. It becomes a convenient focus of company strategy (Metcalfe and Boden 1993), a guidepost
(Sahal 1985) or channel (Georghiou *et al.* 1986), or a vision (Swann and Gill 1993;
Hamel and Prahalad 1994). But it is not uniquely determined by any 'inherent
character' of the technology. In terms of Fig. 3.1, the left-hand set puts limits on
the possible technological paradigms, but there are still a wide range of options.

The importance of the paradigm for the growth of a market can be explained
in four steps.

1. *A common language is essential for the growth of trade.* This first point may
seem obvious, but it is often taken for granted. The growth of trade from the
earliest times required some commonality of understanding between trading
partners, some shared language, and also some common weights and measures. In the absence of these commonalities, trade is just too risky, because
each trader has insufficient understanding of what is being bought and sold and
on what terms (Sullivan 1983; Swann *et al.* 1996).

This observation becomes even more important in a world of rapid innovation. Even amongst those who share a common mother tongue, the ability to
converse about some new product, service, or technology presumes that such a
conversation can be couched in everyday terms. But very often innovation
proliferates jargon. That jargon may or may not be 'efficient' for communication within a particular community, but it is usually an obstacle to diffusion
between communities. If all vendors speak the same technological jargon, then
it may be worth the buyer investing the time to learn what they mean. But if
different vendors use different jargon for the same phenomena, or—perhaps
even worse—use the same jargon to mean different things, then the buyer is
likely to throw up his hands in confusion. We were told of the reaction of a
prospective blue-chip investor on being faced with a highly uncoordinated
message about VR (Swann and Watts 2001). 'It all sounds very interesting. Speak
to us again when you've worked out your story.'

Bacharach (1991)—influenced by the tradition of linguistic philosophy—has
argued that innovations that generate new product characteristics will sell only
if those characteristics can be described in natural (or accessible) language. If
they cannot, then the buyer will not understand the advantage of what he or she
is buying and the vendor will not be able to charge a premium for these
characteristics.

This issue is further complicated in the unique case of VR because of its visual
(and other sensory) methods of communication. Insightful papers such as
those by Sherman and Craig (1995) have highlighted the requirement to adopt

and learn other forms of literacy relating to visual culture and representation. The 'language of VR', and the means by which the benefits of its adoption are communicated, do not rely entirely on verbal or textual methods. Why should we expect them to? VR is principally a graphical medium, and an understanding of its benefits can really be appreciated only once prospective users have experienced the medium itself. Common language in this case relates not only to the associated jargon of the field, but to the artistic and functional expression of the environments themselves. This observation suggests yet another reason why the diffusion of VR has been slow to take off. More recognition of the role of the visual arts in society through targeted education could help break this barrier down. Though contentious, this is arguably one area where the impact of computer games may be positive, by exposing society to new forms of thought and expression.

2. *A common language emerges around a paradigm.* Dalby (1998) discusses the factors causing divergence and convergence of languages. Why do languages diverge? He argues that divergence is a natural and, to some degree, random process of entropy. Arguably it may also be deliberate: divergences in languages or dialects create barriers to competition. Second, why do languages converge? Dalby argues that this is attributable to trade, travel, and communications. Those who travel, for economic reasons or for leisure, learn and imitate the language of others. The same happens when substantial proportions of people pay attention to the press, radio, and television.

   In normal science, the paradigm is accompanied by communication between researchers. No longer 'sole traders', they build up a common model by sharing results and findings. That communication requires a common language, but not necessarily a new one. The same arguments hold when we apply the concept of paradigm to new technologies. The sole trader in finished services who requires no inputs need communicate only with his customers. But alongside the emergence of a technological paradigm we tend to see an increasing division of labour and specialization. Any one company may do no more than add value to a particular part of a system, and hence must communicate with a wide community of suppliers and customers. Without a common language, and without the standardization of concepts and terms, such a division of labour will not work.

3. *The risk-averse buyer faced with undue complexity does not buy.* One of the most telling critiques of modern economic consumer theory is that many practical choice problems are simply too complex for the consumer to be able to optimize in the way that consumer theory assumes (Loasby 1991). Accordingly, the buyer must use simple rules of thumb: for example, to buy a particular brand, or to repeat previous purchases. When it comes to making selections in the area of new technologies, however, such simple rules are unlikely to help. There is no history to refer to, relevant brands are not yet well known, and it is difficult to obtain testimonies from existing users as there are so few of them.

In that case, if the product choice is very complex, the risk-averse buyer may make no purchase at all. There are too many options to evaluate and maybe too many to understand. So, if a technology is too complex or appears too complex (thanks to the lack of a common language), or if it lacks a relatively riskless entry point, then diffusion will not start.

4. *New technologies tend towards unsurveyability without a paradigm.* The problem of unsurveyability can readily emerge in the context of new technologies. To see this, imagine that we use a tree diagram to map different developments in a technology. Suppose that each final node represents a new and distinctive version of the technology or method of application. Imagine also that innovation is continuing, so that each final node of the tree diagram splits into two further branches in every period of time. In that case, by the end of period t a total of 2^t nodes will have appeared. As t increases, this rapidly becomes unmanageable. But Kuhn's normal science (1962) does not proliferate categories as fast as this. On the contrary, normal science would rapidly shed many of the paths/branches of the past. Accordingly, at any time, it may be possible to survey the normal science in 2^k categories, where $k \ll t$ and where k does not expand with t (or only rather slowly). So, even as the science becomes more advanced, it is still surveyable. Contrast this with a pre-paradigmatic phase in which nothing can be discarded, and hence where length of survey is 2^t. Huxley's characterization of science (1963: 35) is highly pertinent here: obsolete scientific expositions 'will go the way of all earlier scientific writings and be forgotten'. But, in the absence of such a paradigm, the field is not surveyable because nothing can be forgotten.

In summary then the paradigm plays two essential roles in the growth of a market. First, along with a paradigm there emerges a common language and that is essential for the growth of trade. Second, along with a paradigm it becomes more manageable to survey a new technology and hence the complexity and risk facing the prospective user is reduced.

Density, Communication, and the Emergence of the Paradigm

Next we need to understand why it is important in economic terms to have high vendor and user density in (some parts of) the intersection if paradigms are to emerge. High density is unlikely to be a *sufficient* condition for a paradigm to emerge. And, indeed, it may not strictly be a *necessary* condition. But we argue that a paradigm is much more likely to emerge as density increases. Given the inherently stochastic nature of the all diffusion processes, such probabilistic statements are perhaps more appropriate than discussion of necessary and sufficient conditions.

In the analogy of the physical metaphor already described, density of molecules was sufficient for 'drops' to form. Moving away from that physical analogy, the process that leads directly towards the emergence of a paradigm is *interaction* rather than density *per se.* But density enables and to some degree *forces* interaction between different vendors and users.

Remember that the density we are speaking of here, as in Fig. 3.1, is density in a technological space: the number of vendors producing similar forms of technology and the number of users using these. However, it will be helpful in what follows to draw out the lessons that can be learnt from densely populated geographical spaces. It is helpful to distinguish between the reasons why density may *require* interaction and the reasons why density can *facilitate* interaction.

Why does density require interaction? The self-sufficient hermit may have little need to communicate with other mortals. The necessity to communicate arises when people share common spaces, whether geographical or intellectual. Moreover, it can be argued that the necessity for communication increases with density of population, because, as density increases, so too do the division of labour and complexity of social relations. As we mentioned before, the sole trader in finished goods or services who requires no inputs need communicate only with his customers. But, with the division of labour, each worker may do no more than add value to a particular component, and hence must communicate with his suppliers and with the next stage in the supply chain. Moreover, in this setting, each trader has not only to communicate with his associates in the supply chain, but must also share a common model of how each component fits into the whole. Traders need to have a common paradigm.

We can see these processes at work in the industrial cluster.[4] As is well known in the literature, location in a cluster brings significant advantages but also some disadvantages. The advantages stem from superior infrastructure, a superior labour market, and the ability to network with other related companies. The disadvantages are the higher costs of labour and real estate, and the greater competition. In the face of this competition, few companies can survive by doing everything in house. Those who do that find they are constantly out-competed by those who contract out 'non-core' activities. Accordingly, to face this more intense competition, companies specialize in areas where they have particular competencies. This leads to an increasing division of labour and the growth of a 'network economy'—where one company's activity depends on the activities of others. Along with this necessity to specialize comes a necessity to interact.

Saxenian (1994) has written of how, in the most vibrant industrial clusters, notably Silicon Valley, people communicate across professions, across disciplines, up and down the supply chain, and across sectors. Some indeed have described the typical Silicon Valley start-up as a network firm in a network economy. The innovative start-up may simply create a link between two branches of the network economy. That may sound trivial but it is not: indeed, Koestler (1969) considered that this bisociation—the bringing-together of two

---

[4] Some have argued that the advent and spread of information and communications technologies (ICTs) reduces the need for and prevalence of clusters. However, as we have shown elsewhere, the reality is more subtle than that (Swann 1999). In some circumstances, ICTs reinforce clustering—an example of the fourth rule of virtuality: 'the more virtual the more real.'

previously unconnected ideas—lies at the heart of innovation. Simon (1985) had a similar perspective. Such innovation is not trivial because it requires the innovator to communicate with two very different and formerly unconnected communities. That requires that the innovator has a command of both paradigms and their associated languages.

These arguments extend beyond geographical space and into technological space. When a technological space becomes more densely populated, the same competitive pressures lead to increased specialism. Instead of trying to supply complete solutions, all developed in house, many companies specialize in particular components or services. But this strategy relies on there being a commonly accepted paradigm for the technology. Any component can sell only if it can be plugged into a system. That requires the other compatible components and services to complete the system, a common language in which to describe the components and services, and a set of standards for interconnection. In the absence of these, no single component will sell, and the specialization strategy cannot work.

That is why density tends to require the emergence of a paradigm. Now we can address the second question: when does density *facilitate* the emergence of a paradigm? Again the literature on geographical clusters helps us. Geographical proximity helps interaction, because it is easier to exchange tacit knowledge exchange and hence develop mutual understanding when interaction is done face to face. This is not impossible at a distance, but it is harder.

Moreover, this argument carries over to communication across technological space. It is generally (though not invariably) easier to communicate research findings to those working in the same field than to others working in disparate fields. The effect is similar though the mechanism is different. The fact that one researcher has accumulated expertise in a particular technology makes it easier for that researcher to understand the research findings of those working in the same field (Cohen and Levinthal 1989). But, as in the case of geographical proximity, density on its own does not generate all the beneficial effects of a cluster. As is well known to geographers, if co-located vendors and users do not communicate, then some of the benefits of clustering are lost. In the same way, those co-located in technological space will generally benefit most from their co-location if they communicate. Of course, co-location does not on its own *force* them to communicate. However, we may conclude as follows: if density is high enough to raise the competitive pressures that make specialization and communication essential, then that density will also make communication relatively easy.

The Pre-Paradigmatic and Diffusion Stages Compared

It is useful to round off by comparing the different characteristics of the pre-paradigmatic and diffusion phases. From the discussion above, and our other

Box 3.1. Comparison of pre-paradigmatic and diffusion stages

Pre-paradigmatic	Diffusion
Lack of consensus about vision; vendor and user expectations out of line	Paradigm/vision has emerged; vendor and user expectations in line
A lot of uncertainty about definitions and ultimate potential	Common language has emerged
Ubiquity is confusing; business failures play an important social role	Technology can be surveyed; wide potential of technology is helpful
Few standards as paradigm does not exist	Some standards have emerged; competition between standards
User investment is highly risky	Risks seem lower to users
High selling costs	Selling costs declining
Technology is not diffusing; users reluctant to invest in adaptation	A variety of diffusion models; something concrete to diffuse, though technology may still evolve during diffusion process
Still waiting for the 'killer application'	Some general-purpose components have emerged

work (Swann and Watts 2001), we have identified some of the most important differences between the pre-paradigmatic stage and diffusion stages in Box 3.1.

These are mostly self-explanatory, but one entry invites further comment. In the diffusion stage, the fact that a technology has a very wide area of application surely helps to expand the market. In the pre-paradigmatic stage, by contrast, the ubiquity of the technology may actually be a problem. If the intersection drawn in Fig. 3.1 is too wide, then vendors and users may be too diffuse to achieve a common focus. We describe this as the *paradox of ubiquity*. This is not to imply that there is one 'right' view or one 'correct shape' for a technology. But the process of market competition tends to yield a few market leaders, even if these are not 'the best' (David 1985), and any technology needs a dominant paradigm if it is to have a chance of success in the market.

IS VR IN A PRE-PARADIGMATIC STATE?

Are the arguments above relevant to the VR market? We shall answer this in three steps. First, we illustrate how the diverse origins of VR have made for a huge and complex technological potential, but difficulty in establishing a common language of VR. In terms of Fig. 3.1, that is part of the 'problem'. Second, we examine the wide diversity of user attitudes to VR and find that, in terms of the right-hand set of Fig. 3.1, this implies a widely diffuse set. Market research suggests that the intersection of these sets is substantial (Cydata 2000), but these are precisely the conditions in which it is difficult to establish a paradigm. Third, we take a look at some other aspects of the VR market that correlate with the stereotypical characteristics of Box 3.1. The implication is that much of the VR market was (in 2000) still in a pre-paradigmatic phase. However, we can interpret some of the collective activities of the VR community as serious attempts to move the technology beyond this pre-paradigmatic stage.

This section draws on a larger study of the VR market during 1997–2000. This included a programme of interviews and visits to some of the main VR vendors and pioneering VR users, participation in several industry shows and conferences and the UK VR Forum (an association of VR vendors, users, and researchers), and a thorough survey of the literature on VR and the VR industry. This work is summarized in detail in Swann and Watts (2001).

Complex Origins of VR and the Language of VR

VR has come to mean a lot of different things to different people. Elsewhere, we have attempted a comprehensive review of the origins and interpretation of VR (Swann and Watts 2001), but here we simply summarize the main strands.

VR is highly multidisciplinary in origin. It lies at the confluence of several traditions. Most histories of VR list around six pioneers or groups of pioneers, who—from very different backgrounds—were instrumental in demonstrating the potential of VR. Though far from comprehensive, these fields are: the computer interface, cinema, art, flight simulation, free thinking, and science fiction. Some would add more: Laurel (1992) writes of VR as theatre. As such, VR draws on the experience and competencies of several different disciplines, industries, and communities. Some members of the VR community in the UK have a background in robotics or CAD; some come from media; some again come from other fields in the arts and sciences. To bring together these distinct traditions into a coherent paradigm for VR is a huge challenge, and at the time of this research an incomplete project.

The term 'virtual reality' was coined by Jaron Lanier, a musician-cum-computer scientist who pioneered the first commercially available VR headset. Lanier, a free-thinker and a very charismatic if unconventional character, did much to draw media attention to the possibilities of VR, but not all of this was helpful publicity. Equally, some of the main ideas about VR have their origins in science fiction, though under a different name. The writings of Gibson (1984) and Stephenson (1993) in particular have been highly influential in shaping how many in the VR community conceive of the future of this technology.

One of the best-known VR pioneers was Ivan Sutherland, a computer scientist who invented the *Sketchpad* in 1962. This was a computer program that allowed the user to draw on a computer screen using a light pen. This invention laid the foundations for the CAD industry, and even more importantly it suggested an entirely new sort of computer interface. Some authors have given Sutherland the title 'the father of computer graphics', in recognition of his contributions to the field (Rheingold 1991; Pimentel and Teixeira 1995).

In 1960, Morton Heilig launched *Sensorama*, an arcade machine not entirely dissimilar to many of today's video games that was intended to portray an extended cinema experience that incorporated features to address all the senses, not just vision and sound (Rheingold 1991; Pimentel and Teixeira 1995). It was one of the pioneering developments in interactive cinema and interactive television. Subsequent variants on this concept—*Aromarama* and *Smellovision*—were less successful, however.

Myron Krueger's art included a series of exhibits that invited participants to question their relationship with computers, and the ways in which they interact with them. Rheingold (1991) captures the essentially interdisciplinary nature of these pioneering works. In his view, Heilig and Krueger 'made a career of falling into the gaps between the conceptual frameworks of scientists and artists, technologists and academics, computer scientists and educators, performers and programmers' (Rheingold 1991: 116).

Finally, Tom Furness III, the director of the Human Interface Technology (HIT) Laboratory in Seattle, a very influential source of research on the potential of VR, worked on visual displays for the military in the 1960s (Moody 1999). In short, these VR pioneers come from many different backgrounds.

At a workshop held as part of our VR study, we were privileged to have a presentation from Angela Dumas (then Director of Research at the Design Council) about her ideas on the role of metaphor in the design process (Dumas 1994). It seemed self-evident to us that this fascinating talk probed the key issues of using graphical models (pre-VR) to enhance the design process. But some members of the VR community at that event did not seem to connect at all. Some felt they had nothing to learn: to paraphrase, 'this speaker is talking about art ... we are doing engineering'. And yet, the whole point of VR, we argue, is that it combines art with engineering and computing. As Moody (1999: 100–1) observes: 'Among the reasons Long and Alexander were drawn to games was a belief they shared with HIT lab director Furness that the effort on the software side must shift from engineering to art if the VR market is ever to grow.' A key point here, in our view, is that literacy in VR requires some literacy, at least, in several of the contributory disciplines (Sherman and Craig 1995). Given the large number of contributory disciplines, that is a tall order. Hence the argument above that *a common language is essential for the growth of trade* is highly pertinent. But it has been difficult to develop a common language for VR.

Dr Johnson famously described the lexicographer as 'a harmless drudge'. While language may be complex and constantly evolving, the lexicographer finds enough stability and enough commonality of understanding that the task of writing dictionary entries is routine if tedious. From this perspective, the existence of a dictionary devoted to a particular subject might be seen as an indication of maturity. And by that measure Latham's *Dictionary of Computer Graphics and Virtual Reality* (1995) could be interpreted as an indication of the maturity of the industry.

However, our strong impression (in 2001) was that the language of VR was still insufficiently developed to overcome the barriers to trade that we have described earlier. Partly this reflects the multidisciplinary origins of VR: people from different communities use different languages. But partly it still reflects disagreement amongst those in the VR community about 'what is VR?' and what is not.

Perhaps the most obvious example of this is in the definition of VR itself. By one of the most common working definitions, VR is *intuitive, interactive*, and *real-time* 3D graphics. This is the definition favoured by those vendors and researchers who would describe their business as virtual reality (defined narrowly), rather than CAD or computer graphics (more broadly). This definition captures quite well the difference between VR and CAD (non-intuitive), physical models (which cannot be modified in real time), and animation (which is non interactive).

But, even if we accept this definition, different members of the VR community interpret it in very different ways. One critic of VR put it to us that much of what is currently marketed as VR is none of these: it is not intuitive, interactivity is theoretically possible but practically absent, any system based on a PC using a standard PC operating system cannot be real time, and VR viewed on the monitor of a PC is not even 3D.[5]

Some *purists* have taken a very narrow definition of VR. To be genuinely 3D and immersive, VR models must be viewed through a head-mounted display, which offers genuine stereo vision. Anything else, from this viewpoint, is not VR. Moreover, purists believe that input devices should be as intuitive as possible for the end-user. VR solutions that incorporate input devices such as position-sensing equipment, data gloves, and other haptic or force-feedback equipment are strongly preferred to solutions using traditional interfaces. These purists tend to be those who believe most strongly that their business is VR (plain and simple).

At the other end of the spectrum are those *pragmatists* who adopt a wider, encompassing definition of VR. They acknowledge that the purist's conception of VR is perhaps the ultimate destination, but also recognize that most of the VR applications selling in the market of 2000 are non-immersive in the purist's sense. The VR models are viewed on PC monitors or on the wide screen of a reality centre, and the inputs used are for the most part the keyboard and the mouse—sometimes, the 'space mouse'. These pragmatists are often people in companies with a rather wider business focus.

---

[5] Such VR models might be better described as offering 2D plus time—that is, in a sense, 3D—but not everyone's idea of 3D. Purists would argue there is a requirement for stereoscopic vision that conventional PC monitors do not permit.

We would not presume to judge whether the purists or pragmatists are right. Indeed, we would argue that there is no 'right' or 'wrong' definition. A more interesting question is to examine these different positions using the framework outlined earlier. Which definition—if generally accepted—is more likely to expand the market for VR?

The pragmatists would say that the current market potential of the purists' conception of VR is very small. It is better, they argue, to adopt a wide definition of VR because then the VR community can point at market data and say, yes, there is a VR market and it will soon exceed $1 billion world wide.[6] Then, when this 'impure' VR market has been established, the purists can start to sell the real VR. The pragmatists worry that, if the industry sticks to a narrow and purist definition of VR, then there will be no perceptible market, and VR will die. In terms of Fig. 3.1, the pragmatists are in effect saying that the overlap between current potential to deliver the purists' VR and current user willingness to buy is minimal.

The purists' views are different. Sometimes, the VR purists seem to argue their case on grammatical grounds. To paraphrase: 'This is VR, and everything else is not. If you call something else VR, then you are inaccurate.' One may not sympathize with this sentiment, but from the perspective of our earlier discussion there is something to be said for it. The purists are perhaps saying (again to paraphrase): 'If you are sloppy and adopt the pragmatists' definition of VR, then the overlap between technological potential and user potential will be very wide, users and vendors will be very sparsely distributed over this large space, and no coherent focus or paradigm will emerge.'

The purists' strategy is to attempt to persuade vendors and users to focus on a small subset of the overlap, as in Fig. 3.1d, hoping that in this way a sufficient density of endeavour can be established to build a paradigm. Indeed, a number of vendors' selling strategies can be seen in this way.

As we look at this in more detail, we find some subtle but important differences in the definition of VR, reflecting the distinct origins and interests of the authors. We can classify these into two groups: the 'hard technological' perspectives and the 'soft communication' perspectives. Amongst the former, definitions of VR describe the interface and the nature of interaction, but tend to portray a somewhat disembodied perspective of the technology.

Virtual Reality is defined as a basic technology that combines computer models, computer-generated images, multimedia and real-time interaction.   (Weimer 1994: 245)

Virtual Reality refers to a suite of technologies which permit intuitive interaction with real-time, three-dimensional databases.   (Stone 1996: 3)

A virtual-reality system should have the three following characteristics: response to user actions, real-time 3-D graphics, and a sense of immersion. It isn't enough to have just one or two of these properties; all three should be present.   (Pimentel and Teixeira 1995: 11)

---

[6] Swann and Watts (2001: ch. 10) take a critical look at market data on 'the VR Market'.

In a virtual environment the human is immersed in a computer simulation that imparts visual, auditory and force sensations...The human operator is allowed to interact with components of the virtual environment through his/her responses being sensed appropriately and coupled into the virtual environment simulation.   (Kalawsky 1993: 7)

The 'soft communication' perspectives, by contrast, describe VR in terms of its characteristics as a medium of communication.

Virtual Reality: a medium composed of highly interactive computer simulations that sense the user's position and replace or augment the feedback of one or more senses—giving the feeling of being immersed, or being present in the simulation.   (Sherman and Craig 1995)

A virtual reality is defined as a real or simulated environment in which a perceiver experiences telepresence.   (Steuer 1992: 76)

Simulation of real development and production processes in cyberspace (Fraunhofer Institute 1997)

Attitudes

Just as the technologists in this market are diffuse, from different traditions and speaking 'different languages', so also the users are very diffuse. In our case studies and case sketches of VR applications, we encountered a spectrum of different user attitudes towards VR (Swann and Watts 2001). This spectrum can be summarized in Box 3.2.

Each row of Box 3.2 indicates a spectrum along which VR use varies. Amongst the VR applications we studied, we can find examples at each end and in the middle (Swann and Watts 2001). The left-hand side represents the more organic and participatory end of each spectrum while the right-hand column represents the more mechanistic and control-oriented end of the spectrum. However, while a particular user might hold several of the attitudes in the left-hand column and another user might hold several of the attitudes in the right-hand column, that does not imply that all these different attitudes are perfectly correlated.

A few of these spectra deserve comment. First, the spectrum running from participatory to control-oriented applications raises some interesting issues. One VR application we examined was a high-fidelity model of a new building, developed to show employees what their new space would look like. However, that model left little or no scope for the employees to interact with the space, to make suggestions, or to modify. They were encouraged to take a 'fly through' and discouraged from making any changes to the model. As such the application did not use the full potential of VR. The problem was not, however, a shortcoming of the technology, nor a shortage of finance. It was an active design choice by the company's management to limit participation, perhaps

Box 3.2. Diverse attitudes to VR use

Organic	Mechanistic
Flat	Hierarchical
Participatory	Control
Empowering	Increased productivity
Generic innovation potential	Specific innovation potential
Mind amplification	Training
Curiosity led	Search the pre-defined space
Open loop	Closed loop
Abstraction	Reality
Metaphor	Representation
Strategic imperative	Strategic scepticism
Disruptive Schumpeterian	Resistant to change
Radical innovation	Continuation of paradigm
VR with everything	Cherished applications
Multidisciplinary	Single discipline
Socio-technical	Scientific management
Arts	Engineering
Media/content	Tool

because they were reluctant to empower their employees to suggest such changes.

Second, the spectrum from generic to specific innovation potential also raises some interesting differences. Watts *et al.* (1998) examined how the innovative organization could use VR to enhance its generic innovation potential, but reckoned that probably only a minority of companies would seek to be innovative in this way. That is born out by the cases we examined. Most use VR to enhance one specific area of productivity (Swann and Watts 2001). However, some of the most exciting applications we saw could be called 'open loop'. In such cases, the user of a VR model does not start out with some particular area that he or she wishes to improve. Rather, the user explores a virtual environment in an open-ended way and then finds some interesting hypotheses that channel future research effort. Interestingly enough, in such examples the virtual environment may be a 'low-fidelity' or abstract VR model rather than a highly realistic or high-fidelity model.

Third, the spectrum from strategic imperatives to strategic scepticism demonstrates the very wide range of views held about the potential and value of VR. One VR user that we visited (a major player in the communications sector) could be said to have a *strategic imperative* towards VR. This organization would try to use VR with everything. We also came across users who could be said to have a *strategic scepticism* towards VR. When we tried to explore what VR could do for the innovative organization (as discussed in Watts *et al.* 1998), the responses were almost entirely negative about VR. To some degree this reflected a surprising but deeply felt belief in the primacy of 2D communication.

Swann and Watts (2001) discuss the implications of this diversity of attitudes. The diversity corresponds to a wide set of user configurations, and it seemed clear in 2000 that no dominant forms of user configuration had yet emerged. Why is this a problem for potential users? Because it is hard for companies to assess which of the many potential applications to pursue. For any company, there may be as many as 10–20 potential applications in areas as diverse as training, product prototyping, marketing, and communications management. Metrics for evaluation are scarce and in the majority of cases participants have not even reached consensus as to the nature of the benefits to be had. Clearly this creates a significant obstacle for the putative product champion. If it is hard to describe the benefits of VR applications to fellow members of the VR community, then it is even harder for the product champion to convince his superiors and peers. As a result, it is unsurprising to find a certain paralysis of action.

Other Indicators of Pre-Paradigmatic Status

Three other observations also suggest that VR is still in a pre-paradigmatic stage. The first concerns the name, 'VR'. Early in our research one of us interviewed the director of a VR company and asked whether his company focused exclusively on VR. The precise detail of the response was less memorable than the manner of it. He started by saying that the company focus was wider, that there was some doubt whether it should be called a VR company or something else. He then memorably dug a piece of paper out of his shirt pocket on which he had written down a rather complex business description, and read this out. Most businessmen have a pretty good, even slick, description of what business they are in. Here was someone who needed a piece of paper to remind him of the precise wording. This ambivalence towards the term 'VR' stems partly from its association with the hype of the early 1990s, but also from some other resonances (which vendors do not like). More recently, some of the leading 'VR' companies seem to have lost confidence in the 'VR' label, and have repositioned themselves. Most prominently, Superscape PLC, which has supplied the much-used *Viscape* 3D web-browser, had in effect removed all references to VR from its company literature by 2000.

Second, it is clear that some of the characteristics of the industry in 1999 matched closely the pre-paradigmatic column of Box 3.1. In particular, the lack of standards is recognized by many in the VR community as a problem—especially the informal design conventions but also technical and interface standards. Moreover, high selling costs are still a major issue for many VR vendors. As one industry observer put it to us: 'Companies are selling VR; nobody is buying it.'

Third, it is clear that some of those in the VR community explicitly recognize the pre-paradigmatic character of their industry. Moody (1999: 148) notes that some in the VR business are clear that it is a big task to work out the 'design grammar' of VR, and will take some time. More bluntly, a vendor doing a sales pitch at a VR conference in 2000 spoke of how his company could guide the customer through 'the VR minefield'. This telling remark begs the question of why any customer would want to walk through a 'minefield' in the first place.

CONCLUSION

This chapter can be summarized in a few paragraphs. When a technology is still in a pre-paradigmatic stage, there is too much ambiguity for diffusion to start in earnest. We have seen that there is a *paradox of ubiquity*: while ubiquitous potential helps to sell a technology in the diffusion stage, it may actually retard the development of a paradigm. At the start of 2000, VR still exhibited many of the characteristics of a pre-paradigmatic technology. Some of the activities of the VR Forum and other VR associations have been directed at trying to achieve the necessary focus through collective action. In a few cases, notably the use of VR models for prototyping in the oil industry and the motor industry, VR has advanced into the diffusion stage (Cydata 2000). Why are these two industries different? Because both are heavy users of CAD already, and in these cases VR is not a new paradigm but an adjunct to the existing CAD paradigm.

How have other technologies made the transition from pre-paradigmatic to diffusion stages? One especially interesting example is the microprocessor solution to the large-scale integration (LSI) 'problem' of the early 1970s. In that case the clear *vision* of a leading vendor (Intel) was sufficiently compelling and credible for users to focus on that, and make their investment plans around it (Swann and Gill 1993). In that case, it was not a matter of explicit coordination to achieve a paradigm, but the emergence of a product leader.

Finally, what does this chapter contribute to the five rules of virtuality identified by Woolgar at the start of this book? The *paradox of ubiquity* has clear resonance with rule 1: that *the current rate of rapid expansion may not continue*. Paradoxical as it may seem, it is the wide generic potential of VR that is holding back diffusion. Some of the attitudes to VR identified in Box 3.2 also resonate with rule 3: that *new technologies can supplement rather than substitute for existing practices*. For those companies whose use of VR could be described as 'empowering', 'developing generic innovation potential', 'curiosity led', 'open loop', or 'VR with everything', rule 3 clearly applies. However, as we stressed above, Box 3.2 defines several spectra, and some companies' attitudes to VR were rather different, suggesting that VR was seen as a substitute and not a supplement.

While we have not discussed the applications of VR at length in this chapter, our case studies have found clear evidence to support rule 4: *the more virtual the more real*. Some of the most powerful applications of VR we saw in our study involved users gathering in the same room to explore a virtual environment on a large 'cinema' screen. Distributed exploration online still happened, but it was much less effective in helping colleagues to surface and share tacit knowledge. VR helps to enrich the 'real' face-to-face meeting, and is not a substitute for it.

How Social is Internet Communication? A Reappraisal of Bandwidth and Anonymity Effects

Susan E. Watt, Martin Lea, and Russell Spears

INTRODUCTION

Internet communication is playing an increasing role in our lives both at work and at home, where it is augmenting or replacing many of the interpersonal and group interactions normally conducted face to face. Approximately 10 per cent of the world's population are estimated to use the internet regularly (McKenna and Bargh 2000). Surveys have often shown that e-mail benefits business by substituting for meetings, and more recently that interpersonal communication is an important home use for the internet. Ninety-four per cent of users report that the internet makes it easier to communicate with family and friends, and 87 per cent use it regularly for that purpose (Kraut *et al.* 1998). Crook and Light (this volume) found that students with networked computers in their study bedrooms use the internet far more for social communication and recreation than for study purposes or for academic exchange.

In addition to helping to maintain existing relationships, the internet also vastly increases the individual's field of eligible social contacts (Lea and Spears 1995). Group interactions through newsgroups and chat rooms are an increasingly important form of internet communication. Indeed, the relative ease with which group interaction can take place on the internet is emerging as one of the most important impacts of this new medium on contemporary social life. This novel form of group communication can take a very real position in people's lives. For example, people with concealable stigmatized identities (for example, being gay or holding extreme political beliefs) gain so much support from belonging to internet groups that their self-acceptance increases, as does their likelihood of 'coming out' or letting other people know about their hidden self (McKenna and Bargh 1998). Internet communications also provide vital social support for people who are isolated through illness or other circumstances (Nettleton *et al.*, this volume).

This pattern of behaviour portrays the internet as a medium characterized by intense social activity. However, this image is in many respects belied by theoretical approaches to computer-mediated communication. These have tended to stress ways in which the medium is *inadequate* for supporting social interaction—or at the very least is suboptimal in comparison with face-to-face interaction. Social psychological theories of new communication media from the telephone onwards have tended to downgrade or even deny the sociality of new media (Short *et al.* 1976; Kiesler *et al.* 1984; Rutter 1987; Walther and Burgoon 1992). A major aim of this chapter is to challenge this conclusion by presenting a theoretical approach, together with supporting evidence, that allows for the full sociality of the internet and is better able to explain specific effects observed in different contexts. In our view, this approach resonates more with the everyday experiences and practices of internet users. This approach also reflects an increasing scepticism in internet research. Initial reactions to the internet have tended to be overly deterministic if not apocalyptic. In our view, a more careful approach to the topic, which takes into account the complexity and variability of the internet as a communication medium, is required.

The structure of the chapter is as follows. We first comment on social psychological approaches that assume computer-mediated communication (CMC) to be socially impoverished in comparison with face-to-face communication, and identify two major themes underpinning these approaches—namely, communication bandwidth and the concept of deindividuation. In the second half of the chapter, we present our theoretical framework (the Social Identity Model of Depersonalization Effects, or SIDE) to explain how reduced bandwidth and anonymity in CMC can *accentuate* feelings of group belongingness and identification, which in our view is central to understanding the internet's social effects. We explain how the SIDE framework is able to account for the variety of social and (apparently) antisocial behaviour observed on the internet, and predict when and why each will occur, and indeed specify circumstances when computer interactions will be intensely social. We describe how social identity processes operate in CMC, and report on various empirical studies to investigate these processes and effects.

Of course, the internet itself is changing—gradually becoming less exclusively text based to involve audio and video communication—just as our views about what the internet is and is capable of are changing. In this respect our research relates to a snapshot in time of the internet, although, if the prior history of mediated communication is any guide, it will be a relatively enduring one. It is perhaps worth recalling that, despite the hype of multimedia internet communication (and indeed the video-telephone before it), it is still the case that the overwhelming majority of internet communications remain text based, as they have been from the start of e-mail in the 1970s. However, it is partly because of this shifting technology that our preferred research method, as distinct from the majority of the research reported in this volume, involves social psychological experimentation in the laboratory. Such experiments seek to isolate critical influences on behaviour by observing people under closely controlled conditions in order to identify causal processes operating in specifically defined conditions. A comparison of behaviour in these different conditions then allows prediction about internet behaviour in particular social and technical contexts. Some of our more recent studies have specifically sought to identify implications for behaviour of the emerging trend towards video communication, and indeed some of our conclusions caution against the imperative to construct the computer medium as an ever-closer approximation to face-to-face interaction.

Finally, our approach is compatible with sociological analyses (such as those that appear in this volume) that acknowledge the potential of CMC to reinforce as well as 'relieve' social relations, and a central objective is to build a theoretical bridge with more concrete analyses of the social psychological processes involved in CMC. Concomitant with the development of this approach, our work has also sought to trace how popular and professional discourses about mediated communication—from the development of the telegraph in the 1840s through to the design of recent computer-supported collaborative work systems—have fed directly into social psychological models and studies of the computer medium, which in turn have helped shape popular and professional ideas about the kind of medium provided by computers (Lea *et al.* 1992; Spears and Lea 1994; Lea and Spears 1995; Lea and Giordano 1997). The SIDE model is just one such contribution, but, as will hopefully become clear, it leads to radically different conclusions about the social nature of internet communications.

Social psychology has generally presented two opposing conclusions about the effects of text-based CMC—positive and negative respectively—both of which assume that CMC is less social than face-to-face interaction. On the one hand, CMC interactions are argued to be more egalitarian, democratic, and liberating than face-to-face interactions (e.g. Sproull and Kiesler 1986; McGuire *et al.* 1987; Dubrovsky *et al.* 1991), and a number of experiments comparing the effects of anonymous CMC with face-to-face communication have found 'beneficial' social consequences such as reduced status and power differentials. At the same time a more pessimistic conclusion has also emerged from similar experiments—namely, that text-based CMC is extreme, impersonal, and antisocial, as evidenced by risky decision making, the use of uninhibited language ('flaming'), and uninhibited behaviour—and concurring with observations made outside the laboratory (e.g. Emmet 1981; Kiesler *et al.* 1984; Stoll 1995; for a case of virtual 'rape', see Dibbeu 1996 and Turkle 1996). Both positive and negative views have received much media attention and been subject to the 'cyberbole' so often applied to the internet, respectively contributing to utopian and dystopian visions of its effects on society (Spears *et al.* 2001*b*).

Despite their opposing conclusions, both arguments rest on the common assumption that a lack of interpersonal cues in text-based CMC creates interactions that are less socially defined, constrained, and regulated—in short, less social than face-to-face interactions. From the optimistic perspective, this is considered to be an advantage because it decreases negative behaviours such as discrimination against people who might be disadvantaged in face-to-face interactions (for example, ethnic minority group members or people with physical disabilities). From the pessimistic perspective, it is considered to be a disadvantage because it decreases positive effects of social interaction such as social regulation and accountability, resulting in more antisocial behaviours. Explaining the heterogeneity of these observations and reconciling the conclusions made from them is one of the challenges of our approach, and, to begin with, we wish to highlight two important conceptual foundations underpinning many social psychological accounts. The first is the engineering concept of *communication bandwidth*, which refers to the relative information-carrying capacity and efficiency of different communication channels. The second concept is *deindividuation*—the psychological state and effects that are produced by anonymity in groups and crowds. The various approaches are briefly discussed next in relation to these foundations (For more detailed accounts, see Spears *et al.* 2001a; Lea *et al.* forthcoming).

COMMUNICATION BANDWIDTH

Communication bandwidth has its origins in information theory: mathematical formulations of communication potentially applicable to any situation of information transfer, by humans or machines. Central to the information theory approach is the idea that communication can be quantified in terms of bits of information required to solve problems of uncertainty (Frick 1959). Research on CMC has been heavily influenced by communications theory approaches grounded in the bandwidth principle, where the equation of technical efficiency of a communication medium with its 'social efficiency' has paved the way for evaluations of sociality based on a mechanistic analysis of information transfer. The focus on information exchange rather than communication of meaning meant that these approaches, collectively termed the 'reduced social cues' perspective (Culnan and Markus 1987; Spears and Lea 1992), were probably bound to underestimate the social dimensions of CMC. Here, theoretical constructs such as 'cuelessness' (Rutter 1987) and 'information richness' (Daft and Lengel 1986) have been employed to quantify the amount of *social* information carried by different media, while the related concepts of 'social presence' (Short *et al.* 1976) and 'psychological distance' (Rutter 1987) attempt to define the relative information-carrying properties of different media in phenomenological terms. From this perspective face-to-face interaction, as full bandwidth communication, is seen as the standard against which every communication medium is measured.

For example, according to the social presence model of communication, media can be distinguished according to the degree of interpersonal contact (intimacy and immediacy) that they provide (Short et al. 1976). Studies have shown that media ranging from letters and telephone through to face-to-face interaction can be rank ordered for social presence by users, and at least one study found CMC to be ranked relatively low (Rice 1993).

A similar construct, media richness, has also been influential in establishing the impression that CMC is less socially rich in comparison to face-to-face communication (Daft and Lengel 1984, 1986). Media richness is defined in terms of how well a medium can communicate equivocal or ambiguous information. In organizational settings, selection of a medium that is inappropriate considering the level of ambiguity in a message results in communication failure. Again, CMC has typically been ranked low in this hierarchy.

Walther (1992) has argued that CMC forces social information into a single, limited-capacity linguistic channel, and that this tends to retard the process of impression formation (though not eliminating it). The social information processing approach proposes that social interaction processes are similar but slower in CMC than in face-to-face interaction, but given sufficient interaction time could be as effective as face-to-face interaction (Walther 1992, 1997).

To summarize, these approaches to CMC each argue in specific ways that the reduced information exchange that results from reduced bandwidth has negative effects on social communication. In general, however, tests of social presence have produced mixed results, or else identified conditions under which social presence effects are overturned. Media richness theory has also been undermined by conflicting evidence (e.g. D'Ambra et al. 1998), and recent revisions have consequently emphasized the symbolic values of different media rather than focusing simply on the information-processing foundations of this theory. Key predictions of the social information-processing model have also not been consistently borne out by research. Indeed, some studies have found people to be less impersonal and more socially attracted to one another in short-term CMC than in face-to-face interaction (Walther 1992; Walther and Burgoon 1992). More recently, extensions to the social information-processing approach have focused on moderating factors that are more social in nature, such as anticipation of future interaction and group salience (Walther 1994, 1997).

In sum, evidence that the social efficiency of CMC can be determined from its technical efficiency is weak. This conclusion holds whether this is cast in terms of social presence, information richness, or social information processing. Significantly, in each case, theoretical revisions have moved away from the central importance of communication bandwidth.

Nevertheless, the belief that reduced bandwidth in CMC means that it is less social than other forms of communication is strongly held both within and beyond social psychology. Indeed, anxieties and concerns about the social

consequences of reduced communication bandwidth were voiced in the popular science journals as far back as the 1890s following the widespread diffusion
of the telegraph and telephone. These concerns tended to be expressed in the
form of anecdotal accounts of dire consequences (such as betrayal, fraud, and
abuse) that befell those who naively treated full and attenuated bandwidth as if
they were socially equivalent. These reports fuelled debates among professional
engineers as to what constituted sufficient presence for a medium to be judged
as equivalent to face-to-face communication (Marvin 1988: 86–96). Some discourses about the new computer-based communication media over 100 years
later are strikingly similar. However, as we shall soon make clear, they depend
upon a circumscribed definition of 'social' in relation to information exchange
in the medium and, perhaps more crucially, an impoverished definition of the
'self' who is interacting in the medium. We develop this latter point in the next
section.

DEINDIVIDUATION

The second conceptual foundation to be found in the reduced social cues
perspective—namely, deindividuation—also has its historical origins in
nineteenth-century accounts of social behaviour. In his classic account of
crowd behaviour, Le Bon (1995) developed the observation that people
experience a sense of anonymity when immersed in large groups. This, he
suggested, creates a loss of personal and social responsibility and of the civi-
lized self, resulting in irrational, violent behaviour and a return to the primitive
self. LeBon's theory was introduced into social psychology by Festinger *et al.*
(1952) and the concept of deindividuation was subsequently taken up by others
(e.g. Zimbardo 1970; Diener 1976) in their attempts to provide an explanation for
various expressions of anti-normative collective behaviour: the crowd's violence,
hooligans' irrationality, and the excesses of a lynch mob. In so doing, the
concept has come to be applied to groups of any size and shape, including
small groups under certain conditions. In one particularly well-known study,
Zimbardo (1970) found that people who were made anonymous by being dis-
guised in baggy overalls and a hood (reminiscent of the Ku Klux Klan) were
more aggressive than those who were made identifiable by wearing their
normal clothes and an identity badge. Zimbardo proposed that these effects
resulted from deindividuation, a state in which reduced self-consciousness had
weakened social controls such as guilt, shame, and fear that would normally
inhibit anti-social behaviour.

More recently, deindividuation theory has also become an influential
approach in accounting for the apparently anti-normative behaviour observed
in CMC and, relatedly, group decision support systems (Kiesler *et al.* 1984;
Jessup *et al.* 1990; Kiesler and Sproull 1992). Like the bandwidth approaches, this

approach also proposes that CMC effects relate to the reduced social dimension in CMC. Importantly, however, this perspective focuses primarily on the relative anonymity experienced in the medium and the psychological state of deindividuation that supposedly results. This in turn affects communication efficiency, participation, relational behaviour, and group decision making. For example, Kiesler and colleagues reported a series of experiments that compared the effects of computer conferencing, e-mail, and face-to-face communication on communication efficiency, participation, interpersonal behaviour, and group choice (Kiesler *et al.* 1984). Significantly, more extreme group decisions were observed in CMC conditions, accompanied by significantly less information exchange. There was also more flaming in CMC (particularly anonymous CMC) in two out of four experiments (Kiesler *et al.* 1984; Siegel *et al.* 1986). In addition, greater task focus and lower attraction responses were found in CMC (Kiesler *et al.* 1985).

Just as with bandwidth approaches to CMC, deindividuation theory resonates with and fuels many popular discourses about groups both on and off the internet (Reicher 1987; Lea *et al.* 1992). However, like other approaches that seek to make general determinations of CMC effects, the impacts predicted by this approach have not been consistently observed in practice. So, while more extreme decision making, anti-normative behaviour, and greater equality are predicted to result from anonymity and lack of social cues, less extreme decision making and greater conformity to group norms have also been observed in anonymous CMC (Hiltz *et al.* 1989; Lea and Spears 1991). The clear implication of these inconsistencies is that behaviour is more situationally specific in CMC than the reduced social cues perspective predicts. Furthermore, evidence has emerged that CMC can reflect and even enhance status-related groupings and norms rather than undermine them (e.g. Weisband *et al.* 1995; Postmes *et al.* 1998; Postmes and Spears 1999).

For example, Postmes *et al.* (2001) reported two studies of specific normative influence in CMC groups. In the first study, participants were physically isolated in separate cubicles. They were then allocated to individuated or depersonalized conditions by displaying photographs of the participants on each computer screen (or not). Their task under these conditions was to use CMC to discuss a dilemma confronting a fictitious hospital. However, prior to their discussions a further experimental manipulation took place—a group norm for either efficiency or pro-social behaviour was covertly activated through the use of a priming technique. The results of this study revealed an interesting pattern of effects. Behaviour in the anonymous groups reflected whichever group norm (efficiency or pro-social) had been activated before the discussions, but this did not take place in the groups where members were individuated. These results showed that, in anonymous conditions, participants were more conforming to the group norm than in individuated conditions.

This finding was replicated in a second study, which also aimed to discover whether CMC is sufficient to establish group norms. In this study only half of the participants in each group were primed with the efficiency-related norm; the other half were neutrally primed. Interestingly, participants in the anonymous condition who had received a neutral prime inferred the efficiency norm from their interaction. They subsequently rated their group as more efficiency oriented. Another study in a more naturalistic field setting using e-mail groups has also confirmed that group norms develop over time, becoming prototypical and distinctive for the group (Postmes *et al.* 2000*a*).

These key studies provide important evidence that visual anonymity in CMC enhances normative behaviour in groups. Parallel findings have also emerged in face-to-face interactions under anonymous conditions. For example, Johnson and Downing (1979) replicated Zimbardo's study (1970) but added a crucial twist. In this experiment, groups of participants were made anonymous either by wearing a mask and overall similar to the Ku Klux Klan uniform used by Zimbardo or by wearing equally deindividuating nurses' uniforms. The results of this study showed that participants in the Ku Klux Klan costume were more aggressive than those in a control condition, but groups dressed as nurses were less aggressive. Thus, it seems that people in these costumes were 'playing a part', conforming to the group norms indicated to them by the clothes in which they were dressed.

Similarly, Reicher (1984) found evidence that people who are deindividuated are more likely to endorse attitudes that they believe are typical of the group than when they are individuated. In a study of attitudes towards vivisection, participants (science and social-science students) were placed in groups according to faculty under conditions of individuation or deindividuation. When individuated, social-science students tended to be generally anti-vivisection, and science students tended to be pro-vivisection. This difference between the groups was increased when participants were made anonymous (deindividuated) by being dressed in baggy clothes and hood. Under these conditions, social-science students were more markedly anti-vivisection, and science students were more markedly pro-vivisection. Thus people's adoption of their own group's norms was greater when they were anonymous than when they were identifiable.

Together, the evidence produced by these studies suggests that anonymous conditions in which individuating cues are reduced or eliminated produce *normative* behaviour. Importantly, the increased aggression found in earlier deindividuation experiments can also be seen to have been influenced by normative cues, such as those provided by the 'Ku Klux Klan' uniform in Zimbardo's experiment (1970). These findings have been summarized in two recent meta-analyses of nearly 100 studies of anonymity in both face-to-face and computer-mediated groups, which concluded that group performance depends on the interaction between specific social context and relevant social norms and system characteristics such as anonymity (Postmes and Spears 1998; Postmes and Lea 2000). Clearly, the conclusions drawn by the studies above are directly opposite to predictions made about behaviour on the internet from the reduced social cues perspective. Instead it emerges that the reduction in social cues and relative anonymity provided by most internet communications are more likely to reinforce socially normative behaviour rather than undermine it. Furthermore conformity to group norms appears to be highly specific to whichever norms are situationally relevant for the interaction.

In the next section we describe our theoretical framework to explain this and other apparent contradictions about internet behaviour, and describe some of our recent work to delineate more precisely the social processes and effects at work in the computer context. Our alternative social identity-based approach offers a different interpretation of these effects, and of the deindividuation concept *per se*. Instead, the SIDE model seeks to explain the *depersonalizing* effects of anonymity in terms of social identity and self-categorization theories. In contrast to the reduced social-cues approach and to limited bandwidth approaches in general, we suggest that CMC is a far more social environment than these perspectives would lead us to believe. Indeed, the social (and prosocial) dimensions of CMC can even be accentuated under certain circumstances relative to equivalent face-to-face situations. We argue that, if we are to explain the variety of effects and to question either positive or negative assessments of the effects, an approach that gives more accord to social context and social influences is required.

THE SIDE MODEL OF COMPUTER-MEDIATED COMMUNICATION

Central to resolving these apparent contradictions is the conceptualization of social cues, the self, and the relation between the two. As an alternative to viewing social cues as a monolithic concept, an important distinction can be drawn between different sorts of social cues that may be present (or absent) in CMC—namely interpersonal cues, and cues to social features, such as group identity and category membership. We argue that, whereas CMC may indeed filter out many interpersonal cues that identify and individuate the communicators, group and category level cues are frequently defined by the interaction context. Moreover, they can be communicated relatively independently of bandwidth considerations and are thereby given more opportunity to influence interaction and the definition of the self and situation. For example, standard e-mail headers may convey information regarding gender, status, or organizational affiliation, but they do not generally communicate personal idiosyncrasies. Despite the trivial quantity of information that these headers represent in information theory terms, they nevertheless are rich in meaning, and a whole raft of self-perceptions and behaviours, as well as perceptions and behaviours of others, follow from their communication. This privileging of group-level information over individuating information in text-based CMC allows a situationally relevant group more influence than in many face-to-face situations where group-level information is submerged by the wealth of interpersonal cues available.

However, when bandwidth and deindividuation approaches discuss reduced social cues in the computer medium, they are primarily focused on the reduction of individuating, *interpersonal* cues. This focus is no accident but reflects the prevailing ideology of individualism inherent in most social psychology, and indeed in most Western societies. In contrast, our approach takes the view that specific group-level cues that are relatively impervious to bandwidth considerations for their communication primarily shape the behavioural differences observed in CMC and on the internet. More specifically we argue that identification of the self with salient groups is the core process responsible for shaping behaviour in these circumstances. In order now to pull these threads together, we briefly describe the theoretical framework for the SIDE model.[1]

SIDE is rooted in social identity theory (Tajfel and Turner 1979), and its sister theory, self-categorization theory (Turner *et al.* 1987). In brief, social identity theory proposes that self-identity is composed of both personal and group elements, and that a person's behaviour in any situation can be placed along a continuum ranging from entirely personal to entirely group based. Self-categorization theory further develops this framework, seeking to show how typical group behaviours (for example, conformity) can be explained in terms of a shift in self-perception from personal identity to social identity. This shift from perceiving the self as a unique person to perceiving the self as a group member is referred to as *depersonalization*. Hence SIDE represents a social identity model of depersonalization effects. It is important to note that depersonalization is very different from traditional formulations of deindividuation. While deindividuation implies a loss of self, depersonalization implies an increased tendency to define the self in terms of the group. In self-categorization theory, Turner *et al.* (1987) argue that depersonalization is the basic process underlying many typical group behaviours (for example, social stereotyping, group cohesiveness, ethnocentrism, cooperation and altruism, emotional contagion and empathy, collective action, and social influence processes). This shift in self-perception, which occurs when a group membership becomes salient (situationally relevant), has important psychological consequences. When depersonalized, people tend to accentuate similarities within groups, and differences between groups, stereotyping others and the self in terms of group attributes. This results in increased adoption of the norms of self-included groups when group identity is salient.

---

[1] For a comprehensive survey of SIDE research, see Postmes *et al.* (2000b). For general review summaries, see e.g. Reicher *et al.* (1995) and Spears *et al.* (2001b). For recent reviews and key theoretical developments in relation to CMC, see Spears and Lea (1992, 1994), Lea and Spears (1995), Lea and Giordano (1997), Postmes *et al.* (1998), Postmes and Lea (2000), Lea *et al.* (2001), and Spears *et al.* (2001a).

According to the SIDE model, anonymity can have two classes of effects, which we have termed 'cognitive' and 'strategic' (Spears and Lea 1994; Reicher *et al.* 1995). The cognitive effects relate to the salience of a particular identity (personal identity or group identity), as described above, and more precisely refer to issues of self-definition. However, the strategic dimension refers to whether the individual or group member feels able to express behaviour in line with a particular identity, given that this is salient. This is particularly relevant in intergroup contexts in which a power relation is present between groups. In this case, anonymity from a powerful outgroup may enable members of the other group to express group normative behaviour that might otherwise be punished or sanctioned by this group. Research on CMC from the perspective of the SIDE model has to date largely concentrated on the effects of anonymity on self-definition in enhancing group normative behaviour, and it is studies of these effects that we review below.

The first empirical tests of SIDE in CMC conceptually replicated in key respects the 1984 study by Reicher, described earlier (Spears *et al.* 1990; Lea and Spears 1991). Here, anonymity was manipulated by either physically isolating participants in separate rooms or by co-locating them in the same room. Group interaction in both conditions was conducted by means of a simple text-based synchronous conferencing system that allowed participants to discuss a range of political issues by typing messages to their group. In a further manipulation, participants in a group-salient condition were briefed that the experiment was a study of groups using CMC and their group comprising psychology students would be compared with other non-psychology groups, whereas those in a personal identity-salient condition were told that the experiment would compare personal differences in communication styles using CMC.

The results supported the hypothesis that normative behaviour in anonymous CMC is increased under conditions of group salience. Importantly, participants in the anonymous condition were more conforming (shifted their opinions towards group norms) when their identity as group members was made salient. This coincided with *less* messaging and issue discussion, undermining the information-based explanations reviewed above. In contrast, when their individual identity was made salient in anonymous conditions, participants were less conforming. They tended to move their opinions away from the group norm—that is, to assert individuality by differentiation from the group.

A significant number of further studies have now expanded the range of anonymity effects accounted for by SIDE theory. In addition to studies by Postmes, described earlier, which were crucial in demonstrating how situationally specific social norms can be communicated and become influential through CMC, other studies have examined group attraction, stereotyping, accountability, support, duty, and power relations in intragroup and intergroup contexts (Postmes 1997; Postmes and Spears 1999; Postmes *et al.* 1998, 2000*a*; Lea *et al.* 2000*a*, *b*, 2001*a*; for a recent collection, see Postmes *et al.* 2000*b*). In each case the specific behavioural effects observed could be accounted for by reference to the social identities made salient in the communication context and the degree of personal anonymity and interpersonal cue reduction associated with the communication condition. This applied to a range of behavioural effects argued by reduced social cues approaches, reviewed above, to be general features of CMC, including extreme decision making, and impersonal task focus. In addition, the linguistic features of group interactions hitherto considered to be either unique to CMC, such as the use of paralanguage (including 'emoticons'), or else ubiquitous in CMC, such as 'flaming', have been shown to be instances of highly situated, group-normative behaviour that is augmented in CMC by anonymity's depersonalizing effects (Lea and Spears 1992; Lea *et al.* 1992; Douglas and McGarty 2001).

Crucially too, behavioural effects in CMC that run counter to those approaches have also been explained by reference to situated social identities within the SIDE theoretical framework. These include increased socio-emotional communication, pro-social behaviour, attraction, and conformity to group norms (Postmes *et al.* 1998; Lea *et al.* 2000*b*, 2001). In the next section we briefly describe some of these recent studies and the specific SIDE issues that they address.

RECENT EVIDENCE

Situated Normative Influence in CMC

One of the central arguments in the SIDE approach is that the effects of anonymity on group behaviour in CMC are closely connected with the context of interaction. This is because anonymity effects in CMC depend on which norms (based on personal or group identity) are activated by the context or communicated through CMC. This marks an essential distinction between SIDE and the deindividuation approach to CMC reviewed above. Whereas the deindividuation approach views CMC behaviour in relation to the *rejection of general norms* prevalent in society, accentuated by the lack of interpersonal cues in the medium, the SIDE approach has shown CMC behaviour to be more consistently explained as instances of *conformity to local group norms*, accentuated by the lack of interpersonal cues.

We predicted that anonymity primarily affects relatively transient identifications rather than identification with pre-existing long-standing categories. The definition of these latter categories and one's relation to them are likely to be relatively enduring and therefore less affected by the contextual conditions of the communication environment. However, our previous studies (e.g. Spears *et al.* 1990) have confounded local group and wider social category categorizations. We therefore tested this prediction in a study of computer-conferencing groups using participants physically isolated in different rooms and operating under two conditions: one in which a wider social category (nationality) aligned with the group identity, the other in which national identity cut across the group. This was done using various procedures designed to present the study as one involving international communication over the internet with participants located in another country (Germany) who were either the same or a different nationality from the other participants. We found that nationality had no effects on participants' self-categorization in terms of nationality or the interacting group under anonymity or identifiability conditions. Various mediation analyses were conducted, and the results clearly indicated that social identity processes activated by anonymity were at the level of the interacting group and were unaffected by perceptions of the wider category (Lea *et al.* 2001).

SIDE Processes Mediating CMC Effects

SIDE research has shown that normative behaviour is enhanced by anonymity under conditions of group salience. According to SIDE, it is *identification with the group* that is the central mediating process that increases normative behaviour in anonymous CMC. Visual anonymity depersonalizes perceptions of self and others; this increases group identification, which in turn increases typical group behaviours. Self-categorization as a group member and attraction to the group respectively form the cognitive and affective components of social identification.

This crucial role of social identification in mediating anonymity effects in CMC groups has been tested in two studies using path analysis. In one study, visually anonymous groups were compared with visually identifiable groups (video mediated). In the other study, nominally identifiable group members (those who were identifiable in terms of their name) were compared with anonymous groups. In these studies, self-categorization was found to mediate the effects of anonymity on group attraction, stereotyping of others, sense of duty, accountability, and conformity. At the same time, some of the crucial mediators predicted by deindividuation theory and information-processing approaches to CMC, such as evaluation concern and impersonal task focus, were ruled out (Lea *et al.* 2000*b*, 2001).

Decomposing Anonymity

Conceptually, a useful distinction can be drawn between two aspects of anonymity within the group: anonymity of self to others, and anonymity of others to self. According to the SIDE model, we would expect anonymity of the self directly to increase self-perception in terms of the group; while anonymity of others should increase the tendency to perceive others in terms of their group memberships, leading to increased perceptions of group homogeneity, of the group as an entity, and the tendency to stereotype others in group terms. Here we report the results of two studies that aimed to decompose anonymity into its constituent elements. The first study was designed to manipulate just one component of anonymity—identifiability of others to the self. In this study, each participant engaged in discussions with confederates using text-based computer conferencing. In one condition, the system was configured so that, in addition to text, the participant received real-time video images of others within the group. In the other condition she received no video. In both conditions, the participant was aware that she herself was visually anonymous to other members of the group (Lea *et al.* 2000a).

Path analysis enabled investigation of the rather complex pattern of effects that occurs when anonymity is asymmetrical within the group. The effect of visibility of others when the self is anonymous activated three different processes. First, identifiability of others directly increased group attraction, reflecting group attraction based upon interpersonal attraction to others in the group. Secondly, identifiability of others increased self-categorization, which in turn increased group attraction; and self-categorization increased stereotyping of others, which also increased group attraction. These latter paths represent the depersonalized attraction process triggered by anonymity that we have previously observed (Lea *et al.* 2001). However, in this case it was visibility of others, rather than complete anonymity within the group, that increased the tendency for depersonalized attraction to occur. In this case, rather than visibility having a primary effect of individuating group members, visibility provided cues for identifying with the group. A likely candidate in these all-female groups is that gender cues, which are readily visible, increased the participant's sense of belonging to the group. We specifically investigated this hypothesis in a follow-up study, which we will describe shortly.

A third process was also evident in an additional tendency of identifiability of others to increase the participant's sense of anonymity of self, which in turn reduced their self-categorization with the group (this latter effect was weak). This may reflect a comparative process produced by the asymmetrical visibility conditions. Visibility of the others when the self was anonymous could increase the sense of the participant's own anonymity beyond the level felt when all group members were anonymous. This in turn distinguished (individuated) the self from the others, creating a sense of being 'outside' the group, different in this respect. Although identifiability of others tended to increase anonymity of self, this in turn reduced the self-categorization with the group. These results suggest that the participant compared herself with the others, and knowing herself to be more anonymous than them decreased her sense of being a member of the group.

In summary, we think that three processes are revealed by these data. First, an interpersonal attraction process increased by the visibility of others; a second, social identity-based depersonalized attraction process increased by visible common-gender cues; and a third, weaker comparative process, in which identifiability of others coupled with anonymity of self causes a separation of the self from the group. The second of these processes was investigated further in the next study, because it seems to question the generality of a common SIDE effect—namely, that anonymity in the group increases social influence.

Reversed Anonymity Effects in CMC: The Case of Gender

In general, SIDE research has found that anonymity increases group-stereo-typical perceptions in CMC, and that stereotyping as well as group norms and social influence are communicated more readily in anonymous CMC. Results also suggest that these effects occur primarily at the level of the local, inter-acting social group. The perceived relations of self and others to pre-existing, long-standing categorizations, such as nationality, are less affected by anonymity in CMC. However, the study reported above also suggests that, when certain identities are salient, anonymity can have reverse effects. This may be because some categories, such as gender, are immediately and easily communicated by visibility, and thus make the category more salient under visible conditions than under anonymous conditions. In other words, we should not assume that anonymity *always* leads to increased group behaviour, as this may depend on whether the essence of a group or category is designated by visible features or not. We tested this hypothesis by comparing, under conditions of anonymity and visibility, self-categorization to a readily visible category (gender) and another social category, nationality, previously shown to be relatively imper-vious to anonymity manipulations (Lea *et al.* 2000*b*).

In this study, groups consisting of British and Dutch, male and female par-ticipants, located in Manchester and Amsterdam, discussed topics using a computer-based video-conferencing system. These topics were designed to make salient either a readily visible category (gender) or a less visible category (nationality), and groups interacted under visually anonymous or video-mediated conditions.

The results indicated that, when gender was salient to the discussion, it was visibility rather than anonymity that increased participants' gender identifica-tions. However, this did not occur when nationality rather than gender was made salient by the discussion topic, and visibility had no effect on national identifications. In comparison with previous findings, these results showed that visibility does not always serve only to individuate, but that, in the specific situation where it provides obvious cues to the salient category, it can enhance perceptions in terms of that wider social category.

CONCLUSIONS

It is inevitable that, in disentangling any question, more twists and turns appear in its fabric. We started out by asking whether the internet is an appropriate place for social interaction, what will happen when people interact over the internet, and whether CMC is capable of supporting group communication. Our theoretical analysis, the SIDE model, was based on a social identity critique of deindividuation theory and its application to CMC. It led us to the somewhat counter-intuitive notion that the relative physical isolation and visual anonymity experienced within CMC may actually lead people to behave in a more socially regulated, normative way. Our programme of research, conducted over more than a decade, leads us to conclude that this is often the case, and that the behaviour so produced is mediated by social identification. However, our aim has not been to produce yet another general determination of CMC effects, but to show how specific behavioural effects are situated and constrained by the social and technical context of the communication and the interaction between these factors. Thus twists and turns, rather than simple conclusions, are precisely what we expect to find and drive the further development of the SIDE model towards greater context sensitivity. In our most recent research we have begun to tease apart the different components of anonymity, to examine separately anonymity of the self to others, and anonymity of others to the self. There we discovered a complex pattern that depends both on the visibility of the group and on awareness about being seen by others. The effect of the visual anonymity of others was also found to depend upon the type of group, and whether it can be easily discerned from visible cues. However, only part of the story has yet been told; we have still to test fully the implications of these effects on identification and behaviour within the interacting group. Further investigations that decompose anonymity into its constituent parts are required in order to understand how anonymity achieves its effects. While we have focused here on studies that simulate under laboratory conditions more naturalistic internet communication, their implications and the theoretical framework underpinning them have been developed alongside observations of discourses and behaviour on the internet and its associated technologies. The next phase, that of combining these two approaches into more naturalistic studies of 'real-life' online interactions in work, educational, and recreational contexts, has already begun (Lea *et al.* 2000*a*; Postmes and Lea 2000; Postmes *et al.* 2000*a*), and will likely turn up yet further twists and turns in the search for greater context sensitivity.

This brings us back to the questions with which we started this chapter—namely, whether the internet and computer conferencing systems form socially adequate communication media when compared against face-to-face communication. A picture, picked up both from theories and observations of everyday usage, initially seemed to suggest that CMC might not do full justice to the social richness of the people using them. However, the analysis and findings presented here should make it clear that communication using CMC is no less social, and may actually be more socially regulated, at least at the group level, than face-to-face communication. Thus, consistent with the fourth 'rule' of virtuality (Woolgar, this volume), virtual interactions in CMC have proven to be at least as real as face-to-face interactions. Similarly, although 'anarchic' in the sense of lacking central regulation, the internet seems to be richly social, regulated by its own inhabitants and by group norms. In this respect, CMC may be regarded as an entirely appropriate medium for group interaction and this conclusion probably helps to explain why e-mail and the internet seem to be, and seem to be experienced as, such social media.

The second general lesson of this programme of research, however, is that it is probably wrong to draw *general* conclusions about effects of media such as CMC. There has been a strong temptation (rarely resisted) by commentators to claim generic effects of new media such as CMC. However, and in line with Woolgar's first rule of virtuality (this volume), these effects cannot be summarized with simple conclusions. The communication effects stimulated by new media are probably no less rich, and certainly no less complex than social interaction in general. By focusing on the communications technology, it is easy to forget the complexity of the social actors and social relations involved, and to fall into the trap of technological determinism (see also Mason *et al.*, this volume). However, to ignore the distinctive character and constraints of the communications technology is equally problematic, and leaves us equally prone to social determinism. Our studies show the benefits of a specific, process-oriented approach, taking into account the nature of identity and the content of associated norms. This allows us to document the complex interactions between social factors and technological features. As a result, we have shown that the anonymous character of CMC will often intensify group-level effects (identification, social attraction, social influence) by depersonalizing perception and self-categorization. However, importantly, it does not always do so. Some social categories are actually more salient when visible (for example, gender, race), and so identifiability can accentuate social effects of these categories. Such specificity is important for understanding the effects of specific media (for example, e-mail versus video conferencing) and specific social categories, and, when necessary, how to tailor one to the other. A social contextualist approach that does justice to the complexity of both social and technical components, and does not abandon conviction in psychological process and theory, is, we think, the best way to understand the systematic variance in the variable effects of the virtual media.

5

New Public Places for Internet Access: Networks for Practice-Based Learning and Social Inclusion

Sonia Liff, Fred Steward, and Peter Watts

THE DIGITAL DIVIDE

The rate of growth in the numbers of people with access to the internet makes any estimate out of date before publication. What does seem remarkably persistent, and a cause of continuing policy concern, is the uneven pattern of take-up across social groups both within and across national boundaries.[1] The *digital divide* has become the shorthand term to capture this concern, which was first discussed in the USA in the mid-1990s. Attention has focused on data such as that documented in the *Falling through the Net* reports (most recently NTIA 2002), which showed significant inequalities of access based on income, gender, ethnicity, urban/rural location, and age. Surveys of internet use in the UK have revealed similar patterns (Booz, Allen & Hamilton 2000). Initially the US public policy approach to the issue of equitable access was framed solely in terms of infrastructural regulation to ensure 'universal' opportunity to connect to the information superhighway (Information Infrastructure Task Force 1993). Similar sentiments could be seen in Europe in the Bangemann Report (Bangemann 1994). This understanding of the digital divide as primarily a technical/financial issue has continued to be dominant, expressed, for example, in the European Union's adoption of the eEurope initiative, whose targets include cheaper internet access and ensuring that citizens have electronic access to government (CEC 2000). The difficulty of making this a reality in a

---

[1] Cf. Woolgar's first rule of virtuality (this volume): the uptake and use of new technologies depend crucially on local social context.

context where many of those currently without access show a reluctance to use PCs has led the UK government to explore whether its commitment to 'universal access' can be achieved via developments in devices already widely diffused such as digital TV and mobile phones (CITU 1998). However, the Institute for Public Policy Research (IPPR 2001) reports that the most optimistic estimates suggest that 10 per cent of the population are likely to remain excluded even from digital TV. Research for the Central Information Technology Unit (CITU) report found that a quarter of the population said that they would not be willing to use any technology they were not currently using to access government services. IT for All (DTI 1999) reported that 12 per cent of the population surveyed said that they had a PC in their home that they never used.

Collectively such evidence suggests that ownership of technology may not be the key issue and has led to a growing recognition of the social aspects of internet access. Research for IT for All (DTI 1999) found that the most commonly mentioned barriers to the use of information and communications technology were expense and lack of access. However, also cited as significant factors by non-users were that ICTs were not seen as relevant or necessary to their lives and that they found them difficult to understand and did not know where to get help. A *Which?* report (1998) found perceived lack of relevance to be the major reason why people were not using the internet. It also highlighted fears about a wide range of threats thought to be posed by the internet, including that it would undermine morality by making pornography available, facilitate fraudulent practices, and be a threat to national security. The 2001 government initiative UK Online, with an awareness of such issues apparently in mind, promotes a new range of public access centres as follows: 'they all have... approachable and experienced people who can help you and can cater for individual needs.... all in a friendly, helpful atmosphere' (DfEE 2001). A recent report from the Office of the e-Envoy (2001) discusses the 'need to put increasing focus not so much on cost and physical facilities, but on raising awareness of the benefits of the Internet amongst certain disadvantaged groups'.

The significance of supportive social contexts to address such issues has been a sub-theme in UK policy debates for some time. A House of Lords Select Committee on Science and Technology (1996) expressed the view that widespread home access to, and use of, the internet would become a reality only if 'special arrangements' were made for public access in order to achieve widespread knowledge, skills, and use of IT. 'Demand for such access', it notes, 'has already been demonstrated in the UK by the spread of cybercafés providing access to the internet, often with personal assistance, known as a "handholding" facility, available as an optional extra, as well as the refreshments more generally associated with cafés' (para. 5.64). Public access continued to be a theme in policy announcements such as *Our Information Age* (Central Office of Information 1999), e-commerce@its.best.uk (Performance and Innovation Unit 1999), and the Learning Centres' initiative (DfEE 1999). But these policies express no clear view as to the relative merits of different types of social setting.

Reference to cybercafés is a recurrent theme, however, all the policy documents cited above note the potential of a range of sites, from colleges and libraries through to community centres.

In practice government support has not been neutral in relation to these different types of sites. Under the UK Conservative Government of 1992–7 an initiative called IT for All was established that listed places prepared to offer a free introduction to computers and the internet. There was no public support for centres providing this service, and so, unsurprisingly, when we analysed the 1,300 sites listed on the web site in 1998, over 60 per cent were schools, colleges, and training organizations and a further 15 per cent libraries. Less than 5 per cent were community-based organizations or cybercafés. This initiative was wound up in September 2000 (including its web site and all associated documents) to be replaced by UK Online. Again no direct financial incentives or support are given to those who join this initiative, although funds have been made available for the creation of new centres in the most deprived areas of the country, including community-led initiatives. However a substantial proportion of the resources continue to go to existing public-sector organizations such as local authorities, colleges, schools, and libraries.[2] The strengths of public institutions, particularly colleges and libraries, as sites for extending access are clear. They have existing buildings, equipment, and staff, an existing public-service role, and are already linked to initiatives such as the National Grid for Learning and the University for Industry (Learn Direct). The focus on such institutions also fits comfortably within a discourse of public provision for literacy and knowledge. But government has also been aware of their limitations. As part of the work of the Social Exclusion Unit, a Policy Action Team looked at the ways adults in deprived communities could be encouraged to gain new skills. They commented that 'too many adults have had a poor experience of compulsory education. A negative experience of school often leaves people disinclined ever to learn again' (National Strategy for Neighbourhood Renewal 2000). Similarly, the government endorsed public libraries' claims to be a 'natural' site for extending access (DCMS 1998), but then issued guidelines reminding libraries of the need to address social inclusion issues (DCMS 1999). The Policy Action Team that looked specifically at ways of increasing access to information and communication technologies in deprived areas stressed the need for provision in community locations such as community centres (Policy Action Team 15 2000). However, unlike the continuing funding provided for colleges and libraries, community-based internet access sites have at best received relatively short-term 'project' funding directed towards the creation

---

[2] This is based on our own analysis of organizations awarded funds under the Capital Modernization Fund rounds 1 and 2. Lists were available at http://www.dfee.gov.uk/ukonlinecentres/news8.htm (accessed 20 Sept. 2000) for round 1 and at http://www.dfee.gov.uk/ukonlinecentres/p2sc.htm (accessed 8 Aug. 2001) for round 2. Neither site is available any longer. The organizations were not classified on the sites but a judgement has been made on the basis of the name of the body to whom the funds were awarded.

of awareness and skills. The assumption seems to be that there is only a transitional need for the provision of such types of access, which will disappear once the internet's value is proved, skills are gained, and costs become manageable. This could be described as the launderette model of ICT provision—a facility that remains but that is used by only a small proportion of people on the basis of need rather than choice.

This view of the attractiveness of internet access in a novel social setting contrasts with the development of internet cafés, which have emerged largely as an independent entrepreneurial activity without any government subsidy. The people who use internet cafés pay for access and appear to do so from choice rather than necessity. This raises the question of whether the provision of internet access in a social context provides something more than a residual provision. Is the pub a better model than the launderette?

REAL SETTINGS FOR ACCESS TO THE INTERNET

This chapter explores the contribution that real social settings make in providing access to, and participation in, the virtual world. Our primary focus is on new social institutions. These new institutions are referred to collectively here as e-gateways and comprise both provision from the voluntary/not-for-profit sector (known by a variety of names including telecottage, electronic village hall, community technology centre) and from the private sector (usually known as cyber or internet cafés). A common characteristic is the provision of internet access in a varied informal and often unstructured setting. Contrary to some expectations, the spread of the virtual world of the internet, a development that many commentators have seen as inevitably leading to a decline in social engagement (Graham and Marvin 1996; Nie and Erbring 2000), has actually been accompanied by a lively process of real social innovation. This development may provide some insights into the contribution of social setting to the provision of internet access.

A consideration of the importance of social settings for who has access to the internet and what they use it for is in line with earlier studies of innovation in communication technology (e.g. Raymond Williams 1974: 43; Dutton 1999: 323). The 'uniqueness of particular settings' is seen to lead to specific 'configurations of heterogeneous technical and social' elements, with contrasting implications for the nature of user access (Robin Williams 1997: 309). These studies emphasize the importance of 'real places' as critical sites for innovations that express different modes of access and where choices 'configure the user' as well as configuring the systems and software (Woolgar 1991).

The number of studies that have extended this form of analysis to internet access are limited, particularly in the UK context. However, US studies suggest that it is difficult to create circumstances that engage some socially excluded members of the community, even when they are explicitly targeted (Virnoche 1998) and that mainstream institutional settings (government, libraries, or universities) are far less likely than the not-for-profit sector to be the source of innovative community networks with democratic and community goals (Harrison and Stephen 1999). In a detailed study of Trinidad, Miller and Slater (2000) highlight the way informal, community-based forms of access and use led to novel and distinctive forms of internet use being developed and sustained. UK community-based practitioner literature has made significant claims for the importance of settings outside the mainstream educational sphere for extending access to the most deprived (e.g. Shearman and Communities on Line 1999). However, they tend not to explain conceptually how this is achieved (Liff and Steward 2001).

A consideration of social learning and the role it plays in the process of understanding the potential of a new technology, and in shaping actual patterns of use, also highlights the importance of social settings. Lave and Wenger's practice-based theory of learning (1991) takes as a starting point the existence of 'communities of practice' defined as 'activity' systems 'about which participants share understandings concerning what they are doing and what that means in their lives and for their communities' (1991: 98). A particular configuration of ICT in a specific social setting may therefore be analysed with respect to a certain group of people who can be regarded as members of a community of practice. The extent of this community depends on the degree to which understandings are shared with other settings.

Learning is situated and occurs when newcomers to this community are treated as 'legitimate peripheral participants' where their 'intentions to learn are engaged and the meaning of learning is configured through the process of becoming a full participant in a sociocultural practice' (Lave and Wenger 1991: 29). This participation has consequences for 'access' to the community of practice in a way that facilitates understanding. This is termed 'transparency' and is regarded as constituting 'the cultural organization of access'. An example is 'the way in which using [technological] artifacts and understanding their significance interact to become one learning process' (Lave and Wenger 1991: 102).

Broader sociological analysis has also drawn attention to the way in which particular social settings impact on the quality of social relations of those who frequent them. Oldenberg (1991) lists many benefits of being a regular visitor to an informal public place such as a bar. These include being introduced to new people and new ideas and developing relationships that lead to a variety of forms of personal support. He terms such settings 'third places' (to indicate a sphere separate from the domestic or the economic). Their characteristics, he argues, can be abstracted from any particular manifestation, as, for example, an English pub or a Viennese coffee house. 'The eternal sameness of the third place overshadows the variations in its outward appearance and seems unaffected by the wide differences in cultural attitudes towards the traditional gathering places of informal public life' (Oldenberg 1991: 20). Being called a café is, of course, not enough. What is needed is a neutral place where people feel comfortable and can come and go at will (as opposed to an interaction based on one being the host and the other the guest) and that is socially inclusive in terms of the criterion for membership, stimulates good conversation, is accessible in terms of hours and location, is frequented by regulars—and it is the possibility of meeting such friends that provides a primary motive for visiting it—is unpretentious in style and in mood, and has many of the characteristics of home without being one's home. In relation to internet access where issues of awareness, anxiety, and the need for new skills have been highlighted as barriers, an access place with such characteristics may be particularly valuable.

INCLUSION THROUGH NETWORKS

Central to our analysis of e-gateways as social settings that support particular forms of inclusion, learning, and participation in the virtual is the notion of social networks. The network of relationships between people in a particular setting, and the relationships those people, individually or collectively, have to others in the wider community, provide a way of understanding the processes of innovation, learning, and sociability discussed above.

It is usual to distinguish between two main types of network relationships: strong and weak ties. Strong ties are those, often with family or those in a close knit neighbourhood, that are multidimensional, intense, intimate, and reciprocal. Studies suggest they are very important for general well-being and particularly for the provision of core support in times of need (see Putnam 2000 for an extensive review of the evidence). Weak ties, in contrast, tend to be more specialized and involve less frequent interaction, but can be a key way in which people get new sources of information and find, for example, new job opportunities (Granovetter 1973). More generally, supporting people's involvement in new networks, and the activities that define them, is likely to involve 'boundary spanning' (Aldrich and Herker 1977)—a way of making links between different networks. Combinations of strong and weak ties may well be important here (Perri 6 1997; Putnam 2000). In terms of e-gateways, it is important to understand what types of social network relations link them to their users and what sort of relations they seek to develop between them in order to understand what, if anything, they contribute to different aspects of access.

Network relationships are important in promoting access to any new product, but they have a further significance for access to the internet. One of the potentially positive outcomes of widening access to the 'virtual world' of the internet is the expansion of the reach of social networks that occurs through the enhancement of the individual user's exercise of communicative power. An extension of the range of a person's networks may be seen as expressing the 'logic embedded in the new technological paradigm' (Castells 1996: 62), with its challenge to the traditional constraints of spatiality, synchronicity, social intermediation, and sectoralism that characterize the 'real world'. Understood in this way, the digital divide is not just about whether one has the technology or not but more about the ability of some people to become active participants in these new patterns of expanded network interactions. If they do not achieve access in this sense, there is a risk that the impact 'could be potentially the reinforcement of the culturally dominant social networks' with the creation of two distinct populations, 'the interacting and the interacted', the 'networkers and the networked' (Castells 1996: 363). In this context it is important to con-sider whether particular social settings for access support users' under-standings of, and ability to participate in, these wider network relations.

The actual form and nature of new relationships between 'virtual' and 'real' worlds cannot be defined or predicted from general theorizing or social analysis. It needs to be explored through 'specific analyses and empirical observation' (Castells 1996: 62). Our starting point is that research on the places where social and virtual networks intersect can provide insights into the actual effects of computer-mediated communication (CMC) use in particular social settings on such networks. The discourse of naming e-gateways—telecottage, cybercafé, electronic village hall, community technology centres—reflects the intersection of the virtual and social and is of particular interest. In addition, their social part draws on existing institutions that are characterized by interaction and communication.

This chapter describes the research we undertook on e-gateways and its findings in terms of the extent to, and ways in, which they succeeded in creating the type of sociable setting described above as third places and the significance of this for forms of access. It further analyses the types of situated practices that were observed in different types of e-gateways and their role in supporting particular types of inclusion, learning, and engagement with the virtual. The chapter concludes by discussing the contribution the research makes to broader debates about the role of the internet in relation to social inclusion and exclusion.

OVERVIEW OF RESEARCH UNDERTAKEN

An investigation was undertaken in the UK to identify existing e-gateway organizations. These were defined as supervised locations offering public access to computers and the internet outside the state sectors of education or libraries. An e-mail survey of the nearly 250 e-gateways identified in 1998 gathered information on what they provided, their approach and use. Responses covering facilities, opening hours, objectives, and user characteristics were obtained from 148 organizations, representing 63 per cent of those iden-tified. Almost all had been created in the previous five years. They were small, bottom-up initiatives run by enthusiasts. Many of the e-gateways promoted a range of activities that could not be tightly delineated within the conventional categories of work, citizenship, education, and leisure.

Based on this initial survey closer study was made of selected e-gateways, which were effective in terms of numbers and range of users and which were also illustrative of distinctive approaches. Short visits were paid to a range of these sites, followed by detailed case studies carried out at four UK locations (both rural and urban). Research included interviews with staff, observation of the site, discussions with clients and funders, and analysis of completed questionnaires from around 300 users and 200 non-users (cf. Wyatt *et al.* this volume) of gateway sites. Questionnaires gathered information on the demographic characteristics of users and non-users, their use of computers and the internet, and their assessment of the e-gateway in question.

The investigation sought to explicate the set of practices situated in these e-gateways that facilitated socially inclusive access to and use of computers and the internet. The exploration of the design and management of a place that enabled new users to gain initial access to computers and the internet was one important issue. The learning process that developed continuing engagement of users was another. The construction of different user roles at the interface between the real and the virtual was the third area where the e-gateway practices were scrutinized. For all of these issues a key objective of the research was to probe the relationship of these situated practices to the social networks of users.

Research was also carried out in the Los Angeles area in the USA and in Finland. As countries that have the highest rates of internet usage, yet with different traditions in the public sphere, the USA and Finland provided an interesting contrast to the UK research. In both locations a wide range of sites providing public internet access were visited. Both countries have also had a longer period than the UK for the generation of a variety of new e-gateways with goals of social inclusion and expressing different socio-technical configurations. LA is an urban conurbation with specific problems of social exclusion, particularly in relation to ethnicity. Finland, along with the other Nordic countries, has been known for a 'telecottage' model based on ICT access in remote rural areas for teleworking and community building. Finland continues to pursue an active inclusionary agenda through the public sector.

TWO SUCCESSFUL BUT CONTRASTING UK e-GATEWAYS

Two contrasting UK e-gateways that were investigated are described briefly to give a sense of the nature of the places themselves.

McNulty's Café is located in central Newcastle close to shopping areas and a metro station. It has a corner location with large plate glass windows on both sides making it easy to look in when passing and see that there are a mixture of computer users and café users. Many people use the place just as a café, coming in for drinks or light meals. The café itself is very relaxed, newspapers are provided, and people use it for getting together with friends or for business or study meetings. As might be expected from this description, there are many regulars among the clientele. The computer and café areas are integrated, providing opportunities for the interest of non-users to be engaged. The layout was such that every café customer was at least in sight of a computer and often sitting next to a computer user, facilitating casual interaction. In addition there were a couple of large overhead screens relaying what was happening on one of the computers, which provided a less intrusive way of observing what could be found on the internet.

Some users said that they had come in over a considerable period just to use the café before finally deciding to 'have a go'. Such 'cross-over' use was encouraged by a cyber breakfast offer where, for a combined price, users bought a cooked meal and half an hour on a computer. Those wanting to use the BBC's self-learning programmes were offered free use of the computers—again during the early quiet part of the day. Staff were not intrusive but were willing to give brief instruction to complete beginners or to those in difficulty. Regular internet users were encouraged to become members, which provided access at reduced cost, developed some sense of shared identity, and provided the management with information about their users, which could be used in the development of services or simply to keep in touch.

Project Cosmic in Ottery St Mary in Devon is based in a disused railway station located on the edge of town, set back from the road. While it is within easy walking distance of the shopping area, it is not in a location one would pass going to anywhere else. Although it was advertised via a sandwich board on the pavement, it would be difficult to judge what type of place it was without going in. Yet it is a popular and highly successful facility because of its active links with its local community. The building is also used for the provision of vocational and non-vocational adult education, which means it is a location already well known to many in the community. One of the other groups that uses the building and has developed links with Cosmic is the local youth club. When they meet, they regularly use the computer facilities for informal activities such as internet searching and participating in chat rooms. They have also had formal sessions leading to the creation of their own web pages on Cosmic's extensive site.

This use has not come about simply through co-location. The original impetus for Project Cosmic had come from young people at the youth club, and the youth worker at that time now runs the computer facility and continues to be actively involved with the club. Cosmic provides trainee jobs for young people writing web pages, and their friends provide another source of regular users. The centre also ran successful business training in the use of the internet and particular software packages. They had strong links with the large number of hotel and other tourism-related small businesses. Members of the board of directors of Project Cosmic (a not-for-profit company) and of the advisory board were active in the local business community, and through them people got to know about the training on offer and, on the basis of personal recommendation, to trust the quality of what was provided. Active links with both the public and voluntary sectors have led to web-design courses for voluntary groups and an input into the way local councils and other groups present themselves on the internet.

These two examples illustrate some key contrasts between different types of successful e-gateway, which were the subject of investigation in the project.

e-GATEWAYS AS THIRD PLACES

Many of the features of the successful e-gateways identified in the research had characteristics that fitted the Oldenburg model of third places. They were 'neutral places' where people could come and go at will, with, for the most part, a lack of formal organized activities. Our UK survey showed that most were open throughout normal working hours. Many, and in particular those with a café orientation, were also open at weekends or evenings. While some places that offered formal training, or had relatively few computers in comparison to the number of potential users, did operate a booking system, the majority allowed users to drop in when they wanted to, and to stay as long as they liked.

The admission policies of e-gateways tended to be socially inclusive. Many e-gateways had no formal membership criteria—although they reserved the right to exclude those who behaved unacceptably in terms of their internet use or social behaviour. Charges clearly operated as a barrier to inclusion for some, but even in the cafés that were attempting to operate commercially they were kept low, and in those e-gateways receiving grants or other forms of public subsidy they were often minimal or non-existent. In some of the LA e-gateways, operating in areas of extreme social exclusion, users were able to undertake voluntary work for the organization in lieu of a membership payment. Access for new users to ICTs was a goal for the vast majority of the UK organizations surveyed (around 90 per cent), but particular types of user were targeted by only a minority (around 30 per cent).

The mix of users was heterogeneous. Around half the organizations surveyed said that they had equal numbers of male and female users, and a significant number (particularly of the non-commercial variety) reported that they had more female than male users. In contrast, the *Which?* Survey (1998) (carried out at a similar time and looking at the entire population of UK internet users, most of whom have home or work access) reported that only 35 per cent of UK internet users were women. In terms of age, the *Which?* survey reported that 58 per cent of UK internet users were in the 15–34 age band, 35 per cent were aged 35–54, and only 7 per cent were over the age of 55. Many of the e-gateways contacted in our survey appear to be reaching a different and more varied age range. Some organizations were particularly successful in reaching older people, and, even where the majority of users were young, few e-gateways reported being overwhelmingly dominated by one age group. From these findings it would appear that UK e-gateway users are more representative of the population at large than are home internet users. This finding is in line with a US survey of users of forty-four community technology centres across the USA (CTCNet Research and Evaluation Team 1998). Data from questionnaires completed by users in our UK case study sites confirm that some organizations, at least, are able to achieve a socially inclusive mix of users. Responses from 292 users showed that the balance of male to female users (of those declaring their gender) was 51 per cent to 46 per cent. Of those declaring their age, 15 per cent were under 18, 45 per cent between 18 and 35, 20 per cent between 36 and 50, and 17 per cent over the age of 50.

A striking finding was the extent to which users of e-gateways were local people. The vast majority of users of our UK case study sites said that they were local residents living less than ten miles away from the provision. These findings contradict assumptions that e-gateways are predominantly used by tourists or by those travelling on business. Users were most likely to have heard of the site via word of mouth (accounting for over 40 per cent of all users). In the case of internet café users, nearly a quarter of users said that they had actively searched for a place where they could use the internet and others had just seen the facility when they were passing. The second most common way (accounting for over 30 per cent of responses) in which users of the community facilities found out about them was through an advertisement or poster.

As a consequence, while each of the e-gateways studied varied in the proportion of casual users they had, all the ones studied in detail did have a core of 'regulars' who were well known to each other and to the staff. The majority of organizations identified were small scale (typically up to ten computers). This is likely to contribute to the ability of regulars to create a sense of place. There is a tension between this characteristic and the goal of general inclusiveness. While the existence of a group of regulars does create a strong, user-focused, sense of place, which is obviously part of its appeal to the 'in group', it may make it less appealing to those who approach as outsiders, particularly if they are demographically different from the regulars. Successful e-gateways seemed to be *either* very open to new users *or* to develop a supportive group of regular users, but found it difficult to do both.

Unpretentious style and mood with the stimulus of conversation and interaction are also key third-place features of the e-gateways. The extent to which these features of a relaxed and interactive environment were valued by users was apparent in their questionnaire responses, through observation, and in interviews with those running facilities. Of users completing questionnaires, over three-quarters in both types of e-gateway said that social factors were very or fairly important issues in their decision to use facilities there. Two-thirds of users said that their understanding of, and ability to use, ICTs had increased and overwhelmingly cited the relaxed atmosphere and help from staff as factors that had contributed to this.

Of course, not all e-gateways could be described as unpretentious in style. Indeed, many were extremely stylish and drew on a computer-related 'high-tech' image to create their own distinctive environment—reflected, for example, in the choice of furniture, decor, music, and even type of food and drink. In some cases they combined internet access with a space for displaying works of art or as a performance venue. Such places were very appealing to some types of users and extremely intimidating to others, again emphasizing that what is inclusionary to some may well be exclusionary to others.

The sense of 'home away from home' was the final third-place characteristic, meaning that people feel it is a place where they belong, feel connected with others, and derive social support (while noting that not all 'homes' in practice deliver these things). Some aspects of this have already been covered in the discussion of 'regulars'. In addition, many of the more community-oriented organizations sought to involve their users directly or indirectly in their management. This was through, for example, participation in advisory boards or drawing up codes relating to how the facility should be used or the definition of acceptable behaviour. One of the cybercafés studied provided regular users with their own web-page space as part of the café's site. These practices contribute to users' perceptions that it is 'their' place. As described above, the ability to use the technology in the same way one would be likely to do in one's own home—for example, risking a cup of coffee next to a computer—is also valued by many. Oldenburg discusses social support in terms of people being generally about each other—for example, noticing if someone does not turn up when expected and checking if he or she is all right. In the context of e-gateways it seems more likely that the type of support that is valued is to not feel alone or abandoned as a participant in a new set of practices and relationships that are created by internet use.

Overall, therefore, the e-gateways displayed a set of attributes that fitted the third-place model of informal public locations. As such their appeal to users was broader than the simple instrumental provision of access to a computer or internet terminal. Our investigations found that many users reported that they had a computer at home or could get access from other places. In one internet café located a mile from a university we found that student users were paying for internet access that they could have had free of charge at their own institution. The conviviality of the environment with music and refreshments was seen by the manager as the attraction over the formal educational establishment's computer labs. The use of e-gateways as a positive choice rather than a last resort reinforces the view that these third-place features provide significantly more that the simple technical provision of internet access.

SITUATED PRACTICES FOR INCLUSION

Our research focused on two stages in the process of inclusion in computer and internet use and the practices situated in e-gateways that facilitated them. Initial entry to the e-gateway and use of the ICT facilities was the first stage. Continuity of new user engagement with these facilities through confidence and motivation from learning and participation was the second stage. They are distinct though connected in important ways. The former is primarily about a sense of place while the latter concerns learning approaches.

It is worth stressing that initial access is not a trivial issue. Far from people rushing to use computers as soon as they are provided for them at low cost, our questionnaires to non-users (those close to the facility but not using the computers—for example, those in a cybercafé just to drink coffee or those in a community centre to seek advice, say on benefits) identified a significant group (20 per cent) who said that they were not currently computer users, would be interested in becoming so, but needed more encouragement than that provided by the facility they were currently so close to. The proportion may well be even higher in the population at large.

The means by which new users were initially engaged is fundamental to the nature of the e-gateway itself. We observed two broad types of organization distinguished by the mode through which users were attracted in the first place: shop-front e-gateways and community e-gateways. Shop-front e-gateways attracted users via a prominent attractive location and facilities. They aim to attract those passing by or those who have come to the site for a specific service. Some people come because a friend or acquaintance has mentioned the facility to them, but most will not know staff or other users initially. Thus pre-existing network links between new users and staff or existing users are at best 'weak', if they exist at all. Some shop-front e-gateways promote themselves primarily as a place to access IT, others primarily in terms of the café or other services they offer. In the case of the latter, this environment helped new users to span the boundary between two different social networks—non-users and users—by providing an opportunity for non-users to observe and assess ICT use without necessarily having made a prior commitment, or even having a specific motivation, to participate themselves.

In contrast, community e-gateways attracted new users primarily on the basis of existing social network links. These might result from the staff's participation in other social groups outside the centre. Such ties encourage boundary spanning between non-user and user networks via a trusted intermediary. Existing social networks such as voluntary groups or business organizations might also be approached. Here boundary spanning was facilitated because a shared interest or concern relating to ICT use could be identified and targeted. In an approach that mirrors the shop-front e-gateways' use of café facilities to get new users close to the computers, many community e-gateways shared premises with an existing community facility. As further evidence that users enter such facilities on a very different basis from shop-front e-gateway users, many community e-gateways are housed in out-of-the-way, often unprepossessing buildings. Entry was often through the 'back door' in contrast to the shop front. They would be intimidating to strangers but attract users who already know what goes on there and hence feel comfortable about entering.

Once inside, successful examples of both kinds of e-gateways are lively and welcoming third places. Again the contrast between the two approaches can be seen in terms of what contributes to the third-place characteristics. In shop-front facilities the physical layout and type of environment created are particularly important. In the community facilities the social relations are dominant.

The mode of initial inclusion used by community e-gateways meant that for them the second stage of keeping users and developing their learning appears a relatively straightforward development. Their users were already often part of social networks with other users, based on shared interests, known as attribute networks, or activities, known as transactional networks (Conway and Steward 1998), which could form the basis for their continued involvement and interaction. However, such developments were not completely unproblematic. Users included those from the most socially excluded groups, including the long-term unemployed, those who had dropped out of formal education, and, in the US cases, those at risk of involvement in gang activities. However strong their initial ties, the retention of such users raises obvious difficulties.

In contrast, shop-front e-gateways generally dealt with a more affluent clientele, more likely to be in work or education. However, they had the difficult task of finding ways to develop new social networks among users who had entered with few previous connections. Such networks were clearly present in some shop-front facilities, but there seemed to be a tension, hinted at above, between strongly bonded regular users and an openness to new users. This was apparent, for example, in cybercafés that had a dominant 'IT club' identity and very few solely café users.

SITUATED PRACTICES FOR LEARNING

Both types of organization reported high numbers of inexperienced internet users when initially surveyed. However, only in community e-gateways was formal training common, in the form of either conventionally taught classes or self-learning programmes that could be undertaken by individuals with support from a tutor as required. Such an approach appeared to be as much a reflection of funding regimes as of commitment to different approaches to teaching and learning. Community e-gateways were often funded to produce 'learning outcomes', either directly through grants or indirectly through subcontracting courses from the formal education sector. In contrast, shop-front e-gateways were normally operating without subsidy and with a clientele who were not willing or able to pay for structured learning support. However, whatever the cause, these differences provide interesting contrasting perspectives on the way people learn in particular social contexts. In turn, these appear to support different kinds of engagement in the virtual world. Users of shop-front e-gateways were more likely to use the internet than those at community e-gateways, both for searching for information and for e-mail communication. Many community e-gateway users were learning more conventional computer skills such as word processing and spreadsheets; 18 per cent of shop-front and 9 per cent of community users had set up a web site for themselves or others.

There was evidence that learning was occurring in all the e-gateways studied, whether or not formal teaching was in place. The majority of users said that their ability to use computers had increased and that they felt more positively about IT than before their visit. Attitudes were generally positive before coming to the site, with 65 per cent saying that they felt very or fairly positive about IT. Around a third said that visiting had not changed their view, but 59 per cent said that their attitudes were now more positive. Of those users answering the question 65 per cent said that their knowledge and ability to use IT had increased as a result of their visits. It is worth noting that over half of all shop-front e-gateway users endorsed this view despite receiving no formal tuition. There appears to be a fuzzy boundary between new and experienced users, with competence better understood as relative in nature rather than absolute. This underlines the importance of staff providing support on a continuing basis and the significance of the social context provided by the gateway organization as an aid to learning. It is also much closer to the Lave and Wenger (1991) description of learning than it is to the conventional model of education/training, with its focus on the transmission of a body of skills from expert to pupil.

The amount of learning support did not correlate simply with the style of learning of different types of e-gateway. Some shop-front facilities offered minimal support and, in consequence, were primarily used by those who were already reasonably competent users. Basic help was likely to be available in such facilities, but to be very time limited, either from financial considerations or through conflicting commitments. Anyone needing more help would probably be referred to a training course. However, there were some shop-front gateways where very high levels of one-to-one unstructured help and support were available, tailored to the needs and interests of the individual involved.

In the UK this tended to arise as a result of enthusiasts offering a service that was not commercially viable. However, in the USA some examples were found where this enthusiasm could command a premium price that, while not necessarily highly commercially successful as a business venture, was sustainable. Those providing support varied in the time they were able or willing to commit to individual users and in the skill with which they provided help, but what they shared was a perspective that started from finding out what the person was interested in doing and giving him or her the confidence to be successful with relatively little formal input. An explanation of the customer closeness found in a number of internet cafés was that new staff were often found by recruitment of former customers. This draws on tacit knowledge of how to create an atmosphere that supports the engagement and learning of some types of new users.

This gave a very different character to the support from that provided by a conventional educational approach, which starts from the assumption that there are certain things one needs to know before proceeding to the next stage. Some community e-gateways were also providing this type of support for their drop-in users or as a supplement to self-learning packages, but it did not fit entirely comfortably with their dominant approach. This is not to deny that informal learning was also important in these locations, nor that the characteristics of the place and the networks of relationships based around it contributed to its success. However, it does indicate that such learning was channelled towards rather different models of the way knowledge is acquired.

It was clear that e-gateway users learned through their use of the technology both from staff and from other users in informal as well as formal contexts. As the communities of practice notion makes clear, learning is achieved through participation in practice—a view strongly affirmed by most users. Formal courses formed a minor part at best in their accounts of what helped them become more competent users. It is somewhat ironic that the community e-gateways were more explicitly oriented to learning yet tended to express this in terms of formal training because of funders' requirements. The shop-front gateways, on the other hand, addressed learning less explicitly yet in some cases were more innovative in the use of mentored practice-based approaches.

The particular socio-technical configurations of user access in different e-gateways were also significant because the specific communities of practice they embodied stressed different aspects of how the internet could (or should) be used. Thus different settings were important in contributing to the broader social shaping of the internet. This is a distinct route from that of promoting alternative visions through policy debate. Instead it concerns the enrolment of users in different sets of practice.

SITUATED PRACTICES AT THE REAL/VIRTUAL INTERFACE

Both types of e-gateways span the boundaries between the conventionally separate spheres of work, education, and leisure. They took advantage of the symbolic isomorphism of the computer interface (Castells 1996) to transcend traditional sectoral specificities. They tended to emphasize the role of their users as participants rather than as passive consumers. The 'shop-front' facilities provided a context that particularly supported social interaction and the development of friendships. Thus the nature of the network bonds that developed between users and that led them to be committed to the e-gateway can be described as primarily affective (Moss Kanter 1972). While such e-gateways did not attempt to encourage particular types of ICT use by their users, the main forms of activity, which included e-mail and chat-room participation, do seem in line with the dominant real relations supported by this type of place.

Community e-gateways also supported the development of affective ties between users. However, the strong ties that link such centres to particular forms of local activities and groups means that users also often share a set of values such as a commitment to improving their community and increasing opportunities for those who live there. These can be described as moral ties (Moss Kanter 1972). In many cases this led community e-gateways to want to encourage their users to focus on 'improving' rather than 'frivolous' activities and reinforced their emphasis on formal learning. In some e-gateways there was little other than learning activities on offer, so using the facility by necessity involved this type of participation. In others, users' choices were structured more indirectly. In one of the LA centres, the woman running the centre expressed the view that those who came to use the computers should be able to do the same range of things that would be available to them were they able to afford their own equipment. However, children who undertook learning activities or ones relating to homework were able to earn points that could be cashed in towards goods or trips, and those who had completed certain courses successfully were then eligible to go on a register of those who would be offered paid work, which was sometimes available when the centre was contracted say, to design and print tickets for a local event.

In some community e-gateways forms of internet use were encouraged that focused more directly on citizen or community-building activities. This involved supporting individuals and groups to be content creators as well as users of pre-existing material. Such activity was relatively uncommon at the time of our research. The Devon community e-gateway, as described above, had trained voluntary groups to produce their own web sites, but these did not generally seem to be leading to any ongoing virtual presence. In the Finnish city of Tampere, academic researchers were working with members of the local community to develop web-writing groups. The groups met regularly in social settings, including a café attached to a public sauna, to develop a web presence that was close to a local newspaper, including local history archives, reports on local events and campaigns, and a small-ads section. This produced an ongoing and sustainable virtual presence in a way not seen as a result of one-off web-writing courses offered elsewhere. In a rather different example, academics were helping local communities develop appropriate and effective campaigns based on the use of a web-based resource, Neighbourhood Knowledge for Los Angeles, that allowed the identification of areas that were in danger of urban decay from publicly available financial and housing data.

Many e-gateways had a limited virtual presence, often with a primary focus on advertising their real facilities. However, some used their own virtual presence—their web sites—to provide guidance for their users. There were examples of both shop-front and community e-gateways that used their web sites to guide users to areas that they thought would interest them. These often included local information but could also be more broadly focused on issues seen as relevant to their users—for example, youth sites, or even just favourites of the people working there. This is an important dimension of access. It is a way in which gateways are giving their users at least some initial signposts into information and services available on the internet. In some instances the centre's web site acted as a collective gateway to sites created by its user groups, but these were rare. Virtual presences often described as community networks, which tend to have as their explicit objective support for excluded communities either through the promotion of economic regeneration, community building, or democratic participation, do exist. However, they frequently had limited 'places' in the real world for engagement with users or potential users.

CONCLUSIONS: SOCIAL INCLUSION IN THE VIRTUAL SOCIETY?

By understanding social settings for internet access as part of a network of social relations, our study has shown how different types of locations can attract particular types of new users. The range of uses for ICTs are not self-evident and we have shown that, through situated practices that encourage and support certain types of real activities, including socializing, e-gateways support the development of different types of activity in relation to internet use and, potentially at least, different virtual roles. The settings of e-gateways have been analysed as a hybrid of real and virtual interactions, which shape the context for participation and learning. In the case of community e-gateways, at least, the form of access facilitated needs to be understood in terms of a policy context that legitimates the targeting of certain types of users and support for specific activities and discourages other users and activities. By understanding the potential of the internet for enhancing communicative power and access as a social process of addressing motivation and anxiety as well as the provision of specific skills, it is clear that different social settings can lead to substantially different outcomes.

Are these outcomes ones that are likely to have a broader impact on patterns of social inclusion and exclusion—either in relation to society in general or specifically in relation to any emergent virtual society? Contemporary models of social exclusion (Bergham 1995; Madanipour et al. 1998; Byrne 1999; Burchardt et al. 1999) emphasize its multidimensionality: it is not only about a lack of material goods but also about an inability to participate in a range of political, social, and cultural processes. The digital divide is sometimes presented as affecting only those who are economically deprived, but this approach suggests that certain relatively affluent groups—for example, the elderly—also find it difficult to participate in the new social networks and activities of those who have become internet users. Social exclusion is perpetuated if people are unable to find ways of connecting to significant social networks with which they currently have no links, and social exclusion can itself be defined as 'network poverty' (Perri 6 1997). One does not have to believe that everyone needs to, or ought to, become an internet user to be interested in the types of circumstances that would allow people to make connections to, and participate in, the networks that would allow them to assess for themselves the relevance of the internet to their lives.

There are long-standing debates over the type of social networks needed for meaningful social inclusion of the individual in a 'community' (see reviews in Wellman 1998; Wellman et al. 1998; Wellman and Gulia 1999), which have led commentators to take divergent positions on the potential of the internet. The traditional view is that, to be effective at supporting inclusion, networks need to be locationally specific and based on strong ties. In this view, most commentators have seen inclusion as, of necessity, a feature primarily of the 'real' world. The internet, particularly if allowed to develop in an unregulated way, can be expected to have a detrimental effect on place-based communities (Graham and Marvin 1996) and hence inclusion. In contrast, Rheingold (1998) and others have argued that strong ties need not be locationally based and that 'virtual communities' can be a powerful basis for inclusion. Wellman and Gulia (1999) argue that inclusion now occurs primarily through dispersed networks and weaker ties and that the internet can play a role in sustaining them. Our findings provide a different perspective on these debates.

The way e-gateways operate shows that local and dispersed networks can be linked in significant ways. First, specific e-gateway locations and their characteristics were seen to be a very important way in which people found a route to access the potential and reality of internet use in relation to reaching dispersed networks. Second, through the community of practice notion we have argued that specific places play a role in introducing people to different ways to engage with dispersed networks—for example, through new forms of communication with their extended family, participation in communities of interest, or new forms of citizenship. Third, the creation by e-gateways of a virtual presence that reinterprets their users' sense of the real place in which they are located and that makes it available to a dispersed social network encourages people to re-engage with local networks, be that through participation in local events, use of local facilities, or engagement in local campaigns (see also Schuler 1996; Tsagarousianou et al. 1998).

Strong and weak ties were both found to be important routes to inclusion of new users of the internet in the e-gateways identified. Community e-gateways attracted new users via strong links, shop-front e-gateways predominantly through weak links. Both were successful routes. Our finding that some community e-gateways were not engaging people visiting other facilities within their building, who nevertheless professed interest in being ICT users, suggests there is a role for them to utilize weak ties to attract users as well as the strong ones that they were currently successfully using. Shop-front e-gateways had the opposite problem—how to build stronger ties between users initially attracted via weak links and thus effectively create the third-place environment within which a community of practice with a shared sense of vision, identity, and support might thrive. This reinforces the view that both strong and weak network ties have a role to play in inclusion.

Similarly our findings suggest that the apparent dichotomy between real and virtual networks may be overstated, particularly in terms of the claimed paucity of virtual social networks in comparison to real ones or in the suggestion that virtual networks will displace real ones.[3] Real networks, in terms of both the social connections that brought people into an e-gateway and those that helped them learn, provided a vital route through which access to virtual networks was achieved. Our methodology did not allow us to explore the quality of those virtual networks in detail, but we did identify e-mail, chat rooms, and web-site access and creation as common activities. These are all ways of engaging in potential significant social networks. Other studies (e.g. Miller and Slater 2000; Nettleton *et al.*, this volume) have shown that such internet use provides some users with important ways of maintaining links with dispersed real networks (for example, Diaspora communities) and of engaging with new social networks that can provide very real support for those whose specific interests or concerns are not shared by those with whom they have 'real' social relations (for example, those with a shared health problem). Again the concept of distinctive communities of practice associated with specific places suggests that real networks can be important for shaping the way people participate in these virtual networks.

Overall our findings contest the polarized nature of much of the current debates about the significance of the internet for social inclusion and show a far greater interdependence of the real and the virtual than is commonly thought to exist. Although not discussing the internet, Massey (1994: 153) also sees locationally based and dispersed personal networks as intertwined: 'on the one hand communities can exist without being in the same place—from networks of friends with like interests, to major religious, ethnic or political communities. On the other hand, the instances of places housing single "communities" in the sense of coherent social groups are probably quite rare.' This does not make the concept of place redundant, as some might argue. Instead, any specific place still has a uniqueness in terms of a particular mix of these diverse social networks. Rather than being contained within physical boundaries, 'it includes relations which stretch beyond—the global as part of what constitutes the local, the outside as part of the inside' (Massey 1994: 5). Our findings relating to the specific role of e-gateways as real places that provide access to the virtual world

---

[3] Cf. the third rule of virtuality: virtual technologies supplement rather than substitute for real activities (Woolgar, this volume).

are in line with this perspective. They show that providing internet access and encouraging internet use should not be seen only in terms of the need to provide equipment or to subsidize its use. Public policy is moving towards understanding the role that public access provision might make in engaging the interest of non-users, overcoming fears, and supporting learning. Whilst endorsing the importance of these contributions, this study of e-gateways has argued that the specific characteristics of real social settings play an additional significant role in shaping the way the internet is used by different social groups, which could influence broader patterns of inclusion and exclusion. As such there is likely to be a continuing role for e-gateways as socially innovative institutions that provide a setting for developing links between the real and the virtual.

Allegories of Creative Destruction: Technology and Organization in Narratives of the e-Economy

David Knights, Faith Noble, Theo Vurdubakis, and Hugh Willmott

INTRODUCTION

To what extent, if at all, can the careers and trajectories of particular techno-logies be separated from the various discourses used to promote or undermine them? The massive growth in information and communications technologies (ICTs) has been closely shadowed by a proliferation of interpretative struggles over the nature, capacities, and likely effects of each new technological appli-cation. In this respect, managers, consultants, journalists, academics, politi-cians, and would-be gurus could all be described as professional producers and consumers of stories 'about' technology, its role and consequences. Clearly such accounts are not in any sense 'neutral' or 'innocent'—that is to say, un-'polluted' by economic, political, or other interests. On the contrary, they enact specific techno-social agendas. It is not, therefore, our intention to attempt to legislate over which story is right and which is wrong. Rather, in this chapter we set out to tell our own kind of 'technology' story: a story about the role of 'technology stories' in framing and producing the objects and events they describe as they invite us to attend to, anticipate, or make 'this' happen while simultaneously neglecting or ignoring 'that'.

The argument developed below draws on an investigation (1998–2000) that focused on the development of, and experimentation with, remote channels of distribution in retail financial services. Financial services organizations, being what Nicholas Negroponte (1995) calls purveyors of bits and not of atoms, constitute a kind of privileged site, a 'critical case' one might say, for observing 'virtualization' in action. We want to argue that an understanding of the processes through which organizations attempt to digest new technologies, and the outcomes of such processes, revolutionary or otherwise, require closer attention to how particular versions of 'virtuality' are (or fail to be) enacted in relation to diverse—academic, consumer, media as well as practitioner—discourses. Of the various such narratives of the 'virtual' in general—and of business to consumer (b2c) e-commerce in particular—jostling for public attention and credibility, two were particularly popular and have been selected for consideration here. These can be summed up as

- the 'future-shock' story (after Toffler 1971), which narrates how extant forms of enterprise and organizing are (about to be) overwhelmed by the changes wrought by the new electronic technologies; if business is to survive in the digital age, it must embrace the vision of the cyberprophets;
- its diametric opposite, the 'emperor's-new-clothes' story, in which it is explained how things are not all they seem (and where various instances of awe-inspiring technological or organizational prowess are 'exposed' as little more than cyberhype).

Hardly a complete inventory. Rather a starting point of an exploration of two particular ways in which narratives are enacted in corporate performances of the 'virtual'.

FUTURE SHOCKS

> The one clear lesson of the Internet is you can't stand still.
>
> (Tony Blair, speech at the 'Knowledge 2000' conference, 7 Mar. 2000)

Future Shock (Toffler 1971) constitutes an adaptation—or, as critics would have it, an oversimplification—of William Ogburn's 'cultural-lag' thesis. 'Cultural lag' is the disequilibrium presumed to ensue from the relative slowness with which non-material culture adapts to technological changes (Segal 1994). Accordingly, we use the label as a shorthand description for all stories of how the technology revolution is triggering fundamental changes in the social environment that threaten a wide range of firms (for example, intermediaries, bricks-and-mortar retailers, and so on) with 'death by 1,000 clicks' (*The Economist* 1999: 23). What follows is an excerpt from such a story, as told by Richard M. Melnicoff, senior partner in Andersen Consulting's eCommerce division:

In H. G. Wells' classic *The War of the Worlds*, an English village awakes one day to discover that it has been invaded by decidedly unpleasant beings from Mars. Panic and confusion seize the villagers as the destructive intent of the newcomers becomes clear. 'All our work undone,' one local cries out. 'This must be the beginning of the end!' Did similar thoughts cross the minds of greeting card companies when E-greetings sent more than 250,000 digital greetings last [i.e. 1998] Christmas Day? What about all those publishers of classified ads looking on as Monster.com stomped onto the nation's desktops?

And it's safe to assume that even the titans of Wall Street were rattled last September 1, the day schwab.com scored 20 million hits. . . . Why do electronic commerce contenders seem so alien? And how is it that highly successful firms, pursuing some of the most carefully thought-out strategies in the world, keep getting caught off guard by them? The answer is these established organizations are still fighting to win a game that no longer exists. Most of them continue to make the assumptions, and accept the constraints, of traditional economics and strategy. But today's electronic economy—fuelled by a unique convergence of computing, communications and content technologies—is subject to an entirely new set of rules.   (Melnicoff 1999: 1)

Certain features of this story are worth noting. *The War of the Worlds* (Wells, 1898/1971) is a narrative of reversals of fortune. Britain, the colonial power *par excellence*, finds itself the victim of Martian colonial aggression. The English are as swiftly and ruthlessly overpowered by the technologically superior alien invaders as they themselves had overpowered native resistance in the course of colonial expansion. As indicated in Melnicoff's account, the disruptive technologies of the new 'eEconomy' are similarly envisaged as agencies of radical reversal. This is after all inherent in the very notion of 'revolution' (e.g. OECD 1998, 1999), which appears to underpin the virtual's utopian and dystopian metathemes. 'In this kill or be killed world [*sic*]. The disrupted companies will be victims as the two laws of the digital revolution [that is Moore's Law and Metcalfe's Law] work in tandem. . . . Today's retail banks will become "the new dinosaurs"' (Heller and Spenley 2000: 75, 129). However, as is often the case with would-be revolutionaries, 'what is to be done', in Lenin's immortal formulation of 1902, may be far from clear:

INTERVIEWER. 'What is virtuality in financial services?'
RESPONDENT (major financial services company). 'I don't know, it's one of these areas and I think there is a lot of terms talking, everybody's got a different understanding of that. . . .'   (interview, 1998)

The speed of this revolution is said to be such that executives—much like the villagers in Melnicoff's allegory—have no time to reflect on developments. As the IT Director for electronic delivery channels at Barclays Bank reports: 'In 1995 we put together a think tank with a remit to look at banking over the next 10 years. Their 10 year view materialised in one year' (Stevenson 1997). Or, as Heller and Spenley (2000: 129) argue, 'in revolutionary times the pragmatist is as much a liability as the conservative'. In the internet era to be pragmatic is to be branded an enemy of the revolution. Consider the banking sector, which, at least according to corporate folklore, is notorious for both its obdurate pragmatism as well as its cultural conservatism.

According to 'Tom', a manager with responsibility for product and business development in one of our case-study organizations, 'Home and Overseas Bank' (HOB)—both pseudonyms:

We probably spent a year just learning to talk the language and getting our heads round phrases like distribution channel and emerging technology and trying internally, this is 'we' the bigger sense, the structure around that and say, well how do we gain an understanding of these areas, how do we go from somebody reading an article and thinking, that's interesting I ought to talk to my colleagues, to actually getting something off the ground, and it has been tremendously difficult because organizationally there is no obvious home and I find that probably HOB is like largely conservative, [HOB's parent banking group] has got a command-control type of structure, almost a military type of structure and that type of structure doesn't react well to changes of this nature. These are the guys who carried on building the steam ships after the airplane was invented, so we are faced with a real problem here in getting insight at sufficient level to sponsor and to fund the necessary work that will prove the case. Because we are conservative and because we are conservative on our IT area, people who work here are generally less exposed to these trends than your average, fairly affluent, up-market earlier adopter consumer, so, part of what I do is persuading people to get a PC, get on the internet at home and take... because, if you don't know what's out there, it's not going to come and find you, you've got to go and find it. But I sometimes fret that all our management know is whatever they read in the Sunday supplement about some teenage hackers, or, you know, it is not giving them the right picture.   (interview 1998)

A gap was rapidly opening up, he argued, between the ever-increasing mobility of high-income, knowledgeable, and technologically empowered consumers and the inertia of banks like his own:

which is a tremendous threat to a Bank that really trades off the fact that, well we have got a reputation, we are big and solid, we've been there a long time, so we don't have to price competitively, we can get away with selling middle of the road products at middle of the road prices and people will give us their business out of financial inertia as much as anything else. The internet is all about, well where can I find a better deal. So I think we are very vulnerable to this sort of knowledge that people are going to go to.   (interview 1998)

Like all stories of the digital age, future shocks come in both positive and negative variants. Tom's fears were mirrored in the high hopes of 'Jon' (again a pseudonym), a manager in another of our case-study organizations, the financial services division of a major supermarket group. The longer banks remained complacent and inactive, he argued,

the happier we are....I don't believe that the banks are going to be able to compete in the long term without some dramatic changes, they are too slow, they are too inflexible, their culture is slow and inflexible, but they have got big pots of money... the resource available to them to, either do something, but as they stand at the moment, I don't think they can compete. The only thing stopping us is size, the rate at which we can grow. (interview 1998)

The new e-economy therefore, appears to offer a straightforward Darwinian choice between adaptation and dinosaur-like extinction. As another one of our interlocutors (a technology manager for a major UK bank) put it: 'I think it was Bill Gates who said that "the world needs banking but it doesn't need banks" ...we have to adapt. And we have to do it quickly. Or else' (interview 1999). 'E-shock' stories then tell of an ironic reversal in roles, where a bank's material assets—its 'old paradigm infrastructure'—which were formerly sources of its strength, are viewed as leaden legacies in an e-economy able to 'live on thin air' (Leadbeater 2000). As one of our interviewees (a senior executive in the California bank Wells Fargo) put it: 'Even a progressive bank like ours finds it difficult to re-invent itself. I think there is reticence about doing that probably because we have so much infrastructure already committed to the old paradigm, so shifting it you have to be incredibly bold to shift because almost inevitably you are going to take a hit' (interview 1998).[1] In the decade from 1999, according to Citicorp chairman John Reed, banks will be nothing more than 'lines of code in a big computer network' (cited in De Kare-Silver 2000: 270).

The stock market is perhaps the most prominent stage on which the various battles between the 'old paradigm' and the 'virtual', 'new', or 'e'-economy one were most visibly played out (Pollner, this volume). Consider, for instance, the *anno mirabillis* of 1998–9, which in the USA was characterized by the seemingly irresistible rise of the so-called internet stocks. In fact the term is something of an umbrella, covering firms associated—no matter how tenuously—with the internet (the perceived medium *par excellence* of virtual organizing).[2] Thus Yahoo came to have a stock-market valuation higher than that of Boeing, while, at $30 billion, loss-making bookseller Amazon.com was briefly worth more than all other US booksellers put together. The experience of Active Apparel, a medium-sized sportswear company, is instructive. The firm's value had fallen to an all-time low of less than $2 million and bankruptcy loomed. Then, on 28 December 1998, it 'went online'—that is, commenced retailing via a web site. Within days, and on the strength of this (rather *ad hoc*) link with the internet, Active Apparel's stock-market valuation increased by a factor of fifty. Similarly in the UK the same drama was being enacted with the ejection of 'old economy' stocks from the FTSE 100 as the symbolic toppling of the *ancien regime*. Thus the profitable Whitbread Group (turnover of about £3 billion) appeared in danger of being ejected by the likes of Baltimore Technologies (turnover £21 million, losses £20 million, market valuation £4 billion). Or, to take another example, in February 2000 a strange conjunction arose in which Dixons, one of the UK's most successful retailers, was valued at less than the company's own stake in loss-making IPO Freeserve, which implied that Dixons' 'traditional' businesses were worth less than nothing.

Information technology, it is often said, 'invariably inverts our models, modes and thinking with surprising and counter–intuitive outcomes' (Cochrane 2001: 8E). In the virtual era accounting and financial disciplines seemed to have been suspended and bottom-line considerations no longer to have the same force.

---

[1] We acknowledge Darren McCabe for his involvement with David Knights in conducting the US interviews.

[2] 'The notion of the "virtual" bids fair to become one of the most over-used concepts of the decade as its use spreads as quickly as the growth of the internet which is, in large part, the occasion for the growing popularity of the term' (Hughes *et al.* 1999: 1; see also this volume).

E-business was viewed as good in itself, and cost a mere inconvenience (Hilton 2000; Knights *et al.* 2000*a*). To critics, 'virtuality' appeared to constitute a looking-glass world in which Amazon.com, the first company likely to lose 3 billion dollars before making any profits, was hailed as a 'revolutionary business model that changed the world' (Spector 2000). Couched in the breathless prose of a sales pitch, such visions of the 'virtual' could have been calculated to provoke scepticism among the ranks of sober academics or hard-nosed prac-titioners keen to disentangle excited hype from mundane reality. Phenomena of this sort provoked a flurry of censorious finger-wagging by the 'Great' and the 'Good', who darkly hinted at the nemesis that hubris cannot but bring upon itself. The market had become 'a lottery', according to Alan Greenspan of the US Federal Reserve. It was in the grip of 'a gold rush' according to Bill Gates of Microsoft. Equally, those suspicious of the notion that new technology is a force that inevitably determines social and economic organization and relationships would no doubt also have felt alarmed at the sight of a share-buying public seemingly in the grip of a bad case of technological determinism.

When it came, the revenge of the bottom line was certainly spectacular. In the immortal words of an IBM ad, it was 'goodbye cheap thrills' (*Daily Tele-graph*, 30 Jan. 2001). The collapse of 'over-hyped' dot.coms such as boo.com or Chickmango and the seemingly unstoppable fall of most of the rest appear to have given critics a warm feeling of *schadenfreude*. Barely a year after the heyday of the internet stocks, the stock options that had replaced profits as 'the critical source of [digital age] investment' (Castells 2000*a*) were rapidly approaching zero value. Meanwhile, many of their owners, the builders of the 'virtual', who had forgone well-paid jobs to join the rush to the e-economy, were back on the job market. At the same time, fears were increasingly voiced that excessive company debts might push the rest of the economy into recession. It is worth recalling in this context that the triumph of H. G. Wells's technologically superior Martians was short lived. The invaders are ultimately undone by simple bacterial infections for which humans have built up immunity.

THE EMPEROR'S VIRTUAL CLOTHES

> *It is important to distinguish hype from reality.* Despite widespread claims about their likely radical effects, it is not clear that the new technologies actually possess the capacities and effects attributed to them, nor that much trumpeted revolutionary changes will necessarily accompany their adoption.
>
> (ESRC Virtual Society? Programme 1999: 5; emphasis in original)

> Hype is not a business plan.
>
> (IBM advertisement, *Daily Telegraph*, 24 Jan. 2001)

We have already glimpsed the importance of the concept of 'hype' (defined by Webster's Dictionary as 'publicity of an extravagant and contrived kind') in the construction and undermining of narratives about all things 'virtual' and 'cyber' (e.g. Stoll 1995). From the point of view of our second type of story, Melnicoff's dark warnings about cyberspace invaders could be seen as equally misplaced as the great Martian invasion panic started in the USA by the Orson Welles radio broadcasts (Haloween 1938) of *The War of the Worlds*.

But how exactly are we to recognize hype when we encounter it? To help clarify what the issue is here, consider the example of Tesco, one of the UK's biggest retail chains and a (relatively) recent entrant into the financial services sector. In November 1996 Tesco launched Internet Superstore/Tesco Direct. This was one of the first home-shopping web sites allowing shoppers to place their orders, and make credit-card payments (including a £5 delivery charge), whereupon the items popped into their superhighway shopping trolley were delivered from a local branch to their home at a specified date and time. The facility was heralded as the dawn of a new era in internet shopping in the UK. The future of shopping, journalists declared, was here and it worked (Collie 1997).[3] The UK was at long last 'catching up' with the USA in electronic retailing.

While the many were dazzled, some were brave enough to investigate. On closer examination of the Tesco Direct ordering process by a journalist from the *European* newspaper, a more familiar and a more complex picture emerged. Once entered by the customer at the Tesco web site, the order was received at the company offices. There it was first retyped and then faxed to the customer's local branch, where it was picked up and passed on to a shop assistant, who assembled the order. The order was then finally handed to the van driver for delivery. 'The leap was not what it seemed. Rather than heralding the arrival of a new era for shoppers where computers and robots merge seamlessly to deliver customers their weekly groceries the site is something of a facade' (Reeve 1998: 6).

This is then a version of the 'emperor's-new-virtual-clothes' story. As in the famous scene from the *Wizard of Oz*, the curtain has been drawn back, and the wizard stands exposed in his den. His awe-inspiring powers are cheap tricks produced with the help of a rather ramshackle mechanical apparatus. The Wizard is a merchant of hype. Tesco Direct's operation on the ground is then 'revealed' as a *performan*ce of (the image of) internet retailing. To the apparent surprise of the journalist (also acting as representative of the reader), the transformative influence of the internet on Tesco's operations amounts to something rather less straightforward than the effortless and unmediated realization of the grand e-revolutionary narratives (cf. Woolgar, this volume).

Of course, it can and has been argued—most vigorously in one of our visits to Tesco's technology suppliers—that this 'expose' is much ado about nothing. This was a *temporary* state of affairs simply representing the fact that the necessary technology—for example, the 'smart trolley' (Bloomfield and Vurdubakis 2001)— was not *yet* in place (otherwise there would be no need for all this retyping and

---

[3] The event merited a special report in the BBC2 *Newsnight* programme.

faxing).[4] Let us, therefore, note down this *yet* as a significant keyword. We can understand the specific technological configuration (e.g. PC/internet/fax/etc.) adopted by the company as an attempt both to minimize expenditure (unlike high-profile fatalities such as boo.com) by utilizing existing assets and at the same time to ensure that appearances keep up with social expectations. It *positions* the firm as progressive and forward-looking with existing and potential customers (especially highly prized ABC1s) and shareholders.

Two things need to be stressed in the context of what has been said here. First, despite losses of around £65 million over five years, Tesco's entry into the semi-magical world of cyberspace has by some criteria been a great success. The area covered by Tesco Direct, and its successor the now independent Tesco.com—unlike that of its competitors—has steadily expanded and today (2000) claims to be the world's leading online grocery business (Grande 2000; Voyle 2000*a*,*b*). Also the firm was among the UK pioneers in offering free internet access, with its web site as the first port of call for those taking advantage of the offer. Second, its ordering process was not untypical of internet retailing in the UK. As *Computer Weekly* put it in 1999, 'Web retailing still means manual labour' (Bradbury 1999: 36). Clearly, if measured against the extravagant visions of certain narratives of the 'virtual revolution', such arrangements might appear as mere parody. The 1999 announcement made by Sainsbury's (one of Tesco's main rivals) that it was restricting its Orderline internet shopping service to sites in the M25 area (Osborne 1999), for instance, sits rather uncomfortably with confident predictions of the imminent 'Death of Distance' (Cairncross 1998). From our point of view, what is interesting about such cases is how they foreground the role played by the imagery of, and the social expectations about, the technologies of electronic shopping and their future role. Tesco's 'impure' techno-social assemblage then did something more than keep the seat warm for the 'real thing'. It performed a vision of the 'electronic shopping experience' so that in 2001 Tesco.com was widely viewed as, in the words of its CEO, 'the only proven business model for grocery home shopping in the world' (quoted in Gannaway 2000: 36).

Whatever one's judgement on the success of Tesco's performance of the 'virtual', one issue of particular relevance to our argument here is the constitutive role of social expectations about what it takes to 'enact' (Weick 1977; Woolgar 2000*b*) the virtual successfully. In this respect, 'hype' stories are as much about social expectations as 'e-shock' ones. Accounts of the emperor having no clothes are often laments for expectations betrayed. In the course of our research, the notion of social expectations has been a persistent refrain in respondents' accounts of 'what is going on': expectations typically performed an important role in explanations of why things might fail to work properly. For example, in the course of reflecting on various UK banks' attempts to join the

---

[4] According to Nicholas Negroponte (1995: 187–9), 'the fax machine is a serious blemish on the information landscape, a step backward, whose ramifications will be felt for a long time'.

'internet revolution', 'Harry' (a pseudonym), a manager in a major international IT supplier, put it thus:

Someone at the top has said, we must have an internet channel because everybody else has got one. No one up there has taken any interest in it at all and it has dropped all the way down to a graduate recruit in the marketing department who happens to be interested in the web and produces something and pushes it out. And the result? Something pretty horrible that doesn't really do anything. So a lot of organizations are now coming to their— well, we've done that bit now so what do we need to do it better? (interview 1998)

As an IBM ad once put it: 'The first chapter of e-business was an emotional one...this next generation of e-business will be a wiser one' (ibm.com/ e-business/uk). The best is therefore yet to come.[5] With the right help, advice, and equipment, the aforementioned banks may now finally look forward to a sort of technological maturity. The emperor in the story may have been underdressed, but only because his clothes were still at the tailors. Let us note, however, Harry's gloss for the construction of those 'pretty horrible' systems 'that didn't really do anything', in the first place: 'Everybody else has got one.' There are high penalties for being perceived as 'falling behind'. We have often referred, or alluded, to the role of particular social 'constituencies' (comment-ators, consumers, shareholders) as being instrumental in promoting and establishing (specific versions of) the potential and existing uses of the new electronic media (Knights and Noble 1997; Bloomfield and Vurdubakis 2001). As one of our interlocutors, a manager in the direct sales subsidiary of HOB, pointed out:

I think there is an appetite for change. You hear that already in political discourse. Well, in the next century, are we going to be doing the same things? It is used to initiate change to validate it. And they are all desperate to show that they are doing it as well, so that the industry is forced to say yes, but look what I am doing. What I am going to be doing by the year 2000. (interview 1998)

It is worth recalling in this context the thesis put forward by Donald MacKenzie (1990). 'Technological trajectories' (Nelson and Winter 1982) are, he argues, best viewed as the institutionalization of particular sets of (self-fulfilling) social expectations regarding technical development, (mis-)use, obsolescence, and so on. It is not then a question of simply distinguishing between '(cyber) hype' and reality, between what is envisaged and what is being delivered. Rather we need to draw attention to the ways particular social expectations (forged in part through the workings of 'hype') are (or fail to be) enacted in technological artefacts. This view is explored in the next section.

[5] This resonates with the discourse on masculinity, where it has been argued that a 'perfect' conquest and control of things is just beyond the horizon of men's endeavours (see Kerfoot and Knights 1996).

FUTURE PROOFING

[The Electronic Commerce Task Force has attempted] to envision how best
Britain should ready itself for the coming world of electronic commerce,
communication and connections....In the maelstrom we have tried to
ignore the noise and identify the fundamentals of the enormous changes
which are just now beginning to be wrought by the Internet to see the fire
and feel the heat through the smoke.

(Jones 2000: 3)

Social collectivities supply specific kinds of plots for use by their members in
defining and organizing the world into meaningful stories. In the preceding
sections, we focused on two commonly employed narratives for representing
the nature and impacts of the new electronic technologies. In spite of their
prima facie opposition to one another, both share the same (perhaps peculiar)
Euro-American preoccupation with sorting out what belongs to the past from
what belongs to the future. Our main focus here has been on the narrative
resources mobilized *in order* to ascribe things as belonging either to the 'old'
order or to the 'new'; as representing continuity or discontinuity. However, two
things need to be stressed in the context of what is being said here.[6] First, this
kind of analysis always runs the danger of reproducing elements of what has
been caricatured as the 'cultural dope' theory of social behaviour. We have
no wish to suggest that the competition between narratives for, say, public
attention or academic credibility can be unproblematically understood as con-
tests between different groups of true believers, 'holding [opposing] but internally
consistent views' (see Woolgar 2000b: 173)—techno-sceptics versus technophil-
iacs. Rather, as Woolgar (2000b) argues, such stories are better understood in
terms of their (differential) availability as discursive resources, drawn upon and
articulated in ways dependent on the occasions of their use, thus giving their
meaning a dynamic and situational character. Secondly, in claiming that these
stories are typical, we do not mean only in the sense of enjoying wide circula-
tion, but crucially as reference points for our interlocutors. That is to say, organizational members routinely employed occasions such as interviews, meetings,
workshops, documents, and so on as opportunities for 'positioning' themselves
(whether as advocates, critics, sceptics, questioners, and so on) vis-à-vis such
narratives. But, as we have already argued, this task of 'positioning' is also performed through the arrangement and use of artefacts rather than 'only' words.
We have borrowed here, in the cause of further clarifying this argument, the
notion of 'future proofing', which the literature of Tesco's technology provider
(anonymized here as 'GlobalStore') sums up as follows: '**Future proof**: By
employing Microsoft Windows NT and *ActiveStore*, GlobalStore has been

---

[6] We would like to thank Brian Bloomfield for his contribution to the development of this
argument.

developed with the future in mind. It supports and will enhance the technology platforms of tomorrow' (*Smart Retailing*, company publication 1999).

Our own use of the concept is a way of accounting for the role performed by the (frequently dysfunctional) business-to-consumer (B2C) systems set up by various organizations *in terms other* than instrumental (in-)efficiency or profit–loss calculations. These are, we would argue, among the means through which the social stigma of 'falling behind' is exorcised. 'At the moment financial services organizations are having to invest in e-business as an act of faith with a view that it is going to have a massive impact. A lot is going to happen over the next 12 months and no-one wants to be left behind but nobody is quite sure of the value.' (PriceWaterhouseCoopers 2000). We have already mentioned how the 'virtual' future's ability to shock the present is typically conveyed through an imagery of creative destruction. The powers of information technology are commonly invoked via terminologies that conjoin the vocabulary of crisis with that of reassurance. We view the concept of 'future proofing' a prime example of this tendency. In IT lore the 'legacy system' (the obsolescent past made durable) plays the role of the rhetorical other of the future-proof one. Whereas the former weighs down the organization with the burden of obsolescence, the latter inoculates against future contingency. The systems of yesteryear are now a drag on the organization, hampering its ability to meet the challenges of, and grasp the opportunities offered by, a future which has already arrived. The systems (and by extension organizations) that are future proof have drawn the sting in time's tail. They represent the desire for security against contingency, for the domestication of *tyche* by *techne* (Bloomfield and Vurdubakis 2001). The technological investments of the present have already anticipated the challenges of the future and absorbed, as it were, its impact. Here is another example from SAP, a supplier of e-business platforms ('Solutions for the *New*, New Economy'):

'Future-proofing' the architecture is another key factor in keeping infrastructure costs down...Any future changes in business direction need to be supported by the existing infrastructure...Future proofing the architecture also means taking into consideration the direction technology will go over the next five to ten years. SAP is already developing applications that will run first—or only—on Windows NT. Many customers and analysts believe that Windows NT will be the pervasive operating system by the year 2002... (www.sap.com/press/magnews/regular/dt_1098e/s40.htm)

Again we have the interesting identification of the Microsoft Windows NT operating system as the technological artefact by means of which the future will be enacted. It is notable not simply because of its 'technical content' (that is, the relative merits of Windows NT vis-à-vis other competing operating systems) but rather because it articulates the set of social expectations that future systems are expected to perform. Moreover, these expectations are legitimated not by being represented as those of suppliers—whether SAP or Microsoft (that is, those with a vested interest in selling their own products)—but by being allocated to 'customers and analysts'. In other words, they are anchored in the knowledge and experience of those who either use the technology in the conduct of their everyday business, or earn their living as reflective producers of knowledge about it. What we have represented here then is the attempt to construct a shared set of social expectations about the future in the sense of MacKenzie (1990)—a technological (and by implication organizational) fix that confers the ability to ride the waves of creative destruction. Future proofing is therefore in our view simultaneously technical practice and social ritual (Pfaffenberger 1995; see also Agar *et al.*, this volume). In contrast, conventional perspectives have long located culture and its rituals outside the boundaries of techno-logical systems. In this context, the usage in our commentary of terms such as 'enactment' (Weick 1977) or 'performance' (Cooper and Woolgar 1992; Law 1994; Bloomfield and Vurdubakis 1997, 1999; Knights *et al.* 2000*b*), with their connotations of the theatrical and the make-believe, may conceivably give offence (Bloomfield and Vurdubakis, forthcoming). This issue is taken up in the next section.

PERFORMANCE

I'll see it when I believe it.

(Weick 1979)

'Future-shock' stories narrate a misalignment between culture and its technology. 'Emperor's new clothes' stories narrate the misalignment between appearance and reality, words and things (e.g. 'hype'). Both topics have been at the centre of the frequently vociferous arguments between so-called constructivists and their critics. For instance, the degree to which accounts of the social shaping of an artefact can, and should, have recourse to some kind of 'technical bottom line'—itself beyond social analysis—has been the subject of much disputation. A frequently cited example of such controversy (one might even say an iconic moment) has been the debate between, on the constructivist side, Keith Grint and Steve Woolgar (Grint and Woolgar 1992, 1997), and, on the realist, Rob Kling (Kling 1992; Ashmore *et al.* 1994; Latour 1999: 176–92). Some of the issues raised in this debate are particularly pertinent to our argument here and deserve a closer look. The proposition to affirm or deny was the claim that 'It is much harder to kill a platoon of soldiers with a dozen roses than with well-placed, high speed bullets' (Kling 1992: 362). Grint and Woolgar rise to the challenge by peeling this statement's postulated 'technological core' like an onion, arguing that 'with enough ingenuity and effort' any ultimate bottom-line argument (shot, injury, death, or even the proverbial hole in the head) can be revealed as a social construction. A succession of false bottoms. 'What counts as technical', they argue, 'is precisely a reflection of the effort needed to show it to be social' (Grint and Woolgar 1992: 376).

The abstract epistemological questions of the precise relation between social and technical, representation and object represented, debated by Kling, Grint, and Woolgar are certainly interesting. However, such debates always run the danger of being perceived as nothing more than exercises in idle intellectual speculation: self-declared 'realists' dream up a formulation that turns, so to speak, the 'world upside down'. They then challenge self-described 'constructivists' to show how it can stay that way. This sets off an endless circle in which increasingly preposterous propositions are constructed (by realists) only to be 'deconstructed' (by constructivists) so the whole thing can start all over again— until both sides lose interest. In this light the social study of technology can appear a rather trivial undertaking. However, what is relevant to our purposes here is the status of the 'guns and roses' proposition as a discursive event; a statement in Foucault's sense of the term (1972: 106). Clearly this proposition is intelligible only under certain (epistemological, social, institutional, etc.) conditions. It is under these specific conditions that it is heard, read, and understood, as an *academic thought experiment* rather than as, say, *practical guidance*. Rather than remain within a discourse of assertion and counter-assertion, perhaps we can speculate as to the context or circumstances in which a proposition like 'guns do not kill' would be taken seriously. *That is under what conditions could it be understood and intended as guidance to the hearer rather than as a self-evident absurdity?*

In his critique of Grint and Woolgar, McLaughlin (1997: 215–16) argues: 'the [constructivist] approach sidesteps the key question of how grievous bodily harm and murder could be accomplished with roses rather than guns. It merely asserts that an actor network could turn roses into effective weapons, but does not demonstrate how this might be achieved'. We understand the spirit of the criticism as a challenge to bring together Woolgar's disparate demonstrations of the social construction of technological facts into a coherent plot—in other words, a demand for a narrative in which roses kill but guns do not, *in the course of a single story*. Although we know of no culture that ever 'enacted' this opposition of roses to guns, it is nevertheless possible to find examples that are not too far off. That requires a return to the colonial experience for which the *War of the Worlds* was meant as an allegory.

In the summer of 1905, for instance, Kinjikitile Ngwale, medicine man in what was then German East Africa, concocted the *maji* (a war medicine made out of water, millet, and castor oil), which rendered the wearer invulnerable to bullets, and proclaimed the rebellion against the Reich. It would be wrong to assume that Kinjikitile's claims on behalf of the *maji* simply reflected a 'native' unfamiliarity with European weaponry. After all, a similar belief in the efficacy of the 'ghost shirt' had become widespread only a few decades earlier among the Sioux, who were highly experienced rifle-users.

The *maji* (Swahili for water) inspired those who used it. As a village headman told his followers: 'This is not war ... We shall not die. We shall only kill' (cited in Pakenham 1991: 619). It was not an altogether impossible objective. There were only a few hundred German officered Askari troops in the whole area of the rebellion: 'For the rebels...August seemed to prove the miraculous truth of all that Kinjikitile had foretold. It was obvious to them that out of the German gun barrels came nothing but water. At a stroke, the Germans were driven from the land of all the peoples protected by the *maji*' (Pakenham 1991: 619).

Even the failure of the rebellion[7] in the face of German machine guns and the arrival of General Gotzen's Marines need not *necessarily* constitute a decisive, knock-out, argument against the claim that European rifles are ineffective against sufficiently strong magic. True, the *maji* had failed but this is not an argument against the whole class of war medicines any more than a computer failure (and there are enough of them) is an argument against the functioning of all computers (Knights *et al*. 2000*a*). In fact, under particular circumstances 'failure' may reinforce belief. An example of this process at work is provided by the study by Leo Festinger *et al*. (1964) of how millenarian sects deal with failure. The sect studied by Festinger was made up by the disciples of a certain Marian Keetch, who sat expectantly while 21 December 1955 passed without the cataclysmic floods predicted by her contact on the planet Clarion. 'The key for them', Festinger notes, 'was to come up with a good reason to explain [this failure].... In this case Mrs Keetch declared that the faith of her group had caused God to cancel the disaster. In these cases failure was no bar to future success. In fact her group became more active proselytizers afterwards' (see Knights *et al*. 2000*a*). In similar vein, we can pose the question about Kinjikitile the other way around. Would *success* have proved the veracity of claims about the power of the *maji*?[8]

Nearly a century later, on 9 December 1990, the front page of the *Chicago Tribune* reported with evident astonishment that 'in the battle ravaged regions of northern Mozambique...supernatural spirits and magic portions are suddenly winning a civil war that machine guns, mortars and grenades could not' (reproduced in Comaroff and Comaroff 1992: 3; see also Strathern 1999*b*). The subject of the report was a motley collection of men and boys named after their leader Naparama. These, in a land awash with Kalashnikovs (i.e. AK47 rifles), were armed with little more than spears and marks on their chests, which, they claimed, were the scars of a 'vaccination' against bullets. Heavily armed rebels

---

[7] The rebellion and its aftermath would ultimately cost the lives of a quarter million Africans.

[8] Compare this, for instance, with the following story, as narrated by Heller and Spenley (2000: 129): 'As in every industry, the survivors (in financial services) will be the visionaries who best read the future. What if the future is misread? This greatly troubled a manager who heard our message about the necessity of "Riding the Revolution". As an engineer he had seen too many predictions of doom and gloom falsified to have much confidence in futurology. Our description of the catalytic, dynamic and dramatic impact of cyberspace on all businesses reminded him of predictions of bug-induced calamity in the year 2000. The ex-engineer expected that the outcome would as usual fall between the forecast extremes. He revealed himself to be a typical pragmatist: someone who waits for proof before committing himself to a view or an action. But in revolutionary times the pragmatist is as much a liability as the conservative who wants only to preserve the status quo.'

and government troops alike were in awe of, and fleeing from, the bulletproofed warriors, while Western diplomats and analysts, the report continued, 'can only scratch their heads in amazement' (Comaroff and Comaroff 1992; Strathern 1999*b*). The head scratching still goes on. Reporting from Sierra Leone's civil war, Sherwell (2000: 29) notes that

magic is a powerful weapon [in Sierra Leone]. . . . Britain is backing a militia [the Kamajors] whose members believe that their lucky charms make them bullet proof. . . . 'Chairman', a 29-year-old ex-university student who now heads the special forces, has no doubt that their supernatural powers and charms and amulets protect them from enemy fire. 'I know they work because I have seen them deflect bullets and make weapons malfunction,' he insisted.

Like the *maji*, bulletproofing[9] medicines 'work' by rendering the enemy unable to use their guns against bulletproofed warriors. It was this perceived ability to disrupt the functioning of the technology of modern warfare that was the key to their 'successes'.

Modern Tanzania honours Kinjikitile as the first unifier of the country (Pakenham 1991: 621). He is, in other words, honoured as a *social* innovator, an organizer or politician. And yet his mobilizing and bringing-together of the disparate clans and tribes, like the successes of Naparama and his army, cannot be easily separated from their key resources *maji* and the 'bullet vaccine', the 'technological artefact(s)', so to speak, through which such 'social' deeds were performed. What is of relevance, therefore, is the politico-practical issue of how a particular representation (in Latour's dual, political as well as semiotic, sense of the term (1993)) of a (technological?) artefact was able to recruit adherents and/or defeat opponents. As Grint and Woolgar (1997) argue, the effectiveness of the 'technology' is the strength of the actor network through which its powers are enacted. In this context, expectations about matters technological shed the superficiality of their conventionally ascribed essentially reflective character (e.g. DTI 2000) and are acknowledged as constitutive of social/technical reality itself.

CONCLUDING REMARKS

The world of Kinjikitile and the *maji* appears far removed from that of Active Apparel and the internet. At the same time they both testify to the transformative power of expectations about, and performances of, technological artefacts in social action. While paying due respect to the transformative role of new

---

[9] A parallel use of the Naparama story is to be found in Strathern (1999*a*). Here she shows the strength of incommensurability in relation to the 'bulletproofing' rituals of university mission statements in Strategic Plans that are used annually in the distribution of funds by the Higher Education Funding Councils.

technologies, we would nevertheless suggest that notions of 'impact' tend to be rather blunt analytical instruments. There is, we would claim, a need to look more closely at how these impacts are realized in practice. In doing so, it is appropriate to focus more directly on the symbolic importance of new information and communication technologies as representations of efficiency, modernization, and progress. We have argued here that the effects associated with any technology are so to speak 'performed'—that is, made real or realized—rather than flowing in a straightforward manner from its inherent technical properties (Bloomfield and Vurdubakis 1997, 2001). This implies that an understanding of the processes through which particular sets of cultural repertoires and expectations are established is central to all questions concerning the nature of the interdependencies between technologies and the (social) 'context' within which they are embedded and acted upon.

Such issues, we have argued, are at the heart of a wide range of ongoing theoretical and practical debates surrounding current developments in remote trading and microelectronic communications. Accordingly, this chapter has been concerned with how the spectre of virtuality (and of those technologies that are said to make it possible, or even inevitable) is invoked to promote or legitimize particular developments and to justify the expenditure of resources. Narratives of the 'virtual' are, as we have seen, at the same time a vocabulary of crisis. This in turn incites discourses of reassurance—as represented in titles like *Futurise your Enterprise* (Siegel 1999), *Net Benefit* (Wingham 1999), *Net Worth* (Hagel and Singer 1999), *Net Gain* (Hagel and Armstrong 1998), *Riding the Revolution* (Heller and Spenley 2000), and so on—on the part of business academics, management consultants, and assorted fellow travellers. It provides an environment in which digital age rituals of 'bulletproofing' (Weintraut and Davis 1999) and 'future proofing' (as advertised by SAP.com or Sun Microsystems) can flourish. The various organizational (re)arrangements and the (often unexpected) technological configurations that firms have set up to interface with the brave new world of all things cyber should not, therefore, be viewed simply in terms of profit or instrumental efficiency (or lack thereof). They are simultaneously public demonstrations that an organization or community (see Agar *et al.*, this volume) has as it were 'absorbed' the impact of the new medium. In their persuasive role they are not unlike the way in which the 'vaccination marks' on Naparama's troops advertised their bulletproof status.

7

Confronting Electronic Surveillance: Desiring and Resisting New Technologies

Brian A. McGrail

INTRODUCTION

The population of the United Kingdom came under the constant gaze of the camera in the 1990s. Whilst other countries were not slow to adopt closed circuit television (CCTV) surveillance techniques, successive UK governments encouraged the establishment of systems to such an extent that the UK, it has been claimed, has double the number of cameras in public places compared to other EU nations (Narayan 1996; see also Graham 1998). As a presumed technique for solving numerous social problems, the camera effectively ruled UK governmentality. Narayan's claim (1996) may well pinpoint a difference between a UK approach to street crime, problem neighbourhoods, and CCTV, and the approach taken on continental Europe. I would not wish to overemphasize this difference, as CCTV is now as important a factor of 'virtual Paris' as it is of London. It could simply be that the UK has led the way on this issue. However, in so far as there has been a difference, with the continental approach to poor housing estates being driven more by 'social justice' policies (Power 1997) than in the UK, it is striking that the other Western country that has rapidly switched to CCTV as a technological solution is the USA (Davis 1991, 1992). The links between Reaganite and Thatcherite administrations, and their similar policies, not only on crime and law-and-order issues, but also on housing and especially state housing (see below) in the 1980s, offer part of an explanation. This link becomes more apparent considering that one of the most influential books on Modernist, state-built housing in the UK during the mid-1980s was Alice Coleman's *Utopia on Trial* (1985), which was directly influenced by the work of

Oscar Newman (1972) on New York's mass housing estates. Both have been viewed as conservative works, strongly critical of public housing, which promoted the need to create 'defensible' private space to determine a better social order and environment. (For a critique of Newman's early work in the USA, see Musheno *et al.* (1978), which empirically analysed what must have been the first ever use of CCTV cameras—though a crude system—on a housing estate.) In terms of CCTV provision, both on housing estates and in general, it is nevertheless significant that the nations that devalued state housing and the rented sector—and also 'civic life'—the most have now turned to the CCTV camera as a means of social control rather than amelioration. That it is a question of mentality and attitude should not be doubted, since this diffusion of electronic eyes is not a purely technological affair—that is, it is not simply about the development of new technologies, with cheap cameras and multiplexes becoming computer controlled. Even the most advanced systems carry substantial infrastructure (capital) and wage (revenue) costs. With regards to a town-centre scheme, which on average costs £500,000 to establish, estimated running costs stand in the region of £80,000 *per annum* (Norris *et al.* 1998: 256). From the author's own research on housing estates (see below), case-study capital investment was as high as £1,000,000 with revenue costs reaching £250,000 per annum. Thus, when, in June 1999, the Home Office and Department of the Environment announced their intention to plough another £153 million worth of public money into CCTV, they were in fact committing a further £23 million a year (for an unspecified time) to operate approximately 300 new schemes. Successive rounds of such public investment indicate that CCTV would appear to be 'worth it' as far as UK governments are concerned, whether this judgement is measured in monetary terms, crime statistics, or votes.

The research reported in this chapter focused on the social and political issues surrounding the introduction of new electronic technologies of surveillance, communication, and remote control such as CCTV, smart keys, and community alarm systems (for example, smoke and burglar detectors) on housing estates, specifically in relation to public-sector housing—the type of tenure and housing most affected by the new technologies.

To give readers some background, housing in the UK is essentially divided into three main sectors: owner-occupation, renting from a private landlord, and renting in the public sector. The public or government-funded side is further split into houses let by state-registered charitable companies and cooperatives, on the one hand, and those let by tax-funded local authorities, on the other. The twentieth century witnessed two fundamental shifts in provision. Before 1920 most houses were built for private rent (up to 90 per cent of houses in cities), but from 1920 to 1970 local authorities became the main developers, such that by the late 1970s between 40 per cent and 60 per cent of all houses (depending on which part of the country you were in) were owned and let by local authorities. The second main shift, through neo-liberal or Thatcherite policies in the 1980s and 1990s, was from renting (in both public and private sectors) to owner-occupation through the expansion of the property mortgage system. This second shift not only meant that most new houses were built by the private sector for direct sale, but also entailed—a key feature of Thatcherite housing policies—the sale of council houses to their sitting tenants.

This brief policy history provides a backdrop to understanding the present social and physical form of UK public housing. For instance, after the 1980s local-authority housing stock shrank in the number of units available whilst waiting lists of those requiring low and reasonable rent homes grew. Those tenants best able to buy their council houses tended to be the economically active, leaving public housing as the tenure of those with little choice in such matters—namely, poorer young people and pensioners. Furthermore, the houses bought by sitting tenants were often the best in the public housing sector—three- and four-bedroom terraced and semi-detached houses. This meant that local authorities' remaining stock was, first, concentrated on smaller one- and two-bedroom houses—raising problems of overcrowding, even when housing a family with only two but different sex children—and, secondly, to be found in less popular areas on less well-built and designed estates. Some of the worst designed houses, because they were largely 'experimental' at a time of general housing shortage, are to be found on post-war and specifically 1960s Modernist estates. These are notable for the mass scale of their construction and the 'factory'-based techniques used, such as prefabrication of all parts and fitments. However, it is not just their construction that turned out to be poor, but also their architecture in terms of social interaction, communication, and management. The main complaint was and is that high-rise flats, or long rows of flats on decks, provide little space for neighbourly interaction, leading to a sense of isolation. This isolation then prevents or constrains social and community action in dealing with issues such as vandalism, break-ins, and other crime, or even poor housing conditions, such as cold and dampness. Hence, it can be argued that, from their inception, this kind of estate had 'uncertain social relations' over who was in control or who could be trusted, and so on even before Thatcherite policies began further to concentrate vulnerable, poor, and troubled tenants on such estates in the 1980s.

A typical Modernist estate in the UK today has the following characteristics. The very largest estates will have between 1,000 and 3,000 units; for example, one case study I looked at, Glasgow's Red Road estate, has 1,444 units split across twelve tower blocks. However, between 400 and 700 units, divided across four or six blocks, is typical or average. None of the estates will have been built after 1978, and most will have been built prior to 1974, with the result that modernization of wiring, lifts, and building fabric is desperately needed, or has *just been* completed (along with or after the introduction of surveillance equipment). A few will still have resident caretakers—a single caretaker who lives in a tied house on the estate—but the majority will have a team of concierges, centrally located on the estate—or, on the most telectronically remote systems, based on another estate. This team will work in shifts, providing twenty-four-hour security, and cover all tasks from surveillance duties to cleaning. In a few cases concierges are divided between more traditional manual tasks and surveillance/communication tasks, on the grounds that the surveillance positions require extra training to ensure privacy, a professional attitude, and so on. Only on the largest estates will these concierges be managed by more than a single housing officer (a nationally recognized position), who deals with cases of disruption, nuisance, policing, and so on, passed on from on-duty concierges as well as applications, terminations, and lettings. The term 'housing officer' is recognized through the various chartered Housing Institutes of Scotland, England, and Wales, requiring qualifications. On high-rise estates, the title can vary, from block manager, to housing manager, to block officer. It is at this level that most contact between housing department and police will take place. Senior management will deal more with finance and policy design rather than implementation. McGrail (1999a,b) provide more in-depth accounts.

It was into this social context that CCTV and other surveillance technologies began to be introduced. Local authorities faced the dilemma of rising crime and neighbourhood nuisance, making certain houses and even whole estates 'unlettable', which further reduced the available stock for rent and their ability to house people. The 'bad-estate' problem became so widespread that central government eventually established several national projects and programmes dealing with the issue, the most significant of which (for this chapter) was the Safe Neighbourhoods Unit (SNU) in 1983. This central government team had the remit of researching and spreading 'good practice' amongst different local authorities, and thus ended up carrying out evaluations of several initial CCTV surveillance schemes, with various mixes between people (security guards) and technology (cameras) (Unit 1985; Skilton 1986; DOE 1988). The original systems were basic CCTV set-ups with no video recording, simply relying on concierges to watch screens whenever they could. These developed during the 1990s into fully automated systems with movement sensors, multichannel links, and recording (even digitally to hard disk in the latest designs), and many new services such as panic buzzers, video interfacing, free on-estate telecommunications, and so on.

Given the social exclusion of those living on many Modernist-designed council estates (Power 1997) with low average incomes, poor education attainment, and age stratification (between the young and the old),[1] the introduction

---

[1] By 'age stratification' I mean a clear division of tenants between young tenants in the 16–24 age group, as heads of household, and pensioners or over-65s as heads of household, with a falling number of tenants in any of the middle categories (25–34, 35–54, and 55–64). As noted above, the most economically active have the ability to buy houses or rent privately. Hence, many local-authority estates are populated by, on the one hand, an older age group, who became public tenants when local-authority housing was the dominant form of tenure and seen as a better form of tenure than private renting (increasingly associated with slums in the post-war period, 1950–70), and, on the other hand, a young age group who are struggling to establish themselves. There has been notable friction between these two groups, as their needs vary. Older tenants will complain that the young ones have parties 'till all hours', and make far

of these technologies was aimed at *both* giving managers and police better control over blocks (Unit 1994, 1997) *and* providing many new telectronic social services (for example, ensuring that even the poorest have access to a phone or emergency alarm button).

These dual aims of the technology indicate an important social trade-off between policing and social welfare. This is highly significant in that, if we stand back from the details for a moment, it is apparent that 'Big Brother' technologies have made their way into public spaces, and even housing estates, with little or no apparent objections. However, the introduction and development of the technologies are not socially neutral, and certain populations, such as adolescents, women, and black people, come under the gaze of CCTV operatives far more than others (Armstrong and Norris 1999). Furthermore, the latest developments, such as miniature cameras, non-hard-wired (infra-red beam) cameras, camcorder arrangements (for mobile filming), key data mining, movement sensing and on-screen tracking, and the use of algorithms (Norris *et al.* 1998) to watch movement—and its meaning—have fundamental implications for the privacy and civil liberties of individuals. This has given rise to notions of electronic versions of Bentham's panopticon (see Bloomfield 1998), often with the 'a priori assumption' (Mason *et al.* this volume) that the new technologies will be used to constrain behaviour and limit freedom (of movement and activity).[2] On the other hand, the availability of new telectronic services—aiming to enhance social inclusion—continues to give hope to beleaguered neighbourhoods, although these may turn out to be an excuse to thin out and downsize services with a traditional human (physical) presence, including policing (McGrail 1998).

Whilst much might be made of the imposition of such technologies on individuals and communities, by the state and other agencies, I will argue that little attention has been given to why such new technologies appear (at least on the surface) to be so popular. My intention here is not to presume that the new technologies 'should be', in an a priori sense, unpopular; that tenants should reject them out of hand and resist any development of an electronic panopticon. Rather, from the standpoint of having undertaken detailed

---

too much noise, etc. However, my research also came across a young family trying to put a baby to sleep through the TV noise generated by a 'deaf' elderly neighbour. This tension is really secondary to the fact that both groups fall into low-wage or fixed-income (benefit-dependent) sections of society.

[2] There are other analogies with Bentham's design. In his panopticon, those being watched have no means of communicating with or recognizing a 'faceless' surveyor. Who is watching and why is beyond the control of the panopticon's inhabitants, and is depersonalized. Electronic technologies, especially of 'tagging', but even those with simple 'surveillance potential' (see Mason *et al.* this volume), are seen to have a similar effect, only over much greater distances and not necessarily reliant on visual contact. In this sense, the new technologies are viewed as updating the existing social arrangement whereby that arrangement is understood to be one of 'surveillance for behavioural control', with benefits accruing to inherent powerful interests.

fieldwork, I want to work backwards from the challenges system commissioners, controllers, and promoters actually face in implementing their plans. These challenges, from whatever quarter they come, generate frictions that help to shape and mould the development, rather than the simple deployment, of the new technologies within a local social context. Hence, in this chapter resistance is understood as 'counter-action' or 'counter-movement'. As it does not exist a priori, resistance should not be presupposed, and it will not come into existence simply because new surveillance techniques are being deployed. However, I take resistance to mean more than counter-action. All too often resistance is seen as purely negative and destructive, about stopping something in progress, preventing something from happening, or undermining social relationships. In the works of both Hegel and Foucault, resistance appears as productive, creating new forms and techniques of social interaction. For Hegel in particular, the product of resistance—which often arises from a state of indignation—is social equality in the form of mutual recognition (a concept discussed below). Thus, technologies can be, and typically are, both popular and resistible at one and the same time. Such an outlook shifts the investigative questions to those of what particular forms resistance can take and why it takes some forms and not others.

This approach contrasts with the viewpoint that surveillance is simply the *opposite* of liberty and helps to answer the question of why there is little concern for privacy or civil liberties amongst target populations of CCTV in a different fashion. Lack of resistance to an emerging panopticon may appear as a 'lack' only because the term 'resistance' is taken to mean conscious and voiced opposition to the deployment of surveillance equipment. Mason *et al.* (this volume) note a similar point in relation to workplace surveillance and the deployment of equipment with a surveillance potential. They stress the theoretical problems and dangers of reading worker resistance into every kind of situation, especially when theory is dictating where and when resistance should be discovered. The difference with CCTV on housing estates is that the equipment no longer has a surveillance 'potential' as it is being introduced with a clear surveillance 'intention'. It is a much more clear-cut case of one person watching the activity of another, which raises the question of fundamental changes in the constitution of agents' authority to watch, to know, and to act. Without presupposing the existence of resistance, its type and form, there are obvious social implications in terms of challenges to existing social roles and the boundaries of authority.

What I would like to do, therefore, is to rethink the issue of resistance by examining the kinds of confrontation that take place (between system commissioners and target populations), specifically relating to Woolgar's second 'rule' of virtuality (this volume): the highly uneven distribution of risks and fears (and/or advantages) of the new technologies. One ironic conclusion is that the first murmurings of resistance (i.e. counter-action) to the now systematic introduction of CCTV actually emanate from those who have desired its effects the most, precisely because the expected distribution of risks and benefits has not materialized. This kind of resistance is the outcome of the *failure* of systems in the eyes of their supporters and carries significant doubts over the future of the technology. For example, overt ('you know you are being watched') surveillance systems—by far the most common to date and a classic self-disciplining technology (Foucault 1977)—actually rely on widespread political support for their justification, and that support is not always sustainable. Thus, it is precisely when the 'Friends of CCTV' start asking 'what is the point of the cameras?' that the political investment in the technology meets its real test.

Given the limitations on space, this chapter draws on a small proportion of empirical data (McGrail 1999*a,b*) to explore questions such as 'Why is CCTV popular?', 'Why is there little outright resistance?' (defined in a traditional, anti-deployment sense), 'Is the technology's popularity (specifically as a placebo) showing any signs of decline?', and 'Do the watched have any real input into decision-making processes?' In terms of the 'five rules of virtuality', the ones of most significance to this chapter are (*a*) the local characteristics that influence the evolution of the new technologies, (*b*) the distribution of risks and fears, specifically in a context of uncertain social relations (such as those, since the 1980s, between housing managers and council tenants), and (*c*) the extent to which CCTV substitutes or supplements existing practices. Consequent on space limitations, there is little room to draw on the empirical data produced by the research—largely based on in-depth interviews—to any great extent. However, the latter is, and will be, available in a number of other publications.

FIELDWORK AND METHODOLOGY

Our fieldwork (carried out between April 1998 and June 1999) examined the social and financial effects of four key technologies (CCTV, remote sensing, databases, entry monitoring) on the delivery of housing services in high-rise blocks. The idea was critically to evaluate improvements in quality of life from a number of perspectives, including those of tenants, housing managers, and other agents such as community workers. How the technologies change 'a sense of place' (for example, perceptions of difficult-to-let blocks), the ways decisions are made about such spaces, and how system designers negotiate collectively identified needs were also key research issues. Focusing on ten case-study estates in Edinburgh and Glasgow, in various stages of development, in-depth interviews (both prospective and retrospective) enabled detailed study of the social processes and experiences involved in introducing the most effective systems and working practices. These materials gave insight to the expectations of various groups about the new technologies and the extent to which reality met their aspirations. The sample estates comprise a variety of landlords, tenant groups, and locations and an associated spectrum of management strategies, housing policies, and other societal instruments for influencing the ability of different localities to use and change the technologies. Finally, further interviews with electrical engineers aided analysis of the manner in which concierge systems are socially constructed over time–space.[3]

A WHOLLY NEW PHENOMENON?

New Surveillance Technologies and their Social Implications

If I start my investigation of the theoretical issues by assuming that there has been *little* outright resistance to the implementation of CCTV in the UK, I present myself with the difficult task of explaining why target populations (including the general public in town centres) appear so unruffled by the gaze of the camera. When speaking to continental academics, who are often shocked by the extent of CCTV coverage in the UK, they will quickly point to their twentieth-century political histories (of the collective experiences of Fascism, Stalinism, or military rule) as a reason for both public caution over CCTV and government unwillingness to tread such a path. This perhaps explains the UK's *easier* acceptance of cameras and other devices, but surely the new technologies carry with them profound implications for the extent to which the police and other branches of the state can pry into people's daily lives? Their potential, at least, should generate cause for alarm. From a traditional human-rights and 'civic-freedoms' perspective, the new technologies have implications we should be concerned with, especially in terms of how many people have access to private information (even if this happens to be an event, like a kiss, in a public space) that can be rapidly processed, communicated, and stored in numerous unreachable, 'virtual' locations. There is, however, the socio-historic argument that such concerns are unfounded, simply because such acute levels of surveillance by the government is nothing new. In the next subsection I will consider both sides of the argument to draw out exactly what changes the new technology has brought about and, thus, what implications it has.

A Tradition of Surveillance: Continuity and Change

Since its inception, the housing profession has always had a surveillance role. This has often existed, fundamentally speaking, at the *non-discursive* level (for

[3] I would like to acknowledge all the interviewees who made this research possible. Whilst there is insufficient room in a note to recognize all 129 individuals, I would, nevertheless, like to acknowledge the help given by Mrs N. Farquhar and the Edinburgh Tenants' Federation as well as Mr Gordon Kane (of City of Edinburgh Council). A full list of acknowledgements can be found in McGrail (1999b).

example, architectural design: rows, bay windows, vistas, etc. (see Hillier 1996)), and been highly localized (for example, relying on tenant self-monitoring via residencies grouped into small dispersions (Hillier and Hanson 1984)), but it has also been highly ephemeral, with no formal records of comings and goings. One of the first problems to arise with the emergence of very large estates in the nineteenth century was that 'personalized' forms of surveillance became increasingly difficult. Hence, with the growth of industrial towns, housing layouts were slowly opened up precisely to aid surveillance from the mobile position of the street (that is, 'beat' policing) (Daunton 1983). However, the high-density tower blocks of the post-war period either re-enclosed communal space (reproducing the policing problems of the earlier 'close' or 'yard') *or* raised the visible street— walkway—into the sky and, hence, away from prying eyes.[4] Subsequently, the 1970s witnessed several attempts at remedying these surveillance and privacy problems through the physical reconstruction of estates and, where reconstruction was inappropriate, electronic media (Musheno *et al.* 1978). This started a trend followed through in the 1980s, with a steady shift from simple, manual controlled CCTV and tenant-controlled door-entry systems towards computer-aided CCTV (with movement sensors), management control of door entry (at a distance), and numerous methods of non-visual electronic tagging, monitoring, and listening (for example, individually encoded fob keys, microphones in elevators, and so on). To bring developments up to date (2001), there is a move to integrate housing management with town-centre and police CCTV systems (e.g. south Edinburgh), whilst new planning permissions in future may contain a requirement for an in-built CCTV/surveillance capacity. This cross-system compatibility is, thus, the latest in police–housing service integration. In summary, housing managers have consistently updated their surveillance techniques, whilst their surveillance capacity has been constantly upset by population growth, higher densities, and changes in tenant time-keeping (that is, shifts in work patterns and so on).

While certain groups within modern societies have always been subject to (or have subjected themselves to) regimes, sovereignties, and territories of intensive or acute surveillance, there have been important changes in the time–space geography of these regimes. The penitentiary, factory, barrack, almshouse, poorhouse, hospital, and school all used covert *and* overt elements of surveillance to segregate, monitor, classify, and process their inmates (Melossi and Pavarini 1979; Markus 1994; Hetherington 1997). However, although their internal surveillance may at times have been covert, these institutions had a distinct physical space and form—they were typically isolated from the 'rest' of society in spacious grounds or a space 'bubble' (Markus 1982). This can be contrasted

---

[4] Interestingly, rather than becoming a means of protecting privacy—taking houses out of public view—this loss of ability to survey an area was linked to a loss of privacy (through the 1970s defensible space debate) because of the lack of security it offered tenants (Newman 1972; Coleman 1985).

with the period since the 1960s, during which the social spatialization just described was, literally, turned inside out. Community care, normalization, and decarceration have been the predominant concepts. These refer to the emptying of institutions (though the older institutions have not disappeared entirely) in favour of diffused programmes of social control and support. According to Stanley Cohen (1985), this has thinned out but nevertheless intensified surveillance activities, often privatizing or personalizing those activities at the same time. The growth of electronic surveillance on housing estates (noted above) would appear to support Cohen's thesis, being a possible mechanism for controlling those classified as in need of help or even a potential danger to society on an 'extensive' basis—the virtual institution, tele-community, and so on. At the same time, such mechanisms represent a departure from convention for those people (individuals and groups) not previously subjected to surveillance but, nonetheless, living within the electronically coordinated neighbourhood.

The New Technologies' Implications

In general, although there is a case for arguing that 'close' surveillance of subjects is nothing new—for instance, the police have traditionally targeted suspects—there is an equally strong case that the latest technology and its introduction onto housing estates have important consequences and entirely novel implications for privacy and civil liberties. Indeed, the latest technologies can mean a number of important social changes. First and foremost, there are changes in legal procedures and processes, with certain procedures becoming less painstaking and formal (as S. Cohen (1985) suggests). For instance, a drive to acquire confessions, and guilty pleas, on the basis of electronic inscriptions can lead to the weakening of *viva voce* evidence (*habeas corpus*) and the demand to acquire eyewitnesses. Second, the technologies may involve redrawing the boundaries between private and public space. For example, outside your front door or standing in your window may be regarded as being in the public gaze, because they are within the frame of a camera. Third, software and its easy exchange can produce an increased number of people *with access* to personal information. Not all of these people may have professional qualifications and codes of conduct, nor have the proper training in dealing with private information. Concierges, who were formerly manual workers with no professional qualifications and received little training in IT management or privacy codes of practice, are a case in point. Fourth, there is usually a recorded tracing of movements, which can be used in any number of ways and not just for tackling crime. If a crime has not been committed, the question becomes one of why such recordings need to be kept in the first place and how they are kept. Commercial gain from sale and/or use of such databases raises the issue of who has the authority to compile the information and make gains from it. Fifth, there is the possibility that access to public/state resources will be removed from those unwilling to undergo scrutiny/inspection, on an arbitrary basis or for whatever reason. This is not necessarily about officials saying 'no' to some-one not on their databases but concerns a form of self-exclusion from public life on the grounds of certain people's 'fears' about having their names and addresses, images, movements, and so on on a database. This could be about evading creditors but could equally be wives trying to escape abusive husbands. Finally, there is the possible concentration of 'problem' people onto estates with monitoring equipment, purely on the grounds that the new technologies are seen as the means of controlling their behaviour. Rather than being treated as a general social problem, the burden of which should be spread equally through society and space, problem neighbours become the concern of specific estates and the residents and managers of those estates.

This is by no means an exhaustive list. It simply reminds us of the potential of the new technologies to change the way we live, work, and think about social ordering. The problem, however, is the manner in which this can be interpreted as a foregone conclusion. Indeed, such interpretations may produce pessimism and apathy, which debilitate certain agents, politically speaking, and enable others to pursue specific developmental channels—to dream up the next stage or enhancement of the technology. For instance, the feeling that the technology is purely repressive may be aligned with a pessimistic recognition of a lack of alternatives, which plays into the hands of the technologists. Perhaps no currently acceptable solution exists, but further technical advances will 'surely' produce a resolution.

FROM TECHNO-DREAMS...

With regards to the social interpretation of technology, much of the literature related to new electronic surveillance takes a far too negative, even paranoid, approach to the expected social outcomes or implications of the technology. Often, in the absence of first-hand empirical study, such claims are based on sales literatures and technical descriptions of how the technology should work and how it might impact on our lives and those of others: 'the flows of images from CCTV systems can now be *easily* switched over broadband networks to cheap labour locations. The World Bank has even suggested that the CCTV systems covering US malls should be monitored in Africa, to take advantage of low wage costs and offer "developmental" benefits to the Continent' (Graham 1998: 501; emphasis added). According to CCTV 'experts', there is no reason why such a system cannot be developed in technical terms. All the various com-ponents are in place, from Atlantic cabling and the internet to CCTV cameras. Yet the technology does not always have to be that advanced to produce such marvellous or fear-inducing accounts. In direct relation to my own area of study—the computerization of concierges—William Mitchell writes the following in his 1995 book *City of Bits*:

As the electronic era dawned, George Orwell presciently anticipated that telecommunications devices would take over these roles [i.e. receptionists and guards conspicuously placed in building lobbies everywhere]; in the world of 1984 the television monitor becomes an ever present instrument of surveillance, and the displayed face of Big Brother was a constant, graphic reminder that he was, indeed, watching.   (Mitchell 1995: 157)

Here, Mitchell is not gazing into the technical future; he is, surely, in the technical present.

This Orwellian image of *1984* is one that is repeatedly invoked, if not eluded to, with regards to developments in electronic surveillance systems. But what is so attractive about it? In my own experience, the 'nightmare' scenario tingles and titillates, producing its own discourse on the risks we (as social beings) appear to be taking. As a story of doom, it shocks! One role new technologies are playing in all of this is in the way such shocks can be distributed more quickly (without due process or reflection), thereby simulating the sudden 'drop' of a fairground roller-coaster. For instance, although it is usually the press that starts and spreads myths and legends about surveillance capacity, I have experienced how e-mail (or mailbases on discussion topics such as surveillance) can spread the fire through academic channels much more quickly than previously. Typically, someone reads a newspaper article—not the most reliable of sources— on a topic like the British police developing facial-recognition software for CCTV (which is true). Within hours or days there can be literally hundreds of e-mails espousing and re-emphasizing the impending doom—'what if?'—on the basis of 'Did you know that…?'. In this fashion, the message of Orwell's novel is reproduced almost daily. But little challenge to the erosion of freedom arises from such speedy electronic communications, and how we might 'do something about it', the topic of concern, is never really explained.[5] Such fears only reinforce the second rule of virtuality (Woolgar, this volume), which is not to take the deleterious effects of technology at face value!

Despite many references to more 'balanced' approaches (e.g. Lyon 1994; Graham and Marvin 1996) and the need for caution, a very Foucauldian view of the world is put forward. We are left

with the indelible realization that power and surveillance are tightly bound up together. [Foucault] repeatedly portrayed society as a giant panopticon, in which power holders

---

[5] The idea that electronic surveillance erodes freedom is another key feature of such 'news' circles. However, as one of the anonymous referees for this chapter pointed out, there is another side to the notion of an Orwellian society with an ever-watching 'Big Brother', namely, the self-promotionist or publicist. That is, the concept of CCTV cameras may be welcoming on the grounds that they give certain subjects the chance to make a name for themselves. Candid camera and fly-on-the-wall documentaries have become increasingly popular over the last few years and the UK's Channel 4 had a massive hit with their 'Big Brother' show, involving contestants living their lives in front of CCTV cameras 24 hours a day, 7 days a week. This 'publicity' angle may well explain the cultural acceptability of the CCTV camera throughout society, however, this point is not, I would argue, central to the social context of this chapter's research, where there is no or little option about living life in front of the camera.

exert surveillance over the rest and in which subjects' *awareness* of constant surveillance is a reminder that punishment awaits if they step out of line. The rulers would know, and they would respond. (Mitchell 1995: 156)

In short, electronic surveillance can apparently do nothing else but extend the power of the few over the many, squeezing out the last remaining possibilities of 'getting away with it' unnoticed (at the time) or on the basis that it can never be detected (in the future). We must, according to this standpoint, act as if we are in Orwell's novel, since the camera is all powerful and resistance is futile.[6]

... TO THE ABSENCE OF RESISTANCE?

Anti-Surveillance and Machine Wrecking

It may seem strange, given such a bleak outlook for the development of surveillance technologies (as the development of elite, instrumental power), that there should then be a search for instances of opposition to the electronic panopticon or Big Brother. Yet, in a sense, this search for heroes is the essential flip side of the coin in storytelling terms. It is a search for a specific kind of resistance and rebellious figure or subject. Within this framework, and this section of the chapter, resistance is specifically interpreted, therefore, as being *against surveillance* and even of being a machine wrecker or Luddite, with the goal of defying authority and asserting one's own power.

The actual existence of such subjects should not be doubted or dismissed. As the following fieldwork quotes indicate, it is possible to discover such forms of resistance and opposition.[7]

[The camera] was stolen by a guy dressed up as Mickey Mouse. He had a Mickey Mouse mask on and he knew exactly what he was doing. We had two taken that way. (Int TA19, *f*, 60)

A lot of it has to do with defiance—a lot of them will do what they do whether the place is bristling with cameras or not. (Int TA63, *f*, 53)

With regards to the 'Mickey Mouse' episode, interviewees assured me that the person was known to them (despite lack of legal proof) and the damage was not about theft of the equipment, but about control of the buildings and the estate. This view was corroborated by vandalism during an unexpected and sudden

---

[6] This is not a point I agree with myself. I am simply pointing out that there are contradictions in overstating the capacity of the technology to control—the point being that overstating the capacity of the technology is part of the knowledge framework that leads us into behaving as if we will, undoubtedly, be caught. We have little option but to act as if we live in Orwell's world if, indeed, we believe we live in such a world.

[7] For interview data the following abbreviations apply: Int = taped interview; Wrt = written response; Doc = manuscript document; TA = tenant association member; HM = housing manager; OP = system operative or concierge; TA19 = unique interview number for category; *f* = female, m = male; 60 = age of respondent.

'wildcat' concierge strike held in Glasgow in October 1998. Whilst items were removed, in addition to built property being damaged, the specialist nature of most equipment made it of little monetary value to the thieves (*Glasgow Herald*, 17 Sept. 1998).

These examples are included on the basis that they may relieve some critics of CCTV of their fears. However, there are three difficulties with such an approach to the whole issue of resistance, and viewing this type of activity as the only form or 'the ultimate' form of resistance. First, in taking a supportive stance towards such behaviour, one can be seen as, and may well be, supporting antisocial behaviour. If the cameras are there to give respite to beleaguered tenants, can one ethically justify such activities on the grounds that it offends or invades the privacy and liberties of those wrecking the technology? The answer is 'possibly', but we need to acknowledge that each unique situation will be different—the answer will sometimes be 'yes' and at other times 'no'. The activities of machine wreckers have no in-built moral or political superiority. Second, instances of this type of resistance are actually few and far between and, thus, fail to explain why even people with doubts are very often in favour of introducing new surveillance systems. Third, such acts of resistance can always be met with a technical response. They may even spur designers and manufacturers on, not simply to overcome current deficiencies—thereby inching towards the 'perfect' solution—but to achieve new heights in the social world of 'science' with consequences for the rest of us. As Mitchell (1995: 208 n. 32) once more reminds us: 'Recall that William Gibson's cyberspace novels postulate head implants as interface devices. When characters offend against the power structure, they risk getting their brains fried. Any kind of forced-feedback device also has the potential to inflict violence.' In other words, outright defiance may be futile in the face of 'evolutionary' knowledge, and resistance can become a game of tit for tat—the few against the rest—with technologies permanently ascribed to one side. This toing and froing does explain some technological adaptation but ultimately says nothing of how those doing the resisting can ever win. Further developments in the field of controls are always possible and science awaits to dazzle us.

QUESTIONS OF POWER: INSTRUMENTAL AND RECOGNITIVE DIMENSIONS

A fundamental problem with the Orwellian (or Foucauldian)[8] view of surveillance, however, is that it is premised on an instrumental theory of power. Those

---

[8] I place the reference to Foucault in parentheses because whether or not one signs up to Mitchell's account of Foucault is an open question. Foucault's account of power is more sophisticated than that of Orwell, being described as the fourth dimension (*à la* Lukes). Also *Discipline and Punish* (Foucault 1977) may be read as an ironic work—it describes systems and mechanisms of power (e.g. the Panopticon) that *failed*.

owning the apparatus and/or doing the watching hold power over others for their own instrumental (economic, political) ends. An instrumental outcome, such as the acquisition of material wealth, whereby others are mere tools in achieving that outcome, is the reason behind the drive to attain power, and technology is the means to that end.[9] Henceforth, to step beyond this interpretation of our social context it is necessary to outline an alternative theory of power.

In Hegel's narrative on the master/slave dialectic *Phenomenology of Spirit* (1806/1977: §§178–96), he suggests that the whole genesis of power or social action (and their contradictions) is precisely that the master cannot kill the slave—to be recognized as 'master', the master must let the slave live. The master's existence as such, as a subject having the ability to rule and act, does not rest on magnanimity, since the meaning and self-conscious state of being a 'master' requires *recognition* of this status by another (Kojève 1969; cf. Gunn 1988). Hence, for Axel Honneth (drawing on Hegel and G. H. Mead) in *The Struggle for Recognition* (1996), power struggles are not essentially instrumental but moral, having to do with our self-belief and formation through feelings of self-confidence, self-respect, and self-esteem. The tripartite distinction is taken from Mead, with each condition arising from a different social/emotional need—to be loved, to be equal, and to be admired. From within this framework, power (social) struggles emerge from our individual and collective experiences of one or more of these conditions being denied and/or lacking. Parity and recognition are the aims and objectives of struggle, not power *over* someone or something. In comparison to the Hobbesian and Machiavellian conceptions of power, social struggles and the desire to establish political order are *not* fundamentally driven by self-preservation (Honneth 1996: 5 ff.).

The first desire in the trinity, self-confidence, for both Mead and Honneth, is primarily individualistic—connected to the love of family and friends—and lack of self-confidence leads us to seek approval from others by changing our personalities, bodies, careers, and so on. The second and third desires, however, are essentially social, having to do with the *moral indignation* and needs of an active group of people. Self-respect and self-esteem cannot be attained from material gratification, but only through the recognition of others (for the freedom and rights of the individual or group).[10] With reference to surveillance and surveillance technologies, I understand this explanation as highlighting how both the watchers (system commissioners, operatives) and the watched (tenants) seek self-respect and self-esteem in and through such systems. Hence, the theory is of particular importance to the first rule of virtuality (Woolgar, this volume) in that the impacts of new electronic technologies are dependent upon a local social context and the quality of relationships between agents in various social roles. For instance, if a housing manager's driving motivation arises from

---

[9] As an aside, Foucault always asserted that he did not wish to answer the question of the *why* of power. He aimed only at describing *how* power operated.
[10] Legal enshrinement means nothing if rights are not lived or *acted* out.

obtaining recognition from their core group of tenants, rather than from their 'boss' and the promotional hierarchy, then the technology may well be introduced in a very different fashion from that originally expected at head office.

The Requirement of 'Justification'

Thus, in terms of interpreting the beliefs (about surveillance technologies) expressed in research interviews, I have found the above recognitive concept of power, with its emphasis on communication (interaction), contestation, and justification, immensely helpful. For example, to sustain one's position as a manager or commissioner or operative, one's actions have to be justified (and authority recognized) within an encompassing social body. It comes as no surprise, therefore, that CCTV is not simply imposed but entails the constant interaction of operatives and 'clients' over the state of play of the technology— is it working or not?, are our/your lives any better? In other words, the technology is constantly 'at stake', leading to a discourse in which the recanting of certain arguments becomes an essential component of the new technology— the latter's existence through ethical or moral justification. Such arguments are nearly always contested and, thus, typically include the following theses and counter-theses.

First, there is the claim that the technologies reduce crime, police, and court costs. Evidence suggests that certain crime levels are reduced, but often on a one-off basis (McGrail 1999*b*). In subsequent years it becomes increasingly difficult to gain reductions, and, although crime is reduced, a new level of 'acceptability' is reached—and on the estates concerned this may still be higher than 'average' crime levels. However, there are large policing and police-industry interests promoting the technology, including the government (on a law-and-order basis). Thus, the tail often wags the dog, with some housing managers being very keen to get surveillance equipment onto their estate because it would give them access to mainstream tax funding—namely, Council Tax funding for conducting police functions in addition to tenants' rents. For example, one manager on an estate with CCTV and fourteen operatives pointed out that 100 per cent of their wages currently had to be covered from tenants' rents when, in fact, about 25 per cent of their time was spent on direct police work. Consequently he was lobbying his employers, the City of Edinburgh Council, to vire the 'policing work' 25 per cent from Council Tax. This would relieve pressure on rent levels and, thereby, increase value for money, as the exact same jobs would be done by staff. Access to such taxation helps managers improve on efficiency (by spreading capital and revenue costs over a wider clientele) within increasingly stringent regimes of accountancy performance measures and housing-quality league tables.

The second claim is that the technologies make areas 'safer'. Whilst most standard tenant-opinion surveys show a reduction in 'fear of crime' after the introduction of CCTV, this variable is highly localized (down to a block-by-block, floor-to-floor scale of approval and disapproval). In other words, it is difficult to generalize feelings of 'safety', and reduce such feelings to the effects of CCTV. Likewise, crime statistics can perversely show an increase in violent/serious crime—perhaps due to the appearance of previously unreported crime on cameras—at the same time as 'fear of crime' falls. Thus, even when crime rates rise, a justification for CCTV is sought in the fact that 'fear of crime' declines—this being a key 'story' in the technology's justification.

Third, it is suggested that new technology will improve management performance. So far evidence is too diverse and split to accept this claim without doubts. For instance, some estates/CCTV systems show much greater efficiency improvements in voids, turnover, and costs than others.[11] Furthermore, 'community regeneration' or demographic stabilization (stated aims of some projects) do not appear to be significant or measurable outcomes. I would argue that more time is required to indicate the truth or falsity of this justification. Where management improvements are greatest, there are usually other management initiatives in place (such as physical refurbishment of housing stock, lettings initiatives, youth development workers, and so on) that need to be taken into account. Again, it is impossible to 'boil it down' to the impact of electronic surveillance systems.

Fourth, the technologies are intended to aid social services and support networks. This is a definite outcome on certain estates (McGrail 1999a). However, such developments also allow social networks and welfare organizations to be 'stretched' across space–time, enabling more clients to be managed without a corresponding increase in staff numbers. For instance, 'panic' buzzers for elderly residents who do not fall into the 'most-at-risk' categories take the pressure off authorities to do constant and repetitive checking. In one field case-study interview, electronic alarms influenced one elderly (age 71) resident's

---

[11] A 'void' is an empty property. Managers are not only measured (for government league tables) in terms of how many voids they have per 100 units (the % rate) but also on the basis of how long units lie empty, with the total number of empty weeks (for all units in an area) being summed up and/or averaged out—e.g. an area might have a lie empty average of 6 as opposed to a government target of 4 weeks. 'Turnover' refers to the number of individual (tenant) households moving through a particular area, and is measured in terms of 'terminations' and/or acceptances. Hence, an area might have a termination rate of 30% per annum, meaning 30% of all tenancies held during the year were terminated in that year. An acceptance rate of 28% is the mirror concept. It has to be kept in mind, however, that a family moving house within the one area would count as both a termination and an acceptance, and that at the beginning of every year a certain number of houses will be voids (empty), so the acceptance rate can be higher than the termination rate. Areas with high turnover rates (both terminations and acceptances) can be interpreted as volatile, with lots of coming and going, but may well be 'popular'. High void rates are a more accurate indicator of unpopularity, often related to fears of break-ins, nuisance neighbours, etc. From the fieldwork there is clear evidence that CCTV can help reduce void rates but does less for volatility and turnover. This indicates that estates with CCTV may be more popular than before but are still viewed as stopgap housing solutions.

decision over her ability to continue caring for an older sister, who suffered from dementia. There are obviously positive outcomes such as this, but an underlying motivation is the reduction of care-worker costs.

Finally, surveillance technologies are part of a wider 'public' social pathology. That is, most housing estates presently (2000) covered by CCTV are seen as troublesome because of 'signs' of social decay (for example, vandalism)—this is part of the reason they received CCTV before other estates. The problem is that the cameras themselves become yet another 'sign' of social abnormality, such that, rather than resolving the 'image' problem of the estates, CCTV simply makes matters worse.

It would be too easy and crass to suggest that the above claims or justifications are made on the basis that those making them simply derive a material benefit from doing so (a Machiavellian or Hobbesian approach). Rather, many housing managers who undertake the arduous task of gaining tenant approval and then manage both the introduction of the technology and its operation (afterwards) make no personal gain other than one of career enhancement and status (which can be categorized as motives of self-esteem in Honneth's framework). Further still, some managers do not even operate out of career-oriented motives, but simply because they want to do the best for the neighbourhoods within which they work—a social or moral sentiment. Similarly, many tenants will give CCTV the nine lives of a cat in terms of 'seeing if it works', on the basis that the concept of CCTV and remote concierges can raise a sense of self-respect. For example, the idea (alone) of electronic monitoring may give the elderly greater freedom of movement, and whether it defeats various crimes is neither here nor there. Yet, there does come the point at which such justifications are not accepted, nor acceptable, and questions about the systems are raised.

ALTERNATIVE FORMS OF RESISTANCE AND OPPOSITION

The technology can, therefore, come up against more internal 'resistance', from those who work *with* managers, than what is faced in terms of a direct defiance or challenge to authority. There may well be sabotage (as described above), but there are also explicit political and administrative challenges from within the process of commissioning and justification. Sometimes the technology (the process of designing it through consultation or simply the technical design of its operation (McGrail 1999*b*)) can be so complex and cumbersome, or understaffed, that it does not work as it should, leading to resistance to management via demands that it should work as promised. I will focus on this particular problem below, but there are many other forms and types of resistance—alternatives to the machine-wrecking stance—that need to be mentioned.

Admittedly, some of what follows may appear as 'resistance' not to the technology itself but, rather, only to the language or discourse of its introduction. For example, going about one's business 'as usual' may be more about non-compliance with the intended outcome of the technology than with resistance to its actual deployment. Some tenants provided stories of how law-breaking residents get round the technology without ever confronting it or its commissioners. The story was related of one tenant lowering stolen equipment out of his first-floor windows, which were on camera 'blind spots'. More secure homes for such tenants also mean more secure 'stores' for stolen goods. For such tenants, life goes on as usual and CCTV either appears not to be such a big deal or a welcome addition to neighbourhood security. This counts as resistance in so far as it challenges the law-and-order intentions of CCTV systems, which are an important aspect of other tenants' support for CCTV.

Another important form to be considered is resistance from staff, who do not want to be seen as police 'narks' and informants.[12] Managers also like to keep their distance from anyone not entirely 'official'. For example, one manager stated that he would provide information on the whereabouts of tenants, to bailiffs or sheriff's officers with warrants or other court papers and to the police, but not to insurance investigators or social workers. Staff can and have been threatened by residents. Such targeting of the human element again shows that the success of new electronic technologies depends on the local social context and the certainty or uncertainty of social relations—or who trusts whom.

Further to the last point, and interestingly, there is occasional resistance to CCTV from police and other professionals at the implementation and planning stages. After all, there are questions of 'turf' and procedure as well as resources at stake. From a policing perspective, housing managers may well have faster and quicker access to information on local crimes. Yet, such knowledge and power are not necessarily of interest to housing managers. One senior level manager even described CCTV as using 'a hammer to crack a nut', and many managers actually wanted resources spent elsewhere—on what were seen as traditional housing activities and budgets.

Finally, there is vocal resistance—with derision undermining operatives' performance—from tenants with experiences of the systems not working when they needed them the most—in an emergency. The example of a child going missing is outlined below, but there were many other instances of tenants' cars being broken into (in front of possible camera angles) and the cameras remaining firmly fixed on the landlord's property. Subsequently, many tenants saw the cameras as purely protection for the landlord's property, not theirs, nor their own personal safety.

---

[12] In relation to Mason *et al.*'s chapter on workplace surveillance, this issue places workers in the 'opposing' role, as surveyors rather than the surveyed. There is no theory, as far as I am aware, that presupposes workers' resistance to a potential enhancement of their powers.

REDEFINING THE PROBLEM: NEGOTIATING DESIRE

For a final, and important, example of how an alternative form of 'resistance' has and may take shape, I will examine how and why 'supporters' of CCTV turn against it—what are the issues they feel strongly about and do they feel they have ultimate control over these? The recognitive theory of power is, again, useful in interpreting how tenants and managers understand the role of the technology (what does it do, what is it intended for) *and* how such understandings are reflected in social practice (agreements and disputes). The following quote, from a strong supporter of CCTV, demonstrates not the 'complexity' of the power/surveillance relation but the simple moral struggles through which the power to survey is negotiated at a local level.

It all depends on what they're using the video coverage for, who's got access to it. If it's there and someone gets attacked in the street and the police have access to it, that's fine! But if it's to nit pick at every single wee thing, if it's someone walking along the street drunk and saying, 'he's doing too much of this in this area', well then, that's kinda selective [i.e. prejudiced] picking on what you're wanting. (Int TA34, *m*, 31)

Such attitudes amongst supporters are not uncommon and demonstrate their ability and willingness to negotiate what surveillance is. It is not easy for system commissioning bodies and managers to ignore their supposedly benefiting constituency—a constituency of reason (including their reason for being behind the cameras). Indeed, it is tenants as 'backers'—often confronting their own experiences of moral indignation—that can cause managers their greatest difficulties, as three further examples demonstrate.

First, when one tenant group felt their concierges were not cleaning the building properly, they asked to see the video footage of the blocks being cleaned. This clearly annoyed managers, who argued that it simply could not be done (that is, surveillance at work is, presumably, organizationally and morally unacceptable or certain 'watchers' are unacceptable). The tenants responded by arguing that, if it was OK for staff to watch them (walking home, going out to buy breakfast), why was it not OK the other way round?

Second, on a case-study estate with 400 flats and seventy-two cameras, a mother could not find her child, who had gone out to play one afternoon. The estate had three tower blocks, each with four entrances/exits, explaining the need for so many cameras. Of course, the point was that all the exits were covered and constantly taped. So, it would not, surely, have taken much to find a toddler wandering around alone. Forthwith, the mother asked the concierges to look for the child using the cameras. However, even this caused a social–managerial dilemma, because, whilst the individual concierges were perfectly happy to use the equipment for such a purpose, the landlord did not want to become known for such an activity in case it came to be seen as liable.

Third, the equipment (and the operators) might not work to tenants' demanded standards and levels of satisfaction. Indeed, the technology rarely meets such standards:

The system, as far as we are concerned, is really the poorest of the poor. Our outside cameras don't move, and there's only one camera in the back stairs and in the lift, and there's two in the foyer. It isn't enough.   (Int TA41, *f*, 61)

Plus the fact that they don't work at night.   (Int TA42, *m*, 46)

Well, they work at night but they haven't got infra-red. They have improved the system a good bit to what it was before, but it's still not adequate.   (Int TA41)

Such dissatisfaction amongst CCTV supporters places managers under pressure to justify existing expenditure on high-tech surveillance (as noted above). Hence, rather than the equipment being used to implement something radical and new, it is typically reduced to the condition of being a supplement to existing activities. However, getting tenants to accept an electronic gadget is not necessarily about 'the gadget' but about whether it can supply the same services as are provided on other estates or as were previously available—that is, where there was less technology but more labour:

My understanding of things is that [the landlord] has a serious financial problem with concierges. . . . and looking at other [landlords], they recognized the financial problems involved in continuing [their own] system. What you had to do was look at the possibility of some alternative . . . this was set up as a pilot project. . . . the idea is that, if it is successful here, it will be extended elsewhere. The cost was something like £560,000—the set-up cost—which is really expensive, but when you consider the benefit of it . . . if there is no 24-hour team with 15 men, there's obviously going to be serious cost savings, so it's probably worth their while doing it, if it works. And it all hinges on this 'if it works'.   (Int HM23)

By 'if it works' this manager means the new technologies being both acceptable to the tenants they will survey—a recognitive interest in the technology—and to senior managers in terms of operating costs—an instrumental interest. However, as the technology reduces costs through 'virtualization'—achieving control from greater distances—it becomes less acceptable to tenants in many ways, such as obtaining physical help quickly. The very concepts of 'control' or 'security'—what these words mean to various parties—is thereby brought into question.

CONCLUSION

The previous section demonstrated some of the ways in which many tenants, despite their obvious lack of outright 'resistance' to the concept of CCTV, nevertheless keep the whole issue of electronic surveillance on the boil. By constantly reminding commissioning authorities of their interests in the new technology, they aim to attain a new sense of freedom—from crime, disability, fear—and thus self-respect. Whilst many critics of CCTV may look to legislative answers to the threats the technology poses to civil liberties, such legislation cannot perform its ultimate role without a coherent body of interested and concerned people to monitor and struggle over such a diffuse technology and its meaning (what it does or is meant to do). One contention would be that such a body of people exists in most localities but that it will not be found in an immediately critical state, and may never reject the technology fully and out-right—in spite of the potential implications. Alternatively, the technologies may well continue to be acceptable to people despite a conscious articulation of their drawbacks and limitations. Or, in the terminology of the second rule of virtuality (Woolgar, this volume), the fears and risks associated with new technologies are unevenly socially distributed.

Overall, my fieldwork suggests that the actual diffusion of CCTV and other surveillance equipment across UK society, and specifically its introduction to and operation on housing estates, does not equate with the image of an Orwellian state. For day-to-day managers, the technologies (even when they work as planned) are not about control, but, rather, take shape in a social context of achieving 'good' for tenants (and others). This, I would argue, is a question of *self-esteem*, and managers and operatives do not want to be seen as spies. This is not to say that abuse (as in any social organization) does not take place (Armstrong and Norris 1999), but that quite often the boot is on the other foot and the drive to survey comes from those being watched. Contradictorily, this latter desire appears to be a movable feast and the promise of the tech-nology (and its commissioners) can often turn out to be empty, even when they meet all the original criteria of their 'clients'—like other 'clients', those who desire CCTV have a prerogative to change their minds. At the same time, the onus or burden of proof as to the effectiveness of electronic surveillance remains on system commissioners to *prove the social value of CCTV* in real terms—by providing measurable and usable services to tenants or other communities.

All of this does not mean that groups of people demanding CCTV are necessarily morally correct—it could be demanded for all the wrong reasons, including elitism, exclusion of others, or ethnic differentiation. However, such a denial of respect for others could only ever produce a new sense of moral indignation—the defiance of the excluded, which one tenant referred to above—rather than a resolution of problems.

8

Getting Real about Surveillance and Privacy at Work

David Mason, Graham Button, Gloria Lankshear,
and Sally Coates

INTRODUCTION

The five rules of virtuality that frame this volume (Woolgar, Chapter 1) seek to capture the ways in which the adoption of a 'positive scepticism' can contribute to our understanding of the impact and potential of new electronic and communication technologies. The five rules represent a shorthand summary of the counter-intuitive findings of the various projects that made up the 'Virtual Society?' programme. The project reported on here is no exception to this general pattern.

It is important to note that the five rules are counter-intuitive in at least two senses. In the first place, they may be said to run counter to common-sense expectations—as they are expressed in everyday conversational exchanges and political and policy discourse. The first and third rules might be said to exhibit these features in respect of the commonly voiced expectation that the rate of expansion of information and communications technologies (ICTs) will continue apace, supplanting and rendering obsolete existing ways of doing things. There is, however, another sense in which the rules are counter-intuitive. This is because they summarize findings that, in many instances, also run counter to a number of orthodox positions in the academic literature.

The findings reported here embrace both these senses of counter-intuitive. One aspect of this is perhaps not surprising. As we shall see, the research was designed to some degree from a standpoint of analytic scepticism towards a number of influential academic traditions. However, whilst the researchers anticipated that their findings would be likely to enable serious questions to be asked about those positions, they were less prepared for the fact that, from an early stage, the data also ran counter to their own, common-sense, expectations. Nowhere was this clearer than in relation to the apparently low priority accorded by our respondents to the question of privacy at work. Indeed, so unexpected was this finding that it gave rise to an early crisis of confidence within the research team, and an urgent reassessment and redesign of the research strategy.

THE RESEARCH AND ITS BACKGROUND

In this chapter, we report on the findings of a research project designed to investigate how surveillance-capable technology impacts on, and is framed by, the social relations of work. The original stimulus for the research was the burgeoning academic interest in, and the practical problems thrown up by, the increasing deployment in the workplace of a range of electronic technologies that have the potential to be used for the purposes of audit and monitoring. These have given new prominence to questions concerning empowerment, surveillance, privacy, and resistance that have long been the focus of sociological studies of the labour process and of managerial strategies. We refer to these technologies as 'surveillance capable'[1] because, in the course of operating, they collect and store data on individual activities that are potentially available for surveillance purposes, whether or not they are actually utilized in this way. We are not, it should be clear, primarily concerned with technologies that have been explicitly designed with surveillance functions in mind, but rather with a much larger class of innovative systems present in the modern workplace. Indeed, as the research progressed, it rapidly became clear that technologies having these characteristics are much more widespread and diverse than might be supposed from the literature that focuses on surveillance conventionally defined.

The research identified a continuum of surveillance-capable technologies. At one extreme are those designed primarily with a surveillance function (such as closed circuit television (CCTV) security systems).[2] At the other are systems that

---

[1] We should make it clear that we use this term as a convenient shorthand to describe a range of different kinds of technology, with diverse functions and purposes, that can be found in modern workplaces. The term seeks explicitly to distinguish the technologies in which we are interested from those specifically designed and deployed for surveillance purposes. We make no great theoretical claims for this distinction, recognizing that designers' intentions are not themselves unambiguous. Our category of surveillance-capable technology is, then, no more than a device for alerting ourselves, and others, to the potentialities of a range of technological systems beyond those characteristically invoked by mention of the term 'surveillance'. We are concerned more with empirical understanding of the way in which technologies are folded into the ongoing social relations of work than with the adequacy of theoretical abstractions.

[2] Even here it should not be assumed, however, that such systems are necessarily installed for disciplinary reasons. Thus CCTV systems may be intended to monitor customers' behaviour rather than that of employees, to manage access, or to monitor safety.

SURVEILLANCE AND PRIVACY AT WORK   139

are designed with non-surveillance functions in mind (such as workflow control technologies) and where the capacity to monitor individuals' work is a by-
product. In between are those where a surveillance or audit function has been
intentionally designed in, but where the relative emphasis on various system
capacities is dependent on local needs and implementation strategies. Indeed,
as the research proceeded, it rapidly became clear that almost any modern
electronic technology in common use could, if desired, be utilized for surveillance purposes.

Characteristically, lay and social-science responses to these developments
have been framed within one or more sets of assumptions. The first suggests
that technological developments exercise decisive influences over the way in
which organizations function and develop. This essentially determinist position
assumes that the very availability of a technological capacity will lead to its
deployment and that this, in turn, will transform the way the organization
functions. The second set of assumptions concerns the nature of the employment relationship itself. Here it is assumed that the workplace can be characterized as one of struggle and conflict and that relations between management
and employees are intrinsically oppositional. In such a model, the logic of
management as control makes the deployment of the enhanced surveillance
capacity of technology inevitable. When put together, these sets of assumptions
give rise to a characteristic debate about the degree to which employees are
able to resist the managerial consequences of enhanced surveillance capacity.

It is possible to discern a number of recurrent themes in debates around these
issues. A key one concerns the question of whether employees are empowered
or disempowered by the increasing deployment of technologies of the kinds in
question. In much management discourse, such developments are represented
as empowering. They are frequently seen to enhance the capacity of individuals
to contribute to organizational goals—often by underpinning and facilitating
more effective team working. Such arguments are characteristically found in
management texts extolling the virtues of people-centred forms of human
resource management (HRM), or in the rhetoric of businesses themselves. Hughes
et al. (this volume) report interestingly on a situation driven by assumptions of
this kind. As their discussion makes clear, the reality is frequently more complex.

A diametrically opposite view is to be found in the literature deriving from the
labour-process tradition. Authors in this tradition either stress the persistence
of 'harder' forms of HRM (Storey 1989) or seek to uncover the manipulative
character of modern management techniques, revealing in particular the ways
in which they promote self-discipline in the working behaviour of employees.
Here modern electronic technologies are conceived as tools deployed in support of managerial control either by offering the opportunity for closer forms of
direct supervision or by providing auditable data in the light of which individuals and groups of employees discipline themselves to pursue management
goals. Perhaps the seminal paper in initiating this debate was Sewell and
Wilkinson (1992). This paper, in its turn, gave rise to a further debate within the

labour-process literature about the extent to which such systematic dis-empowerment was inevitable and ubiquitous or, to the contrary, was capable of being resisted.

Sewell and Wilkinson (1992) sought to draw attention to the apparent paradox that modern developments in the labour process and managerial strategies have given rise to decentralization and devolution of responsibility for tactical decision making, while at the same time generating higher levels of centralized, strategic control and surveillance. This has occurred because devolved systems *require* the development of countervailing techniques of surveillance and loci of control to ensure that the actions of employees, collectively and individually, are continually focused on the productive goals of the organization. In other words, despite apparently radical changes in the organization of work, management retains, and continues to pursue through new means, its traditional interest in challenging worker empowerment and autonomy. Sewell and Wilkinson's argument amounts to a claim that employees are increasingly locked into an 'electronic panopticon' (cf. Webster and Robins 1993: 244), which effectively disempowers them in the face of managerial attempts to assert control of the labour process. By contrast, Thompson and Ackroyd (1995) accuse Sewell and Wilkinson of overdrawing the panopticon model and underestimating the scope for, and level of, worker resistance. They call for a return to the traditional focus of industrial sociology on employee resistance to ever-changing strategies of managerial control. Despite the differences between them, then, both of the positions just described are based on the fundamental assumption that the employment relationship is intrinsically exploitative, oppositional, and *essentially* conflictual.

The research reported here was framed in terms of the assumption that the questions raised by the existing literature could be addressed only if more attention were paid to the *empirical* features of the ongoing social relations of work. In this context, it is important to note that the project did not set out to investigate instances of surveillance at work. Rather, it was concerned with the increasing ubiquity of technologies having what we have called surveillance capability. Much of the popular and academic literature on these issues offers a somewhat apocalyptic vision of the future, in terms of both the implementation and the impact of surveillance-capable systems (see Lyon and Zureik 1996; Sinclair 2001). Against this background, the project was concerned with questions such as: whether and how employers deploy surveillance capacity; how employees define the boundaries of legitimate and illegitimate surveillance, particularly in relation to issues of privacy; and how they perceive and mobilize techniques of control and/or resistance in the context of definitions of legitimacy. We may specify each of these questions more closely.

First, it is important to ask whether managers and employers are conscious of the surveillance capacity of systems they commission and use. What influences their decisions to utilize or not utilize this capacity? If they use it, why do they do so? If not, why not? Secondly, we need to know whether employees are aware of the surveillance capacity of the systems they use. Do they see such capacity as a threat to their privacy or autonomy? What determines whether they regard actual or potential intrusions into their privacy as legitimate or illegitimate? Thirdly, and in the context of the above, we may ask how employees respond to the deployment of surveillance capability. Do they experience feelings of disempowerment? Do they resist and, if so, in what ways? Do they respond with resignation or apathy? Finally, in the event that employees are seen to engage in acts of non-compliance or circumvention, we need to ask what goals they are pursuing. Can we simply assume, in line with some of the theoretical positions reviewed above, that they are *resisting* management control in the pursuit of private objectives? Alternatively, are there circumstances in which apparent resistance is better understood as the development of alternative strategies in pursuit of organizational goals?

A series of case studies of actual work situations was, therefore, undertaken with the aim of revealing how the individual responses and social adaptations of both employers and employees arose from situationally specific perspectives, located in the day-to-day conduct of work. Specifically, the methods were designed to: map patterns of technological innovation; explore the intentions, motivations, and perceptions of those centrally involved in the introduction, implementation, and operationalization of technological solutions; identify the social relations entailed in day-to-day operationalization; investigate the ways in which managers and employees implement, circumvent, or manipulate technologies in the realization of organizational goals; identify instances of resistance and/or sabotage; catalogue coping strategies deployed in the context of competing demands and opportunities offered by the technology; and map the implications for human and organizational performance.

Case studies were conducted of the following: a print shop utilizing workflow management technologies; a public health laboratory using a computerized reporting system; a council tax office utilizing a computerized billing system; two call centres deploying computerized call management systems and audio monitoring technologies; a power station utilizing a range of relevant technologies including swipe-card entry, CCTV monitoring, and a computerized management information system. In addition, a cord blood gas analysis system and a computerized instructional package in a maternity hospital environment were also studied and information was generated about an instance of e-mail monitoring in a university. Finally, a mail survey of trades unions was conducted, designed to determine the scale of employee concern about privacy issues, as measured by the frequency with which these matters were the subject of member complaints.

The case-study approach adopted entailed several elements. The precise mix depended to some degree on such matters as the size of the organization and the duration of the research that was possible. This varied not only according to the access that it was possible to negotiate but also in terms of unpredictable exigencies of the research process. Wherever possible, however, the research followed the following stages. First, the investigators sought to become fully conversant with the overall structure and objectives of the organizations and specific work situations to be studied, as well as the nature and ostensible functions of the electronic technologies deployed in the work environments to be focused on. This was accomplished through such means as interviewing key personnel and scrutinizing documents such as organization charts, organizational policies of various kinds, and technology strategy documents. Second, a series of semi-structured interviews was conducted with managerial staff and employees in order to elucidate perceptions of the nature, purposes, and utility of technological innovations. These were designed, *inter alia*, to map the boundaries of what was considered legitimate surveillance and what were the privacy expectations of those concerned. In the third phase, observational studies were conducted of selected work situations, identified on the basis of preliminary access negotiations and familiarization. These sought to uncover and understand the actual work practices that had been developed in response to technological innovation and, where appropriate, in the context of perceived surveillance and surveillance potential.

As we have seen, some interpretations could lead us to conclude that those employed in modern workplaces were caught in an embattled situation in which they were either subdued by panoptic surveillance or faced with a constant struggle to devise resistance strategies in pursuit of individual and collective autonomy and privacy. At the same time, there is a widespread tendency to characterize all apparently non-compliant acts by employees as instances of resistance aimed at asserting control contra management interests or requirements and at protecting individual privacy and autonomy.[3] The result of our work, however, tends to suggest that, although employees were aware of its potential, their response to this technology, and to the management structures within which it was deployed, was much more complex than portrayed in such accounts. This was true also of the responses of managers themselves. Both employers and employees were, therefore, caught up in complex social relations of work within which technology was variously deployed, struggled with, sidelined, manipulated, circumvented, and appropriated, often in surprising ways.

MANAGING WITH TECHNOLOGY

The first point to make is that the availability of a technological capacity does not mean it will necessarily be deployed. In some cases, managers appeared unaware of the surveillance potential of systems in use or could not conceive of ways of deploying them. In others, they made calculations about the likely

---

[3] See, for example, the discussion of these issues in Edwards (1988: 191–2); Delbridge (1995: 812–13); Webb and Palmer (1998: 617–22).

impact of implementation in terms of employee reaction, judging the benefits of utilization against the costs. There was evidence of a reluctance to 'stir up unnecessary trouble' and of different attitudes to implementation among different groups of workers. In the case of a computerized reporting system in a public health laboratory, for example, senior managers were wary of utilizing the surveillance capacity of the system, even in what they regarded as a benign way, lest doing so should disrupt generally harmonious working relationships. Indeed, attempts were made to enlist the research team in assessing likely reactions of employees and in 'selling' the system's use. In general it appears that, the higher the status, or greater the organizational 'clout', of employees, the less likely management is to mobilize surveillance potential.[4] Perhaps inevitably, given the characteristic placement of women and men in the occupational structure, there seems to be a gender dimension to such calculations. Thus, in the public health laboratory studied, the utilization of surveillance capacity was mooted only in relation to clerical data inputers (all of whom were women). There was no suggestion that the higher status laboratory staff (who comprised both women and men) should be included.

It seems that surveillance capacity was most likely to be deployed where there was a perceived problem (for example, of health and safety, security, or stock wastage). A number of respondents suggested that routine use of surveillance capacity in the absence of an identified problem would be too 'resource hungry'. Moreover, even where some degree of surveillance was routine, as, for example, in call centres, whether or not sanctions were applied for procedural irregularities depended on judgements about their impact on the achievement of organizational goals. It is also important to note that there were differences of view among managers and supervisors depending both on position in the organizational hierarchy and on functional responsibilities. Often lower-level line managers and supervisors appeared to have a closer appreciation of the realities of day-to-day working than senior managers who were some way removed from them.

This draws attention to a frequently overlooked fact—namely, that managers do not constitute an undifferentiated category. Even if 'management' (an inevitably reified category) could be said to have a disciplinary interest in the minute control of all aspects of work, it is not at all clear that all *managers* will share that interest in any simple way. To the extent that they do, it will be attuned to the exigencies of their day-to-day lives and the targets that they are

---

[4] This said, it is important to note that, in the case of a prototype decision support tool for use in a maternity hospital environment, it was envisaged that the system would be deployed in relation to the work activities of a range of professional staff, including consultants. Unfortunately, delays to implementation of the system did not permit the researchers to study what happened in practice. However, this case does point to the potential that modern electronic systems have for drawing a wider range of employees, including professionals, into the purview of systematic day-to-day monitoring than has, perhaps, been traditionally recognized in the sociology of work.

expected to achieve. This is a particularly important point given the increasing tendency for what were once called 'supervisors' (shop-floor staff promoted to coordinating roles) to be renamed 'managers'. Such individuals may be particularly likely to be locked into forms of interaction with former peers that inhibit the deployment of disciplinary sanctions. This may be a consequence of affective attachments or a result of the internalization of the discourse of 'team working' and a related collaborative conception of the management-labour relation (see the discussion in Lankshear *et al.* 2000).

In addition, it should be noted that managers at all levels frequently have contradictory targets in terms of which they are judged. Call centres provide good examples of this problem. Thus, there is a widespread tension in call-centre operations between *quantity* and *quality*. On the one hand, a high value is attached to processing the largest number of calls possible in the shortest time. Often there are targets in terms either of call duration or of call throughput. In the case of those call centres that contract to undertake outsourced work for other companies, these targets are related to the pricing strategies adopted to secure the contract. At the same time, there is also a need to maintain the quality of calls, ensuring that customers' needs are met in a manner that makes it likely they will use the service again. Sometimes this entails the use of 'scripts' to which operatives are expected to adhere when interacting with callers. Balancing these objectives entails making decisions about whether, how, and when to apply sanctions for deviation from expectations in respect of either measure. It entails judgements about their relative importance, both globally and in relation to the performance of any individual member of staff. (For a fuller discussion of some of these issues see Lankshear *et al.* 2001.)

STRUGGLING WITH TECHNOLOGY

Contrary to popular portrayals of technologies as omnipotent, infallible, and superhuman, in many (if not the majority of) instances, technologies fell short of their design expectations. They frequently required considerable effort and ingenuity to implement and, in some instances, were rapidly abandoned or scaled back. In this respect we found that considerable individual and collective energy was expended in actually making the technology work rather than in circumventing its supposed negative effects. Thus, as the research proceeded, we encountered a number of situations in which planned implementations of technologies either did not go ahead to schedule or where extensions of use were abandoned or suspended in the face of unresolved problems. In the council tax office studied, for example, the implementation of a computerized record and billing system was seen, in part, as a trial for the more widespread adoption of the system in the higher work-volume environment of a benefits office. In the event, the difficulties of making the system work effectively led to a decision to defer a further roll-out beyond the lifetime of the research project. In this case, as in the workflow system encountered in the print shop, the problem was not primarily that the system did not work as designed, in a technical sense. Rather the issue was that the design had failed to take account of, or adequately address, key features of the working environment. (For a fuller discussion of a case in point, see Button *et al.* forthcoming.)

In circumstances where this was the case, we found that managers and workers frequently worked together in order to use the technology effectively to achieve the organization's goals. Thus, not only did employees commonly identify overtly with those goals but frequently went beyond the call of duty in seeking to realize them. At the same time, managers commonly colluded with practices that in strict terms broke organizational rules in order to maintain the day-to-day working relationships that made the achievement of organizational goals possible. We have already noted features of the call-centre environment that inhibited the deployment of disciplinary sanctions. In other cases, 'coalface' managers appeared better placed than those more senior to identify the dysfunctional consequences of technological innovations. Thus, in the printing operation studied, it was evident that the introduction of computerized workflow management tools actually disrupted the production process, slowing the pace of work and imposing a number of unplanned overheads. In this case, the result was direct collusion by management and employees to circumvent the system in order to re-establish the former order and productivity of the print room. A by-product was that the system's capacity to facilitate surveillance was at the same time undermined.

CIRCUMVENTING TECHNOLOGY: RESISTANCE OR APPROPRIATION?

Even where they were not simply pursuing organizational goals in a straightforward way, it was not the case that employees' orientations to the technology were framed in terms of simple resistance to its demands. Thus we found many instances where employees *appropriated* the technology in order to achieve a variety of individual and collective goals. For example, some respondents saw the apparently objective and auditable data produced by technological monitoring as a protection against unfair work distribution or accusations of dereliction. This may be because it is seen as being more disinterested and warrantable than the potentially arbitrary judgements produced by traditional modes of work observation and monitoring. As one respondent in the council tax office, commenting on the system's potential for ensuring a fair distribution of work and highlighting effort, put it: 'If you have not got anything to hide then there is no problem with it. That is my opinion on it. Not that we have a problem with it any more but there always used to be times when people weren't pulling their weight. Now that would be highlighted.'

Another example of this kind of appropriation was provided by a trade-union respondent who told the researchers of a supermarket chain that had stopped using its electronic point of sale systems to set throughput targets for checkout staff. The reason given to us for this development was that such targets, and the data stored in the system, could be used to support claims by employees against the company in respect of repetitive strain injury.

Moreover, even where employees expressed concerns about, and opposition to, the introduction of monitoring, initial hostility often abated as fears were allayed and staff appropriated the technology to their own purposes. A good example of this process at work was encountered in the power station studied. Here, the twenty-four-hour operation of the plant required that maintenance personnel be able to access spare parts and tools at all times. The stores, however, were not staffed at night. Those requiring items during this time were required to sign out any equipment or materials taken. In practice, this did not always happen, with the result that the inventory was often inaccurate, leading to a failure to reorder vital items. (There was no explicit suggestion that theft or other illegitimate removal of materials was a concern.) In order to address this, management installed CCTV cameras in the stores area with the aim of producing a record of its use when unstaffed. The initial reaction of stores staff was hostile. They were concerned either that they were suspected of impropriety or that the system could be used to monitor their activities when on duty. Management sought to allay these fears, but the opinion of stores staff was finally swayed when they realized that they could recruit the system to their own purposes. Because the system monitored the counter area, where 'customers' would arrive to seek items (or to sign them out at night), it generated an opportunity for stores staff to deploy their time more effectively. Thus, instead of having constantly to be present at the counter, they were able to undertake other tasks, in other parts of the stores, relying on the CCTV monitors to alert them to the presence of 'customers'. This example also shows how technologies that had overtly surveillance functions evoked other responses that could be categorized as 'resistance' but that might equally be described as 'putting the technology in its place'. Here recourse was often made to humour and the technology recruited to episodes of playfulness, which are common at work, even if frequently overlooked in academic studies. Thus, for example, the response of one employee to the introduction of the CCTV system was to don a large paper bag to conceal his head whenever he entered the stores area.

Even where employees circumvented or manipulated systems, we should be wary of assuming that they were engaged in acts of resistance, as conventionally defined in the literature. In the print room studied, for example, employees (in collusion with management) found ways to circumvent a workflow management system that not only changed the way they worked but actually made the task of meeting production targets more difficult. In re-establishing traditional forms of work organization, employees were not resisting management control or reasserting their autonomy *for the sake of it*. Rather, they were seeking to re-establish a method of working that actually met organizational goals more effectively. The example of a computerized instructional tool in the maternity hospital studied makes a similar point. The package was intended to improve the capacity of staff to interpret the data output from patient monitoring systems. In order to use the system, staff would be issued with individual PINs to enable them to log in. As they used the system, a record would be generated of their usage and of their performance in a number of simulation exercises. It thus had a monitoring capacity and data had been used for these purposes as part of the system's design and evaluation. It was conjectured that, in the longer term, it might also have an accreditation function. One aspect of the system's use that, at the time of the research (1999), militated against this, however, was the fact that staff would routinely 'borrow' others' PINs—effectively their identities. As a result, it was impossible to know to which staff members the recorded data referred and this undermined its utility for both surveillance and accreditation. It would be easy to see this as an example of the kind of resistance posited in labour-process debates. Interviews with staff, however, suggested that other explanations were possible. In the pressurized working environment of the maternity ward, time for training activities was at a premium. There was evidence that a number of staff who were keen to use the system during lulls in their work were inhibited by the need to find time to get themselves issued with a PIN. It was easier simply to 'borrow' someone else's identity in order to snatch a few minutes on the system and this is what at least some of them did.[5] That it was felt necessary and appropriate to do so was itself related to midwives' commitment to providing the most high-quality care for patients. As one respondent put it: 'I am delighted to do the package. I can only see advantage in it for me. I have a responsibility to be competent. I need to know what that information means.'

CONDITIONAL COMPLIANCE: BEYOND THE EMPLOYER–EMPLOYEE DYAD

This stress on a responsibility towards patients alerts us to a further issue of importance. Contrary to a common portrayal of work as defined only by the relationship between employers and workers, we found a number of cases in

---

[5] The system was not formally deployed either as a monitoring or as an accreditation tool during the period of our research. Indeed, those responsible for its technical design were wary of using it for accreditation since this had not been part of the original design specification. As a result, they argued, it would not be robust if deployed in this way. However, we should note that, were the system to be formally deployed for accreditation purposes, staff might not be willing to swap PINs quite so readily. We can, of course, only speculate about this. It is probable that such deployment would, however, also undermine the utility of the system as an instructional tool and thus pose other dilemmas for both staff and managers. For a fuller discussion of these issues see Lankshear and Mason (2001).

which one or both parties was also orienting to significant other players. Perhaps the paradigm case was that in which employees were involved in an interface with customers. In these cases, it was difficult to understand key features of employee responses to electronic monitoring without taking cognisance of the significance of what was effectively a three-way social relationship. We encountered two extremes. In one case, the print shop, employees colluded with managers effectively to deceive customers. This deception was a by-product of their mutual circumvention of the workflow control system, which was designed, in part, to produce an auditable record of work done. In another, employees' relationships with customers had implications for their responses to different kinds of management demands. In this latter example, a call centre, it is noteworthy that management demands themselves were frequently contradictory. As we have seen, a stress on speed in processing calls often ran counter to the demands of quality. In addition, however, quality measures in turn often ran counter to demands for more aggressive selling of products. Moreover, management's own performance indicators were often in conflict (as when a concern with productivity ran up against the need to keep down labour turn-over rates). In the case in question this created the organizational space in which employees could develop and defend their own definitions of 'professional' conduct by invoking obligations to customers.

It is worthwhile dwelling on this example for a moment, since it illustrates some of the weaknesses of seeing all apparently non-compliant acts by employees as instances of a global tendency to resist management requirements. In the call centre in question, which was part of a company selling travel and holiday packages, agents frequently reiterated a desire to be professional and give a good service to customers buying a 'happy product'-people like themselves whom they wanted to please.

On the surface, then, agents' orientations to customer care were clearly congruent with management objectives. However, other evidence suggested that it was too simple to see this as an internalized form of self-discipline. Evidence that matters were more complex is provided by the difficulties Holidayco senior management had in persuading agents to increase revenue by being more sales oriented. As one manager put it: 'We've tried time and again to get them to sell and they won't do it. They do everything else we ask them to do, but *they will not sell.*'

Despite the introduction of a complex bonus scheme, there was a remarkably consistent attitude to selling among agents, as revealed in interviews:

I am not in favour of the bonus scheme. I think that every phone call you take is just as important as a booking, whether it is a person who is concerned about their booking and you spend half an hour with them, or whether it is a £5,000 booking and you spend ten minutes.

I don't think you can [sell to clients]. People have limits on what they can afford. You are trying to organize their holiday.

Thus, although employees may appear, on the surface, simply to have internalized company objectives, their attitude to selling suggests something more complex. Employees clearly possessed their own conceptions of professionalism, which involved striking a balance between corporate and client interests, and acting with a sense of ethical and personal autonomy. Their own definitions of professionalism and good performance were, therefore, neither at complete variance with, nor simple clones of, management definitions. Rather they represented a negotiated outcome in a context where both sides enjoyed relative, but restricted, autonomy. (For a fuller discussion, see Lankshear *et al.* 2000.)

REINSTATING THE SOCIAL IN RELATIONS AT WORK

Finally, we should note that a defining characteristic of almost all the technologies encountered in the research was their tendency to construct work as an *individual* activity. Even where the collective nature of work was taken into account in technology design it was typically conceptualized as an aggregation of individual effort. The task of technology, then, was to coordinate those individual efforts to produce a collective outcome. This fails to recognize, however, that what appears to be individual effort is itself frequently the outcome of collective and collaborative interactions. The social context of work, and the contribution that this made to individual performance, appeared frequently to have been overlooked by technology designers. This feature frequently accounted for the difficulties encountered in its implementation. In these circumstances, the responses of employees (and indeed of managers) often make sense only if they are seen as part of an attempt to re-establish collective dimensions of work in the face of the individualizing tendencies of technology. The example of the print shop is a case in point. Prior to the introduction of the workflow management system, staff had routinely shared work, watched others' machines, and swapped tasks in order to optimize both their own efforts and the flow of work through the plant. The workflow management system, by contrast, had been designed on the presumption that work was an individual activity. The work of the print room was conceived as consisting of identifiable tasks that could be separated, timed, and sequenced. As a result, the operation of the workflow management system was premised on the allocation of particular 'jobs' to individual operatives. One of the reasons for the failure of the system to deliver on its objectives, and indeed why it significantly disrupted production, was that it individualized tasks that had previously been accomplished collaboratively. The response of operatives in circumventing the system, and re-establishing the productive order of the print room, can be seen as in large measure consisting of the re-establishment of the collective character of work—a task that required the circumvention of the system. This was accomplished by manipulating the input of data required by the system in a manner that misrepresented the actual flow of activity in the plant, while ultimately producing an auditable 'record' in line with the requirements of the system and those who had installed it.

It is probable that similar processes account for other aspects of our findings. In cases where management has colluded to some degree with employees, failed to implement rigid disciplinary guidelines, or declined altogether to implement surveillance capacity, it is likely that cognisance of the collective character of work has played a part. Indeed, it may even be the case that the design of many technological innovations is running counter to the emphasis of modern HRM on work as a team activity (Hardingham 1995; Pokras 1997). It may also undermine attempts to recognize and harness individual differences—as in the currently fashionable emphasis on managing diversity (R. Thomas 1991; Kandola *et al.* 1995; Kandola and Fullerton 1998).

This widespread conceptualization of work as a collective enterprise may also help to account for the marked lack of concern for issues of privacy that we encountered among our respondents. If work is indeed seen as collective and collaborative, privacy as a property of individuals may well be seen as irrelevant to the work situation—an issue for non-work time.

PRIVACY AND AUTONOMY AT WORK

A key finding of the research is that almost all employees in our case studies appeared to recognize, and indeed accept, that monitoring and surveillance was a routine aspect of their working lives. Few, if any, appeared wholly unaware of the surveillance capabilities of systems they used, while many more saw them as little more than an extension of traditional forms of monitoring. There was a widely expressed acceptance of the legitimacy of such monitoring, not only where there were perceived problems but more routinely. As one call-centre agent interviewed put it, 'If you are going to have their wages, then I suppose you have to work to what they want.' In contrast to the concerns of much of the literature and a good deal of public discussion,[6] there is little evidence in our research of employees regarding technological surveillance systems as a threat to privacy. Not only did almost no respondents in our study express such concerns, but a mail survey of trade unions (followed up by a number of interviews) suggested that concerns of this kind were not widespread. Unions reported few complaints from members and, while they remained wary of future developments, generally appeared to accept that monitoring of work performance, as well as security, is legitimate. A prime concern, however, was

---

[6] See, for example the following press articles: A. Barnett (2000); Bresler (2000); Inman (2000). For a contrary view more in line with the findings reported in this chapter, see Sinclair (2001).

that such activities should be open, subject to collective agreement, and conducted within the law (cf. Ford 1998). Providing these conditions were met, the potential for a mutual benefit was recognized. Often initial concerns had been allayed following experience of implementation, and early opposition sometimes turned to support. In some cases, surveillance systems had been used to address questions of concern to unions and their members, as, for example, when monitoring of e-mail was used to trace those responsible for abusive or indecent postings.

Only in one case did we encounter expressed concerns about privacy in the context of electronic monitoring, and the manner in which it was expressed may indicate something about the way the distinction between privacy and legitimate monitoring is conceived more widely. In one of the call centres studied, where there appeared to be a general acceptance of monitoring for the purposes of assessing performance, there was, nevertheless, great sensitivity about the potential monitoring of private phone calls. Such an eventuality was regarded as representing an invasion of privacy by the agents and was viewed as very disturbing. The problem was exacerbated by the absence of facilities for making or receiving private calls. There was no suggestion that the monitoring of private calls was routine or an aspect of company policy. Rather, agents were concerned about accidental intrusion into private matters. What is of particular interest, however, is the clear distinction that agents made between this *illegitimate* trespass into matters that were regarded as occupying the realm of personal privacy and *legitimate* monitoring of occupational performance.

Before we leave the issue of privacy, there is one further issue worthy of note. Much of the literature on privacy treats it as a 'good', an important value, something to which all human beings have a right. Any infringement of that right must, from this perspective, be ethically problematic, as must developments that threaten, or facilitate, such infringements (Westin 1992; Spinello 1995; Ottensmeyer and McCarthy 1996; Rule 1996; Ford 1998; Introna 2000). However, our evidence suggests that approaches to the ethical implications of surveillance-capable technologies that divorce them from their organizational and social settings are unlikely to be able to capture the complexity of the ethical dilemmas experienced, and struggled with, by participants. Thus, in the case of the medical instructional package discussed above, discussions were in progress about the appropriateness or otherwise of utilizing the monitoring capacity of the system for monitoring or accreditation purposes. There were even some senior staff willing to raise the question of whether any such monitoring should be covert rather than overt. Such debates must, however, be set in the context of a medical environment where the right to privacy was literally competing for ethical priority with considerations of life and death (see the discussion in Lankshear and Mason 2001). In such circumstances, blanket claims for the priority of privacy as a value seemed less than wholly convincing. What is of interest, however, is that for many of our respondents the balancing of privacy with the competing claims for legitimacy of other principles of workplace organization seemed routine and unexceptionable. (Compare the discussion in Marx 1998.)

CONCLUSION

The findings reported in this chapter, we believe, indicate the importance of empirical studies in understanding the implications of technological innovations for the social relations of work. In this respect they are consistent with the first rule of virtuality—the impact of new technologies depends crucially on their local social context. Moreover, in line with the overall theme of this volume, our findings are counter-intuitive in both the senses we identified above, although not perhaps always in the way we might have expected. That they both confirmed and ran counter to some of our own initial expectations has already been indicated. In other respects, however, they may not be as unequivocally counter-intuitive as might be imagined. Thus, set against much press commentary, and the literature of bodies such as the Institute of Employment Rights (Ford 1998), our findings regarding employees' views on privacy at work are certainly counter-intuitive. However, set against the perspectives of many of our respondents, they appear unexceptional. For them, the distinction between those matters that are relevant to the world of work and those that are genuinely matters of personal privacy seemed self-evident. As a result, they frequently appeared uncomprehending of our early efforts to raise privacy at work as an issue.

This does not mean, of course, that issues of privacy are everywhere irrelevant to the world of work or that views currently expressed might not change in response to developments in workplace social relations. It may even be, as writers in the labour-process tradition might well charge, that our respondents were victims of a false consciousness that blinded them to the underlying realities of the workplace. While it would be foolish to dismiss such a possibility entirely out of hand, our data suggest that, in most cases, our respondents were, in fact, very clear about both the power relations of work and the capabilities of the technologies with which they worked. This discussion does, however, illustrate that the second rule of virtuality—the fears and risks associated with new technologies are unevenly socially distributed—may have a particular resonance for our results. These suggest that such fears and risks may be most commonly expressed among those who have a stake in maximizing their perception. Given the contrast between such views and those of our respondents, the question may be usefully posed, 'If false consciousness is indeed an issue in this area, where does it most commonly manifest itself?' We submit that, though not perhaps decisive in any such debate, the accumulation of empirical evidence about the ongoing day-to-day relations of work, and their perception by participants, is a key to approaching an intellectually defensible answer.

9

Virtual Society and the Cultural Practice of Study

Charles Crook and Paul Light

INTRODUCTION

The university community has become keenly aware of 'virtual society'. There is no shortage of commentators urging the appropriation of information and communications technology (ICT) into higher education. Political analysts identify issues of economy and enfranchisement: arguing that virtual education may both cost less and make possible greater social inclusion (Hague 1991). Principals and vice-chancellors uneasily observe the growth of corporate universities and the accreditation of for-profit institutions with no bricks-and-mortar identity (Duderstadt 1999). Educational managers sense a danger of being left behind as they see neighbouring universities develop new technical infrastructures (Oblinger and Rush 1998). The ICT industry promotes positive images of computer-supported learning. Not least in significance, a number of academics are publicizing their own teaching achievements, which involve the new tools of ICT (White and Weight 2000).

Consequently, undergraduates entering universities now can expect learning to be organized in a context that is increasingly fluid. They may find that the community of higher education feels more virtual, as staff are drawn to new learning practices that ICT makes possible. Yet it is by no means clear what the prospects are for such new forms of higher education. In this situation it may be tempting to extrapolate from the various localized successes of distance education, where these virtual methods are more developed. However, this may be unwise. For the motivations, aspirations, and life circumstances of most distance learners are very different from those of the typical student transferring directly from the secondary to the tertiary sector. Moreover, while there are virtualization success stories involving this more traditional community, they typically refer to piecemeal innovations that involve just parts of the total system. There are still very few universities—distance or otherwise—whose use of virtual practices can be said to be comprehensive.

In discussing these uncertainties here, we shall draw upon experience from our own research concerned with virtualization as it is gradually being adopted in traditional higher educational contexts. After Richardson (2000), such contexts may be termed 'campus' universities—that is, settings that are largely full time and, often, significantly residential. Thus, we have not been studying fully virtualized institutions. Instead, we have considered the process of transformation as it is gradually taking place in circumstances that are more familiar: circumstances that largely involve students fresh from secondary education who are entering universities that are still firmly bricks-and-mortar institutions.

The empirical work we outline later in the chapter draws attention to how difficult it can be to establish virtual-learning practices among undergraduates. Evidently, it is important to understand why this is so. Thus, the first half of this chapter is concerned with establishing a conceptual framework that may help with that understanding. In particular, we are keen to establish that study is a culturally distinctive form of human activity: a cultural practice. Where cultural practices are firmly entrenched, interventions can be problematic. We argue that this may be the case for attempts to engineer new forms of virtual learning.

THE VIRTUALIZATION AGENDA WITHIN HIGHER EDUCATION

Going virtual entails core institutional activities becoming more distributed in time and space. For universities, this means modifying traditional practices such that they may support students who will rarely congregate in shared spaces for study. Such students may also wish to extend their education over longer periods of time. At first sight, trends of this sort suggest a form of higher education that seems less participatory. Going virtual may thereby make university teaching less about orchestrating a kind of communal experience and more about properly pacing the delivery of learning materials. Indeed, this apparent commodification of educational practice is increasingly visible in the language of senior academics. For example: 'A knowledge economy connects the producers and suppliers of knowledge to the consumers of their product, and to the provider of related services such as tutorial support, assessment and certification' (MacFarlane 1998: 84).

These students/consumers will need new forms of resource to support their learning in the virtual society of higher education. They will require materials that can be readily dispatched to their chosen private study spaces—for where they choose to work might not form part of any designed environment of labs and libraries. Moreover, these materials will need to be authored to match the framework of use dictated by the computer desktop. Yet MacFarlane's reference above to 'tutorial support' reminds us that higher education in a virtual society may still aspire to the intimacy of tutor-to-student contact. Achieving that goal must depend upon other potential uses of new technologies—in particular, uses that allow communication where engagement at the same time and place is not possible (that is, 'asynchronous' communication). So, personal computing will not simply be a materials delivery technology; it will also be implicated where practitioners need new techniques to protect the sense of community within their teaching.

The principle of education freed from constraints of shared places and times is often celebrated in economic or social-inclusion terms. However, enthusiasts for virtual education may also refer to the quality of the learning experience itself—sometimes characterizing it in liberational language. Such visions are captured in the following claim about virtual education: 'When students can get cash at 2 a.m., download library materials at 3 a.m., and order shoes from L. L. Bean at 4 a.m., it is only educational inertia that keeps them convinced that they must learn calculus by sitting in the same classroom for fifty minutes three times a week' (Blustein *et al.* 1999: 21). Yet while this observation at first sight seems to get to the heart of virtualization, it also should encourage us to think about what is involved in the activity of 'learning'. In the quotation, learning seems framed as a distinct domain of human activity, self-contained in a way that makes it potentially comparable to shopping. So, by analogy, if the purchasing of shoes is just one possible activity drawn from the larger domain of 'shopping', then the study of calculus is just one possible realization of the larger domain of 'learning'.

It is an intriguing notion that the convenience of purchasing shoes at any time we fancy could provide a model for educational reform. Such manifestos for virtualization argue that opportunities to study should be accessible with the same consumer-friendly convenience as opportunities to shop. However, the analogy is an uneasy one. This is not just because of the commodification implied, for a virtualized 'loosening-up' of education does not *necessarily* require that knowledge should become merely a delivered commodity. The real problems with the analogy may arise from the fact that, as an activity system, learning is significantly unlike shopping. Just as it is also unlike climbing or singing, or any variety of these more circumscribed human pursuits. The nature of the difference between them is worth highlighting.

Suppose there are people who feel that being in a bathroom is the only time and place that they should sing. Then, we can imagine new cultural practices that might empower them to sing more freely—just as new cultural practices might be designed that liberate people to do their shopping at 4 a.m. However, *learning* is not necessarily fluid in the manner being claimed here for shopping and singing. Arguably, the analogy is attractive because these latter activities seem to us more self-contained: there is nothing particularly problematic about exercising them. Once we have decided, say, to shop, we simply get on with it.

However, learning does seem different: perhaps it is better considered as 'activity-in-context'. How easily we can 'do' it depends more upon an environment being in place that is more structuring of the activity—an environment designed for configuring a form of participation. Learning is not activity to be readily abstracted from context, such that it might be calmly executed at other arbitrary times and places, although this is not to imply that such dependencies are to be rigidly felt forever. The activity–context relationship of learning may evolve for the learner. Experience of learning in some domain may empower the student to become more versatile in managing these environmental relationships, more emotionally comfortable in entering them. Indeed, this is part of what successful educational contexts may achieve. However, the autonomy of this learner 'becoming' may not be easily won. Appropriate experience must be gathered and, so, environments must be crafted to support such progress. It is this embedding of learning in a cultural context that defines a significant challenge for virtualization—or any initiative that radically re-mediates the underlying practices.

The conceptual language of psychology may have played some part in tempting us towards this decoupling of learning from context. Psychology has encouraged analyses of human action in terms of 'behaviours'. Attention is thereby narrowly focused on observable forms of action. More recent developments in psychology, particularly in the form of cultural psychology (Cole 1996), offer a different perspective. The cultural perspective invites us to view human activity as everywhere embedded in a medium of cultural resources. When we set out to understand it, human activity should not be decoupled from the artefacts, technologies, symbol systems, institutional structures, and other cultural paraphernalia within which it is constituted. Moreover, some forms of activity have evolved to be particularly well binded into particular cultural conditions. This may be so for learning.

Invoking this cultural theorizing creates a significant stocktaking point in our argument about learning and its potential for virtualization. The claim about learning being firmly embedded in contexts is really a claim about it being a special form of cultural practice. Yet this is confusing if a further distinction is not kept in mind. That distinction concerns what may be termed the 'formal' and the 'informal' in relation to learning. There is a sense in which human beings are learning all the time—as developmental psychologists are keen to point out (Wood 1988). This is a claim about people's dynamic relationship with their environment: they are constantly being changed by its influence. On such an analysis, learning is certainly not a form of activity episodically carried out, like shopping or singing. It is pervasive: something that just happens to people as they engage with the world. The sense of learning under discussion here (and the sense potentially challenging for virtualization) is more circumscribed. It concerns the case of learning as cultural practice: as a particular form of activity-in-context. It concerns circumstances where the pervasive capacity to learn is allowed to be orchestrated by others—often in an institutional context.

Such distinctions invite reference to 'formal' learning, because what is meant applies to situations where some type of culturally organized activity is going on. Circumstances have been formalized in the interests of promoting learning that is deliberate or intentional. This sense of learning might be more naturally called 'study'; indeed, that term has been our preference for the title of this chapter.

A somewhat glib summary of our thesis is that learning-as-study is often a *difficult* thing for students to do. Certainly it is expected to be much more demanding than shopping. What 'difficult' means here is that, to be stimulated and sustained, the activity of study depends upon an embedding in certain cultural settings: it is activity-in-context. So, if learning is successful, this is often because (educational) institutions have fashioned a supportive context that works in sustaining the engagement. Perhaps participants in education become numb to the presence, structure, and importance of this context—rather as the proverbial fish is the last to discover water. This possibility is considered below when we comment on a slowness in the adoption of virtual-learning resources by students. We argue for understanding their reticence in terms of designers failing to notice how the activity being re-mediated (with ICT) was firmly grounded in a context of practice—a context that may be unhelpfully disturbed in the virtual transformation.

Once it is decided to theorize the activity of study in terms of cultural practice, then it is natural to consider educational experience in terms of 'enculturation'. In fact, this is a perspective that is already well developed within research on apprenticeship learning (Lave 1988) and research on learning at work (Wenger 1998). It is a perspective that invites seeking insight from the broader literature concerned with psychological processes of enculturation during development (e.g. Valsiner 2000). Here we find an interesting emphasis upon how individuals experience the interface between new systems of cultural practice and those with which they have become familiar. So, influencing the enculturation of others may often concern the careful management of an interplay—namely, that between novel and entrenched modes of acting. We turn to this issue next: considering how such an interplay may arise in the domain of higher education.

THE NATURE OF STUDY: ACCESSIBLE REPRESENTATIONS

Here, we wish to consider what this contrast between established and novel cultural practices might mean within the context of entering higher education as a student. In particular, we dwell upon the dynamic relationship between 'everyday' or familiar cultural practices and the practices of study. This discussion will better contextualize the successes and difficulties of virtualization.

To capture the relevant contrast, it is tempting to employ the distinction between curricular and extra-curricular. Yet we are uneasy about the term 'extra-curricular' as a description for one pole of the distinction at issue here. This is because it seems to be constrained to activities that are, by definition, quite independent of study. Instead, a distinction is needed that seems to refer less to differences in the content of the activity and more to differences in the conditions governing its conduct. Accordingly, we invoke again the distinction introduced above: suggesting that living in an educational context comprises the 'formal' and 'informal'. This contrast is still broadly about life within the curriculum and life outside it, but the contrast seems more readily to admit a possibility of traffic between the two activity settings—something we believe needs to be understood. In a sense, the 'informal' remains a pole of the distinction that is defined by exclusion: it is activity that is *not* directly managed by the institutional demands of a curriculum. It is what students are doing 'the rest of the time'. There is a risk of implying that such activity does not have 'form': that there are *no* forces shaping its content. This is not intended, although what is implied is that the content of informal student activity is felt by students as being more under their own control—that is, it is guided by choices that are more continuous with an individual student's history of personal concerns and preferences.

Having just made a distinction, we now wish to blur it a little. Formal learning may appear a sharp enough polar term in this distinction. It seems easy enough to identify when it is in progress: students are seen immersed in texts, attending lectures, contributing to seminars, or systematically manipulating apparatus. Such contexts for engaging in the formal (texts, lectures, seminars, apparatus) are a natural extension of what people persistently do during their 'informal' lives (for example: reading, listening, talking, playing). This continuity identifies a 'blurring' of the distinction that is inevitable but useful, for the formalizing of learning involves cultivating in students a certain *stance* within what is already well-practised activity—a certain kind of required adjustment to otherwise traditional frameworks for interacting with the world, social or material. That stance comprises a willingness to arrange such established interactions into new formats—formats intended to concentrate engagement with disciplinary material. So, the well-practised activities of reading, listening, talking, and playing become subject to explicit management. They become focused, sustained, directed, and variously coordinated towards goals imposed by the cultural device of a curriculum. This describes how humans (uniquely, perhaps) are led to learn by design. Therefore, what educational enculturation achieves is the engineering of already established repertoires of human communication and interaction: orchestrating them towards serving the more particular goals of an instructional agenda.

Within our project, we tried to make visible these continuities: the links between a cultural practice for interacting with the world called 'formal learning', and people's otherwise spontaneous and improvised interactions. In doing this, we considered how learning has become publicly represented. Specifically, we examined how institutions created visual images that portrayed learning. University prospectuses provided a rich source of such material and we analysed all the relevant photographs from a random sampling of ten UK institutions. Pictures accompanying departmental entries often illustrated students purportedly studying. Yet their activity rarely corresponded to the canonical images of formal learning discussed above. They were rarely shown in lectures, libraries, or states of private study with texts. Rather, the prospectus student was engaged, active, exploratory, often out of doors, and, above all, social. Indeed, it might sometimes be hard to judge what these photographs were about—if the viewer had not been tipped off where they were taken from (see Fig. 9.1).

The reason these images 'work' is surely because they celebrate a grounding of formal learning in everyday cultural routines: informal activities that potential students already recognize and find comfortable. The images are reassuring, for they promise that learning will be a version of familiar and agreeable cultural experiences. It will be about conversational engagement; it will be about taking part in communal activities; it will be about investigating and exploring material things. And so it will be. However, if there is any dishonesty in all this, it is the mild form associated with being selective. So, the critical viewer may spot the failure to include many examples of learning as potentially a solitary and more passive activity. They may also spot another missing ingredient: something selective about the *attitudes* portrayed. Students in promotional representations are decidedly upbeat. It will never be suggested that learners can lack confidence, that they become frustrated, or that they may sometimes encounter a stressful impasse in their explorations. Yet we do expect students to experience these things, simply because the demands of formal learning will often be difficult and relentless. It might be said that formalizing everyday interactions into learning often involves turning those everyday interactions into routines that become 'hard' for us. Formalization involves orchestrating and channelling familiar interactions such that they become dense and probing encounters with disciplinary material. Sustaining such activity—adopting the stance of a learner—may not always be an easy or welcome invitation.

The emotional demand of formal learning is edited out of promotional material. This happens easily (and perhaps innocently) enough, because the static quality of pictorial imagery conceals some of the formalization guiding what is being portrayed. For example, learning conversations (say, tutorials) may be represented; but the conversational moments captured in photographs cannot easily suggest that managing learning talk between expert and novice (tutor and student) might often be problematic. Similarly, in showing students engaged in more solitary explorations, there is no indication that these are embedded in a (perhaps stressful) regime of deadlines and time management. There is no hint that the learning resources might sometimes be arid, or that the necessary engagement with them could be lengthy and tiring, or that these explorations have to be accompanied by stylized record-keeping.

In short, the familiar interactions captured in popular images of studying deny the intensity, persistence, and focus that is often demanded when

Fig. 9.1. Images of learning from a university prospectus.

learning-by-design. A central ambition of institutional life must be to create conditions for learning that make tolerable the felt pressure of such demands. In this spirit, institutional contexts start from the everyday repertoire of learners (narrative, conversation, play, and so on) and formalize it such as to support purposeful learning (lecture, tutorial, investigation, and so on). First, this will entail exposing learners to a curriculum—an organized passage through some syllabus of disciplinary material. Second, formalization also involves designing a physical environment that supports the management of time and effort. This architecture helps focus and sustain activity towards disciplinary exploration: it will include spaces with specialized functionality, including suitable insulation from competing forms of activity (Jamieson *et al.* 2000). Finally, institutional design for formal learning includes creating occasions for exercising the discourse of a disciplinary community.

It is these features of an educational environment that come to mind when learning is framed as 'cultural practice': when it is formalized. The curriculum, the material setting, and the community that makes up educational institutions together provide a set of resources to make learning happen. These are the artefacts, technologies, and specialized spaces of institutions—as well as the rituals, routines, and roles that comprise their bureaucratic traditions. An established motive and energy for sustained learning cannot be taken for granted in most intending students (Newstead 1998). Institutions have evolved in the terms we have described so as to engineer learners' behaviour towards the disciplinary goals set by educators. The success of educational practice will often depend on the skill with which these 'learning sites' (Bliss *et al.* 1999) are designed. We have argued that such design entails a skilful weaving of informal cultural practices into the formalized investigations that comprise 'studying'. The risk of new learning technologies is that they disrupt rather than support the process of enculturation—by creating experiences of discontinuity.

THE NATURE OF STUDY: STUDENT DIARIES

Discussion in the previous section was largely focused on the formal—that is, study as a special set of cultural practices into which students are drawn. However, we were anxious not to over-sharpen distinctions; in fact, it was the *continuity* between the formal and the informal that was more at issue. The content of promotional imagery was used to make visible how educational practice might 'work'. It works through the possibility of grounding the design of formal learning in the familiar and informal communication practices of everyday experience. In the photographs that populate prospectuses, this continuity is implicit as an ideal—one that portrays the events of learning as having an agreeable familiarity and spontaneity. Admittedly there may be a romantic flavour to this suggestion of a particularly strong continuity between the informal and the informal, for implying that this idealized experience of study is *easy* to enculture could be a bold promise.

However, a model of learning-as-enculturation must do more than just declare that there is a grounding of the sort discussed above. The model must also address a dynamic associated with this grounding—a dynamic concerned with traffic at the borders between the formal and informal. This traffic moves both ways. Thus, while the formal gets to be grounded in the agreeably informal, there is also an influence in the reverse direction. Put simply, successful enculturation into educational practice will also entail the cultural practices of the formal coming to reconfigure activity within the informal. The intellectual conventions of analysis, investigation, and discourse that students practise in an institutional context may be appropriated into their more everyday interaction. In short, students come to act and talk more generally in ways that echo their disciplinary experience in learning, perhaps this is exactly what is entailed in their becoming authentic practitioners. Indeed, it seems to be traffic from the formal to the informal that inspires some theorists to dwell on learning as a matter of shifting *identity* (Wenger 1998).

In the previous section, we were concerned with idealized representations of learning such as those in promotional imagery. Now we consider students' own reports of how they spend their time. Sketching this investment in general terms provides a vehicle for introducing the study contexts that have provided settings for our own research on virtualization. The lessons of this research are then discussed in the remainder of the chapter.

We obtained self-reports of study activity by recruiting a sample of forty-eight second- and third-year undergraduates from one campus university. This university has made particular effort to develop ICT for teaching: for instance, all its study bedrooms now allow network access for student computers. As this initiative was in development at the time of our project, it conveniently allowed sampling such that half the students were networked this way, and half not. Care was taken to recruit learners across all academic disciplines and very few students we approached declined to take part. The research we were able to do involved personal activity diaries, interviews with the students, cataloguing of e-mail traffic and, for those with networked computers in their rooms, continuous system logging of how they used this technology. We shall draw on this material below. We also refer to other cohorts of students at a second university who took part in various initiatives to establish computer-mediated seminars.

One thing the students did for us was keep diaries across a full week; logging, in fifteen-minute intervals, details of their activity, location, and any study resources that might be in use. Figure 9.2 is a typical summary made possible by these records: it displays three forms of aggregate measure. Across the whole sample, it describes the probability of recording within successive units of time each of three general activities: being in class (tutorial, seminar, fieldwork, and so on), being engaged in private (solitary) study, and studying with a peer (out of any classroom context).

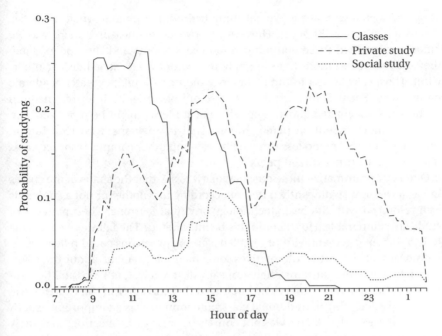

Fig. 9.2. Distribution of study time from student diary records.

Investment of time is evenly spread between classes and unscheduled study periods. In principle, this class time could be targeted for virtualization (with, say, network-delivered lectures, laboratory simulations, and so on). These methods had not been pursued at this campus university; indeed, they remain uncommon more generally. Yet, such virtualization of study may be taking place *indirectly*. Indeed, the liberational claims for virtualization might imply that this would readily happen. As staff increasingly offer course-related web resources, students may thereby chose to make this more the basis of their engagement with a course. Students may even elect to follow their own route through the curriculum by combining these course-designed network resources with opportunities provided by their internet access—thus taking more control over the assembly of learning material.

However, this did not seem to be happening. To notice this, the comparison between bedroom-networked and un-networked students is useful. The former have intensive access to local and global network resources. So they can adopt more virtual modes of study in the manner just proposed. Their networking allows access to learning material at times they choose and in a place (their own room) separate from the formal spaces of institutional learning. There was no doubt that the networked students spent more time using this technology. Indeed, during the typical afternoon and evening period there was around a

50 per cent chance that the typical study-bedroom computer would be active (Crook and Barrowcliff 2001). However, in two other measures there was *no* difference between these computer-resourced students and their peers. First, they did not spend more time in study-related activities (scheduled or otherwise). Thus, easy access to the technology did not stimulate greater academic productivity. Second, their study practices did not migrate into this medium in the sense speculated above—namely, that students might be more active in designing independent curricular routes. That is, they spent no less time in scheduled classes and no less time in libraries and other campus resource areas than did their un-networked peers.

One way to summarize these observations is to say that the shape of the curves in Fig. 9.1 are not significantly different according to whether or not a student is well resourced with the basic technology of virtual learning. Their patterns of study are comparable. How should this be interpreted? The failure of accessible ICT to shift engagement with timetabled learning occasions could reflect either the poverty of the virtual alternatives, or something precious about the traditional formats that sustains their appeal. Most likely, both possibilities are involved. Certainly, our interviews suggested that the latter of the two was real enough: participating in traditional classroom formats was an important experience for these students. This was not entirely because those meetings inevitably exposed students to brilliant lectures, animated tutorials, or engaging practicals. Perhaps sometimes they did. What students more often remarked upon was the organizing discipline that this timetable imposed on study. They also referred to the opportunities class meetings provided for peer contact: such contact was important to them for its casual feedback about personal progress and targets (Crook 2001). The failure of virtual tools to re-mediate this communal dimension of learning is a theme developed further below.

So there may be something quite precious in the traditional formats. Whether their continuing appeal also reflects a poverty in the virtual alternatives is harder to assess. All modules at this campus had web pages, but not all staff made use of them. Of course, students also had full access to the internet, but perhaps the scope of the learning materials to be found there is limited.

One form of network-based resource that was unquestionably available and encouraged was text-based communication tools. Moreover, these are central to the virtualization agenda and they were certainly widely used by these students. For these reasons, we give closer attention in the next section to forms of virtualization that are based on this form of computer-mediated communication. We were particularly interested in how far such tools would come to re-mediate traditional modes of academic communication—those involving students exchanging with each other and with tutors. Hence, below we discuss the fate of the interpersonal dimension of learning when it encounters virtual tools—that is, we consider the virtualization of informal collaboration, tutorials, and seminars.

VIRTUALIZING THE PERSON-TO-PERSON EXCHANGE OF STUDY

In comparison with, say, video conferencing, the textual and asynchronous nature of e-mail may suggest an impoverished form of computer-mediated communication (CMC) (see Watt *et al.*, this volume; Brown and Lightfoot, this volume). However, e-mail tools remain prominent in virtualization agendas, very much *because* of their asynchronous property. The liberational promise of virtual education—to free learners from the constraints of time and place—rules out any communication medium that assumes students will *congregate*, such as would be required for conversational styles of contact. Asynchronous text messaging is, therefore, an attractive medium because it does respect the principle that individuals are free to choose the times and places of their participation. Moreover, where several learners are involved in a communication, e-mail can preserve the history of the ongoing exchange, such that newcomers may easily enter at any point in its development.

Here we shall comment on the use of e-mail in two formats. First, in its traditional design: that is, private text messaging between individuals (students to students as well as students to tutors). Then, in the following section, we shall consider a more orchestrated design: namely, text conferencing or the coordination of e-mail traffic among a group—on the model of a seminar. Here, a web-based tool can be used to collate and systematize e-mail contributions from individual participants, thereby creating a sense of a single, evolving discussion.

If a traditional educational community is receptive to the virtualization of its learning, then the accessibility of e-mail makes it a resource that should easily be adopted to support study. Our observations of students (and staff) in such a campus university suggest that this appropriation to study is not quick to happen. To research this take-up, we must discover how students actually use their e-mail. However, such patterns of use are hard to expose. Asking to look directly at people's mailboxes seems an unreasonable invasion of privacy; yet relying on their own remembered summaries of use is unlikely to be reliable. We opted for a compromise procedure. A computer program was written that would organize the inspection of a student's mailbox message by message, allowing each to be classified in respect of origin, content, and value. The resulting description could then be systematized. This tool was sufficiently accessible that students could process their own mailboxes on our behalf—following a short session of introduction.

The findings most relevant to our present discussion are these. All students welcomed and made use of e-mail. Students with networked computers in their study bedrooms were significantly heavier users. However, the profile of use (what messages were about and who they were from) was not different between the networked and the non-networked groups. Extending network access caused more use of e-mail but it did not seem to change what the tool was used for. Most significantly, the nature of that use was mainly social or recreational. In coding the main purpose of messages, students reported that less than a third (29 per cent) of incoming mail made any reference to study. Moreover, only 6 per cent of the total mail was judged to reflect academic debate—asking questions or otherwise discussing course-related matters. So, most e-mail with any academic content was not an alternative version of exploratory learning conversations: instead, the course-relevant mail was largely exchanges of a purely administrative nature. The same observation has recently been made with US students (Gatz and Hirt 2000).

This finding fits our own experience gathered across a longer period. One of us was attracted to the potential of e-mail as early as the mid-1980s (Crook 1988). From that time, colleagues and students in the author's department elected to use e-mail for coordinating routine communication. In looking back on a long period of encouraging students to adopt such a practice, it seemed that e-mail was accepted with enthusiasm, yet never became widely used for tutorial or peer discussion about study (Crook 1994). The idea arose that this could be because access to the tool was never optimal: perhaps it was never to hand when it might be most needed—say, as difficulties were encountered during periods of private study. Consequently, as a stronger test of its tutorial potential, computer-based course materials were designed that incorporated an easy method for sending e-mail to the appropriate tutor (Crook 1997). Specifically, hypermedia revision materials were composed for two courses that were shortly to be examined. Embedded within these materials were links to the appropriate course tutor: in effect, an e-mail launcher inviting students to pose queries in a text box on screen, and expect replies later via their normal e-mail account. Logs revealed that the study materials were used by most students and sometimes quite intensively. Yet the feature of 'just-in-time' e-mail facility was not used—apart from some requests that these computer-based materials might be made available on *paper* (Crook and Webster 1997).

Perhaps e-mail fails to stimulate study-related dialogue because existing face-to-face opportunities for talk already meet students' needs. However, we also know from research on university essay writing that students infrequently discuss such work with peers or take full advantage of staff availability for informal tutorial support (Crook 1994, 2000; Hounsell 1987). With hindsight, our simple expectation as innovators was that this new medium would, as it were, 'unblock' whatever obstacles were impeding scholarly conversation. Thereby the natural energy of informal human communication would be released and channelled towards formal academic goals. Our metaphors for thinking about these matters have now almost reversed. Many of the institutional factors previously seen as 'obstacles' now appear more like scaffolds. The natural energy of human communication seems to need appropriation rather than release. It is the scaffolds of institutional learning practice that help stimulate this process of enculturation.

Here is the simple principle we are promoting. The success of a new communication tool within an educational community depends on how effectively
it recruits informal practices of exchange (with which members are comfortable)
into an organized structure of formal communication (such as tutorial talk or
collaborative investigation). Designing for this, therefore, should be based upon
a good understanding of existing patterns of interchange and, in particular,
how the borders between formal and informal communication are managed.

Our research findings allow us to pursue this line of reasoning in relation to
the particular case of sluggish e-mail take-up for study. We have other observations relating to the nature of existing communicative practices within the
campus community. It was noted above that earlier research implied many
undergraduates traditionally have rather little informal course-related collaboration with either staff or peers. This might imply the virtualization problem is
one of confronting a too-deeply entrenched inertia. However, the situation is
not that simple, for a claim about inertia would be based on observations about
collaborating that take it to mean well-orchestrated out-of-class meetings.
During interviews, our students confirmed that such meetings were relatively
unusual, but they still reported quite frequent occasions of discussing study
(Crook 2001). However, such occasions were brief and somewhat improvised or
serendipitous in character. They typically took the form of snatched conversations made possible by the routine of campus life—say, encounters between
lectures, in libraries, or in cafeterias. Often these moments allowed traffic in
course-related tips and warnings as well as (much-valued) opportunities to
benchmark one's own progress on assignments. These could be so casual that
we suspect few of them figure in the diary records summarized in Fig. 9.2.
Nevertheless that figure might imply that rather a lot of peer collaboration took
place. This summary suggests modest but significant investment of time in
private study with others ('social study'). However, closer analysis suggests that
these exchanges were often associated with co-presence in institutional spaces
(such as computer and resource rooms). Such collaborations again seemed
serendipitous in nature, although they were definitely made possible by a
cultural context. That is, they arose within the design of the curriculum and the
material architecture for learning.

This identifies two versions of extra-curricular collaboration. Typically, they
are each characterized by informality and a lack of organized intent on the
students' part. However, both of them arise out of the cultural context of
institutional design. First, students launch their brief collaborative conversations as they move across the campus in pursuit of their social and classroom
schedule. Second, the more sustained episodes of 'social study' (in our diary
records) are constructed in those class-related spaces that afford spontaneous
cross talk: labs, libraries, resource areas, computer facilities, and department
common rooms.

Such is the status quo into which electronic communication tools are placed.
If e-mail makes only a modest impact, this seems to reflect a mismatch

between the design of the tool and the structure of the practice that it seeks to re-mediate. Existing collaborative conversations about study seemed supported by the cultural context of the community (visiting a resource room, heading for lectures, meeting at lunch, and so on) and, when they did occur, they seemed unplanned. However, sending an e-mail is not at all like triggering one of these conversations. The point at which an e-mail is composed is not one of a shared cultural context with the correspondent. Asynchronicity denies this mutuality. Moreover, the decision to communicate in this way and the medium of composition (text) creates a sense of formality that is dissonant with the more improvised exchanges that have evolved as the familiar style for informal collaboration. So, however informal the tone of e-mail messages, the conditions and medium of their composition creates a formality that seems to have been resisted in established extra-curricular collaboration.

This also applies to understanding the low exchange of e-mail between students and staff. Again, this was not simply a question of inertia arising from low baseline levels of existing communication. The students whose e-mail use we monitored were also interviewed about staff contact. Almost half of this sample reported at least one out-of-class exchange with a staff member during the preceding twenty-four hours. Yet few of these seemed planned. As with peer conversations about study, they arose in the spaces between curricular activities or as a result of chance encounters during the normal course of moving about the campus. We suggest that the implicit formality of an e-mail message does not complement the pattern of interaction that has evolved. In focus-group discussions with students as to why they did not open more e-mail dialogue with tutors, it was common to hear of concerns about 'interrupting' or 'disturbing' staff (Crook and Webster 1997).

These points need to be integrated with our earlier remarks concerning study as enculturation and the management of continuity between the formal and informal. E-mail relates to learning as a form of *conversation*. Being a student involves exposure to a range of conversational opportunities. At one extreme of formality is the tutorial meeting. This has evolved as an arena for motivating, structuring, and sustaining a certain kind of investigative discourse. At the other extreme is the very informal: the various spontaneous conversational exchanges that arise from simply living amongst others. Successful enculturation will involve a certain disturbance of the gap between these points. So, talk in tutorials may draw upon some of the fluency and confidence of everyday conversation—as participants become more comfortable with their developing shared knowledge, while, in turn, everyday informal talk may be shaped to reflect the formal—as participants appropriate topics and modes of discourse encountered in study settings. Earlier, we noted that much campus collaborative talk was unplanned. However, we also noted that the design of the institutional context supported these improvised possibilities for interleaving the formal and informal. Arguably, the management of that design is important to understand if the learner is to be encultured into new communities of practice.

The asynchronous and textual nature of e-mail may obstruct its potential as a resource at this interface. Yet, other electronic media may be better matched to what is needed. For example, our computer logs from students in networked bedrooms revealed that three-quarters of them made intensive use of 'instant messaging'. With such a tool users can maintain on their computer desktops a list of other users with whom they routinely communicate. Names become 'active' when that person's computer is connected to the local network (although individuals can block their visibility). Then, as individuals do become visible, so there develops a traffic in text, images, audio files, or web-site addresses. This species of CMC seems closer to the character of the familiar and informal. A user's responsivity for communication can be assumed from his or her 'visibility', and, while the medium does involve distance between the communicators, the text exchange itself is more conversational. Instant messaging systems were more attractive to these students than the official electronic communication (e-mail) promoted by their university. We believe this preference echoes a point made above—namely, that, in this community as it stands, the most valued peer interaction often remains contained within brief and serendipitous exchanges.

Unfortunately, e-mail resonates with a simple but seductive model of communication: packets of information efficiently going to and fro among conversants. If educational discourse is conceived in these terms, e-mail may inspire great hopes. Yet it is clear that such hopes are not easily delivered in practice. Insufficient attention has been directed towards the way in which a formalized mode of communication (a learning conversation) remains grounded in familiar traditions of the informal (spontaneous conversation). Similarly, it is important to understand the reverse: how spontaneous conversation is exposed to openings that allow appropriation of elements from the formal. Then, on reflection, working on these continuities with new media may well seem fruitful. However, some such tools may offer a better 'fit' than others: in this case, more might be expected of instant messaging than electronic mail.

This argument has been focused on the relatively intimate setting of tutorial exchange; next we consider the more communal quality of group or seminar discussion.

VIRTUALIZING THE GROUP COMMUNICATIONS OF STUDY

A seminar may be reconstructed in virtualized form by arranging that members of the group can send contributions to a common e-mail address. In this way their views are circulated: messages sent by any one member to this address are automatically distributed to the other participating members. The resulting exchange is gathered and made browsable to all. Of course, the asynchronous nature of the exchange means that these discussions can last much longer than traditional seminars. However, this may be judged an advantage—if the consequence is to cultivate more measured contributions. This illustrates an important point: the re-mediation of electronic seminars entails a different kind of experience. As such, in comparison with traditional seminars, the resulting exchange may be enriched in some respects, yet impoverished in others.

We noted modest take-up of e-mail for person-to-person exchanges about study. Is an e-mail configuration for *group* interaction any more attractive? Questions about user reactions will be difficult to answer at a stage when most students will never have tried the resource. At the present time, the virtual seminar has not been widely adopted by university staff and, therefore, not widely experienced by students. Of course, neglect by staff may not signal poor functionality; it may merely suggest that the effort required to get *started* is, at present, unacceptable. This suggests studying contexts where that overhead is intentionally made very small. Such a situation held at one of our rescarch sites. Here an e-mail discussion tool had been incorporated into the local web space created for each module taught at the university. Yet, although these electronic seminar spaces were easy to enter, they remained unused by over 90 per cent of the modules. Moreover, where they were used, that use appeared to be dom-inated by small numbers of individuals and they were tending to make only routine two-turn queries directed at tutors.

This might imply that there is indeed a problem that goes beyond the effort of getting started. This encouraged us to create an organized comparison between experience in conventional group discussions and experience in a virtualized seminar. Accordingly, studies were carried out with a number of classes—again in the context of a conventional residential university setting (Light *et al.* 2000). Despite their inevitably slow pace, these virtualized seminars still allow com-parisons with face-to-face alternatives. When we did this, we found a different pattern of participant contributions across the two formats. Electronic seminars generated a better gender balance in the exchange and encouraged less dom-ination of discussion by particular individuals. However, two other aspects of the resulting discussion deserve mention, as they may relate to why this format for discussion is demanding. The first relates the interactional management of the discussion; the second to the text-based nature of the medium.

First, managing the talk. With virtual seminars, the initiative for launching and sustaining the discussion may reside much more with students themselves. Indeed, this autonomy may be something that is seen as a potential strength of the resource. The practical issue here is whether or not the electronic discus-sion should be moderated. We studied virtual seminars in which moderation was rigorous and pervasive, as well as others in which it was totally absent. Where there was no moderation, student participation tended to lapse into abrasive exchanges, irrelevance, and irreverence. Again, this makes visible the subtle discipline that often underpins activity in the formal contexts of education— even where what is happening on such occasions looks very similar to an informal equivalent (in this case, casual peer-centred conversation). In a con-ventional moderated seminar, the intrusions of, say, a tutor serve to fashion and shape practices grounded in informality: directing free-wheeling conversation such that it is recruited to promote learning. In the absence of this management, the playful volatility of spontaneous conversation seems to surface quickly— often at the expense of aspirations for focus and direction in the talk.

Accordingly, expectations for virtual seminar discussions may be over-optimistic, at least if it is not noticed that dissuasions of this general sort usually depend upon skilfully managing the formal–informal axis. The labour of doing this in the virtual case may be an important demand that leads teaching staff to neglect this tool. However, even when virtual seminars are taken up and moderated by tutors, it is clear that there are other factors that influence success. This introduces the second issue that struck us in the groups that we studied— namely, the text-based nature of the exchange.

In a conventional seminar, speech equips participants with a resource that all human conversation allows: a capacity to improvise, experiment, and self-correct as prompted by events in the evolving discourse. Experience of informal conversation prepares students for doing this, although it needs to be done more systematically in the formal arena of a seminar. On the other hand, realizing a conversation as a sequence of typed contributions has no strong parallel within everyday interactions. If any parallel exists to guide a student's activity, it is probably the writing of essays or answering of exam questions. Accordingly, many participants in these electronic seminars invested much effort in carefully crafting their written contributions. Thus, the slow pace of turn-taking and the lasting and visible log of these contributions led to a very measured style of participation—quite different from that typical of synchronous conversation. Ironically, although contributors had fellow students in mind as their potential audience, students in general placed little reliance on the textual comments of their peers. The net effect could be unrewarding, and yet quite demanding of effort.

The two issues mentioned here pose problems for the development of virtual group discussion among students. Again, we suppose that the root of the problem is a neglect of the subtle way in which the established cultural practices of education have evolved to manage the gap between formal and informal experiences. In the case of moderation, the problem is one of neglecting the need to manage conversations that have academic goals. This is about recovering the formal. The second issue—the textual character of the discussion—is about the reverse: that is, recovering the informal. Conventional seminars go well because they are grounded in our everyday experience of talking. This is usefully appropriated to a curricular agenda, thereby importing the versatility of spoken conversation. Text-based seminars can be problematic because they do not have this natural rhythm. Moreover, the nature of contributions is far from transient: indeed the visibility and permanence can sometimes be intimidating to the novice.

None of this should imply the medium is *intrinsically* problematic. These issues may not arise for some constituencies of students, and, in any case, they are issues that invite strategies for management. Thus, success is quite possible

(Tolmie and Boyle 2000). Indeed, in our own sample, by the third year of exposure to virtual seminars a much more positive attitude among users was becoming visible. This might be taken to imply adaptation to the demands of the tool. However, it might also reflect the enculturation of these students into a more confident relationship with the cultural practices of learning more generally. The borders between informal conversation and the formalities of seminar discussion may have shifted sufficiently to make coping with the challenges outlined here more manageable.

VIRTUALIZING PRIVATE STUDY

In this final empirical example, we continue the theme of virtualization acting at a point of discontinuity between formal learning and students' everyday informal lives. The case concerns private study, which our diary records (see Fig. 9.2). showed to be a more common use of undergraduate time than lectures, seminars, practicals, or other corporate occasions of formal learning. Private study is liable to virtualization because of the increased use of networked computers. We studied a group of thirty-four students who had network access in their study bedrooms; all their computer activity was logged over a period of one week (Crook and Barrowcliff 2001).

In what particular ways does a networked PC used in a conventional university illustrate a trend towards the virtualization of private study? It could be argued that networked students merely have access to a large corpus of distributed information (internet and intranet) and that they act towards it no differently from the way they do in using a conventional library (although some will argue that students will use it *more*—as information has been rendered more accessible). However, compared to a library, the networked PC is far less circumscribed as a space for studying. What it 'contains' is far more diverse. Moreover, its networked status makes it highly interactive. We believe that this combination of properties can create obstacles for the student. The versatility of the networked computer cultivates forms of use that mean there is more at stake than just accessibility gains. To explain this concern, it is necessary first to locate private study as another cultural practice of formal education.

Solitary investigation geared towards learning (private study) may resemble *public* discourse geared towards learning (the seminar) in that they both demand forms of management. We noted above that the seminar moderator acts to manage the boundary between a formal and an informal conversation. There is a sense in which private study must also be protected, although this protection is more often by the design of spaces and the exercise of self-imposed rituals rather than through the intrusion of human moderators. In fact, libraries are particularly effective spaces—designed such that study can be concentrated and sustained in the direct presence of relevant resources. The concept of a study bedroom may also be supportive of the formal learner in that it is also situated well in respect of learning resources, yet ensures a certain degree of privacy for focused study.

Our diary records revealed that the networked students did concentrate private study on their computers. Almost half of the time given to such study was computer mediated. However, they reported spending even more time in computer pursuits that were recreational. We expected this to be long sessions of video gaming or web surfing. However, neither of these patterns was very common. Instead, what was striking from our logs of computer activity was the variety of *different* things that would get done in any one session. It could be said that students' use of this technology was highly animated. Often our logs showed an active task that was clearly related to study (say a word-processed document) but one that was present on the desktop with many other active applications—all of which would be in strong competition for the user's attention. Some of these applications almost *demanded* attention, notably e-mail and instant messaging. But others simply had very strong affordances for unplanned interaction. Thus, students would frequently leave a focal task to tinker with a media player, or do some recreational web browsing, or check a news ticker, and so on.

Put simply, private study on a networked computer can be very distracting. However, it is not that *simple* claim that we wish to labour here. What the example illustrates once again is the grounded and subtle nature of the activities constituting formal learning—in this case, activities of private study. In the institutional settings of education it is expected that private study will be focused and sustained. So, we may cease to notice that the achievement of this depends upon the design and cultivation of various institutional spaces and practices (as well as personal techniques of self-management).

However, this balance between the more disorderly world of informal pursuits and the disciplined world of pursuing formal learning needs to be better understood. Here, we are drawing attention to the way in which virtual practices break some of the helpful *insulation* between the two. Nevertheless, such insulation is not always and inevitably helpful. We have noted distracting ways in which networked technologies encourage vigorous movement between different applications. Yet this mobility could also define the very kind of exploration that supports active research around some study topic. Ironically perhaps, the same opportunities of technology design that can empower a student's study can also undermine it. From our own observations we were more struck by the disruptive than the empowering dimension of interactivity.

CONCLUDING REMARKS

The impression left with us as researchers is that virtual practices in higher education are not easy to get going. This is certainly not because students are unfamiliar with the technical tools, or hostile towards them. In fact, many students are vigorously using these tools for routine writing and computation, and certainly for recreational purposes. If there is a problem of take-up, it arises from the ways in which virtualization involves doing things differently. (This is consistent with what Woolgar (this volume) calls the third rule of virtuality: virtual technologies supplement rather than substitute for real activities.) This point is familiar to those studying other areas of human–computer interaction: 'new technologies seldom simply support old working practices with additional efficiency or flexibility. Instead they tend to undermine existing practices and to demand new ones. In this disruption, subtleties of existing social behaviours and the affordances upon which they rely become apparent, as do the new affordances for social behaviour offered by technology' (Gaver 1996: 112).

In this chapter we have dwelt upon Gaver's 'subtleties of existing social behaviours' that apply to the domain of undergraduate study. We have argued that such study is often *difficult* not just because the concepts being studied are themselves difficult, although often they may be. There is another layer of difficulty associated with what is required in orienting towards those concepts. Deliberate learning involves engaging with exposition, orchestrated discussion, research, systematic annotation, the focused reading of text, and a variety of other directed activities that many students may not always find easy to mobilize and manage independently. Sites of formal education have evolved structures that sustain and coordinate such activities with a scaffold of cultural resources: timetables, curricula, designed spaces, discourse rituals, and so on. We argued that making progress within this infrastructure amounted to a process of enculturation. Students are confronted with the various arenas of study as formalized versions of activities well rehearsed in their informal lives. The enculturation of knowledge is then a subtle management of the interface between the demands of the formal and the fluency of the informal. Successful education involves making students comfortable with the activities demanded by formal study: encouraging them to allow their repertoire of informal cultural practices—listening, talking, investigating, and so on—to be formalized in ways that then support learning.

Where educational experience is particularly successful, notions of changing identity may be invoked; students are thereby said to 'become' disciplinary practitioners (Wenger 1998), at which point, the cultural practices of learning are transformed from hived-off occasions dependent upon the institutional scaffold. Instead, such practices become visible in the repertoire of the informal: they are imported into the individual's spontaneous concerns and thereby demand less formal scaffolding. However, such transformations may still be slow. The important point remains that formal learning can be very difficult for the novice. The orchestration of deliberate learning is an extraordinary human achievement—perhaps a uniquely human achievement (Premack and Premack 1996), it would be surprising if the structure of those activities involved was not a sensitive fabric. Our argument is that ambitions for virtual learning must be grounded on a better theorizing of these matters—and, then, more informed design of the tools and the associated practices.

Yet we do not wish to appear unreasonably negative over future prospects for virtualization. The difficulties we have documented relate to conventional university settings with their conventional constituency of young learners. The motives and lifestyles of other intending learners may be better oriented to studying in a virtual environment. Moreover, there is another way in which the virtualization of learning may become more easily realized. If the activities of formal learning are grounded in students' more informal cultural experiences, then dominant practices of individual socialization will help explain what tends to happen. Learners confronting virtual methods today have one sort of personal history for interacting in the material and social world. The methods of formal learning try to make contact with that history. Learners in the future may more readily respond to virtual tools of instruction than they do now—for they would recognize them from their own informal enculturation.

10

The Reality of Virtual Social Support

Sarah Nettleton, Nicholas Pleace, Roger Burrows,
Steven Muncer, and Brian Loader

> As communication technology, biotechnology, transgender networking, and
> networks of individuals, develop in parallel, as key elements of social
> practice, they are interacting, and influencing each other. Thus the internet
> is becoming a very instrumental tool of management of new forms of life,
> including the building of on-line communities of support and collective
> learning.
>
> (Castells 2000*b*: 21)

> The risky and uncertain conditions of modern life often call on us to sort
> out many of our problems ourselves, without the help of institutions, and
> even to help others to do the same.
>
> (Slevin 2000: p. x)

INTRODUCTION

It is now well established that there exists a strong relationship between levels
of *social capital* and *social support*, on the one hand, and levels of health and
well-being, on the other (Callaghan and Morrissey 1993; Cooper *et al.* 1999). It
can be demonstrated that variations in certain aspects of psycho-social life—
such as sense of control, perceived social status, the strength of social affiliations,
social support, self-esteem, feelings of ontological (in)security, and so on—lead
to variations in a number of health outcomes (Wilkinson 1996; Elstad 1998;
Lomas 1998; S. Williams 1998). In short, people who display a high degree of
social participation and/or have good social and community relationships tend,
ceteris paribus, to have better physical and mental health.

The implications of this fact are profound for the analysis of processes of
social change. To the extent that systems of social support can be viewed as a
crucial buttress against an otherwise dramatically changing world, any social

changes that impinge upon these systems become of the utmost importance for the social analysis of health and well-being. There is, of course, much evidence that the processes of social change we are witnessing at the start of the twenty-first century do indeed alter both the form and the content of the systems of social support to which we are able to gain access. The acceleration of processes of globalization, detraditionalization, and individualization with concomitant increases in levels of both manufactured risk and reflexivity—often characterized together as processes of *reflexive modernization* (Beck *et al.* 1994)—are all altering the fundamentals of how we go about our everyday lives, how we feel about ourselves, and how we establish and maintain social relationships. Furthermore, there seems to be developing a profound elective affinity between these processes of reflexive modernization, on the one hand, and developments in information and communications technologies (ICTs)—the internet in particular—on the other (Slevin 2000: 11–26; Burrows and Nettleton 2002). Emerging virtual social systems and flows are becoming ever more enmeshed with other social dynamics, to the extent that any useful distinction between the 'virtual' and the 'real' has all but collapsed.

This all means that how we both experience and provide social support is changing. Not only will the patterns of social interaction within which social support is implicitly embedded be subject to the forces of a more reflexive modernity, but it will also be increasingly mediated by various forms of ICT. In this chapter we want to examine how people are beginning to experience computer-mediated social support and how it articulates with other aspects of their social lives. This is an important undertaking because hitherto much of the literature that relates to this topic has been polarized into statements of either enthusiasm or criticism allowing little analytic space in which to view computer-mediated communication (CMC) as a social technology that is likely to be ambivalent at a number of different levels. As Wellman and Gulia (1999: 167) put it, the

Manicheans on either side of this debate assert that the internet either will create wonderful new forms of community or will destroy community altogether. These dueling dualists feed off each other, using unequivocal assertions of the other side as foils for their own arguments. Their statements of enthusiasm or criticism leave little room for moderate, mixed situations that may be the reality.

Our concern in this chapter is to examine empirically some of the 'moderate, mixed situations that may be the reality' in relation to emerging patterns of computer-mediated social support as they are being experienced by members of the online public in the UK. In previous publications we have examined this issue by studying various forms of online interaction in computer-mediated forums that have been expressly established in order to provide social support in relation to topics such as physical disability, parenting, and housing debt (Burrows *et al.* 2000), eczema, child immunization, and worries about the safety of food (Burrows and Nettleton 2002), depression (Muncer *et al.* 2000), problems with alcohol (Pleace *et al.* 2000), and diabetes (Loader *et al.* 2002). In this chapter we come at the issue another way by offering an analysis of qualitative interview data with a range of different users of different types of virtual social support. In the next section we outline in more detail what we intend by the concept of social support and outline what forms virtual systems of social support currently take. In the third section we outline some of the details of our research. In the fourth section we offer an analysis of some of the data we have gathered on people's experiences of using various forms of virtual social support. The chapter then concludes with some more observations on the data and a brief discussion of some of the broader implications of the analysis.

SOCIAL SUPPORT

There is a considerable technical literature relating to what social support actually is and how it should be measured (Dean *et al.* 1994). However, here we draw upon a widely used and accepted definition articulated by Cooper *et al.* (1999: 9) as follows: 'the companionship and practical, informational and esteem support which the individual derives from interaction with members of his or her "social network", including friends, colleagues, acquaintances and family members.' Social support has been hypothesized to function in two ways: the *main effect* social-support hypothesis suggests that social support has a general beneficial effect on people at all times, whilst the *buffering* hypothesis suggests that social support functions to 'buffer' people against the effects of stress (Cohen and Wills 1985). In the first case it is believed that the size of one's social network provides a feeling of integration and self-worth. Buffering can work in two ways; first the perception that you have social support may bolster your ability to deal with a stressful situation, and, second, adequate support after the stressful event may ameliorate its effects. There is strong evidence to support both hypotheses (Cohen and Wills 1985).

Clearly the internet may impact upon the size of social networks, and it may also increase the number of potential 'buffers' that can be useful in times of stress. Certainly, there is evidence that the internet can be used to gain information and solve problems (Constant *et al.* 1996). This would then be 'received' and 'perceived' social support. The former refers to support that is tangible—for example, when there is someone there to listen to problems, worries, and so on. The latter refers to whether or not a person perceives that significant others genuinely care about them and would offer them emotional support in times of anxiety or stress.

Early experiments in the use of computer networks for social support were conducted in the USA by academics and medical researchers testing both the utility of such networks as a means of professional service delivery and their potential usefulness in providing patients with self-help and support networks

(Boberg *et al.* 1995; Feenberg *et al.* 1996; Weinberg *et al.* 1996; Bass *et al.* 1998). The potential of CMC for self-help and social support was, however, soon seized upon by people using these technologies for themselves. Perhaps not surprisingly, what has now become a global activity (Burrows *et al.* 2000) originated in the USA (Finn 1999). As Norman Denzin (1998: 113) has observed: 'We cannot imagine America without its self-help groups. And, we cannot imagine an America that is not in love with technology. Cyberspace and the recovery movement were meant for each other.'

Virtual social support employs a range of CMC using the internet and USENET network (M. A. Smith 1999). Perhaps the main forums are the newsgroups that were originally established on USENET, but which are now accessible via web sites such as deja.com. Newsgroups allow asynchronous communication between the people using them. The newsgroup functions like a large electronic notice board, on which individuals can place or 'post' a message and other individuals can post messages in response, establishing a dialogue. Newsgroups order messages on the same subject by their title, so an original post and all the subsequent posts on the same topic are grouped together. This group of messages is called a thread and a newsgroup will often have several threads running at once. While this technology is relatively old, it remains the main means by which virtual social support is provided, with newsgroups functioning as online self-help groups for just about every health and social problem imaginable (Burrows *et al.* 2000). Other forums for virtual social support include e-mail-based mailing and discussion lists and various forms of synchronous communication that are perhaps best characterized as typed conversations. Examples of synchronous forms of CMC used for social support include internet relay chat (IRC) rooms (Pleace *et al.* 2000) and multiuser domains (MUDs) (Mousund 1997). However, given the trend for different forms of CMC to coalesce with web pages to form more integrated systems of information and online support (offering perhaps web-based information services alongside integrated provision to join mailing lists, discussion groups, and/or to engage in real-time chat), the virtual geography of systems of social support is constantly in a state of flux.

Finn (1999) has argued that the sheer proliferation of these virtual social-support groups on a global scale could be taken in itself as evidence that people are getting some sort of benefit from participating in them. Yet until this exploratory study, the impact and the use of these forums have remained relatively unexplored, particularly within the UK.

METHODS

The data reported below were collected as part of a larger exploratory qualitative study of people's experiences of computer-mediated self-help and social support in the UK—what we have termed on previous occasions *virtual community care* (Burrows *et al.* 2000). As part of this study, we have gathered data from a number of different sources. First, and as we have already indicated, we have analysed online interactions from a wide range of newsgroups, discussion lists, IRC rooms, web sites, and the like, all of which claim to offer various forms of self-help and/or social support. We have also sought the views of health professionals on the nature of some of this material (Loader *et al.* 2002). Second, we have interviewed a number of originators, contributors, and users of different forms of virtual social support. Third, we have interviewed a small number (fifteen in total) of medical practitioners about their experiences of interacting with clients who are users of the internet for health-related information, advice, and support. In this chapter we draw upon the data gathered by way of face-to-face, telephone, and computer-mediated interviews with fifty-one people who have made use of different forms of virtual social support.

The fifty-one people interviewed were recruited to the project in a number of different ways. Some agreed to participate after being approached by us by e-mail following our observations of their postings on a number of the newsgroups and discussion lists we were studying.[1] Others were recruited by 'opting in' to the study following postings made by ourselves to a number of different newsgroups directing participants to the project web site. The sample is thus unlikely to be representative of all UK-based users of virtual social support, but is hopefully diverse enough to represent a good range of attitudes and experiences. The sample contained twenty-one men and thirty women based throughout the UK with a diverse range of ages, incomes, household circumstances, and many different health and social-support needs. All had in common some experience of using the internet during 1998 and/or 1999 for virtual social support of some kind. The greater number of women than men in the sample may simply reflect the nature of our sampling strategy and the form and content of the virtual forums from which the sample was recruited. However, and perhaps not surprisingly given what we know about the highly gendered nature of informal health and social care work, health is the one category of online information that is accessed more commonly by women than by men (Eysenbach *et al.* 1999), and, consequently, we may also expect more women than men to populate this particular area of cyberspace.

ACCOUNTS OF EXPERIENCES OF VIRTUAL SOCIAL SUPPORT

Cohen and Wills (1985) and Wills (1985) have developed one of the most commonly used typologies of social support. They make a distinction between four dimensions of social support: *social companionship* (various kinds of social

---

[1] For a discussion of some of the ethical implications of this procedure, see Pleace *et al.* (2000).

activities); *informational support* (the provision of necessary information); *esteem support* (social contact that increases feelings of esteem); and *instrumental support* (assistance with material tasks). Whilst it is possible to separate these dimensions of support for analytic purposes, in practice there is invariably some degree of overlap. In some of our previous analyses of online social support (Muncer *et al.* 2000) we found the first three of these dimensions to be a helpful way of categorizing our data. In this chapter we apply a parallel analysis using these three categories but this time using data derived from interviews with users of virtual social support. In virtual contexts we have found very few examples of instrumental support, and this is perhaps not surprising given the nature of virtual communities. Unlike other forms of support group, within online support there is often no one available to render physical assistance or provide other instrumental support. While there is, of course, always the possibility that someone else in a virtual group may live just down the road and can drive one to the hospital, it is equally possible that they live on the other side of the globe.

Companionship Support

Social support of this type refers to the sharing of recreational and leisure pursuits with a broad range of people or 'companions'. For many people we interviewed, the internet provided the opportunity to establish and extend social networks. This meant that they were able to spend time 'chatting' to others beyond their immediate social environment. Obviously a feature of the internet is its global reach, as this subscriber to a Chronic Fatigue Syndrome (CFS) newsgroup, a woman in her 40s, makes clear: 'I would say 98 per cent of the internet is very friendly... I mean I talk to people all over the world. I've got friends in India. I can't think of a country that I can't talk to somebody in and I would say 98 per cent of them are polite and courteous and friendly.'

Of course, the extent to which widening one's social network has the potential to enhance one's well-being is questionable, and some writers have suggested that fewer and more 'close' relationships are likely to be more beneficial than larger social networks that comprise acquaintances (Thoits 1995). However, for a number of the people we interviewed, the opportunity to extend their social network was invaluable. This was especially so for those who were socially isolated because of their geographical location, disability, or social circumstances. For example, a woman in her 30s who also suffered from CFS reported that: 'In many ways I have more of a virtual life than a real life. I'm not able to get out of the house sort of as much as I would like and it means that I can sort of have a life within rather than without.' And again, from another woman with CFS: 'The internet has been and is a lifesaver for me. I don't have that much real life any more in some ways, but I have a great virtual life.'

A mother of a 2-year-old child in her 20s also found CMC was an important means of securing companionship. She related how the internet and newsgroups in particular had given her access to

most of my social support since I've been at home...I want to be at home with my daughter but I, yeah I don't want to be doing housework and washing and that every day...it doesn't take away the intrinsic loneliness of being at home with a small child all day with whom you can't have an adult conversation, and obviously it's not live. But, you know, if you're really tearing your hair out you can, you could run up and write down a post and even, even if nobody responds you've still written it down and it's there in the public domain, which probably doesn't make much difference, you could probably just go and write it all down in a letter and throw it away just to, you know...it's just a method of venting some emotion I suppose. But yeah it's nice if people do respond and you can occasionally get, you know, light-hearted things just to cheer you up a bit...I mean I do live within walking distance of my local town and everything but yeah it makes a difference. I'm very aware of using it for sort of social interaction and support but it's a secret part of my life really...well not that I'm doing it sort of, in a sort of closet fashion or anything just that...I don't really talk to anybody about it. I mean I talk to my partner about bits on the newsgroups every now and again but, you know, we've got lots of other things to talk about and it's just something that I do that's just for me, it's, I suppose it's, you know...part of my personal time...even though specifically on the parenting things I'm obviously researching things for the family but...yeah it's, it's kind of 'me' time really.

And again, a woman who had moved from an urban to a rural area noted: 'It can help you feel less cut off...you feel a bit out of it down here. In some ways the attitudes, peoples' attitudes down here—they're a few years behind what they would be in London, which is where I came from'; and another that 'I am a regular on a newsgroup which discusses new information and gives people support on every aspect of living with ME. This is also a large part of my social life.'

There is a strong sense here therefore that a virtual social life may form a further dimension to a person's 'real' social life. It provides further opportunities to meet other people and to establish social networks. Some respondents described how they found it an especially useful means of meeting other people. Very often this was because users were contacting others who had shared interests or experiences. But in some cases the medium of exchange served to facilitate communication, as this man who was blind explained.[2]

I suppose...being blind, it's easier than meeting real people. You're not always addressing, you know, if you go out, I don't know say you go to a pub or whatever there's always somebody coming over and patting your guide dog and wants to talk about the dog or wants to talk about you being blind or wants to talk about how you got there and how you find the buses and this sort of thing. On the internet you don't get that, people

---

[2] A range of technologies exist to assist partially sighted and blind people in using the internet. These include voice-controlled browsers that can read the content of newsgroups, e-mails, and web sites to their users. However, these technologies can sometimes be inaccessible, as they can add substantially to the cost of basic computing equipment.

don't know about you so you can talk about what you want to talk about. You're not constantly trying to turn the conversation round your way or whatever.

A further distinctive feature of companionship is the availability or 'ready access' to friends and contacts. As many users pointed out, one can log on at any time of the day or night and you do not even have to leave the house. As one woman in her 40s with CFS put it: 'The benefit of my newsgroup is that there is always someone around to answer a question or just to listen.'

Many respondents related how the internet provided an opportunity for social exchange, comfort, laughter, and encouragement within what many perceived to be a supportive environment. This extract from a computer-mediated interview with a woman in her 60s with ME communicates this well:

The mailing list MECHAT...in particular has been a real lifeline. I check mail several times a day. I have been able to discuss things with people who understand...important as ME is an especially misunderstood illness...make new friends and share experiences and laughter...It is a real comfort if any trauma or upset occurs—death or illness of a loved one, relapse, relationship problems, or even just thoughtless remarks from folks who do not understand ME, which we would otherwise have to bear alone. It is also great to be able to contribute by giving support and friendship to the others—nice to be useful!...The MECHAT group are a very friendly group and the hard core of us who post frequently (when health permits) I would count among my friends. I have spoken to some of the group, who are well enough to talk on the phone, and corresponded with several. I haven't actually met any yet as I live out in the wilds but would love to.

Informational Support

The provision and exchange of information is perhaps the most readily obvious source of social support on the internet. It has been defined as follows:

a process through which other persons may provide information, advice and guidance. Network members may serve a supportive function by providing independent assessments of the locus of the problem (for example, which party is more at fault in a marital or parent–child conflict), by giving suggestions about the respondents' decisions or problem-solving approach, or by giving information about community helping agencies. (Wills 1985: 69)

Certainly, using this definition we found numerous examples of informational support, with people providing each other with information on issues to do with health, illness, parenting, disability, welfare benefits, and so on. What is perhaps striking are the resources, time, and effort that some people put into providing informational support. For example, some people we spoke to had set up web sites to provide information on matters about which they had strong views. One woman had set up a site dealing with 'bullying' after she had accumulated a wealth of knowledge and experience on this issue after her son had been bullied at school and she had successfully taken the school to court. She talked about the support she offered:

I run [the web site], which gives information and personal advice to parents and children...It is quite expensive to run, about £54 per month. You can get free web space from other firms but we have a bulletin board and paying a fee gives us immediate access to remove any dubious messages and enables us to reboot the server when it crashes. The actual phone cost of running... [it] ... is very small as it only takes seconds to download e-mail and I write replies offline—say £10 per month. However, I often do research, for instance when a parent says his child is being put on an individual education plan, and I need to download all the info from the relevant government site, so that I give up-to-date replies. Sometimes I also download OFSTED reports on a particular school to see if anything there will help a particular parent. I try to keep up with new sites on bullying. For instance, there is an excellent group... dealing with homophobic bullying and young people and I have referred people there as they have more experience of that aspect than I have. A surprising number of adults also contact me about their school bullying ordeals and so do adults who are currently being bullied at work. Bullying at work is not my forte so I refer those people to another first-class site...I also regularly use the government education pages, which are excellent to research latest guidelines.

Another woman ran a special-needs site, and in this instance her online activities were a clear extension of her other support and advocacy work—illustrating again the observation that 'real' and 'virtual' relations of support are becoming ever enmeshed with each. As part of a computer-mediated interview she explained:

I use the internet to gain information, to give information. I have my own web sites...I also publish a special-needs e-mail newsletter and for mutual support. I have my own e-mail...discussion list too...Because of all my voluntary and advocacy work I do for families affected by [this] I use the net to go get information to pass onto others. Also I do lots of networking...speak with eminent authors, mental health professionals and paediatricians. I am on very friendly terms with other internet community leaders too as I do like to network as I say.

Esteem Support

Esteem support refers to that support that helps people deal with threats to their self-esteem. It involves: 'Having someone available with whom one can talk about problems; this supportive function has variously been termed *esteem support*, emotional support, ventilation, or a confident relationship' (Wills 1985: 68). Interestingly, from the point of view of our study, Wills suggests that because talking about negative problems involves revealing negative aspects of the self, most people tend to limit their discussions to people they feel particularly close to, such as a partner, a family member, or a close friend. In our research, however, we can observe that people found 'virtual contacts' to be particularly valuable for esteem support. Users described how their virtual friends had provided them with much emotional support. Furthermore, giving emotional support to others was often perceived to be a source of esteem. Users spoke about their virtual communities being 'mutually supportive'. As this man in his mid-50s involved in various disability groups described:

Using newsgroups has enabled me to make a lot of friends with common interests such as disability and caring and many of these have been 'mutually supportive'. For example, I have been able to support an American woman through the long-term terminal illness of her husband—in return she has encouraged me in periods of depression. There are significant advantages in having the facility to 'open your heart' to another, almost anonymous person who may have already been through what you are suffering. I can liken it to writing down your problems in a personal, yet interactive, diary!

This man also explained how the medium of exchange itself facilitates support—the anonymity in particular. Unlike other forms of interaction, one can 'dive straight in' as it were—no need for social niceties, introductions, and so on. For example, a woman involved in a stillbirth list had found it very difficult to talk to her friends after the death of her baby. Furthermore, she pointed out that they did not know what to say to her. For her, the net provided a lifeline, a means by which she had immediate access to others who could offer appropriate emotional support:

I mean that's one of the advantages for bereavement is that people, people want to contact you but they don't know how to. You know when people have phoned me up and said 'oh I'm ever so sorry to hear . . .' and I said, and all you can say is, 'well thank you' and where do you go from there. Whereas the e-mails that I've received, and I've kept them, I've printed them all off and kept them, you know for the future. They have been wonderful because people have been able to say things that they really feel that perhaps they wouldn't say in a conversation. People, people I think as a nation, the British are quite reserved aren't we and we don't say; oh you know 'I'm sending you all my love and I, I really feel you know I'm here, blah, blah, blah.' Whereas in an e-mail people were able to express exactly what they felt without embarrassment, or, or fear of saying the wrong thing if you like and that also made me feel a lot better as well, because the love and support that I got from people that way was a lot better than anything else I could have had. Only very close family that were picking up the phone, other people obviously find it difficult, so without those e-mails I'd have felt you know pretty isolated.

As we can see here in this woman's account, it was a combination of the shared experience and the anonymity that contributed to the quality of the support. People using virtual systems of social support engaged in offering emotional support to others on the net, support that in 'real' life we might imagine would be limited only to close friends.[3] As this young women explained:

It's hard to explain. I used to get very depressed but being with other people on the net has helped a lot. People are very supportive and club together. If I see something that I know someone else on the groups I use would like, I either post it or e-mail them

[3] In line with the third rule of virtuality (Woolgar, this volume), this provides an interesting example of the ways in which the new communication channel supplements the existing ones—the 'virtual' supplements the 'real'.

privately depending on what it is and others do the same. We provide emotional support for each other too and some groups meet in real life every now and then.

Thus the boundaries of real and virtual life are sometimes transcended. As this woman who suffers from MS explains:

When I am going through a hard time with my disability or personal life they can be very helpful. It can be very therapeutic to talk to virtual strangers, although I have met some of them. I am in a brilliantly supportive chat room for MS sufferers, as we all have the same illness even though it has many manifestations. We support each other. You always know someone will be there for you and we are all good friends. Unfortunately, as it is not regulated, we do sometimes get the odd nutter, but we simply ignore them and after a while they go away. One or two of the others I have tried don't seem to be as good. I think sticking to a specialized one is better.

ANTI-SOCIAL SUPPORT?

As this woman points out, there are hazards associated with online support, the most obvious perhaps being unsolicited and aggressive exchanges. Most of our respondents spoke about aggressive posts or 'flames' and the problem of what many referred to as 'nutters'.[4] However, in general, the people we interviewed said they simply dismissed and ignored them. It is important, however, to note that it may be that those people who found these aspects of net use to be particularly disturbing may well have opted out of using newsgroups, chat rooms, and so on for this very reason, and so their views were not heard by us. Certainly some previous research has found that cyberspace can, on occasion, be an uncomfortable place, and some people feel alienated and excluded within it (Sudweeks *et al.* 1998). A majority of people reported how their group would come together to support each other in the face of aggressive posts, and, as such, systems of social support were strengthened by such interventions. These two extracts from interviews are indicative:

We do get occasional spammers and flamewars, but not too often. When flamewars develop, it is very distressing to most of the regulars on the group. We try to maintain a supportive atmosphere. I don't actually think I would be here without my newsgroup. It has seen me through some very difficult times with practical advice and emotional support.

On the Newsgroups there is often flaming but that goes with the territory. The advantages far outweigh the disadvantages, as, if one is liable to feeling isolated, those feelings are quickly dispelled when on the newsgroup. For every flamer there are a dozen people who are willing to offer help and support, even if only moral support.

---

[4] See our earlier discussion of such instances within the context of systems of virtual social support (Burrows *et al.* 2000; Muncer *et al.* 2000; Burrows and Nettleton 2002).

DISCUSSION

Within our sample of users, the great bulk of accounts of the experience of virtual social support were positive. This may, of course, be a reflection of those who were willing to participate in the study. For the people we interviewed, the internet provided an important dimension of social support for certain aspects of their lives. In the main, virtual social support was of a specific rather than a general nature in that it was sought on the basis of a particular need at a particular time, in relation to, for example: parenting; disability; illness; or bereavement. Some people moved through a number of different contexts by using it, for example, for both parenting and health matters. Many were also using the net for entertainment and participated in groups to do with gardening, television soaps, cooking, and so on. Nevertheless, it is clear that virtual social support can be of a far more strategic, precise, and focused type than that which is available offline.[5] Online support involves more than simply providing information and advice about particular matters; it also provides esteem and emotional support. This is achieved by way of a dialogue with other users, whereby people have to narrate their personal stories, their experiences, and at times ongoing life events. In this sense online support may also contribute to ontological security whereby individuals have to create and recreate their biographies, and can reflect upon them in the light of the reactions and experiences of others. Furthermore, the history of the process itself may serve as a reflexive resource. As we have already discussed, users often kept their exchanges as a record, a keepsake of their experiences.[6] The woman whose child was stillborn recounted how she had done this.

I've found writing the e-mails has been almost cathartic to me because I've been able to express my feelings. I wish I wrote a diary or a journal but I don't, so perhaps the e-mails have, have become if you like my journal. I've been telling other people what's been happening because obviously over the past three weeks a lot has happened from losing the baby to the various other stages that I've had to go through and tests and you know and a funeral . . . I've been able to, every couple of days, put it all together and e-mail and send it to the various people, rather than writing a journal, so this has become my journal I suppose . . . I've actually now sort of kind of created a folder and kept all of the e-mails about this subject—to and from—in that folder and then sort of in the future I suppose I will just wrap that up and keep it, take it, take it off the machine, but I will keep it again for sentimentality perhaps when I look back on this episode in my life so that I can see what's been happening.

As Walter (1999: 125), in his book *On Bereavement*, has argued, 'bereavement is like the rest of contemporary life, a reflexive process checking that one is

---

[5] Here we note how the virtual supplements the real (Woolgar, this volume).

[6] As a result of virtual social support, participants wound up with an extra 'real' record of their exchanges. Cf. the fourth rule of virtuality (Woolgar, this volume): the more virtual, the more real.

doing okay...The democratization of grief, like the democratization of marriage, may be an advance in freedom, but the flip side is an increase in chaos, anomie and uncertainty.' True of bereavement, and, as Walter notes, true of lives in late modernity more generally, from work to welfare, from parenting to politics, our views, actions, and beliefs are not so fixed as they were, they require constant negotiation and verification. Indeed, other researchers have examined in some detail the reflexive nature of experiences of health, illness, and emotions both in terms of seeking out and assessing information, resources, and therapies, and also in relation to reassessing notions of self and identity in the light of the onset of (usually chronic) illness (Kelly and Field 1998; S. Williams 2000).

We see then in empirical explorations of social support, health, and illness the everyday life impacts of those broader social changes associated with late modernity, the contours of which have been outlined by Giddens (1991, 1998), Beck (1998), and Castells (2000*b*). Within the context of a post-traditional order and the concurrent emergence of 'institutionalized individualism' whereby 'people are invited to constitute themselves as individuals: to plan, to understand, [and] design themselves as individuals' (Beck 1998), the internet adds to this by being perhaps the ultimate reflexive resource. But, as we have seen from the data discussed in this paper the internet is used *together with* other resources and becomes meshed into people's social lives.

As a reflexive resource, the internet can be both liberating and constraining, of course. It provides us with the space to exchange experiences, knowledge, and information, it enables us to seek out information on virtually any topic we choose to investigate to the nth degree. In this way it contributes to the uncertainties associated with the reflexive process. But, on the other hand, it also provides a space for support and the formation of 'communities', however transient, which can provide a buffer to these uncertainties (Slevin 2000; Burrows and Nettleton 2002). Thus those tensions that are inherent in the risk society are especially poignant when considered in relation to the realities of engaging with the virtual world.

11

Real and Virtual Connectivity: New Media in London

Andreas Wittel, Celia Lury, and Scott Lash

INTRODUCTION

This chapter argues that processes going on in the virtual society(?) are to a large extent continuations of those going on in the real society. It thus exemplifies the fourth rule of virtuality (Woolgar, this volume): 'the more virtual, the more real'. It argues that social processes in 'the real' and 'the virtual' are increasingly characterized by the phenomenon of 'connectivity'. We base this argument on a discussion of case studies of real and virtual connectivity drawn from a largely ethnographic study of the new media sector in London. We have observed this sector more or less from its inception in the mid 1990s, conducting intensive ethnographic work from 1998 through the first half of 2000. More particularly, we mapped the 'biographies' of a number of virtual products, as they were conceived, developed, and distributed, moving between new media producers, their clients, and end-users.[1] We continued less intensive study of the sector up until mid-2001. The research was thus a 'real-time' study of the rapid and accelerating transformations of an emergent sector. We are now witnessing, at the time of writing in May 2001, a levelling-out of growth in London's new media

---

[1] In this study we had planned to track a small number of virtual objects as they moved through networks of small firms in London's Shoreditch, Soho, Clerkenwell, and Islington. These were conceived partly along the lines of the new industrial districts of webs of small firms in alliances and producer–client pairings (Becattini 1990). We would trace the objects through these networks of producer–client and producer–client–consumer relations. This would be different, we anticipated, from a purely economic study. And that is because the objects that were being transformed and built through the networks were also cultural objects. In contrast to objects made and circulated in the silicon valleys, silicon alleys, we assumed, made *content*, which was not just reprocessed, but *interpreted* in its movement.

that has not yet hit the level of lay-offs or decline in revenues of its closest comparable counterpart—that is, New York's Silicon Alley. This chapter will, in addition to looking at real and virtual connectivity in London's new media, attempt to draw implications for the present and future of the new economy more generally.

Our notion of 'connectivity' in this chapter is in some sense a concrete indication of the significance of the 'imperative to connect' identified by Green and Harvey (1999). It draws on both the emerging characteristics of virtual communication and the work of organization sociologists and geographers in the USA and Germany on the 'heterarchic organization'. We will present below brief descriptions of four case studies in London's new media, involving different combinations of real and virtual connectivity. The real connectivity has to do with the organizational form that production takes, that of 'networks' and 'projects'. Connectivity here is different from hierarchy or bureaucratic organization and its conditions of 'dependence'. It is different from market governance and its defining property of independence. Production through connectivity is characterized instead by *inter*dependence (Stark 1999). In each of our case studies below there is an interdependent connectivity, either between new media firms and clients, or between networked producers and clients, or both. Such connectivity enhances production not through hierarchies or markets, but through networks and projects. At the same time there is virtual connectivity. Real networks produce virtual objects—from 3D chat rooms, to intranet games, to online banking sites, to interactive television programming—that also serve purposes of real and virtual connectivity. They connect the client firm normally to consumers, users, and audiences. They also involve users/audiences in an experience, not primarily of narrative, as in old media, but one instead of connectivity itself.

CONNECTIVITY, HETERARCHY, NON-LINEARITY

The idea of the heterarchic organization, as developed by Powell (1996) and Grabher and Stark (1997) has its roots in complexity theory and notions of non-linearity.[2] The heterarchic organization is a non-linear system—'heterachies are complex adaptive systems'—in the same sense that the more traditional hierarchy is linear (Girard and Stark 2001: 9). And in the sense also that the neo-classical economics of market governance presume linearity of distribution and communication. Linear hierarchies have single equilibrium points, heterarchies have multiple equilibrium points. Hierarchies are closed systems governed from above, heterarchies are open, autopoietic systems. Heterarchies are also

---

[2]   David Stark was the second social scientist named as a Fellow of the Santa Fe Institute, and some of the seminal papers on heterarchy (e.g. Grabher 2001) were first presented at seminars at Santa Fe.

reflexive in a sense that hierarchies are not. Heterarchies are characterized by an 'underdetermination' of organizational structure. In heterarchical organizations there is continual self-monitoring, interpretation, and evaluation of the organization by the organization. A particular hierarchy may result from a 'search for the one best solution'. Heterachies are not a result of this search; they are a result 'that is better at search' (Grabher 2001: 358). Heterarchies are continually involved in search: as part of their reflexivity, they are continually scanning the environment, continually coping with 'unpredictable strategy horizons' (Girard and Stark 2001: 9). Heterarchies are about 'distributed intelligence'.

With the dominance previously of a logic of structure (Castells 1989), linear systems could adequately respond to environments. Now, with a dominance of the logic of flows, non-linear systems are more able to be adaptive. Complex, non-linear systems are better at coping with an environment increasingly characterized by unpredictable flows. Heterarchy may characterize relations both inside a given organization, and within an organizational configuration that is a network of organizations. Heterarchy in either case works through the connectivity between interdependent agents, through the flatness of distributed intelligence. Unpredictability is channelled best through the flows and stoppages that constitute such complex systems. Heterarchy and thus connectivity are particularly prevalent in the new sectors or creative sectors—so, for example, Powell *et al.* (2001) has described them in biotechnology, Grabher (2001) in advertising, and Girard and Stark (2001) in new media. And, while the idea of heterarchy is taken originally from natural science, its prevalence in creative and new economic industries is a consequence of the ways in which such sectors—for reasons of both appearance and substance—are required to innovate more intensely than others.

At issue then in this chapter are three types of connectivity. First, a real connectivity between and among new media organizations, and of new media firms with their clients. This is a non-linear form of production and a shift from previous linear forms of production. Second, a virtual connectivity of the objects produced, in each of our four cases below connecting (or intending to connect) the client firm with its consumers. This is also non-linear, and may be contrasted with earlier models of communication in the media. Normally, and linearly, media work on a model of producer–message–consumer, or sender–message–receiver. The message itself may be mediated through say a television set or a computer. But the movement of virtual objects from place to place, from producer to marketer to distribution in a variety of countries, through a set of different technologies and markets, defies this linearity. Indeed, this transformation in media was shown in our earlier study of global culture industries (Lury and Lury, forthcoming), in which we tracked the movement of eight cultural products—Nike, Swatch, global football, internet portals, Young British Art, *Trainspotting*, Wallace and Gromit, and *Toy Story*. The linearity of producer–text–reader is being succeeded by the non-linear connectivity of real networks and virtual objects in discontinuous time and space.

In terms of the third sense of connectivity, we can speak of connectivity partly displacing narrative as a mode of making sense out of culture for users. Narrative here is more or less linear, while connectivity is less linear. Narrative is comprised of actions, connectivity of communications. Connectivity has to do not with meaning and interpretation, but with operationality and functionality. When a microprocessor is put in say a TV box, you can do something with it,—that is, it is no longer just a question of meaning but of functionality, or operationality. This is much more than a question of an 'active audience' interpreting the various meanings of lean-back broadcasts. Indeed, it is not a matter of *meaning* at all, but of *doing*, of performing. As one of our interviewees succinctly puts it, 'When people get to a site they want not only to see something. They want to do something.' The audience or reader becomes a user. This is also the case with non-virtual forms of what might be called technological culture, such as Nike shoes and apparel. Such objects are not about the *significance* (or meaning) of style, but more—as also in the case of mobile phones—a matter of *doing* style, of operationality or performativity.

CASE 1. IMPERFECT COMMUNICATION AND CONNECTIVITY

We tracked the first multimedia object ethnographically. This was a three-dimensional multi-user chat environment, which is a combination of a chat area and a so-called virtual world, itself comprising several different sub-environments to navigate. The user is represented by an avatar and will encounter other avatars (other users) as well as two bots on his or her journey through the world. This virtual object, T-world, was produced by the Shoreditch-based firm Alpha for Broadcast, a major British non-terrestrial broadcaster, and specifically for the web site of their youth cable channel, Trouble.[3] Prior to this, the channel's web site featured a 'conventional' 2D chat area. Asked why they needed to add a 3D chat world to the already existing 2D chat area, the Channel's web producer said:

I've always regarded 3D with a certain fascination and I also believe that it will replace 2D. I think the fact that, for example, the way the games industry has increasingly gone 3D is significant and playing games is very immersive and I think that the internet and particularly chat will go that way. I think the games industry clearly points in that direction. Apart from anything, it gives you quite a lot of credibility because it's so cutting edge. It's quite good to do something and invest in something which shows you're moving with technology and you're not static and relying on one system.

The production process of T-world lasted about nine weeks. During these nine weeks we conducted intensive fieldwork at Alpha, studying the production

---

[3] In this chapter we use real names for some of the individuals and firms we discuss, but not for all.

of T-world from scratch to the last stages of its completion as a prototype. During these nine weeks we observed the production process, taking photographs of the work environment, the employees, and the different stages of T-world as a virtual object. We videotaped and audio-recorded meetings (internal meetings and meetings with the client), conducting interviews with Alpha employees and Broadcast employees. Further, we collected the e-mail correspondence relating to T-world (the correspondence between Alpha employees, between Alpha and Trouble, and between Alpha and other new media firms who were involved in building T-world, such as Blaxxun, a new media firm in Munich that provided the technological platform). After the launch of T-world we focused on its users. We conducted interviews with Trouble's web producer, a freelancer who was employed as a host for T-world, and Trouble's public-relations manager. We analysed some of the log files that stored the users' (primarily teenagers in so far as it was possible to establish identities) communications in the 3D chat room. Later on, one of us went to Munich and interviewed one of Blaxxun's employees who had collaborated on the building of T-world from a distance.

Tracing T-world through different social settings and studying the environments of these social settings gave us the first insights of our enquiry. A virtual object cannot be traced in the same way as many other objects because it does not exist as a singular, somehow original object (even as a prototype). Instead, it exists simultaneously in a multitude of copies and a plenitude of physical places (computer screens) simultaneously. The production of a digital object is not a linear process that consists of different temporal phases, but a project, a complex and flexible, that is, heterarchic, interaction of tasks and firms. As a consequence of inevitable technical problems and a lack of routine procedures, the production of T-world could not and did not follow a structured order. Furthermore, a good deal of the work was not done in the Alpha offices. It was done in external places such as the employees' homes (one of the designers mostly worked at home, but regularly communicated with her colleagues by e-mail, telephone, and through web sites) and bars and cafés (most of Alpha's 'internal' meetings took place in a nearby café called The Bean). To put this more abstractly, at the same time as its production was underdetermined, the boundaries of the object were indeterminate. Moreover, the biography of the object was not to have a clear ending, a 'failure' that we came to find was commonplace.

As the weeks progressed, it became clear that more or less constant communication was essential to the production of T-world, since no one could rely on existing knowledge: much of the work was non-routine and a great deal was based on trial and error. Everybody in the project team had to be informed about the current and ongoing difficulties and obstacles. Thus the production of the virtual product, the 3D world, can be described as a constant but discontinuous flow of communication, of real connectivity. This flow involved e-mails, phone, web, and face-to-face communication, including official team meetings as well as unofficial meetings of a part of the group with a frequently changing configuration. It included bilateral talk at the workplace as well as numerous formal and informal presentations (called 'show and tell' by Alpha employees).

The communication flows between Alpha and Trouble were particularly instructive. In these interactions, the boundaries between producer and client could blur. So, for example, during the main production phase the web producer of Trouble was frequently at the Alpha office. She visited about twice a week and stayed for several hours. Additionally she was almost continuously in contact with several team members through e-mail and phone. She was deeply involved in the production of the T-world. She came up with ideas and suggestions; she discussed technical problems and possible changes. She was so deeply involved that to all intents and purposes she actually became part of the production team. This aspect of the indeterminacy of the virtual product—its openness to revision—is crucial to its capacity to provoke connectivity, since it facilitates an 'imperfect', non-linear model of communication, in which what is heard is not always what was said, but something more interesting. This imperfection of communication through virtual objects is part of the non-linearity of connectivity.

Surprisingly or not, when T-world was launched, it failed to attract many users. This was despite the fact that the channel spared no expense in promoting it. It launched a substantial advertising campaign for the new web site. It employed a 'hostess' to look after teenagers visiting the 3D world and to convince teenagers in the 2D chat rooms to check out the 3D world. It funded several attempts to redesign the 3D world for two further years following the launch. Yet during most of this time the site remained empty. The 3D world was a failure in so far as it has not attracted substantial numbers of teenagers, the desired audience. Nevertheless, the study of such an unsuccessful virtual object is instructive as it illustrates the necessary limits to imperfect communication if connectivity is to be possible. It suggests, on the one hand, that a certain kind of indeterminacy or openness of virtual objects is vital to connectivity. Yet, on the other hand, no kind of connectivity is possible if certain minimum conditions are not met, including access and a match or fit in terms of technology.

A further way in which the failure of T-world is instructive is in relation to the commercial success of 3D products and VR as a whole. In 1998 the Managing Director of Alpha was a true believer in 'virtual reality'. He was a co-founder of the 'London Virtual Reality Group' and the group's chair. The firm, which was initially primarily focused on the building of 3D environments, was established in 1997. In this initial year, however, the company struggled for survival. The principal problem was finding clients willing to pay for 3D design on their web sites. This in turn was partly due to the inaccessibility of the application software it was necessary to download to enter into 3D environments. In this first year, the firm did not get enough commissions to survive financially. However, the MD and all employees were convinced that its time would come soon. After

the production of the above-mentioned 3D world—the firm had been in existence for more than a year by then—the crisis grew to a point where the MD
seriously considered liquidating the firm. In a collaborative effort to continue, a
decision was made to move away from an exclusive focus on VR and to attract
clients with more conventional needs. The crisis of the company soon ended,
and longer-term steady growth set in. However, the production of 3D
environments does not play a significant role in its current financial success.
Instead, it is involved mainly in creating brand identities, in facilitating online
marketing, in developing business-to-business (b2b) web sites, and designing
interfaces for music publication. It designs web sites that are highly interactive
(for example, Stephen Hawkins's web site), but relies more on 2D applications
such as Flash, Shockwave, and Director than 3D ones. Like many other new
media companies, it has moved from being merely creative and/or technological towards the integration of consultancy work into its professional practices
(of which more in the final two case studies).

CASE 2. PLAYING AT CONNECTIVITY

The second biography of a virtual object we traced is that of a computer game,
produced by the new media firm Pop for the financial services company Origin
(a division of an established bank that describes itself as providing services
'tailored for the individual'). According to one of the PR officers, the Origin
corporate philosophy is about 'getting [customers] to a point of loyalty where
they will actually become an advocate, they will actually through word of mouth
bring in new customers for us'. The game was specifically designed for use in
training employees in 'customer management'. In mapping this biography we
recorded videos of meetings, within Pop, between personnel in Origin and Pop,
and within Origin, conducted interviews with key personnel, and collected
visual documentary data of the conception, development, and implementation
of the game.
    In the first stages of this game's development, its form—quite what kind of
product it was to be—was explicitly indeterminate. This indeterminate product
was, though, defined in terms of its function, which was to promote awareness
of the philosophy of customer advocacy within Origin as a whole. Thus it was to
be a medium of communication, a means of connectivity; indeed, the virtual
was seen as a means of extending the real. So, for example, one story about the
decision to make the product into the game was that it was a way of getting the
whole firm behind customer advocacy. In this story, the form of the product as
a game emerged from a more general philosophy in Origin: 'the word game
stuck as a word for the whole process ... turn from a game in what we're playing
into a game in the sense that we're playing' (Peter, Customer Advocacy). What
is suggested here is that the reason that the product became a game was that

the organization defined and recognized itself in game playing. And certainly to some extent a conception of playing the game was indeed already part of the company philosophy; so, for example, company literature is concerned with 'moving up' levels of relationship with the customer—through awareness and satisfaction to loyalty and advocacy. But the belief was that the game that Origin is playing in the financial services market would somehow be made more securely part of the organization if the product itself took the form of a game. They would play even better.

The ability of this game—aptly called Loyalty—to make connections—that is, to recruit players—was shown in one of the meetings we observed. At this meeting there was a demonstration of the product's prototype. The representative of the new media firm that was commissioned to make the game did not need to 'sell' the product as such, since, as one of them joked, one of the client's employees was 'already an expert'. Indeed, at the meeting to discuss the prototype it was he who actually carried out the demonstration, tutoring his colleagues in the rules of the game. As this and our other biographies suggest, then, a virtual object is likely to be successful if the recipient of the interpretation that it enables becomes lodged in it, infusing him or herself into the encounter. As the Pop representative put it, 'the key thing is the emotional impact. You can immediately see the customer is happy, you've got customer satisfaction, got an incentive, gone up a level—my score's higher!' For us, this indicates one of the ways in which representation in the new media differs from the representation of older forms of cultural production: the distance between, for example, a painting and a viewer, a novel and a reader, or a film and a spectator does not exist here. Instead, the spectator is a player, an interactant. Without this lodging of the subject in the object, the network of connectivity the product creates as it moves forward would be vulnerable to break up.

While, as just noted, this power of connectivity is in part related to the gamelike quality of the product, it is also related to the distinctive characteristics of communication as it is developing in the new media. These characteristics are perhaps most clearly visible in what is called viral marketing: 'a Net strategy built on the premise that a product or service can self-promote and propagate. It's a way of engineering a fad, of making word of mouth pay' (Wieners 1999: 60). One of the characteristics of messages on the internet is that they are not only representations in the sense of re-presentations of something that has happened (before or elsewhere or not at all), but also *represent themselves to further interpretation and indeed to action*. This is not unique to internet communication: indeed, it is a characteristic of all communication (Peirce 1991). What is distinctive, however, is that this second aspect of representation dominates. Indeed, it is often the point of internet communication that it is to be further interpreted—added to, copied, extended via hyperlinks, or simply passed on. Then again, it is often this characteristic that is the subject of anxiety, restriction, and attempted control. Nevertheless, this ability to connect, to make networks, is a consequence of the ways in which the internet makes it possible to appropriate this second aspect of communication in ways so as to provoke connectivity.

Such provocation relates to the more or less purposive nature of communication that is produced in interactivity. Consider, for example, the temporal sequencing of actions required to buy books on Amazon.Com, or purchase theatre tickets through lastminute.com. Consider the structured online sequencing of the exclusive intranet connections through which major traders in currency markets work. But also consider—and more detail is provided below here—the less purposive nature of interaction that is computer gameplay. In each case, such purposive sequencing is dependent upon the presentation of information drawn from a database, the cultural form considered by Lev Manovich (2001) to be at the heart of new media. Manovich argues that databases have no development, thematically, formally, or otherwise, to organize their elements into a sequence. For him, databases are collections of individual items, where every item has the same significance as any other. In connecting the back end to the front end,[4] it is the interface that constructs the sequencing of interactivity between the client companies (or owners of a web site) and the customers (or users of the web site). As Manovich (2001: 37) puts it, 'A number of different interfaces can be created from the same data. A new media object can be defined as one or more interfaces to a multimedia database.' More specifically, it is the interface that comes to structure a sequencing of activities, the connectivity between the virtual and the real.

Interactivity is, of course, a term whose meaning is much contested. On the one hand, while computer-based interactivity may be seen to be more open or dialogic than conventional cultural forms such as narrative or image, in comparison with *interaction* it is restrictive. Thus, instead of being ordered by a mutual influence that is as peripheral and trivial as is characteristic of interaction, the interactivity of the computer interface is typically 'a highly structured form of mutual fatefulness' (Goffman 1961: 35). As in a game, each move or response is selected from a small number of possibilities, these being largely determined by the previous move of the opposing player, just as each move largely determines the possibilities next open to the opponent. Indeed, this mutual fatedness is what explains both the strength and the fragility and frustration of the virtual connectivity we describe here. The selective and

---

[4] In the net industry, practitioners differentiate between front-end and back-end programming. Front-end programming refers to the visible parts of a web site, to its design and to user experience and user perception. Front-end programming is closely connected to those who look at a web site and interact with it. Back-end programming is invisible to the user. It refers to the structure behind the design of a web site, the information design, and the information architecture. Thus it is closely related to work processes and to the organizational structure of the firm itself. Front end seems to refer to design and back end to technology. Digital design is understood as 'front-end' work. It is putting the design on the screen. It was in the first instance the 'cool web site'. The image, indeed the *content*, is the front end. Front end is about 'user experience' and 'usability'. Front end refers to 'human–computer interface'. The 'back end' has to do with technology, with code, with functionality.

sequential ordering of interactivity produces a world of its own. Yet this world is highly conditional. Let us return to the specific example of the game being discussed here to illustrate this since what the case of Loyalty suggests is that such restrictive interaction may be the only link, within a sequence of interaction, interactivity, interaction, of real and virtual connectivity. And, moreover, this embedded sequencing of real and virtual connectivity suggests that play— as a particular kind of operationality or performativity—has the potential to combine the restrictions of mutual fatefulness and the flatness of distributed intelligence with the possibility of hierarchical levels of risk and reward.

In the course of observation, for example, it became apparent that in the process of developing Loyalty, the two companies—the new media company and its client—were themselves effectively engaged in play. Meetings between the two sides seemed to be both the representation of a contest and a contest for the best representation of something (Huizinga 1950). The new media product could thus be seen as a game within a game within a game, or as one level within a multilevelled game. What was important to all the players, as we followed the product through the course of its development, was how interaction (the meetings) could be transformed into interactivity (the new media product). Such interactivity would, it was hoped, in turn structure relations between the client company employees and their customers—that is, it would lead to further interaction. The interface was to provide the basis for the selective and sequential organization of the embedded sequences of interactivity/interaction. Such sequences are, we suggest, characteristic of connectivity, combining underdetermination and purposefulness.

The representative of the new media company, Pop, following an especially tense meeting with the client, acknowledged this. In this meeting the previously agreed rules of the game had been overturned, with substantial revisions being demanded. On returning to her offices, she reported, somewhat regretfully, that the newly agreed version of the game now had to

affect their behaviour. Not the behaviour of them [the customers, as represented in the computer game itself]—it affects the way you play the game [that is, the game the client company is playing]. [What the client wants] to affect is the way these people work.... He wants them to pick up the phone and say, 'Hello Mrs Blah. Is it your birthday? Happy Birthday!'

She insisted that this development meant that the product was no longer a game at all: 'they're not thinking of it as a game, but thinking of it as a training tool, and whether they're getting their message across.' But, from another point of view, she had simply been outplayed, in part because she had not made the best use of the prototype in negotiation at the meeting.

Let us try to explore this example more analytically. Many discussions of play consider that it must take place in a closed world, a world detached from purpose. Indeed, Gadamer (1993) describes play in terms of non-purposive rationality. He maintains that the movement that characterizes play is not tied down to any goal, but this does not mean that it is not intended: 'the end pursued is certainly a nonpurposive activity, but this activity is intended. It is what the play intends' (Gadamer 1993: 23). Nevertheless, so he argues, in so far as we play, we participate in excess, a superabundance, and in this excess we may outplay the capacity for purposive rationality. Or, to put this another way, in so far as we lose ourselves in play, we may find 'something more'. This 'something more' may, in part, explain the value of play and other kinds of connectivity to contemporary businesses, especially the creative sectors; it calls up 'something more' than means–end rationality, something more open-ended, something experimental and affective. But Goffman provides another interpretation of play. He argues that what some perceive to be watertight rules of irrelevance are better conceived as a particular subset of the rules of transformation, which may be either inhibitory or facilitory: 'The solid barrier by which participants in an encounter cut themselves off from externally based attributes now seems to be not quite so solid: like a sieve, it allows a few externally based matters through into the encounter' (Goffman 1961: 30). In the example we are discussing here, the transformation rules of gameplay were represented in the interactivity afforded by the interface, connecting not only the front end to the back end, but also the company managers to their employees to the company's clients, in a sequence of interaction, interactivity, interaction.

For Goffman, the rules of transformation enable the selective introduction (and alteration) of externally based attributes into the game and the transference of locally realized resources out of the game. Seeing the rules of transformation in this way is important for Goffman. It 'tell[s] us what modification in shape will occur when an external pattern of properties is given expression inside the encounter' (Goffman 1961: 33). In this case, following the tense meeting, the new rules were to be designed to enable the game not only to provide an engrossing experience; they were intended also to 'lift out' its players from the everyday routine of selling products, of merely responding to requests. Indeed, while the product was never (either before or after this change in rules) an especially complex or well-developed game, any player is forced to intervene continually in a proactive as well as reactive manner if the game is to continue. Once engaged in the game they are challenged to 'get the message' and give their customers 'care-events' (say 'Happy Birthday Mrs Blah'), stepping outside already given sequences, initiating interaction.

What makes a game successful for Goffman is the combination of two principles: a problematic outcome and the sanctioned display of attributes valued in the wider world. Indeed, he suggests that uncertainty of outcome gives the player a shield behind which he or she can work into the interaction attributes that would threaten the workings of the game if openly introduced. This shield does more than simply provide a defence against claims of self-interest: it provides a means by which intent can be disavowed temporarily only to be claimed, retrospectively, as aim or purpose, if the player is successful. In short, in so far as the rules of transformation—the interface—enable the selective and sequential—but not necessarily meaningful—organization of interactivity, they may result in virtuoso performances amongst new media players. For such skilled players, the boundary between play and non-play is not a wall at all, but an interface—that is, both sieve and shield. Indeed, our research suggests that interface design is vital for the ways in which connectivity operates across and between real and virtual worlds. It is what organizes items of information, themselves without meaning or significance, into the possibility of sequences of interactivity and interaction that enable imperfect but more or less purposive communication: in short, (real and virtual) connectivity.

CASES 3 AND 4. MISCONNECTIVITY: RETAINERSHIP AND FRACTURED ALLIANCES

Let us now present briefer accounts of two linked case studies, neither of which, at the time of writing, had reached the stage of the production of a virtual product at all. In the first of these cases, the project nature of connectivity became reabsorbed in the quasi-permanence of a retainer relationship, reminiscent as much of hierarchy as heterarchy. This would correspond well with Green and Harvey's (1999) never quite realized 'imperative to connect'. In the second, issues of dis- and misconnection were as important as those of connection. We want to claim nonetheless that both cases took place in the register of connectivity, and that the latter was an important heuristic through which to understand developments in new media and in the culture of the now crisis-ridden new sectors more generally.

The first of the two linked cases is focused on another of London's new media firms—MIX-IT Studios. A number of leading London-based new media firms—such as Razorfish and Icon Media Lab—are substantial offices of non-British firms. The latter—along with foreign-based venture capitalists—have a formidable presence in London because of the location of so many corporate headquarters, or European head offices of multinational firms. The latter have become—more than old media clients—the primary clients for new media firms. MIX-IT was, alongside firms such as Deepend and the Manchester-based Eunite, among the home-grown leaders in the sector. All three were in the top ten (including foreign firms) in the UK in terms of revenues and numbers of employees.

MIX-IT began very much as an art house, a content house. It was founded by a well-established London designer with strong connections to the record industry. The company became a computer design house in 1993. It was one of the earliest 'multimedia companies', on the ground two or three years before the establishment of Razorfish and Icon Media Lab in London, and initially located in Shoreditch. We first established contact with MIX-IT at the end of

1995, at which time it was not at all clear that new media firms would work primarily for clients. There were no dot.coms at that time and contemporaries looked just as much to final consumers as to clients in order to establish an income stream. The company undertook a number of one-off projects, many of which paid little or no money at all, and functioned via a connectivity in which there was little hierarchy in terms of relations between partners. In early 1996, for example, the company carried out one of the first web broadcasts of a pop festival, the Phoenix festival. There was the beginning of a relationship with the Institute of Contemporary Arts. MIX-IT was also doing web and design work with *Dazed & Confused*, a leading independent fashion and photography magazine in London.

D&C itself was and is a money loser, a loss leader (McRobbie 1999). It was established in the mid-1990s by a young successful London fashion photographer, who pays for the magazine's losses from his income as a more mainstream fashion photographer. The magazine has been in effect a quasi avant-garde showcase for photographers, models, and designers who through it come to the notice of the commercial sector and later develop remunerative careers. MIX-IT also developed 'pink' web sites for Britain's nationwide gay community. In alliance with some Glasgow-based publicans, it began to develop national web sites that could be used locally for pub quizzes. Even its relationship with big players like BT—including an initiative to digitize 25,000 adverts—was non-profit making. At the time it, like other new media firms, became involved in various public–private, especially European Community, research (and development) consortium bids. All of these cases were one-off projects in which the company related to more or less equal partners, working roughly along the lines of the model of heterarchy described above.

Five years later, in the early months of 2001, things changed. MIX-IT now had seventy-five, not thirty-five employees. It had been acquired in 1998 by Havas, the global advertising network with revenues of approximately $8 billion, and moved into new offices—from SE4 to W1—in 2001. The company was now close to Harley Street, to Soho advertising agencies, and to the Groucho Club, an infamous media watering hole. Rents in Shoreditch had risen to £35 per square foot per month. In W1 they were £55 per square foot per month. The move of MIX-IT and other new media companies to the environs of Soho, or in this case the even more upmarket district directly south of Regents Park, was part of a wider process in which even finance-sector firms moved from the City to Westminster. In any event, in 2001 MIX-IT occupied 10,000 square feet and nine conference rooms, with revenues growing at about 50 per cent per year. (In 2000 revenues stood at about £3 million.)

More widely, even by the end of 1996 and beginning of 1997, a new business model was beginning to emerge for new media firms in London, New York, and elsewhere. Money was to be made by billing clients. Primary interest was less and less in products to be produced for the market and more and more in clients. New media firms were increasingly working by billing clients and competing with other firms for new business through 'pitches'. New media firms had thus become business services rather than businesses selling to consumers. Their focus was no longer on the 'cool' content of web sites, but on their list of clients, and, in this respect, their ethos was 'the bigger the client the better'. New media companies now no longer describe themselves as 'cool' content houses, but as more sober and buttoned-down internet solutions providers. Thus firms like Agency.Com adopted their name not because they were dot.coms, but because they were self-branding like an advertising agency.

At the end of 2000, one of the Creative Directors of MIX-IT estimated for us that only about 25 per cent of the firm's work was creative, blue-skies business, the rest being for major clients such as a national bank, Nokia, and NTL (the UK's leading cable TV company). Indeed, the company is a main developer of a national bank's online banking strategies. On a recent visit to their new offices, seven of the company's nine conference rooms were taken up with meetings with various bank representatives. In 2001 creative directors spent less time putting together local network projects and a lot more time with the major clients, cementing the relationship and keeping them as clients. This is very much like the model prevalent in advertising. If you are a successful new media firm, you have four choices: internal income generation, venture capital, flog, or float. Deepend and Eunite have grown through the retention of revenues. Icon Media Lab and Razorfish floated and have been very badly hit by the Nasdaq and European technology-market crashes. Razorfish peaked at $55 per share in February 2000, hit bottom in April 2001 at about $0.40, and recovered slightly in June 2001 at $0.85 (www.nasdaq.com). MIX-IT Studios chose the flog option. The result is that it has moved away from a project-based connectivity model and towards one that privileges clients, one that is very much like an advertising agency, a 'retainer model' based on long-term and continuous client relations. Thus there is a tension in new media between the emergence of heterarchy and a reinstatement of hierarchy through retainer relations. In the case of MIX-IT, the move from a more heterarchical to more hierarchical organization paralleled the translation of an initial accumulation of symbolic capital based on 'cool' content into an income stream of economic capital.

The second, linked case here is also of connectivity, but one that underlines (the productivity of) processes of misconnection and de-connection. It is an example of the building of a project network for a project of mixed public-sector and private-sector funding. The project is to create interactive television content and appropriate it to broadband internet and mobile phone microsites. It was, at the time of writing, under consideration by the DTI and the ESRC for funding. The project will also collect data on 'audience usability' of programming in this context. The initial partners in the research and development coalition were ourselves, a team based primarily at Goldsmiths College, and the just described MIX-IT Studios. It was conceived in August 2000. MIX-IT brought in a TV, film, video, and advertising production firm called Zone

Productions. Zone's Managing Director, Astrid Martin, had worked closely for years with one of MIX-IT's Creative Directors, Tony Jones. Indeed, at one point Zone was considering moving into MIX-IT's new offices. And NTL, a MIX-IT client, was at this point listed as our most likely end-user partner. (Martin had also worked closely with NTL's Commissioning Editor.) But falling market capitalization had recently forced NTL to spend less on programming. Further, its Liberate platform had been less than fully functioning. Thus NTL withdrew at an early date in January 2001. The project then included one-half private-sector funding. Logical prospective end-user partners were now the broadcasters and BSkyB. The participation of any broadcaster would also mean extending the network to include a carrier (since broadcasters must sign deals with carriers to be able to use their platforms for digital broadcast).

Goldsmiths along with Channel 4 partly funds the Cultural Entrepreneurs Club at the Institute of Contemporary Arts. Simon Jameson, of C4, is on the governing board of 'the Club'. He works with C4's brand development team and put us onto some commissioning editors. But they were not interested. We contacted BBC New Media, whose director had been an executive at Trouble previously. There was some interest, but we did not follow it up, partly because Martin, Zone MD, preferred to work with a private-sector client because of the sponsorship and online purchase possibilities of the study. Further the Head of BBC online was an old colleague/friend of one of the founders of MIX-IT. We mentioned this to our contacts at MIX-IT, but perhaps significantly they did not follow this up. Further, the BBC has not yet decided which digital carrier (or carriers) to work with and will need to choose a platform (or platforms) when they develop and broadcast interactive content. Astrid Martin began to approach others at C4 and E4. A few bites but no luck. She also was approaching Sky, Nokia, and others. It seemed that Zone was doing all the work in attempting to find the coalition end-user clients, and that MIX-IT was doing very little. The Independent Television Commission (ITC) began to take an interest in participation via its Engineering Division, which was already funding psychological research on perception in 3D virtual environments at Goldsmiths. NTL itself had previously been part of the ITC. Then the ITC, which is not a state, but a charitable sector organization, funded by fees from private-sector broadcasters, split up its operations into regulation, on the one hand, and transmission, on the other. The transmission wing underwent a management buy-out to create NTL, which was subsequently acquired by a New York company. NTL also own a substantial portion of present and future 3G mobile phone masts.

As for the ITC, it was due to be merged with the telephone regulators, OFTEL, to become OFCOM, which would have some regulatory powers over the commercial broadcasting sector and the BBC. Patricia Hodgson, ex-BBC prime mover of non-terrestrial broadcasting and of BBC digital operations, had been made Director of the ITC and was likely to be the head of OFCOM. The ITC was a great enthusiast for broadband multi-platform universal access. Further, it was keen to join our network because it seemed as if BSkyB would be a partner. BSkyB has consistently refused to talk to the ITC and typically only meets it in court. The ITC was keen to find any venue for dialogue with BSkyB. A week later BSkyB said it did not want to sit at this sort of table with either the ITC or the DTI. A few weeks later still, on the evening before the project application was due, the ITC said it would not join the coalition. Since Zone (not Goldsmiths or MIX-IT) was becoming the initiating partner in the network, BSkyB became interested, as did Channel 5, which was about to sign a deal with BSkyB as its exclusive digital carrier—that is, C5 would exclusively use BSkyB's proprietary Open platform. This was at about the same time as ITV's deal with OnDigital, the terrestrial digital carrier. OnDigital will become increasingly identified with the ITV brand.

Nokia was still interested. It was up to MIX-IT to bring it into the coalition. But MIX-IT protested. 'Nokia is our client', it said. It was precisely because Nokia was its client that it could bring Nokia into the coalition. What MIX-IT meant was that it did not want to *spoil* its client relation with Nokia by trying to bring it into the project network. The writing was on the wall. MIX-IT withdrew from the coalition, stating it found it insufficiently coherent (although it had played a leading role in designing it). It further said that it was involved in much bigger things with clients. And indeed this was the case (see above). When Zone moved offices, it was to a Soho venue and not to MIX-IT's premises. Zone said the reason was that 'it [MIX-IT] would bleed us'—that is, although Zone would pay no rent, it would be obliged to enter a series of perceived disadvantageous partnerships with MIX-IT. In the event Zone was able to find another technology company for the project: the Manchester-based Eunite. Further, Zone was able to bring Yes Television, a video-on-demand company into the coalition. Its set-top boxes use a non-proprietary platform that, unlike Open, actually works from IP protocol and uses a web browser and gives internet access.

The point here is that the literature on new sector production through project networks, heterarchy, and connectivity usually describes the successful networks. It rarely describes the de-connections and misconnections involved in network building. The point is also that, after the de- and reconnections, the project itself, what is yet to be produced and researched and developed, seems to be almost an unintended consequence of failed intended connections. It is significant, moreover, that this network passed through a set of partnerships that include private, state, and voluntary sector organizations in quite fascinating permutations. We suspect that this is a more common phenomenon in the UK and Europe—and much less common in the USA—then is generally recognized. There is a contradiction between the private-sector ideology of the DTI, the regulators, and various EC bodies, and the mixed reality of public–private coalitions. This deviant and possibly unsuccessful case may be the rule. In short, connectivity may be just as much about the failed connection as the successful connection, but still takes place in the register of the 'imperative to connect' that is characteristic of new media and other emergent sectors.

THE NEW ECONOMY?

We have data only on the handful of firms that we have studied intensively. But perhaps a few observations should be made in this context. The initial firms to crash in the technology sector were the dot.coms. Dot.coms are not *per se* new media firms. Dot.coms sell online to consumers. New media firms in the strict sense sell to clients who are businesses. Amazon.Com, Boo.Com, and lastminute.com are paradigmatic dot.coms, while Razorfish, Icon Media Lab, and say Agency.Com are leading new media firms. New media firms now call themselves 'Internet solutions providers'. Our entire sample was new media firms providing services or products for business clients, not for consumers like the dot.coms. The dot.coms' online purchasing facilities were exorbitantly expensive to set up and maintain, apart from the advertising to establish a client base. New media firms have lower fixed costs. They do not need to advertise on the same scale. Their clients come largely from word of mouth. They create products. Dot.coms sell things to consumers that other companies have made. Dot.coms do not make virtual objects. They hire new media firms to construct their web sites. Eunite, a leading UK new media firm, declares proudly that none of its main client firms was or is a dot.com. Yet the new media firms themselves have lost value. The market capitalization of Razorfish has declined most precipitously. The market capitalization of Icon Media Lab has also declined. Most new media firms in London have had neither IPOs nor used venture capital. There have not been the redundancies in London new media that there have been in New York's Silicon Alley.

The Nasdaq crash began in April 2000. Some six months later, client firms in business began cutting down on all IT expenditure. From 1995 to 2000, investment in IT equipment and software had been rising at an average annual rate of 25 per cent per year. In the first quarter of 2001 in the USA it fell by 6.5 per cent (*The Economist* 2001: 99). Microsoft, for example, whose revenue growth from desktop applications had been consistently 30 per cent per year, grew at less than 7 per cent to $2.26 billion in the quarter to 31 March 2001 (*Guardian* 2001: 24). The exception to this is the continued spending increase in online advertising, which suggests that new media firms may be better placed in some important ways than other technology firms. Further, online purchasing looks very likely to increase in the long run, especially with the expansion of broadband. The penetration of broadband (in 2001) was still very low in the UK, but in countries like South Korea over 9 per cent of the population was online with broadband (McIntosh 2001). This should also favour new media firms when compared with the rest of the technology sector. The development of micro-sites for broadband, 3G mobile phone networks will increase demand for the services of internet media solutions providers. The growth of interactive television should also increase demand, especially as it shifts to IP protocol. Thus new media in the strict sense—that is, the 'Silicon Alley firms' that have been the subject of this chapter—may be quite well placed in the technology sector for the medium term. The new media firms rose during second wave growth of the ICT sector, as the centre of technological gravity moved from desktop computing to communications. Communications infrastructure has been lain in this growth burst from 1995 to 2000. And new media firms—not computer firms such as Dell—should be the beneficiaries for at least a decade.

Most importantly there have finally been gains in labour productivity through the whole economy. From 1995 to 2000 in the USA labour productivity grew at twice the rate (3.0 per cent) it had done in 1975–95 (1.4 per cent). A certain proportion of this is due to the significant increase in IT spending by firms in all sectors from 1985 to 1995. A certain proportion is due to the massive increases in technology spending on internet-related technologies from 1995 to 2000. The increases in productivity are comparable to those experienced in other technological revolutions such as the automobile, the electrical industry, or railways. In each case these resulted in 12–15 years of strong gains in productivity. Most of the productivity gains are attributed to capital deepening—that is, an increase in capital expenditure per worker in the labour force. Less seems to have come through efficiency gains, though it seems as if there has been a reduction in transaction costs (*The Economist* 2001: 102). Companies ran up very high stocks of IT equipment. It is likely that this capital deepening will lead to increased productivity for several years at relatively low rates of investment in IT equipment (and services). It has made sense to cut back in this area of expenditure. These reductions corresponded to the much sharper and more drastic decline in 'exuberance' of stock market investors.

The Nasdaq crash—after its peak index of 5,048 on 10 March 2000—was a very serious business. From April 2000 to April 2001 the Nasdaq Index fell by 59.2 per cent. There were some huge losers in market capitalization (MC) here. MC is a measure of company strength that is based on neither revenues, nor assets, nor profits, but instead on how much investors are willing to pay for shares of the company. It is the value of a company's outstanding shares as measured by shares times current price. Cisco Systems, makers of internet hardware, were the world's number one company in March 2000, with an MC of more than $500 billion. In April 2001 Cisco's MC stood at $109 billion. During the fourth quarter of 2000, the MC of server manufacturer Sun Microsystems fell from $147 billion to $49 billion. The share price of Amazon (the world's leading dot.com) fell, for example, from $400 to $12 and in June 2001 marginally recovered to $16.95 (*Wired* 2001: 110, 130, 132). Internet portal Yahoo suffered a similar spiralling fall, its revenues—drawn mainly from advertisers—also hit by the crash of the dot.coms. Yahoo peaked at $230 per share in December 1999, fell to $11.50 in April 2001, and slightly recovered to $19.46 in June 2001 (www. nasdaq.com). The European telecoms have moved into massive debt. Wireless network firms such as Vodafone and Orange (many owned by the de-nationalized telecoms) have run into debt through buying 3G spectrum from governments. They will have to spend as much again for the construction of 3G network infrastructure. As company demand for IT and software fell in the first quarter of 2001, substantial layoffs resulted at Cisco, Charles Schwab, Disney, Motorola, Ericsson, and elsewhere.

It is significant that the discourse concerning the 'new economy' spread not during the PC-based dynamic growth of computing, dating from the early 1980s, but from the internet-inspired expansion from the mid-1990s. Thus in a sense the 'new economy' is the internet economy. The steady expansion of the new media firms described above dates from 1995–6. This corresponds to the growth in expenditure of client firms from all sectors on internet protocol (IP) technology—on intranets, B2C and B2B e-commerce facilities, database, net advertising, and web sites. The firms that we studied ethnographically reported growth in revenues and in some cases profits of 25–100 per cent per year over this period. The rapid increase in MC sets in from 1995–6. It is at this point that the business press begins to speak of firm size in terms of MC rather than turnover. This was symbolically signalled by Netscape's 1995 IPO of $4 billion–5 billion. Then there is very strong growth in stock market investment and the Nasdaq Index from 1995 to 1998; the period of delirious 'irrational exuberance' described by Alan Greenspan from 1998 to 2000 and then the crash after March 2000.

Yet even more than a year after the 'dot.bomb', investment in technology stocks remained unusually strong. The ratio of MC to sales, profits, or net profit margins was still much higher in Nasdaq firms than in the old economy. In old economy firms there was often a 1 : 1 ratio of MC to sales. For example, for Sony from April 2000 to April 2001 both MC and revenues stood at about $62 billion. Even after the debacle, Yahoo's ratio of MC to revenues was about seven. Oracle's MC has halved but in April 2001 it still stood at $86 billion on sales of $10.1 billion. Sun's MC stood at $49 billion; its sales at $17 billion; Vodafone's MC at $169 billion on sales of $12.7 billion. Microsoft's $298 billion MC compares to sales of $23 billion. AOL-Time-Warners' MC stood at $158 billion. Cisco's MC was still at 5–6 times its revenues. Nokia's MC was $101 billion, its sales $28 billion; Intel's MC $173 billion, and sales $34 billion. The Nasdaq Index as a whole stood at only 3.5 per cent below its 1998 level (http://quotes. nasdaq.com/quote).[5]

The technology sector, between 1995 and 2000, found itself swimming in liquidity. What happened to all of that surplus investment? What happened brings us back again to connectivity. The years 1995–2000 saw a very great deal of investment of shareholders' money by technology firms in communications infrastructure: into laying fibre-optic cable, expanding broadband. The rise of the computer sector (computers, software, microprocessors) was about

---

[5] The Nasdaq Index has increased marginally since the *Wired* report of 2 Apr. 2001. Cisco, for example, was valued at $76 per share in March 2000, Sun Microsystems has also recovered by a small amount since its trough of April 2001. Sun peaked in September 2000 (http://quotes. nasdaq.com/quote = CSCO, SUNW).

information. In 2001 the shift was to communications, to connectivity. This communications infrastructure has comprised hardware, software, and networks—including mobile phone handsets and other wireless devices as hardware. The construction of 3G networks was a question of mobile phone communications hardware, much in the sense that Cisco was a network hardware company for the Internet. This infrastructure included the business database construction in which Oracle and IBM were sector leaders. This company database infrastructure included applications software for sales, procurement, and marketing; it included their knitting-together in a database, and it included the servicing of these products. This servicing accounted for some 50 per cent of Oracle's sales (http://host.businessweek.com/businessweek/Corporate_Snapshot.html? Symbol = ORCL). Applications themselves were increasingly built into the communications network. Hence the success of Sun's Brazil, a toolkit for building net-based applications. Hence Intel's long-term strategy of developing communications silicon: networking silicon, data centre silicon, non-PC client silicon. Hence Microsoft's attempts to escape the desktop ball and chain by developing .Net, an XML-enabled architecture for applications that reside on central servers, and to deliver software as a subscription service rather than as CD-roms. This parallels Sun's developments with Java. At stake in all of this was the laying of infrastructure for connectivity.

So what can we conclude? Irrational, even rational exuberance is a thing of the past. There is a big question mark indeed in terms of the breakneck pace growth of the virtual society(?). We have tried to argue that the non-linearity and connectivity of virtual culture is more or less an extension of the logic of emerging non-linear production organization in the real economy. This is a phenomenon of the new sectors generally and new media in particular. These non-linear project networks, we have claimed, often misfire through misconnectivity or dis-connectivity, but they do operate in the register of connectivity, of the imperative to connect. The virtual objects that production networks in the real economy produce are often themselves tissues of connectivity—intended to establish bonds between client firms and consumers. Finally the cultural experience of consumers is increasingly also driven by connectivity, by 'data demand' rather than a need for sustaining narratives. This hunger for data seems only to increase the more that we are surrounded by the noise of the data. Will this data demand of consumers finally reach its saturation point and transform into what French anthropologist David LeBreton (1997) has called an 'aspiration towards silence'? Will the imperative to connect finally run its course?

12

Presence, Absence, and Accountability: E-mail and the Mediation of Organizational Memory

Steven D. Brown and Geoffrey Lightfoot

REMEMBERING AND THE ARCHIVE

In Western thought there is a long-standing link between the practice and tools of remembering: *memoria* and *techne*. Take, for instance, the two pivotal moments described in that great work of memory, *À la recherche du temps perdu*. The first is the legendary scene where the taste of the tea-soaked madeleine restores Marcel to his childhood bed, awaiting the tread of his mother's steps on the stairs. The second, however, is far less celebrated. During his return to Paris from the sanatorium, Marcel stumbles on uneven courtyard stones. The effect is the same—an instantaneous transport into the depths of memory. On both occasions what proves decisive for Marcel is the act of engaging with a particular object. The effect is peculiar. It is as though the memory emerges by way of the object itself and not by way of thought at all—'all anxiety about the future, all intellectual doubts disappeared...I had followed no new train of reasoning, discovered no new decisive argument' (Proust 1981: 899). The sensation then appears to Marcel to originate not within himself, but as 'given to me by the two uneven paving-stones' (Proust 1981: 900).

Much has been made of Proust's treatment of memory by cognitive psychologists (see Engel 2000; Delacour 2001), who propose that his text describes the

Earlier versions of this chapter were presented at the XIth meeting of the European Association of Experimental Social Psychology, July 1999, the Society for Social Studies of Science 1999 conference, and various 'Virtual Society?' gatherings. Especial thanks are due to Ron Day and other participants who commented on a previous draft at the 'Virtual Society?' seminar on 'Network, Scale, Memory and Play' convened by Sarah Green, Penny Harvey, Celia Lury, and the authors.

link between the context of recall and the content of what is recalled. But memory, for Proust, involves more than this. All of Marcel's prodigious feats of memory are mediated by his engagement with everyday objects. This includes not only the madeleine and the paving stones, but also telephones, handwritten notes, timetables, and perpetually unfinished articles. There is then a way of approaching memory, following Proust, that focuses on the mediational role assumed by artefacts as much as it does on the putative cognitive mechanism involved in recollection (see Radley 1990; Brown *et al.* 2001). But a strange paradox exists in this linkage of memory and technique. In *The Republic*, Plato famously remarks of writing that it is a means of forgetting. What is alluded to here is the way in which a technology such as the written word enables both the preservation and the disposal of memory. For example, a diary both conserves the past and relieves the diarist from the burden of keeping his or her recollections alive within him or herself.

This tension between preservation and displacement has been much remarked upon. Ong (1988) proposes that the advent of writing disturbs the way in which the past is brought into being in the present. In an oral tradition, the past must necessarily be brought to presence through the repeating of traditional stories and narratives—in short, through myth. Such myths are not the sole property of the teller, they are communal accomplishments, and the right to narrate myth—the past—may fall to any number of individual speakers or indeed be done on an entirely communal basis. But when writing comes to dominate the activity of remembering, the past comes to be recorded in the form of written inscriptions. This provides the means for storing up the past as a resource, a kind of stockpiling of memory. As historians of accounting have shown, this shift to treating the past as a resource can be seen to confer material benefits on the one who is able to access and interpret such records (see Hoskin and Macve 1988; Ezzamel 1994). The storage and mobilization of the past as archived inscriptions are then a decisive moment in the emergence of what we now recognize as modern commerce.

The archive—the place where the past is consigned and stored up for use in the present—occupies a powerful place in cultures dominated by the written word. In a very public way, the archive demonstrates to a given collective the way in which it manages the tension between remembering and forgetting. Thus decisions around what ought to be recorded, the form that record should take, and the way in which it should be subsequently preserved and made available take on increasing importance. Derrida (1997) explores this subtle link between judgement and the storing of records. He notes the etymological roots of 'archive' in *arkhē*—a classical Greek term that means both 'commencement' and 'commandment'. Commencement is the positing of origins, the establishing of the original, authoritative version of something. Commandment is the issuing of law, the practice of judgement. These two senses of *arkhē* are embodied, Derrida claims, by the figure of the *archon*—a magistrate who takes charge of the archive and is granted the power to practise law on the basis of the authoritative records that he alone is allowed to store, review, and interpret. Working from this link, Derrida then proceeds to explore the role that the archive plays in how we think of both law and human memory.

We will return later to Derrida's text, but for now let us carry forward the idea of the consigning of records to an archive, and the subsequent interpretation of those records by those privileged to do so. As Lynch (1999) notes, this practice has increasingly become a site where struggles over interpretation are fought out. Lynch offers the example of the 'Irangate' Senate hearings in the USA, which turned around the relationship between Oliver North and the public documents he claimed to have shredded (see Lynch and Bogen 1996). The central issue here is how an authoritative version of the past can be reconstructed when the archive has been systematically corrupted by the very individuals charged with its safekeeping. Stripped of its wider political import, this constitutes a mundane organizational issue: how can the past in the form of records survive through time? Or, put another way, how can the archive be best designed to prevent its future destruction?

A recent solution to this problem comes in the form of networked computing. Linking together multiple sites for the storage of data offers the opportunity to preserve multiple copies of records. Indeed, one well-worn story of the very origins of the internet describes the original rationale of its forerunner (that is, ARPANET) as being precisely that of ensuring the preservation of government data from destruction by distributing the sites of its storage. Networked computing can then bring about a kind of multiplying of the archive. Instead of one single site, the archive may be divided into numerous copies, all of which may be distributed and made generally available. Much of the enthusiasm for the introduction of networked computing in organizations then comes from the idea of an 'opening-up' of the archive, which will purportedly result in a whole new way of creative working:

The computer is the means by which many of us pull ideas together and organize information. Once, only a few were able, with difficulty and time, to access and converge information resources for the purpose of creative invention; today using networked computers, the many can search for and discover interrelationships of increasing complexity. Technology represents a potential platform from which humanity can take a quantum leap in intelligence, creativity, and achievement.   (Khoshafian and Buckiewicz 1995)

What Khoshafian and Buckiewicz describe is a situation where the *archon*—the privileged interpreter of the archive—loses his or her exclusive power. Every competent user of new technology in an organization may in principle access and interpret archived records. Or, to borrow a phrase from Lynch (1999), networked computing becomes an 'archontic infrastructure' that potentially enrols all organizational users into its upkeep.

In this chapter we want to explore these claims about the way in which new technology fundamentally changes the way organizations relate to their own past. We will concentrate on one particular—and now near omnipresent—technology, that of e-mail. As a written form of communication that affords an immediate and relatively easy way of storing up the past in archival form, e-mail is increasingly being treated as a formal business record. Witness, for example, the appearance of mandatory disclaimers as to the content of a message that many organizations now insist appear at the end of any e-mails sent from company addresses. Or the recent legal battles in both the USA and Europe over the ownership of individual e-mail records.[1] Our concern here will be to display how, given this evolving context of e-mail as a formal record, organizational users actually make use of the possibilities for accessing and interpreting the past that the archiving of e-mails provides.

THE ORGANIZATIONAL USE OF E-MAIL

We will be drawing upon empirical materials from a study of two organizations at different stages in the implementation of networked information systems. The first organization—which we have given the pseudonym 'OilSite'—is a major constructor of oil industry infrastructure (that is, oil rigs petroleum refinement plants). OilSite is based in the UK, but has a complex system of international ownership, which means that it has parent companies in the USA and in Japan. From its UK headquarters, OilSite directs operations around the world. The complexity of these kinds of operations has lead OilSite to develop an organizational structure based around a core group—which deals with the routine running of the company—and associated project groups. The lines of responsibility between and within these groups are constantly shifting. Indeed, the project groups themselves expand and shrink in relation to the nature of existing projects and less controllable variables such as the global price of oil. As a large-scale organization, OilSite relies upon a myriad differing information systems. In the UK headquarters alone, over 2,000 different software systems are installed across the company networks. E-mail—in the form of Lotus CC mail associated with several distinct systems—has been routinely used since 1990. There are, for example, a number of continuously running distribution and discussion lists within the company.

The second organization, which we are calling 'ReadyAds', is the publisher of a weekly advertising newspaper. ReadyAds has several offices throughout the major cities in the UK, but also has interests abroad (for example, in the USA). Much of the 'frontline' work at ReadyAds consists of filling advertising space and taking information for putative advertisers. This is handled by shift-based teams of telephone operators, who are physically organized in a 'call-centre'

[1] At the time of writing (2000), for example, the Council of Europe had just made public its backing for a law mandating the archiving of all e-mails, internet usage, and web sites for up to seven years.

fashion within each regional ReadyAds office. ReadyAds also uses a wide range of information systems to link telephone operators to editorial staff and electronic print setters. All members of the organization, including shift workers, use e-mail on an everyday basis. The packages commonly used to manage e-mail in ReadyAds included Microsoft Outlook.

In both companies e-mail is used for a variety of purposes. For example, communicating between offices and countries (different place/same time) or between shift workers or project teams who work at different times (same place/different time). In this sense, e-mail is often used in preference to the telephone in an attempt to end the kind of 'telephone tennis' associated with leaving answerphone messages. This use of e-mail has been widely reported and studied (see Sproull and Kiesler 1998). E-mail is also routinely archived by users in both companies. Those e-mails that are posted to discussion lists or via the intranet services that exist in both organizations are automatically archived and made accessible. But individual users also develop their own personal archiving practices, such as storing e-mails they are sent on the company server, or on the hard drive of their PC, or simply by printing out and manually filing messages. Here it would seem that it is the written memo rather than the answerphone that serves as the model for how users treat e-mail.

The first point we want to make, then, is that, for all its novel appearance, users in both organizations fashion the way they use e-mail upon a previously existing practice, such as answerphone messages or filing memos. We may then suspect that in both cases the introduction of e-mail did not lead to a fundamental change in business practice. Rather, users drew upon existing practices when adjusting to the possibilities offered by this new medium. Berg (1997) makes much the same point in relation to the introduction of electronic patient records in medical settings. New technology does not displace previous ways of working, instead it becomes assimilated and shaped by those extant practices. At a wider level, we argue that, following Woolgar (this volume), e-mail sits alongside things like sending memos and acquires, for users, something of the same character. To a certain extent e-mails become treated as though they actually are memos sent by other means.

Nevertheless, users in both organizations were able to describe two distinct uses that they made of e-mail. The primary use was for *informing*. This ranges from the support of workflow and the exchange of data, through to more complex tasks around the retrieval and dissemination of information. Common examples of informing include making requests ('asking whether or not something has been completed', 'can you get feedback on this?') and issuing instructions ('this is how we are going to go about it, this is what you need to look out for, try it this way if it doesn't work'). Users also referred to e-mail as providing an improved sense of 'being in the loop'. That is, as having continuous access to potentially important or at least interesting information circulating on the company network, often across sites ('you can be up to date with what is going on all the time in every centre'). As McGrail (this volume) describes, the reverse side of this sense of belonging is an awareness that one is continually accountable for what goes on in electronic communication. Failing to respond adequately to a request made by e-mail, for example, or being seen to have not fully contributed to an e-mail discussion that touches upon one's area of responsibility or expertise, is an accountable matter. This generates anxiety amongst users over keeping up with the volume of e-mail they receive. For example, one OilSite respondent described taking a work laptop computer on a family holiday, and furtively logging onto his e-mail account once his partner and children had gone to bed.

Alongside this informing, users also pointed to how e-mail could enable all kinds of *relating* activities. The archetypal piece of relating is the short warm message sent to a co-worker or subordinate, praising his or her work or simply establishing contact. This, again, was particularly important as a means of maintaining relations across sites and or within groups of mobile workers. Many users considered this relating use to be part of an informalizing of relations. Whereas previously access to higher level managers could be difficult to establish, now it was far easier simply to copy them into an e-mail discussion, thereby drawing their attention to a particular matter. In turn, managers in both organizations were keen to stress that time spent in relating activities with e-mail was not in any sense wasted: 'sometimes I can be crackling off for half an hour and you have not necessarily achieved anything concrete, but what you are achieving especially when you are new to a team is forging a relationship with those people so they can determine what you can expect and vice versa' (ReadyAds, New Media Manager).

However, at the same time there was also a general sense that this kind of relating work could have its limits, and that a certain amount of face-to-face work needed to be invested in a relationship, particularly in the initiation phase. In this sense, not one single respondent we talked to in either organization entertained the idea that e-mail could ever replace face-to-face interaction. Indeed, the relationship between these two communication media was often described in a complex way. For example, one respondent pointed to the importance of face-to-face interaction in building trust:

sometimes it is important to see people because I often cannot do business with people I get a bad feeling about and that is often, over the years, I realize it had got a basis with something and that if I think that someone is a bit smarmy or someone is a bit odd or if it turns out that someone does not produce the goods, they lie, I think that it is important that face to face that you get impression of them and then you can do business with them.   (ReadyAds, Project Manager)

Just prior to the above extract, the respondent recounted a story describing a progressive breakdown in the business relationship with a supplier. A pivotal moment in the story was where the supplier began sending 'inappropriate' e-mails to the manager, such as slightly risqué jokes. For the manager concerned, these e-mails served to confirm her existing mixed feelings about the supplier (the business relationship was subsequently terminated). What the extract then emphasizes is a difficulty in managing business relationships via e-mail. People, she claims, can make misleading promises or lie with relative impunity in an e-mail message. In order then to make these kinds of relationships work, the manager emphasizes the importance of including face-to-face meetings. The implication here is that, rather than replacing face-to-face interaction, e-mail actually stimulates or encourages more of such activity. Or, as Woolgar (this volume) puts it, 'the more virtual, the more real'. What this also suggests is that the nature of e-mail interaction in both companies needs further disentangling.

E-MAIL AS FORMAL INTERACTION

Much of the research on e-mail and other forms of computer-mediated communication (CMC) in organizational settings since the mid-1980s has sought to identify the potential benefits and distinctiveness of the media in relation to other modes of communication (see Rice and Love 1987; Walther and Burgoon 1992). A common early finding is that CMC such as e-mail results in a democratization of workplace communication (Kiesler *et al.* 1984). Features such as visual anonymity and a more relaxed turn-taking structure have been described as allowing for wider contributions from users, resulting in forms of interaction that cut across existing organizational structures. Recent research, however, has tempered these findings somewhat. For example, Watt *et al.* (this volume) have shown that visual anonymity results in an increased, rather than decreased, awareness of evolving group norms in CMC. A number of empirical studies (such as Brigham and Corbett 1997; Ngwenyama and Lee 1997; Romm and Pliskin 1999) have concluded that e-mail can be used as a fairly blunt managerial tool for enforcing particular kinds of power relations. The message seems to be that, as Mantovani (1994) puts it, CMC is not intrinsically apt to bring about workplace democratization. It all depends on the local context in question—a finding that is echoed throughout the current volume.

In the case of OilSite and ReadyAds such an ambiguity about the potential benefits of e-mail was widespread across respondents. On the one hand, few had any doubt that e-mail was now an essential feature of their everyday working life. It was difficult to think of life without it. But all respondents were able to point to instances of problematic practices that had evolved around e-mail. For example, strategic attempts to exploit the same place/different time ability of e-mail were described, which had as their objective the maximization of the impact of delivering sensitive pieces of information. One manager likened this to 'dropping bombs': 'And I think that possibly it is also a way of letting something go as a bit of a bombshell and the following morning someone comes in and logs in and they have logged in overnight or before they left or something' (OilSite, Project Manager).

Now this ability to 'drop bombs' is not an exclusive property of e-mail. Doubtless this is a managerial strategy that has been honed by managers well used to a culture built around office memos.[2] But what is peculiar to e-mail is not only the ability to 'drop bombs' from outside the office itself (for example, by logging onto the system remotely overnight), but also the way that this can be done more or less instantaneously. This places the recipient of the 'bombshell' in a difficult position. A common reaction is to reply immediately, but many users rapid learn that this can have personally damaging implications and go on to evolve strategies of deliberately 'sitting on' e-mails they judge to be offensive or provocative:

I received an e-mail myself once which I took great offence to, I found it absolutely patronizing. What you learn with e-mail is that if you are annoyed do not fire it off straight away, sit on it for twenty-four hours and collect your thoughts. This last time I sat on this e-mail and took it home and showed my partner and he read it and said that he agreed with this person actually. (ReadyAds, New Media Manager)

Delaying a reply gives the respondent time coolly to craft an appropriate response. That is, a response that he or she will later be able to justify and that will not serve further to inflame the interaction (an accountable matter). But this practice also allows the respondent to pick out precisely what he or she finds objectionable in the previous turn, and to home in on this in his or her reply. This may lead to prolonging the debate. When each user has the ability to dwell at length on the conversation and to craft his or her reply to maximize impact, this inevitably leads to a long and often complex exchange with each party paying particular attention to his or her own subsequent accountability for potential outcomes. This, we claim, is what makes e-mail communication in both OilSite and ReadyAds a highly formal interaction.

In support of this claim, we offer the following extended example. This is a sequence of e-mails generated at OilSite. It was selected from a series of e-mail exchanges we collected. This exchange was comparatively recent at the time of the research, so we were able to check our interpretations with participants. The exchange was also cited by several participants as a 'good example' of problems in e-mail interaction—hence its relevance to the argument we are mounting in this chapter. The topic that is under debate is the claiming of 'backcharges' from a supplier ('vendor'). Because of the project-based nature of OilSite's business, schedule is always a primary concern. An oil refinery must be up and running by a prearranged date. A delay of only a single day may have tremendous financial implications for the end-user. These will be passed back

---

[2] Culture is not really the right word to use because at OilSite the organization of social relations between project groups is modelled on the same modular design deployed in building oil refineries. So relations between people are reciprocally patterned on relations between things. Which means that it is difficult to explain the use made of e-mail at OilSite by referring to an existing organizational culture, since this culture is already modelled on things. We unpick this more elsewhere (Brown and Middleton 2002).

to OilSite as financial penalties. Thus OilSite pays especial attention to identifying the source of delays to build schedules, and wherever possible it applies 'backcharges' to vendors who fail to meet their commitments, deliver substandard goods, and so on.

The exchange opens with a message from David Richards, a middle manager overseeing the backcharging process, in relation to one particular project based at the TMB yard.

Subject: TMB Backcharges
Author: David Richards at OilSite-F
Date: 12/5/99 9:24 AM

All,

It is noted from the latest report from TMB Yard that Engicom are still to submit their final VORs against MSR, JG Welden and Savanti.

When in receipt of these costings we confirm that we shall pursue claims against the respective suppliers.

However, it should be noted that this equipment was delivered to the TMB Yard between September 1998 and January 1999. The MERs for this equipment do not identify any action required by the home office. To date we have still not received any formal notification of backcharges with estimate of costs.

The Equipment Purchase Order Terms and Conditions, GCIII, Art.15. clearly states that when the Company has rectification work performed by a third party the Supplier shall immediately be informed.

According to our records this procedure has not been followed in all instances. Our ability to recover the costs of this rectification work may be restricted should Suppliers refer to this clause.

To assist with our pursuit of claims, and to counter Supplier's protests, it would be most appreciated if the TMB team could forward any correspondence to demonstrate that the above Supplier was notified of re-work and given the opportunity to remedy at its cost.

David R.

David Richards's initial enquiry into claiming backcharges against a supplier is phrased formally. It is also copied to a number of recipients across the company—hence the generic 'All' as the opening. The e-mail begins by identifying a problem ('Engicom are still to submit their final VORs'). But this problem is rapidly displaced by a second, more pressing issue, involving a possible failure to notify a supplier of 'rectification work' done by a third party on equipment it supplied to the TMB site (presumably to meet the demands of schedule). This is potentially damaging to OilSite, because the supplier may use failure of notification as a loophole to wriggle out of responsibility for paying backcharges. Richards then asks the TMB team to forward any evidence they may have that procedures were actually properly followed with which to build a case against any future protests from suppliers.

The phrasing of this e-mail is quite subtle. It appears simply to point out a problem and request information. But there are numerous features of the message that provide grounds to suspect that this is not the only possible reading. Why, for example, has Richards chosen to distribute the message widely, rather than simply e-mail the TMB team directly? Why are the regulations ('GCIII Art.15') prominently noted, when all recipients of the message are aware of exactly what the established practices and regulations are in the back-charging process? Our interpretation is that this e-mail is designed to be read as an accusation, as a kind of marker of potential blame. But Richards exercises considerable caution in not explicitly making an accusation—which would make him, as the accuser, accountable for providing formal evidence.

This interpretation is supported by the response to Richards's e-mail sent by George Wallis, head of the TMB team. Wallis clearly does read Richards's message as an accusation, which he sets about immediately rebutting.

Subject: Re: TMB Backcharges
Author: George Wallis at OilSite-K
Date: 12/05/99 11:41 AM

DAVID,

FOR THE DURATION OF THIS CONTRACT I HAVE REPEATEDLY INFORMED BOTH OMAR AND YOURSELF THAT BACKCHARGES WOULD BE DIRECTED AT VESSEL VENDORS AND YOU BOTH ASSURED ME THAT THE P.O.s WOULD NOT BE CLOSED OUT TILL YOU HAD ALL THE BACK-UP EVIDENCE TO SUBSTANTIATE AS SUCH.

I NOW FIND MYSELF SURPRISED AND ANGRY TO FIND OUT THAT IT NOW APPEARS EVIDENT THAT FROM YOUR C-C TODAY THAT IT IS CLEARLY EVIDENT THAT THE VENDORS HAVE NOT BEEN INFORMED AS I WAS LED TO BELIEVE.

I WAS TOLD FROM THE ONSTART THAT YOUR DEPARTMENT DEALT DIRECTLY WITH THE VENDORS AND THAT I HAD NO DIRECT DEALING WITH THEM.

THE M.E.R.s YOU QUOTE WERE FOR VESSEL BODY INSPECTIONS ONLY, THE BACKCHARGES RELATE MAINLY TO REMEDIAL WORKS TO PLATFORM PROBLEMS WHERE THE PLATFORMS WERE NOT SHOP FITTED AS IN ACCORDANCE WITH THE CONTRACT PRIOR TO SITE DELIVERY.

I COMPLIED AS REQUESTED AND NOW I FIND THAT YOU ARE TELLING ME THAT IN ACCORDANCE WITH THE P.O. TERMS AND CONDITIONS, GCIII, ART 15. WHERE THE VENDOR SHALL BE IMMEDIATELY INFORMED OF SUCH REMEDIAL WORKS THAT THEY WERE NOT INFORMED.

GEORGE WALLIS

Wallis provides a careful response that states an entirely different account of the recent past. In Wallis's story, he has done his utmost to keep Richards and colleagues informed of progress at the TMB yard. Indeed, he claims to have received assurances that the backcharging process would not begin at all until Richards himself gathered the relevant evidence and also that Richards would have sole responsibility for dealing with vendors (that is, suppliers). Wallis also questions which particular pieces of documentation are in question (the MERs), with the clear implication that Richards is confused in his original request. Finally, Wallis is very precise in managing the emotional tone of the message. He may be 'surprised and angry', but he still takes time to point out calmly that he is perfectly well aware of the nature of 'P.O. Terms and conditions, GCIII, Art.15'.

Why does Wallis go to such detail in his response? Might it not suffice simply to point out the error over the MERs? Why, in other words, does his response attend so formally to questions of accountability? At the time of responding, Wallis, it is safe to assume, may not necessarily know who is present in the audience to which he is addressing his response. The original message had been sent to a large distribution list, all of whom could be copied in should Wallis choose to do so. And this is, of course, what Wallis does. His personal accountability has been publicly questioned, and he must be seen to respond in an equally public way. But, because messages at OilSite are routinely forwarded around the organization, Wallis cannot at the time of writing be sure who will end up reading his reply. It must then be designed for multiple recipients. Hence the level of detail in his rebuttal of Richards's original account aims at making the reply robust enough to survive its journey around the inboxes of colleagues throughout the organization—who may be either supportive or potentially hostile.

The details then serve to work up the facticity of the response (see Potter 1996). But there are risks involved in this strategy. The inclusion of more detail offers up more points that other recipients might seek to question. His account becomes, we might say, potentially more 'falsifiable'. And this is what appears to happen next, when Arthur Brayburn, a senior manager who has overall responsibility for both Richards's and Wallis's operations, posts a contribution to the evolving e-mail thread:

Subject: Re[2]: TMB Backcharges
Author: Arthur Brayburn at OilSite-K
Date: 12/05/99 12:49

GEORGE/TONY

FURTHER TO MY CCMAILS ON THIS ISSUE THERE IS FUNDAMENTAL QUESTION WHICH NEEDS ADDRESSING IN THE FURTHER REVIEW THAT WE ARE UNDERTAKING.

THE CROSSKEYS MCR SYSTEM IS AN EXCELLENT METHOD OF IDENTIFYING AND HANDLING EXCEPTIONS WHEN AN ORDER IS SHIPPED. FURTHER MORE, BY DEFINITION, IT HAS THE VENDOR'S AGREEMENT.

IT SHOULD ALLEVIATE THE NEED FOR MER's UNLESS SOMETHING HAPPENED DURING SHIPMENT.

CAN YOU ADVISE TO WHAT EXTENT THE CORRECTIVE ACTIONS TAKEN AT THE YARD WERE COVERED BY THE MER. FOR EXAMPLE SHIPPING PLATFORMS LOOSE AS OPPOSED TO SHOP FITTED IS A GOOD MCR ITEM.

DID THE MCR IDENTIFY IT AS SUCH IN THIS CASE? IF NOT WHY NOT?

Arthur Brayburn's posting then offers comments on the MER documents. Recall that the MERs were at the heart of Richards's initial query, and in response Wallis was obliged to add more detail about their use. Brayburn opens up this issue still further, by questioning their use in the first place and pointing to the possibilities offered by an alternative system (the 'Crosskeys MCR system').

This contribution by Brayburn then serves to do two distinct things. First it lets George Wallis know that Brayburn is monitoring the debate and not simply deleting the mailings. That is, Brayburn constitutes himself as an active member of the audience in front of whom this exchange is being played out. Second, it is worth noting that the e-mail, although sent to everyone who is now listed on the e-mail header field, is addressed to Wallis personally, raising again the issue of his own personal accountability. There is an additional twist here. Along with 'George' (Wallis), the message is also addressed to 'Tony' (Johnson). Now here we need to invoke some additional local knowledge. Tony Johnson is a company trouble-shooter. He sorts out messy situations. What Brayburn does here is to signal to George Wallis that Tony is being briefed (and copied in) to the debate around the use of MERs in backcharging at the TMB yard. The implication here is that, if Wallis does not resolve matters to Brayburn's satisfaction, then Tony Johnson will be brought in to do so.

The next posting in the thread, by the initiator David Richards, appears to display an orientation to just such a scenario:

Subject: Re[3]: TMB Backcharges
Author: David Richards at OilSite-F
Date: 12/05/99 13:38

Arthur,

Following discussion with Tony Johnson your comments have been noted and I confirm on behalf of all those involved that the MCR system has been used where there was known carry-over work. In fact the MCR you were reviewing with Roger Stewart earlier this week covers one of the deliveries by Foresight to the TMB yard. George has advised us that Foresight have been to site to complete the sign-off of this record.

With particular reference to your example re: platforms shipped loose we advise that this was always the case on this project. The Engicom contract covers the receipt of steelwork loose for assembly and fitting by Engicom at the TMB yard. Therefore this is not an MCR item as it was always in the yard scope. Should there have been problems identified after receipt and start of work, I believe, this would be covered by the Site Query/Instruction Procedure.

I confirm receipt of the VOR package today 12.05.99 from the yard and we are now reviewing in accordance with your previous instruction.

David R.

Richards addresses his reply to Arthur Brayburn alone (although the message itself is copied generally). Note that Richards has not publicly replied to George Wallis's robust response to his initial query. We may suspect from this and from the offline discussions mentioned in the posting that Richards is making it clear where he now believes the power to resolve matters lies—with Brayburn and Tony Johnson and not with George Wallis. In fact, Richards does not acknowledge in any way Wallis's version of events. He deals solely with the matter of the MCR system mentioned by Brayburn. Now this can be read as a further slight aimed at George Wallis. Certainly that is how the next posting in the thread treats Richards's message:

Subject: Re: TMB Backcharges
Author: Oliver Bellings at Crosskeys
Date: 12/05/99 14:30

David,

I am very surprised by your E-mail.

An MER was not sufficient to identify shortcomings in many instances because defects were not immediately identified. For example wrong dimensions of platforms ladders etc are only discovered at fit up some time after delivery of vessel.

As far as I am aware George was very conscientious in informing London EEP, usually Omar, whenever there was a problem with a vessel.

In fact I have been very disappointed with amount recovered from suppliers when I have seen with my own eyes the defects and known them to have been reported formally and Supplier summoned to the Yard at first opportunity.

Oliver B

This posting marks a turning point in the thread. The discussion has moved on from a detailed analysis of the use of MERs to a discussion of the use of the MCR system. In the course of this discussion, George Wallis's original robust defence of how MERs are used at the TMB yard has been passed by. Now, however, Oliver Bellings of Crosskeys (which is responsible for the MCR system) makes a contribution. He staunchly defends George Wallis ('very conscientious'), thereby displaying an orientation to the slights aimed at Wallis during the thread, and criticizes Richards for bringing up the issue of MERs in the first place. Bellings concludes by shifting attention to the way Richards has managed the backcharging process from a position outside the TMB yard.

A brief summary of events. David Richards opens the thread by questioning MER practice at the TMB yard. George Wallis, TMB head, provides a robust defence in the form of an alternative account. Arthur Brayburn further questions MER practice and brings in the issue of the MCR system. He also brings in Tony Johnson. Richards now ignores Wallis and addresses himself to Brayburn and Tony Johnson. Oliver Bellings starts posting in support of Wallis and with an entirely different take on backcharging via MER or MCR.

Things now start to look messy! Recall again that this entire thread is being conducted in public. No one knows precisely who else is now monitoring the debate, watching with interest as a growing number of colleagues squabble amongst themselves. It is at this point that Arthur Brayburn asserts himself:

Subject: Re[2] TMB Backcharges
Author: Arthur Brayburn at OilSite-K
Date: 12/5/99 6:44 PM

GEORGE/DAVID

IT DOES US NO GOOD TO WASH LINEN IN PUBLIC.

I SUGGEST THE FOLLOWING:

1. GEORGE TO PREPARE A SUMMARY OF BACKCHARGES ON EACH VENDOR AND CCMAIL TO THE RECIPIENTS OF THIS CCMAIL BY CLOSE OF BUSINESS 13/5. GEORGE TO CALL TONY JOHNSON IF THIS CAN NOT BE MET.
THE SUMMARY IS TO BRIEFLY IDENTIFY THE NATURE OF THE BACKCHARGE, ITS VALUE AND DATE/REF. PREVIOUSLY ADVISED TO LONDON PROC. IF AVAILABLE.

2. TONY JOHNSON TO REVIEW WITH APPROPRIATE BUYER AND TO DISCUSS WITH ME BY CLOSE OF BUSINESS 17/5 ON HOW BEST TO PROCEED.

3. I WILL DISCUSS WITH OLIVER ON 18/5 AND SUGGEST FURTHER ACTION.

4. NO MORE MESSAGES PLEASE.

We may reasonably interpret this message to display an acute awareness on Brayburn's part that his ability to be seen as someone who can effectively manage his own people is under threat. He then shuts down the thread ('no more messages please') and issues direct instructions. Or kicks asses and takes names, as it is more commonly known.

THE 'POLITICAL USE OF E-MAIL'

The e-mail thread we have discussed above is an example of what participants at OilSite (and also at ReadyAds) described as a 'political use of e-mail' or more simply as 'ass-covering'. This use was held by participants to be distinct from 'informing' and 'relating'. It was also seen as one of the principal problems with e-mail communication in both organizations. From our analysis of the interviews and selected e-mail threads like the one above, we propose two defining features of the political use of e-mail. First of all there is a tendency to copy others into the debate. Typically these others are senior figures. Thus a common pattern is for a dispute to develop between two parties at an equivalent level within the organization—like David Richards and George Wallis—followed by the rapid copying-in (or CCing) of respective line managers. Other kinds of people who may be copied in include members of collaborating teams or projects, colleagues who attend particular kinds of relevant meetings, or people simply known to have an interest in the topic under discussion. In all cases, because of the way the e-mail systems allow for the Forwarding, Copying, and Blind Copying of messages at both OilSite and ReadyAds, it is nearly impossible for any one participant to know exactly who else will be monitoring his or her messages—or, for that matter, storing the messages,—a point to which we will return.

Debates and disagreements are then usually focused on reconstructing what has happened in the past. This is not a matter of simply collating information. Nor is this some form of communal ritual in which the past is brought to presence through a process of collective prompting and recalling. No—here versions of the past are hotly debated. Others are copied not only because they may have some interest in the matter at hand but also as witnesses who will provide further evidence for opposing versions as they are put together by participants. The audience—those people actively contributing or monitoring a thread—may be appealed to by the principal disputants as either potential allies or else as a baying crowd before whom the dispute will be fought to the bitter end. One OilSite senior manager offered us this understanding of the practice: 'If someone in the reporting line or one of my guys has got a dialogue going he will copy me with it. Some of that is appropriate, there is an issue or a dispute or something to resolve that I might not know about and I will just read it and see that it has been completed. You do get the opportunity to stick your oar in. I do get copied a lot of stuff, but I just don't need it' (OilSite, Manager Executive Development).

The manager here neatly summarizes the two aspects of copying in. On occasion it is useful; it delivers information to him that he might not otherwise acquire. It also provides an opportunity to see how his people cope with the kinds of routine skirmishes that go on between departments and projects. He may even seize the opportunity to make a few points of his own in the course of the debate. But the cost is that of a massive increase in the amount of e-mail traffic coming in his direction. Other managers offered a more cynical view:

Yes, yes it is also a terrible medium to waste people's time [laughter] because you will not only remember the little gemstones but you are going to get a load of crap in there too. I mean anyone who says any different is a liar [laughter]. I am afraid that the e-mail is the worst junk mail in the world ever, source of junk mail and always will be and you have got to take the long view that if you are going to throw it out there then you have got to be prepared to tolerate everyone's feedback. And some feedback is not as enlightening as others [laughter]. (ReadyAds, Managing Director)

The 'little gemstones' are the useful nuggets of information that can be acquired in the course of debate. For example, George Wallis's description of the MER practice at the TMB yard offered both Arthur Brayburn and David Richards further ammunition for their own separate evolving arguments about the MCR system. But uncovering such 'gemstones' requires continual vigilance. One has to read an awful lot of e-mails. Which leads us to the second aspect of the political use of e-mail—deliberate attempts to prolong a debate for as long as possible. This typically occurs when an e-mail is sent between a series of parties, all of whom automatically copy all of the preceding messages into the body of their current message. The result is a message that is several screen lengths or many pages long. But worse still is the kind of practice described in the following excerpt:

you get the thing where they are trying to insert comments on text that has already been written and of course they are using different colours and then someone has gone in and used capitals and the whole thing then becomes a bit of shambles. Then someone prints it out and you have no clue what the history is and what has been going on in this message and that does happen. (OilSite, Manager Project Definition)

Here participants edit all or some of the previous messages in a thread, resulting in a mélange of text where it is difficult to work out who said what to whom in whichever order. Contrast this with the standard model of face-to-face conversation, where the whole interaction can be seen to unfold its own form of order on a turn-by-turn basis, with a mutual sequential orientation being displayed by participants. Here previous turns in an e-mail thread are chopped up and reformulated directly. Participants may orient to what was said weeks or even months ago as much as they do to more recent turns.

Now discursive studies of how people jointly recall the past have described at length the ways in which the relevancy of particular details is worked up and argued over by conversational partners (see Buchanan and Middleton 1995; Middleton 1997). In face-to-face interaction this is achieved by a skilled management of talk on a turn-by-turn basis. But with the kind of e-mail interaction described above, simply working out what words constitute the current and preceding turns can be hard enough. Add to this the difficulty of reconstructing a sequentially accurate record of the interaction due to the cut-and-paste editing performed on the message(s) that are being batted back and forth, and the work of recollecting on e-mail appears substantially different. Indeed it might be more fitting to understand it as an ongoing 'hermeneutics of suspicion', where each e-mail is treated as a potentially unreliable text to be scrutinized for inconsistencies, errors, and subtexts.

For example, in ReadyAds, an acrimonious dispute between a site manager and the IT director of another office flared up around the issue of purchasing a new piece of computer hardware (a server). The dispute was initially conducted on e-mail, producing a lengthy document incorporating numerous turns from both participants. At an apt moment in the dispute, one of the participants copied in the ReadyAds CEO. However, the message copied to the CEO was an edited and truncated copy of the exchange, which constituted both a highly partial version of the dispute and of the recent events under debate. Interestingly enough, the matter was eventually settled at a face-to-face meeting, where the offended party flourished a hard copy full transcript of the exchange, which then resulted in a settlement of the matter.

Some points are worth noting. First, the idea that e-mail can replace face-to-face meetings is erroneous. The previous and many other examples we were offered suggest that not only are roughly the same amount of face-to-face meetings held in both organizations, but also that meetings are now held precisely to deal with problems that emerge in e-mail discussions. Second, that, where disputes do occur, producing complete hard copy transcripts or other forms of documentary evidence appears to be the way of settling matters, notably when the dispute occurs between colleagues at the same level of seniority. This then creates a need to be continuously maintaining ongoing archives of such documents. Finally, we can see how the practice of extending debates as long as possible reproduces itself. The longer the debate runs, the more chance there is of revealing inconsistencies or, alternatively, 'little gems' to be stored away for future use. We can sum this up with the mundane observation that, in both organizations, users experience e-mail not as an informal system of messaging, a simple replacement for the telephone, but as a highly formal space of inter-action where issues of personal accountability are constant and pressing. One's standing in the organization can be literally at stake in such debates.

How then do users manage to do anything when they are so caught up in this collective hermeneutics of suspicion? We should, of course, note that a great deal of e-mail traffic is just the kind of innocuous trading of information imagined by system designers. And, despite the often high stakes involved in the political use of the medium, users do evolve their own procedures for man-aging particularly difficult interactions. Sending short standard responses that are designed to curtail debate is a widespread strategy. For example: 'Thanks for your input', 'Let's call a meeting about this', or simply 'Phone me now'. Just as in the past, users of memos evolved ways of working that took this written technology into account, so contemporary users of e-mail find methods for managing the potential pitfalls and risks to their own personal accountability that it poses. We will now address the implications of the hermeneutics of suspicion around e-mail for a particular group of users.

DISCONNECTION AND SELF-EXCLUSION

We began this chapter by referring to Derrida's analysis of archival practices as having the twin aspects of 'commandment' and 'commencement'. Derrida's concern is with how this archival logic finds its way into our understanding of memory, notably the Freudian model of the unconscious. Central to this logic is the exchange and storing of handwritten documents, which have a claim to be the original material destined for conversion into archival stock. Indeed he conjectures at one point that: 'in the past, psychoanalysis would not have been what it was...if E-mail, for example, had existed. And in the future it will no longer be what Freud and so many psychoanalysts have anticipated, from the moment E-mail, for example became possible' (Derrida 1997: 17).

The thrust of Derrida's argument is that our understanding of memory, which is dominated by psychoanalytic notions of selective forgetting, repression, and sudden recall—witness, for example, the debates around false memory— remains structured by an ancient archival logic. We see this in Proust (and hence the cognitive psychologists who seek to reclaim him). Think of the role played in *À la recherche du temps perdu* by chance encounters, missing or frag-mentary messages, and handwritten notes. These materials need to be archived because they are so fragile, so prone to corruption or casual destruction. Once archived, only a trusted few are authorized with the power to interpret what they say and thence to legislate on this basis.

It is this ancient archival logic that, Derrida claims, is being threatened by technologies such as e-mail.[3] Through its rapid dissemination, e-mail in effect opens up the archive by making the exchange and storing of messages everyone's business. And, as we have tried to show through our analysis of e-mail use at OilSite and ReadyAds all e-mail users may be potentially enrolled as interpreters and legislators of stored e-mail materials, either through practices of copying-in or as direct participants in extended e-mail debates. If e-mail changes how people work, it does so in part by changing the relationship users have to the archiving of the past. How so? One immediate instance is the way in which e-mail allows users to build up their own personal archives:

I am probably the most hated in IT because my e-mail, my e-mail file is bigger than probably the rest of the company [Laughter]. I wish I was joking it is huge. I never delete anything. I get regularly erm nice messages from [IT manager] saying can you please take your file to less than ten gigabytes [laughter]. I will show you I mean, if I show you my e-mail trees erm there is my basic list of e-mail folders (laughter) okay, and then I can show you each element just for the purpose of the tape recorder erm Geoffrey is now looking at a tree which is about erm shall we say you can see (laughter) we are looking at a tree of e-mails of maybe fifty folders deep. (ReadyAds, Managing Director)

This may appear to be an exceptional case. Ten gigabytes worth of stored messages sounds implausible. But even one gigabyte is still around 10,000 or so e-mails. An awful lot of archived material. We found that the practice of storing this number of e-mails was fairly widespread in both organizations (see Brown *et al.* 2001). Why so? Because archiving materials is demanded by what we have been calling the hermeneutics of suspicion and our participants call 'ass covering'. Participation in the formal space constituted by e-mail demands that users constantly maintain their own personal archives of everything they send and much of what they receive (either as direct recipients or when copied in).

This demand is termed 'archive drive' by Derrida. This is the press towards the storing-up of the past, or consignation to the archive. Consignation—the process through which things are made fit for storage—involves a form of standardization. Or, as Derrida puts it, a form of repetition. Each piece of material must be drawn within the archive in the same way. It is assigned a place in an identical fashion to the last piece and the coming piece. Repetition, or standardization, is then an expression of archive drive. But, as Derrida notes, in classical Freudian theory, repetition is also the hallmark of another drive. Repetition is the deadening return of the same. It is the annulment of creativity, of difference, of life itself. Repetition is then also an expression of the death drive.

[3] 'Electronic mail today . . . is on the way to transforming the entire public and private space of humanity, and first of all the limit between the private, the secret (private or public), and the public or the phenomenal. It is not only a technique, in the ordinary sense of the term: at an unprecedented rhythm, in quasi-instantaneous fashion, this instrumental possibility of production, of printing, of conservation and of destruction of the archive must inevitably be accompanied by juridical and thus political transformations' (Derrida 1997: 17).

So the neat paradox Derrida finds at the heart of archival logic is this tension between standardization and mind-numbing repetition. Or, more simply, between preservation and destruction, for what repetition also expresses is the desire simply to have done with the archive altogether, to escape from its endless proliferation and incorporation of all new materials. This is what Derrida calls 'archive fever'. One seeks to break free of the past by destroying its traces, by razing the archive to the ground. That which gives rise to the desire to store things up also creates the opposing desire to destroy whatever is stored.

Again, with necessary changes, we see this tension in both OilSite and ReadyAds. Users are caught up in the project of creating and maintaining archives of e-mail messages in order to cope with the demands of participating in a formal space of communication. But they are also, in a sense, shackled to their archives. Their latitude for future action, the kinds of moves they can see themselves making, are necessarily tied to the kinds of records they have in their e-mail archives (and that they know exist in other people's e-mail archives). George Wallis, for example, found himself tied into the project of maintaining MER documentation once his initial posting on the topic became disseminated. He could not readily free himself from his initial e-mail.

This leads us to what we consider to be the central question: how can anything new get done when e-mail makes the past so readily available? Here is Derrida's answer (1997: 11): 'There is no archive without a place of consignation, without a technique of repetition, and without a certain exteriority. No archive without outside.' Archives require a place where materials can be consigned. But they also require a technique of repetition, of standardization. This technique sits alongside the archive, it is to a degree separate from it. One might, for example, consider reordering the archive using an entirely different set of standards. But there is also another space that is outside both the archive and its standards. This 'certain exteriority' remains outside. It never really enters into the archive. For Derrida, archival logic is founded on this relation to an outside that cannot ever be entirely incorporated. It is this outside that holds the promise of something new, something that is not and will not be part of the archive, but that nevertheless stands in relation to it.

That is a difficult idea to catch hold of. So here is our version of the same answer. At OilSite we were struck by the way in which very senior executives make use of e-mail. Or rather by the way in which they seem to avoid e-mail as far as possible. The CEO of OilSite, for example, does not respond to e-mail messages. He does not do business like that. He is not available for e-mail exchanges. He is, in effect, disconnected from the system. That is an interesting phenomenon. We tend in general to be more concerned when the less powerful, the socially excluded, are disconnected from electronic communication (see Liff *et al.*, this volume, McGrail, this volume). But there is another kind of disconnection going on involving the self-exclusion of the very powerful—that is, those managers in both OilSite and ReadyAds who can take the opportunity to exit from the formal space of e-mail communication. In so doing they ensure that what they have to say can no longer find its way directly into the manifold e-mail archives that are mushrooming around them. They free themselves from the past by leaving nothing behind to be generally archived.

Take the following long extract from an interview with a senior figure at OilSite. The topic under discussion is the meetings held by the executive Operations Management Group (OMG):

INTERVIEWER. The impression that we seem to be getting is that a lot of the strategy type meetings are being done very informally, since there are not a huge lot of formal minutes being taken at the meetings?

OILSITE MANAGER EXECUTIVE DEVELOPMENT. The meetings I go to, very rarely are they minuted, very rarely. And that is OK, to me it would not be appropriate. We had one meeting a few days ago where we did record it because it was a project action and I actually just sent around that meeting note today formally, but that is quite unusual actually for myself. But in the job that I am doing now it does not come up.

I. We have got the picture especially with the OMG, perhaps they meet ten times a week, but minutes are never kept?

M. That is an internal, that is a fairly informal grouping. It is informal but it is basically four operations managers, you have to bear in mind. But no there are never... no secretaries there. There are four or five managers working together on issues around the table progressing some issues. But no, we never record minutes. Absolutely unnecessary. It is not that sort of a meeting and that is typical of the meetings that go on. There are very few internal meetings of projects that get recorded formally, in my opinion.

I. It is intriguing, as that is entirely where the big decisions are made—in meetings— therefore you would record them in the minutes? It seems that, you are OMG and must be making decisions all the time though, and they are not recorded?

M. Yes. You know you are basically colleagues together. There is not any, you do not want to leave that meeting having to defend what you have decided at the meeting against others. If there was something that came up at OMG which was divisive, there was not an agreement or there was something like that, it would go to another level. I have never been to one of those meetings. It tends to be a consensus pretty well.

What emerges in the course of the extract is that very senior meetings, the places where big decisions are made, are rarely minuted. This is felt to be 'absolutely unnecessary'. The reasons for this, as offered by this particular manager, is that at that level 'you are basically colleagues together'. Which is to say that matters of routine accountability are handled very differently. One is not expected to have to mobilize extensive evidence to defend one's position. As such there is no need for the present to be continually consigned to the archive through a supplementary mechanism in the form of minutes. The joint recall of these 'colleagues together' suffices.

What we are presented with here is the space prior to the place of archiving, the space from which archiving is itself commanded, but which stands outside the archive. This is a space that is not bound by the usual rules of audit. Managers here keep no formal records, save a few notes in their own personal workbooks that are never entered into the organization's wider archives. Since their own past is not captured in any archive maintained by the organization, senior managers are able to claim that these archives are merely supplementary, that they do not capture the real essence of the business. That they fail to express the guiding vision or project of the organization. But—and this is crucial—such a claim can be launched only if managers simultaneously have complete access to the organization's archives. Because it is only through access to such archives that these managers are able to make their own moves in the organization. Thus these senior managers never entirely escape from the e-mail archives. They are continually being dragged back by way of CC'd and Forwarded messages. And by their own sense of the archive drive that impels users to store up the past.

CONCLUSION

Our central argument in this chapter is that e-mail is experienced by users in the two organizations we have studied as a formal space of communication, one where personal accountability is constantly at issue. One of the principal features of this space is what our participants called 'the political use of e-mail', which involves widespread copying in, prolonging debate and storing of messages. We suggested, drawing on Derrida, that this practice needs to be understood as a transformation in the relationship of users to archives and archival logic. Nevertheless, this same logic allows us to understand why it should be that certain kinds of users choose to exclude themselves from e-mail communication (Brown and Lightfoot 1998). Disconnection—another theme running through the volume—is what now appears to us to be the central issue. We no longer need to explain why organizational users adopt e-mail—they are simply impelled to do so, as we have described at length—but rather how and why they are able to give it up.

13

Inside the Bubble: Communion, Cognition, and Deep Play at the Intersection of Wall Street and Cyberspace

Melvin Pollner

INTRODUCTION

I had heard of neither the Iomega Corporation nor the Motley Fool until dinner with a friend in the late autumn of 1995. My friend told me that his life had changed after purchasing shares of Iomega Corporation whose (then) new product was a portable computer storage device, the Zip Drive. Surprised by the amount of money he had invested earlier in the year, he was even more surprised when the shares soared in value. His new wealth, he continued, had affected every aspect of his life: his emotions, thoughts, and even his dreams were now different. If I was interested, he suggested, I ought to visit the Motley Fool (www.Fool.com), an online personal finance and investment site then based at America Online (AOL). Aiming to 'educate, amuse and enrich' individual investors, the Motley Fool hosted message boards devoted to discussing particular stocks, one of which was Iomega. My friend's enthusiasm and success amplified the cultural clamour that adults not participating in the 'incredible bull market' and the 'new economy' were financially irresponsible or naive and, most assuredly, losers. Moreover, as we ate, I tasted the truth of Kindleberger's adage (1989: 19) that 'There is nothing so disturbing to one's well-being and judgement as to see a friend get rich.' Thus motivated, I subscribed to AOL, clicked to the Motley Fool, and then to the Iomega message board.

The Motley Fool proved to be a fount of engagingly written and seemingly savvy financial information and advice—at least to this novice. The message board discussions of Iomega—the company, the stock, and the Zip drive—were often lively and informative. On occasion, the forum became more of an arena in which posters 'long' or 'bullish' on IOMG—Iomega's ticker symbol at the time—contended in varying degrees of civility with 'shorts' that argued that the stock was overvalued. Interest in the message board was not limited to posters and investors. *The Wall Street Journal* (Fleetwood 1996), *Time Magazine* (Abbey 1996). *Fortune* magazine (Nocera 1996), financial TV networks, and major market gurus commented on Iomega stock, the message board, and the increasing popularity of The Motley Fool. According to one recurrent refrain, the rise of Iomega stock was due to the 'hype' on the board: the 'Iomegans,' as posters were dubbed by *Fortune* magazine (Nocera 1996) had a 'religious fervour' not unlike a 'cult.' Regarded as the desperate attacks of an outflanked Wall Street establishment or the machinations of investors 'shorting' the stock and who stood to gain if the price fell, offending commentators were sometimes inundated with vociferous on- and offline criticism.[1]

The net effect, so to speak, of my exposure to the Iomegans was to purchase shares in the Iomega Corporation. In short order, I found myself a newby, lurker, and participant in the Iomegan village. I was making both money and ethnographic observations as Iomega and the Iomegans rapidly ascended a financial Everest. The value of a single share of Iomega bought for $1.17 in April 1995 was worth $56 (adjusted for splits) on 23 May 1996, outperforming all the stocks on any of the major exchanges. Alas, 'Do you know how to make a small fortune on Wall Street?' goes the question: 'Start with a big one', goes the retort. Although I bought shares before Iomega stock began one of its dramatic ascents, I subsequently bought additional shares on the morning of 22 May 1996, a day before Iomega was to reach its all-time high—and begin its precipitous decline. I was so confident of Iomega's bright future that at the very point when the clarity of hindsight shows that I should have sold not only did I buy additional shares but I encouraged my teenage son to make his first investment by purchasing Iomega stock. Thus, I went up and down—financially and emotionally—with the rise and fall of Iomega and recruited my son for the downward leg of the journey.

I use my experiences among the Iomegans to three ends. First, I suggest that the economic, cultural, interactional, and reflexive features of sites at the intersection of investment and the internet (such as the Iomega board) make them sociologically interesting. Second, I offer reflections on how this newby—me—came to make what might be characterized in the words of the US Federal Reserve Board chairman Alan Greenspan as an 'irrationally exuberant' investment. My enthusiasm, I will suggest, partly reflected the communal, cognitive, and emotional attractions of the Iomegan village. The village offered participation in an 'imagined' community (Anderson 1983), a plausible if not persuasive version of the prospects of the Zip drive and Iomega stock, and the emotional

---

[1] Iomega was one of the most heavily shorted stocks in the market.

charge of vanquishing what was characterized on the Motley Fool as the moribund, manipulative institutions of Wall Street. The subsequent (mid-2001) dramatic decline of the entire stock market suggests that my experiences may reflect and prefigure processes that subsequently unfolded on a grander scale (Schiller 2000). Third, I suggest that, if the investment/internet (I/I) intersection is a new sociological domain, new concepts may be required for its analysis. Some venerable analytic concepts—say, 'self-fulfilling prophecy'—are not significantly different from those that I/I participants use to make both sense and cents. Thus, the discourse at the I/I intersection diminishes or 'deflates' the analytic purchase and power of sociological concepts that might otherwise be used to analyse that discourse. To the extent analysis relies on or overlaps the concepts already used by participants in I/I, sociological analysis is more likely to elicit a knowing 'uh huh' than an epiphanal 'ah hah.'

THE INTERNET/INVESTMENT INTERSECTION

The market and the internet intersect in many ways. Until the market downturn that began in the year 2000, the high-technology corporations using and servicing the internet were the darlings of investors: Amazon, Cisco, AOL and eBay are among the most familiar corporate names in the USA. Developments on the internet have facilitated investment in the market. Online trading is often easier and cheaper than trading through 'brick-and-mortar' brokers and online sites and services make available financial information once the privy of wealthy or professional investors. Finally, the internet enables individual investors to interact with one another—as they do at the Iomega board at the Motley Fool (and other financial/investment sites such as Silicon Valley and Raging Bull).

The I/I intersection is of sociological interest in several respects. First, stock forums are consequential nodes in the nexus of corporate–market–consumer relationships. One measure of their potency is the relative ease and impact of stock fraud. Misinformation is hardly new to the market (Lejeune 1984), but the I/I intersection facilitates its dissemination and amplifies its effects. A Houston day trader, for example, was arrested and charged with posting a fake earnings warning for Lucent Technologies Inc. on a Yahoo internet message board, reportedly driving Lucent stock down 3.6 per cent and reducing the company's market value by $7 billion (*New York Times*, 31 May 2000). In response, corporations monitor stock boards and chat rooms to control 'cybersmearing'— the posting of unfavourable, inappropriate, or erroneous information and have pursued legal action to identify, restrain, and even jail posters. Catering to corporate concern is itself a cyberspace cottage industry. Netcurrents (www. netcurrents. com), a company that advertises itself as the 'premier internet intelligence agency', for example, offers to manage the 'cyberperception' of corporations by monitoring 50,000 message boards and chatrooms for damaging information.

Second, the forums at the I/I intersection are conduits through which what MacFarlane (1987: p. xvi) calls the 'cultural system of capitalism' flows into the 'mentality, morality and emotional structure' of everyday life. As perhaps never before, the culture of the market suffuses the everyday lives of the American public. A small but telling illustration of the penetration of market discourse into everyday life, observed by David Gardner (1997), occurred when a sportscaster on a major TV network likened a champion collegiate basketball team to a mutual fund to a national audience: 'If they were a mutual fund, they'd be a balanced income fund with a high margin of safety.' In contrast to the traditional use of sports to describe the opaque financial world, the commentator felt sufficiently sure of his audience's familiarity with the market to illuminate the world of sports through the discourse of the financial world. Market culture and discourse flow into everyday life through the media, of course, but also through the capillaries radiating from the I/I intersection (cf. Frank 2000).

Third, I/I sites are windows onto an aspect of the social processes of investing. The situated dynamics of everyday investment decisions have received relatively little attention from sociologists (Adler and Adler 1984). As Boden (1990) notes, however, movements of the market are mediated, if not constituted, by situated interactions. Focusing on professional and institutional investors, she observes that, when

the New York Stock Exchange dives precipitously in a single trading day, it is to the traders on the floor, the analysts at their computers, the account executives at their phones, and the institutional buyers in fern-filled offices across the country that we look. It is their actions, impressions, conversations, rumours and reactions that constituted so-called Black Monday in October 1987.   (Boden 1990: 257)

We must now include ordinary investors at their computers incited to investment by the very sites whose public accessibility provide a window onto the interactions through which investment decisions are made.[2]

Fourth, the I/I intersection includes novel forms of cyberspace life. To be sure, many of the processes and practices found on forums devoted to non-financial matters are found at I/I (Phillips 1996). As Giddens (1991) has suggested, however, the stock market is perhaps the most reflexive institutional domain in all high modernity. The potential reflexive relation of stock talk and stock prices endows talk about the prospects of a stock with special significance: what posters say about the price of a stock is arguably capable of affecting the price of the stock.

The reflexivity is illustrated by an episode during the course of my involvement with the board. With one exception, my 'cyberethnography' of the

[2] A number of studies focus on the context and practices of institutional brokers, market traders, and financial managers: C. W. Smith (1981), Abolafia (1996), Knorr-Cetina and Bruegger (2000).

Iomegans did not amount to much more than the activities of an interested newby. I read posts, occasionally communicated on and offline with other participants, and attended an annual stockholders' meeting of the Iomega Corporation in Salt Lake City also attended by a contingent of 'Fools'. At the Iomega stockholders' meeting, however, I distributed a questionnaire to other 'Fools' in attendance. Along with queries regarding demographics and online activities, respondents were asked to share their prediction of the 'next IOMG'—that is, to identify a stock likely to have a similarly glorious future. The summary of the results, which I e-mailed to respondents, identified Amati Communications (which merged subsequently with Texas Instruments) as the most frequently nominated prospect. In the afternoon of the same day, the price of Amati (whose ticker symbol was AMTX) stock spiked upwards. At least one poster conjectured that the sudden increase was due to the dissemination of the results of the survey that Amati was the 'next Iomega:'

Here's my theory. Around 2 pm somebody leaked to the Wise MPollner's post on the results of the Fool survey taken in Salt Lake City. On the question 'Care to share your prediction of the next Iomega?', AMTX got 9 votes blowing away all others, next highest was 2 votes ... Wes ; >)

For some, beliefs about the prices of a stock may comprise noise that deflects attention from the fundamentals of the company, but for others they present opportunities to be used or exploited (e.g. Soros 1994, 1998). At the very least, participants' awareness that information 'about' the price of a stock can affect the price of the stock introduces practices and concerns not found on forums whose topics are less reflexively tied to the talk about them as, say, chat about baseball batting averages.[3]

THE IOMEGAN VILLAGE: COMMUNITY, COGNITION, AND DEEP PLAY

The Motley Fool is one of the oldest and best-known financial and investment sites at the I/I intersection. In 1993, Tom and David Gardner, brothers then in their early 20s, published an investment newsletter for some forty-eight subscribers, mainly family friends. The Gardners began to respond to investors' questions on an online message board. By February 1994, these discussions were so popular that AOL contracted the brothers to host and develop the Motley Fool site in AOL's personal finance area (Gardner and Gardner 1996). The site grew to include investment information, services, and message boards discussing a wide range of market and investment matters and individual

---

[3] Fox and Roberts (1999) consider the heightened reflexivity of ethnography in cyberspace communities.

stocks. At the time of my involvement, some 125 unpaid volunteers—whose screen names were prefaced with the letters 'MF'—had responsibility for housekeeping tasks and monitoring boards for terms of service violations.[4] The volunteers also participated in online discussions.

The Gardners chose the name 'the Motley Fool' to highlight the boldness of the medieval fools who spoke the truth to the king. In the slightly inversionary and occasionally carnivalesque world of the Motley Fool—the Gardner brothers wore jester's caps in their public appearances—participants refer to themselves as 'Fools' and the tenets of the Motley Fool as 'Foolishness'. Foolishness—with a capital F—is explicitly contrasted with the practices and 'conventional wisdom' of institutional financial managers, brokerages, and allied media—the 'Wise of Wall Street.' The Wise, according to Foolishness, are characteristically concerned with commissions, churning accounts, and short-term profits and are not held accountable for their advice and recommendations. Online interactivity, however, offered an unprecedented tool for sharing and evaluating information, increasing accountability and empowering the ordinary investor. One of David Gardner's posts to the Iomega board lauds the power of online and its implications for the Wise:

The online medium is the champion of the individual investor, and a threat to the established apparatchiks of 'information dissembly', namely the Wall Street analysts and brokers who enjoy access to information that you and I have heretofore been restricted from. (The previous comment by a fellow Fool about the advantages the establishment has—Peter Lynch gaining access to top company officers and then sharing it all with Fidelity fund managers—is right on the money.) What has happened in this folder is that a bunch of small-time individual investors (among which I proudly number myself) has energetically and somewhat zealously cobbled together information from a multitude of sources. What has resulted is a beautiful patchwork quilt of cooperative education (and profit to boot) which also just happens to be the Ultimate Information Machine with regard to Iomega stock specifically, and Iomega Corp. to a lesser extent [parentheses in original].

The Motley Fool investment strategy (since modified) encouraged investors to consider a progressively more sophisticated mix of investment strategies. Investors were encouraged to develop a portfolio that included Vanguard's S&P 500 Index Fund (instead of mutual funds); the then popular 'Dogs of the Dow' (the lowest priced of the highest yielding stocks on the Dow); and small-cap companies selected in accord with Foolish criteria, which included high-profit margins, a low 'Fool Ratio' (the price-earnings multiple divided by anticipated growth in earnings per share), and leadership in their industry or market sector. More generally, investors were encouraged to adopt a long-term perspective, invest in industries, companies, and products they 'know', and to 'do your own research.' They were invited to consider 'shorting' stocks and cautioned against day-trading and purchasing on margin (Gardner and Gardner 1996).

---

[4] The Motley Fool subsequently replaced volunteers with paid employees and later introduced an annual fee for access to the previously free discussion boards.

Iomega—the message board, company, and stock—played a special role in the early days of the Motley Fool (Fischer 1996). Several posts to the Iomega message board were cited by the Gardner brothers as embodying the spirit and potential of investors coming together online. In one post, an engineer described what he observed on a fifteen-minute tour of the Iomega factory. He apparently did it so well that company management accused him—a complete outsider— of providing inside information (Gardner and Gardner 1996: 8). Another poster asked his parents who lived in the area to look at the company's plant in Roy, Utah. They reported that the employee parking lot had been full on a Sunday— an indication that the factory was operating to capacity (Gardner and Gardner 1996: 8).[5] Inspired by the discussion on the Iomega message board, the Gardners purchased shares of Iomega for one of their model investment portfolios. The subsequent rise in Iomega's value (as well as that of AOL in which the Motley Fool had also invested) contributed substantially to the portfolio's unrivalled success in 'beating the market'.[6]

The diversity of issues considered on the Iomega message board defies easy cataloguing, but a significant proportion involved one or another aspect of Iomega, the stock, the corporation, or its products. Posts included detailed analyses and arguments regarding the Zip drive, Iomega management, financial and business plans, personal experiences with the Zip, and analyses of competitors and their products. One popular type of contribution was a 'channel check', which reported on the sales of Iomega's Zip and Jaz (which had greater storage capacity) drives at various outlets.

Results of visiting four retailers in Durham NC this week, next to Research TrianglePark where many techies reside and work, plus several major universities. Office Max. Get three to four zips at a time, they sell quickly, currently out of stock. Jaz drive unseen as yet. Best Buy. Asked about HP computer with Zip. Salesperson checked their order list, didn't find it anywhere. He didn't seem overly impressed by IO products. 'It's a nice add on device.' Jaz drive hasn't arrived there either.

Posters were concerned about major ongoing or impending events: a withdrawn secondary offering of shares; estimates of future earnings; the inclusion of Zip drives as an option by one or another computer manufacturer; comments about Iomega on major financial networks; computer shows where Iomega products were displayed; a rumoured SEC investigation of the Motley Fool. Interspersed among the putatively on-topic posts were innumerable subsidiary issues

[5] The Iomega message board at the Motley Fool evolved into one of the most active sites on AOL. The average number of daily posts during the period I describe was about 130, though the number soared as high as 600 posts and 100 posters in a single day.

[6] Following the installation of Kim Edwards as CEO in 1994, the Iomega Corporation developed several new products, of which the most successful was the Zip drive (which stored 100 MBs of memory on a single magnetic disk—some seventy times the capacity of a standard 3.5" floppy). The company also developed the Jaz drive, which (then) stored a gigabyte on a single removable cartridge. These products received exceptionally strong reviews in trade and popular journals, and revenues increased from $141 million to over $1 billion within two years.

and topics, which were regarded by some as serious and costly div€
Posters complained of what they characterized as the increasing am
'garbage,' 'trivia,' or 'drivel and dreck' that had to be scrolled past to get t
information and discussion. Some declared that they would no longer read posts
or warned that truly knowledgeable contributors would refrain from posting
unless there was discipline regarding the quality and focus of posts (and, in fact,
some posters organized an e-mail group to circumvent what was felt to be an
increasingly less informative board).

I entered—or, more appropriately, lurked about—the Iomegan cybervillage
and went native. I put my money where my mouse was: I bought shares at a low
price, but I also bought shares at virtually the highest price Iomega stock ever
attained. Within a short period of time, I had been transformed from an utter
novice to a novice who put his—and eventually his child's—money on the line.
As I reflect back—and as I sensed over the course of my involvement—my
commitment and confidence were buttressed by the communal, cognitive, and
emotional embrace of the Iomega village.

Communion

The exchanges on the Iomega message board offered the experience of a
community. More appropriately, posts provided the resources for 'imagining' a
community. As Anderson (1983) notes, groups in which members are not in
continuous face-to-face contact require acts of imagination to cultivate the
sense of we-ness. Nationhood must be 'imagined because the members of even
the smallest nation will never know most of their fellow-members, meet them
or hear them, yet in the minds of each lives the image of their communion. In
fact, all communities larger than primordial villages of face-to-face contact
(and perhaps even these) are imagined' (Anderson 1983: 6). In the real world,
the imagination of community is stimulated by maps, museums, and memor-
ials. In cyberspace, the resources for imagining community are writing/reading
practices that presuppose and imply a community. Conceiving the construction of community as an inscribed achievement entails attending to how direct
and indirect references to the features of a community—putatively shared
history, common values, operative norms, and the like—potentially provide a
sense of commonality and connectedness.

'Community' was inscribed through direct references to the board as comprising a community. The Gardners (Gardner and Gardner 1996: 31) themselves
framed discussions in exactly those terms: 'They are investors—bulls and

---

[7] Several of Louis Corrigan's useful commentaries (1996) on Iomega in 'The Rogue', an
occasional feature at the Motley Fool, are accessible at the the Motley Fool archives
(www.Fool.com).

bears—who become a sort of community unto themselves, with distinct personalities, shared interests, and a common history based on news developments and price fluctuations of [e.g.] Apple and its stock.' But the elements contributing to the sense of community were also inscriptively insinuated into the fabric of exchanges. Posters inscribed 'history' into the developing text of the Iomega board, for example, by suggestions that newbies consult the archives of prior postings for issues previously considered. In response to a newby's concern about CDR read/write devices as a competitive alternative to the Zip drive, one poster writes: 'We have been over and over and over this time and time and time again... Please read the old folders... it has all been hashed out over and over and over again and again and again... BTW, welcome to the Iomega world.'

The sense of community was further cultivated in exchanges that implied that the board was frequented by commonly known personalities. Particular contributors to the board were referenced in ways implying not only sufficient familiarity to identify their characteristic perspectives but suggesting that such characterizations were collectively appreciated and recognized. On the one hand, posts might explicitly reference MF Chiros as one of the most informed and informative contributors; Cynical Guy as relentlessly bullish: DIOMEGA as an ardent short; Huibs as the board humourist. On the other hand, oblique references might be embedded in the construction of a message implying a shared understanding of why they were referred to. The following post, for example, presupposes and reaffirms consensual appreciation of Huib's penchant for puns through an allusion that Huibs would recognize the sexual innuendo of 'get longer'.

Since I am long and want to get longer (no pun intended, Huibs), I would welcome the opportunity to get in at yet lower prices. I think this is possible considering that option expiration time is still looming (I guess the lowest price might be close to 31 if we do go lower). So at least temporarily I'll say 'go shorts!'.

Similarly, putatively shared values were displayed (if not constituted) in the (w)rites and reads in which the principles and policies were expressed, challenged, or implied. One straightforward instance of an assertion of the values of the Iomega board occurred in an especially turbulent context. Sometimes cast as part of the conspiracy of the Wise to undermine Iomega (and even the Motley Fool), media commentators were often subject to a barrage of phone calls, e-mails, and faxes. Some communications apparently moved beyond edification to vilification and intimidation. At one point Dan Dorfman, a TV and print financial commentator whose critical comments were believed by some to be on behalf of 'shorts', suffered a heart attack. A number of Iomegans expressed their pleasure in on- and offline communications. In this context, MF Chiros exhorted others to refrain from such actions and explicitly called for a return to the 'real subject of the board':

And, I will state publicly that whatever Dorfman did, he deserves our best wishes while he recovers from his heart-attack. We are talking about his life here.

Now, I was on the forefront of fighting off the short campaigns. I put more hours posting against false information harder than anyone here. Now, we need to drop the 'siege mentality'. The stock is now in the institutional hands. The story phase of this stock is beginning to turn into real performance stage. The bottom line performance will determine the stock's future now.

We need to restore respect and dignity to this board. To all those who have benefited from my analysis, I call on you to ignore the shorts and side issues. Yesterday and today's posts concerning this issue is my first post of such nature. Please. Let's get back to solid research. Otherwise, this is just another chat board. Why spend any time or energy just chatting and chest-thumping???

The inscribed resources for imaging community are also found in expressions of obligations and responsibilities. Ventura Bay, a well-known sceptic and reputed short, posted information about low sales of Zip drives in a major computer outlet in his neighborhood. LazC, however, reported that he had checked the same store and found that sales of Zip drives were brisk. LazC declared that Ventura Bay's report was a 'bold-faced lie' and that his claims should henceforth be ignored. Capnwilly commended LazC for his good work but cautioned against simply ignoring 'the Ventura Bays', because other readers could be misled:

It would be nice if we could ignore the Ventura Bays, and I would really like to, however, there are too many people reading the boards who do not know who or what to believe. So I feel we need to keep exposing their lies. The work that you did in telephoning and exposing this lie in a short period of time is to be commended and is what we need to show these people that they will get caught in their lies.

These explicit and implicit references, at least for a reader so disposed, provide the textual resources for imagining a community of others bound together by common history, shared values, and mutual obligations. The 'image of communion' was further constituted and confirmed as posters extolled the communal power of the board: 'I am in awe in the presence of Foolishness,' exclaims one; 'The kinship of Foolish investors cannot be overstated,' writes another.

In addition to posts *inscribing* community, various offline meetings *incarnated* community. The annual stockholders' meeting in Salt Lake City was preceded by extensive online discussion among Iomegans regarding questions to ask at the actual meeting and how Fools should comport themselves. At the meetings, Iomegans were pleased when the Iomega Corporation, which had been regarded as distancing itself from the Motley Fool and Iomegans, left tote bags with the Iomega logo filled with pens, pads, and other items at a Fool reception. At the stockholders' meeting itself, Fools, some wearing the jester's cap, praised Kim Edwards, then CEO, and the Board of Directors for the company's success and thanked them for their new wealth, which enabled the education of their children, the purchase of their homes, and the prospect of early retirement. The day concluded with a banquet organized by Fools, featuring a pantheon of Foolish luminaries, including one of the first brokerage analysts to report on Iomega stock, the revered MF Chiros, and the Gardner brothers themselves.[8]

Cognition

For investment-challenged newbies such as myself, the market was intimidating and chaotic. Until one became familiar with the culture of the market, the meaning of arcane ratios and margins, issues of management and marketing, the importance of institutional investors, options, expirations, secondary offerings, floats, shorting—let alone the technical details of a Zip drive and its competitors—were obscure or confusing. If the flow of commentary and information incited confusion, it also contained the resources for order and sense. Read with a certain bias, the post and posters provided charts to navigate a cognitively turbulent sea.

For example, Iomega was a so-called story or concept stock. The 'story' was that success was inevitable because the vast amount of information that would soon be downloaded from the net required the increased, portable, affordable storage capacity of the Zip. The Zip would eventually replace the 3.5 disk as standard equipment in new PCs and, just as the profit in razors is in selling the blades, Iomega would forever profit from selling the storage disks. A stream of positive information could be pointed to as documenting the current and future reality of Iomega: increasing sales and revenues, Zip drives offered as options by computer manufacturers, and rising stock prices.

Adept narrative efforts—'bullwork'—emerged in the absence of confirming evidence or in the wake of disappointing news, such as when the price dropped, adoptions by computer manufacturers did not occur, Iomega executives sold their shares, traditional measures of valuation—such as the P/E ratio—defied conventional wisdom, competitive products emerged. At virtually every turn, artful interpretations emerged that minimized or explained away the negative implications or recast them as actually positive. Thus, for example, a drop in price might be recast as normal consolidation to be expected of a high flying stock: 'I can't believe some in here are starting to worry because we are in a respite mode from the recent explosive upward momentum. GEE WHIZ, people, it's called a CONSOLIDATION.' Far from being a disaster it is an opportunity to purchase shares of IOMG at a bargain price prior to the next big move upward. Oldtimers brought their experience to bear:

Been a shareholder of IO for a long time now...I remember weathering the 30%+ drop back when Dorfman and the bit did their cut on IO...I just have to say that this is nothing compared to back then. I feel unwaveringly confident about IO at this point.

---

[8] Communion in the real world, however, did not always trump the virtual world: a Fool in the lobby of the hotel that was the veritable epicentre of what was happening at the meeting said: 'I'm going to my laptop in my room to find out what's happening.'

There was concern about IO's earnings during that correction...to me, that was something to worry about...Today and recently, we have the overall market declining... storage stocks undergoing a normal correction...but nothing *nothing* has changed my mind about IO. I have added to my position in a manner that will allow me to take advantage of the recent buying opportunity...

To be sure, the alternative interpretations were often contested. Sceptics offered sophisticated critical analyses of the prospects of the company, the product, and the future trajectory of the stock. Some might even analyse the practices through which Iomegans maintained their belief in the prospects of Iomega stock and the Zip drive. Bullish analyses might be deconstructed into rhetorical, self-fulfilling practices through which some Iomegans transmuted ostensibly negative events into grounds for optimism. A post sarcastically commenting on the 'objectivity' of Iomegans builds to a characterization of the Iomegans as a religion:

The overwhelming majority of IOMG posters on this board are without question the most objective posters on AOL. You care for nothing except truth and fairness. You respectfully listen to all opinions. Even when you disagree, you are always courteous and civil and never engage in any form of personal invective. Dissenters (bears) are encouraged to voice their opinions and only their (faulty) logic is criticized, never themselves. You are generous to a fault with all views that differ from your own...Iomega is more, much more than the greatest corporation on earth. Iomega is a...RELIGION!

Given the resources and opportunities for scepticism, the sense to be made of Iomega was not dictated by the posts. The narrative that sustained the confidence of an investor such as myself—who did *not* do his own research contra various admonitions—required a reader privileging certain information and analyses while discounting critical asides and cautions.[9]

Deep Play

The roller-coaster movements of the market induces highs and lows of exhilaration and despair. In the words of posters, the soaring price of Iomega is: like sex;

[9] The problems of textual analysis become more subtle and complex as posters become more subtle and complex and write ironically, allusively, technically—or do not write anything at all. Moreover, interpretative reading involves innumerable editorial decisions in weighing the good, true, central, and significant from the bad, false, peripheral, and trivial. Variants of these issues were themselves debated and contested on the board. A related complicating issue is not only how these posts are read but whether they are read. The bulletin board presents a chronologically ordered sequence of posts. While some posters may read them in that order, others read selectively. In the end, the generalizability of my reading of the texts—the resources I selected and the inferences I made—is highly problematic. As is perhaps evident from some of the posts that variously deride or castigate the Iomegans and that themselves provide part of the overall text, quite different readings are possible. Moreover, even the term 'Iomegans', which itself originated in a somewhat derisive context, might be seen as a reading striving to imagine an imagined community.

better than sex; a rocket ship—buckle-up, hang-on; Wow; Wheeee. As the price plummets, posters write of stomach-turning anguish, of throwing up and defecating: 'This thing is in free fall. Grab your guts folks.' The emotions involve not only net-worth but self-worth. Investing is often described as requiring self-discipline and composure to 'beat' the market, which is itself portrayed in animalistic or jungle metaphors (Neal and Youngelson 1988). Framed in these terms, the market is an arena for what Goffman (1967) refers to as 'action': situations in which individuals take fateful chances as their response is judged to reveal aspects of character such as composure and courage (Abolafia 1996). Daniel, buying additional shares of Iomega as it plummets: 'Well, I bought some more at 26 5/8, but that was after I puked. I don't know about the rest of you but this is a test of faith for me.'

Motley Fool and the Iomegan village laminated another layer of significance and emotion onto the ups and downs of Iomega. In his classic 'Notes on the Balinesian Cock Fight' Clifford Geertz (1973) described how owners and audience waged large sums of money on the outcome of ferocious fights between spurred cocks. In such 'deep play', writes Geertz, 'more is at stake than material gain: namely esteem, honor, dignity, respect—in a word status'. Two chickens fighting in a dusty arena has implications for status because the cocks represent divisions within and between communities. Bets identified the bettor not only with a chicken but with a particular faction in the village or some other village entirely: the battle between chickens is endowed with transcendent meaning.

The board was internally divided between 'longs' and 'shorts', between Foolishness and other investment strategies. Read through the prism of Foolishness, the board as a whole was positioned against the media and financial institutions of the Wise. When framed in terms of the divisions within and between factions in the world of Iomega, playing the market and investing in Iomega became deep play. When Iomega succeeded, the Fools were not simply making money but triumphing over forces—a combination of 'shorts' and the Wise—cast as actively attempting to subvert Iomega and the new form of investor empowerment pioneered by Motley Fool (cf. Corrigan 1996). David Gardner's commentary following IBM's announcement that the Zip would be an option for its new line of computers frames the stakes in the Iomegan cockfight: vindication of Foolishness:

It's hard not to be 'in your face' emotional about this, since so many humiliated elements of the fading old media have centered their attack on the new medium by using Iomega ...Iomega being all just a bunch of hype, of course, just internet hype, no business, no real prospects, just a whole bunch of idiotic individual investors who are creating hysteria by talking about the stock online. [But], the truth will always out, and history will demonstrate the truth and beauty of the Foolish viewpoint.

Congratulatory toasts celebrate the significance of the rise in price: money, personal character, and collective triumph: 'I toast to all The IOMEGANS ... past and current ... that had the guts and the vision to see this thing for what it really is, before Wall Street got it ... this is a HUGE victory.'

Isaac Newton invested in the mother of all bubbles: the South Sea Bubble. After selling his initial stake for a profit of £7,000 pounds, Sir Isaac reinvested and lost £20,000, much to his puzzlement: 'I can calculate the motions of heavenly bodies, but not the madness of people' (Kindleberger 1989). I too made a substantial profit from my initial investment in Iomega and reinvested only to lose an impressive—depressive—sum. I have tried to calculate the 'madness'. My analysis suggests that it was partly this newby entering the Iomega village and succumbing to its communal, cognitive, and emotional attractions. These processes converged with unusual intensity on the morning of the day I made my final purchase of shares. Iomega had lurched upwards dramatically in the preceding days and posts in the morning suggested that yet another computer manufacturer was about to incorporate the Zip in some of its new models. Involved in an imagined community, braced by the dominant narrative and energized by the deep play, I bought shares and encouraged my son to do similarly.

DEFLATION OF THE CONCEPTUAL BUBBLE

As the value of Iomega shares deflated, so too did the value of certain concepts for analysing life among the Iomegans and, indeed, at the I/I intersection. I should like to illustrate the notion of 'conceptual deflation' by reference to well-taken calls for analytic scepticism regarding the excessive or ungrounded claims about the nature and prospects of virtual society—Woolgar (this volume). Clearly (in hindsight), some of the claims about Iomega, Zip drives, and the future of technology were cyberbolic and would have benefited from a sceptical attitude. But the Motley Fool and posters on the Iomega message board recurrently issued calls for scepticism: investors were reminded to do their own research, to be on the alert for 'hype', and that claims made about Iomega might prove to be, well, cyberbole. Our subjects—though they do not use the charming term—are themselves sensitive to cyberbole and cultivate scepticism. Thus, in raising the possibility of cyberbole and the appropriateness of analytic scepticism, one is advancing a variant of a position voiced by some of the participants at the I/I intersection. The position is not wrong—far from it—but it does not deliver a distinctively penetrating insight: it is one among a variety of posted positions. In so far as the value of an analytic stance is found in how it permits seeing new things, allows seeing old things in a new way, or jostles taken-for-granted assumptions (M. S. Davis 1971), the value delivered by the sensitivity to cyberbole and the cultivation of analytic scepticism is deflated.

In this spirit, I suggest that the capacity of other analytic claims, concepts, and metaphors to provide insight or irony are deflated when applied to the internet, especially at the I/I intersection. For example, consider how the material organization of the internet and the World Wide Web deflates the insight provided by the sociological concept of *social networks*. The metaphor of networks invites construing society *as though* individuals were interconnected in the manner of a fishing net or spider web. In social life there are no actual threads, cords, or wires binding one to another. Thus, social analysts stretch—even do intellectual acrobatics—to see what 'networks' might mean in the social world. The cognitive acrobatics are one index of the value of such metaphors. When we speak of the internet or World Wide Web, by contrast, there *are* actual glass and copper threads connecting computers or households to one another—or at least to the routers spinning out the packets that show up on our screens (Hayes 1997). To propose that the internet should be viewed as a network is almost literally correct: it does not take cognitive acrobatics to appreciate the hard wiring (at least until wireless technology makes greater inroads). For that reason, the analytic value of 'network' deflates when applied to the internet.

Narrative, constructionist, deconstructionist, ethnomethodological, and reflexive approaches—perspectives I regard as my analytic bag of tools and tricks—seem especially vulnerable to analytic deflation when applied to the internet. Derrida's 'there is nothing outside the text' (1976) requires intellectual acrobatics to see what the claim might mean in a world in which things are obviously outside texts. The claim requires less intellectual dexterity to apply to cyberspace: virtually everything is a text. Precisely because it is so plausible and true, the analytic puissance of the deconstructionist precept—its promise to deliver insight—is deflated: it is one thing to say everything (for example, my refrigerator) is a text, quite another to proclaim 'e-mail is a text'. The latter pronouncement does not induce an 'ah ha!', but rather an 'uh huh' (or, perhaps, a 'huh?').

Similarly, if you take the narrative turn and hold that selves, society, and reality are constituted through the stories told about them, you will not be met with incredulity in the I/I world. The I/I intersection—the Iomega board in particular—provides ample illustrations of how narrative shapes the price of a stock—and that participants are aware of the process. Again, admonitions about hypesters, tipsters, and touts are testaments to participants' appreciation of the power of stories and narratives. In fact, narrative and more generally a constructionist sensibility are explicitly employed as an investment strategy. In contrast to 'positivist' strategies holding that the value of a stock is ultimately a reflection of business fundamentals, others place their bets that the price of a stock is what others are willing to pay for it, which is related to what they believe and/or believe others believe are the value and prospect of the stock—those beliefs being shaped and constituted by the constructions, interpretations, and stories developed. Thus, a narrativist–constructionist stance is not a source of ironic analytic insight but the heart of a known, albeit arguable, investment strategy.

The form of reflexivity, known to sociologists (and most of the public) as 'the self-fulfilling prophecy', was initially recognized through observation of the financial world. The 'parable' offered by Robert Merton (1957) as the canonical case of the self-fulfilling prophecy recounted how a rumour of insolvency—once believed by enough depositors—resulted in the actual insolvency of a flourishing bank: 'The parable tells us that public definitions of a situation (prophecies or predictions) become an integral part of the situation and thus affect subsequent developments' (Merton 1957: 423). Merton acknowledged that the bank manager readily recognized the process, but that it was a valuable way of understanding similar processes in other domains of social life.[10] When the concept is brought back to its home—the world of finance—the self-fulfilling prophecy is virtually common wisdom.[11] In fact, prophets in search of profits set in motion self-fulfilling prophecies. With some regularity, I receive an e-mail from 'Explosive Pick' recommending the purchase of a particular stock—based on virtually no rationale other than that, if enough of the e-mailed investors buy the stock, the price will increase.

The internet, particularly the I/I nexus, literalizes, intensifies, thematizes, or appropriates the processes and perspectives that are ordinarily in the *analyst*'s traditional bag of tricks. As this occurs, depending on the sophistication of the audience, the power of the tricks to illuminate cyberspace is diminished.[12] Rather than furnishing an analysis of the I/I nexus, these concepts are deflated to echoes or descriptions of participants' voices (cf. Mesny 1998). In the parlance of ethnomethodology, some analytic constructs are no more than members' concepts.[13] Of course, these dynamics prick and deflate the bubble of my own analysis. I have suggested, for example, that my commitment to Iomega stock may be sustained through the rhetorical practices that invited and sustained confidence in the prospects of Iomega in the face or wake of ostensibly negative events. As we have seen, however, the Gardners and posters to the Iomega board might well identify what I and other Iomegans were doing in kindred terms.

[10] The Nobel prize winning economist instrumental in creating a hedge fund whose failure threatened to collapse the global economy is sociologist Robert K. Merton's son, Robert Merton, Jr.

[11] Reflexivity itself is a key concept in George Soros's investment strategy (1994, 1998).

[12] An 'uh huh' or an 'ah hah' reaction depends on the knowledge and assumptions of the audience. Sociological concepts and characterizations of I/I practices might be 'news' to audiences with little or no knowledge of such practices but not to adept practitioners who would hear what they already know.

[13] The potential conflation of concept of participants (or 'members') and researchers' (or 'analysts') is a familiar ethnomethodological concern. In sophisticated professional environments, practitioners may be familiar with and even invoke the discourse of analysts. Latour and Woolgar (1986), for example, show how practising scientists variously invoke versions of philosophical and sociological accounts of science to frame and describe their activities.

By substituting the 'price of a share of stock' or 'the market' for 'social facts' and 'investing' for 'sociology,' Garfinkel's respecification (1967: p. vii) of Durkheim reads as a concise statement of investors' reflexive relation to the market: 'the objective reality of social facts [the market] as an ongoing accomplishment of the concerted activities of daily life, with the ordinary, artful ways of that accomplishment being by members known, used and taken for granted, is for members doing sociology [investing] a fundamental phenomenon.'

CONCLUSION

In 2001 the entire equity market mimicked the trajectory of the rise and fall of Iomega shares. The Nasdaq Index, which had risen so dramatically during the 1990s, reached an all time high in 2000 and plummeted by some 60 per cent in less than a year. In his prescient *Irrational Exuberance*, Shiller (2000) suggested the growth of the 'bubble' (he correctly anticipated was about to 'burst') was partly due to the amplification of a heady optimism regarding the inexorable progress of the market. In effect, the stock market was functioning as a 'naturally occurring Ponzi scheme'. Successive waves of investors were induced to enter the market by a variety of psychological and cultural processes, which included a 'cascade of stories' of success disseminated by the media and academia. Thus, the dynamics in which I was implicated on the Iomega board might well be seen as a particular expression of more ubiquitous processes affecting the larger investment community and indeed society as a whole.

Another bubble—a conceptual bubble—may also burst as traditional concepts are brought to bear on the intensely reflexive domains at the I/I intersection. Castells (2000*b*) recently expressed scepticism that extant sociological concepts (and perhaps the current scholarly cohort to whom they are dear) could comprehend the new 'network society'. The reflexive world of cyberspace may require new ways of thinking about developments that have usurped or surpassed and thereby deflated our older ways of thinking.[14]

[14] If claims about virtual society are cyberbole, it would be interesting to consider the contexts and practices that encourage, permit, and sustain them (see Wynn and Katz 1997).

14

The Day-to-Day Work of Standardization: A Sceptical Note on the Reliance on IT in a Retail Bank

John A. Hughes, Mark Rouncefield, and Pete Tolmie

INTRODUCTION

Exploring the relationship between technology and organization has for long been one of the central interests of sociology since the classic statements of Marx and Weber, so it cannot be any surprise that during the 1990s one of the predominant interests has been the relationship of information communications technologies (ICTs) to the major transformations in the social and economic environment in which organizations now operate (Lash and Urry 1987; Castells 1996). In brief, the claim is that in a more global economic environment organizations need to 're-engineer' themselves and become more flexible, knowledge based, and better able to survive and prosper in marketplaces that are less predictable and prone to rapid change (Hammer and Champy 1993; Nonaka and Takeuchi 1995). Meeting these requirements will mean, it is argued, abandoning traditional bureaucratic forms of organizing work activities and, instead, embracing organizational forms that better serve the new conditions under which organizations have to operate. Such forms would need to empower the workforce more, rely far less on hierarchical structures and more upon temporary and often distributed networks of expertise. The underpinning to these 'virtual organizations' is ICTs (Casey 1995; Zimmerman 1997).

In view of the critical role ascribed to ICT in the development of such forms of work organization, banks are particularly interesting, not least because they have been at the forefront of distributed IT and 'expert systems' for some decades as well as undergoing major organizational changes of the kind just described (Fincham *et al.* 1994). Accordingly, they offer an opportunity to investigate how 'virtual organizational forms' are instantiated in the day-to-day work of the organization. This chapter reports on just such a study of a major UK retail bank, a study that had the express focus upon how a strategic orientation towards developing a more 'virtual organization' was actually realized in its day-to-day work.

The retail bank first adopted the notion of the 'virtual organization' as an informing principle in the early 1990s as part of a long-term programme of systematic organizational modernization called the 'Delivery Strategy' (Hughes *et al.* 1995).[1] This was nothing less than a strategy to impose concurrent changes on the organization, changes in organizational structure and working practices, technology and culture. The separation of front- and back-office processing and the establishment of independent functionally specialized units coordinating their activities through IT was an early phase of the programme. A more recent phase of restructuring—'Building the New Retail Bank'—created specialized regional centres dealing with millions of customers and which functions, such as Lending and Securities, were further centralized. Concurrent with the above organizational restructuring came efforts to move away from, or at least complement, the traditional 'good husbandry' practices of banking towards much more emphasis on selling the goods and services that the bank had to offer its customers. All of these changes were predicated upon an increasing reliance upon IT-mediated means of communication and, integral to the strategy, upon IT-mediated representations of customers through the development of more sophisticated relational databases, and decision-making and risk-assessment packages. The day-to-day task of implementing and operating these changes fell to (and in 2001 were still the responsibility of) 'middle management', who, in effect, constitute an interface between the 'virtuality' of IT, and the 'real' world of organizational relationships with customers and with banking staff.

We had been studying various aspects of the bank since the early 1990s and, accordingly were well placed to contextualize the changes in 1999. The central aim was to investigate, in detail, the move towards more virtual organizational structures and, in particular, to explore the relationship between the new technologies and organizational change. We were interested in the 'hands-on' work of building virtual organizational forms, the impact on everyday work activities, and the ways IT was used to facilitate teamwork and coordination. Related areas for investigation were the development and use of computer-based representations of customers increasingly employed as support for decision making. During the course of our fieldwork we studied the work of a number of middle managers in a range of settings: a business centre, a customer service branch, a lending centre, and a service centre. The fieldwork involved shadowing

---

[1] Since the early 1990s, various people have been involved in the ethnographic study of various aspects of the bank. These have included Dave Randall, Manchester Metropolitan University, Val King, St Martin's College, Lancaster, Jon O'Brien, EuroParc Cambridge, as well as the authors of this chapter. See the following for further details: Hughes *et al.* (1995, 1996*b*, 1997, 1999, 2001); Randall *et al.* (1998*a,b*, 1999); Tolmie *et al.* (1998*a,b,c*, 1999*a,b*, 2000).

individual managers and team leaders throughout their working day, recording in detail their activities and interactions. We observed and recorded a gamut of routine activities—meetings, interviews, computer use, telephone use, training, advising, modelling, and so on—that constituted the 'working day' of the middle managers.

THE PURSUIT OF STANDARDIZATION

A key problem for any highly distributed organization is how to coordinate non-co-located workers, and provide them with some sense of what their responsibilities are in relation to others. The bank was no different in this respect. In the virtual organization literature an ideal solution to this is to have a negotiated set of responsibilities shared amongst virtual team members, who flexibly coordinate their activities through IT (Lipnack and Stamps 1997a,b). In the bank the solution was somewhat different. Emphasis was placed upon process-driven arrangements with a high degree of specification of task accompanied by a pervasive rhetoric of standardization. This was one of many ways in which the actual realization of the notional ideal of the virtual organization was set aside for more conventional, 'trusted' business solutions to the organizational problems of coordination. As indicated, the move was to standardize as many processes as possible so that, despite the centralization of many of the bank's functions away from the high-street branches, and despite the lack of co-location of many of the staff involved in the many processes constituting the bank's activities, there would be some assurance of an identity of service and practice across the distributed operations of the organization.

Such a rationale for standardization, it has been argued, was the *sine qua non* of the development of modern rational organization and exemplified in so many domains from bureaucracy, the military, mass production, public services, education, measurement standards, and so much more: a process that has been characterized and theorized about in numerous ways.[2] What makes the process interesting from our point of view was that the standardization of many of the bank's activities had to be achieved during a period of major organizational change. In many cases this involved migrating many of its procedures from the old to the new forms of organization, but in other cases it meant creating standardized procedures anew in the context of new emerging organizational forms. One of the major casualties of the concentration of many

---

[2] One might argue that the more mature sociological reflections on standardization derive from Weber's work on the rise of rational organization (Weber 1954), but, of course, it is implicit in Marx's analysis of the logic of capitalist production. Historically such processes pre-date the development of capitalist economic organization, though were much hastened by it. It is also a strong theme in Foucault's work (see e.g. Foucault 1977).

of the 'back-office' functions previously undertaken by the high-street branches into regional functional centres was the loss of knowledge of the locality and local management discretion over many of the bank's services, not least the making of loans. It was anticipated that over the years ICT technologies could substitute for this acknowledged loss.[3] However, an almost inevitable tension was created by the emphasis on personal customer service prominently stressed in national advertising campaigns and in injunctions to staff.[4]

In what follows we will discuss two aspects of standardization, the first as it relates to customer-facing work in the bank, and the second the process of attempting to standardize working practices in a changing working environment.

STANDARDIZATION AND CUSTOMER-FACING WORK

Exhortations to standardize were common throughout the various activities within the bank, and it was applied equally to both staff procedures and customer policy. There was an ongoing attempt, for instance, to 'reconfigure' customers by embedding typologies or models in decision support systems (Woolgar 1991). Alongside the development of this expert software, tight parameters were placed upon managerial lending discretion. However, where standardization was applied to customer behaviour, the unpredictability of such behaviour meant that formats had to be continually and contingently revised.

In high-street branches, since most of the 'back-office' work has now been transferred to regional centres, the main function of the branch is to deal with customer requests of various kinds. While such requests are very often routine, they are unpredictable both in terms of the nature of the request and how it is delivered to the bank official. As a matter of course customers would deliver their requests in a variety of ways, sometimes making a series of requests in one go, sometimes making additional requests after the first one has been dealt with. Nor can customers always be relied upon to furnish all relevant information without prompting (Randall and Hughes 1994). This inherent unpredictability of interactions with customers had relevance not only for face-to-face interactions

---

[3] We say 'acknowledged', but the crucial question is, by whom? Certainly most of the middle managers we studied recognized that the loss of knowledge of the locality was a significant problem, and, as we shall see, a number of IT initiatives were intended to provide adequate substitutes. Inevitably these would lack the nuanced character that can be provided by personal experience of the locality and, importantly, customers. See our papers on the phenomenon of 'organizational memory' (Hughes *et al.* 1996*a*; Randall *et al.* 1996).

[4] A rather nice irony that emerged recently (2001) is that, although the retail bank that we studied was one of the first to initiate the organizational changes summarized earlier in the chapter with the loss of a large number of high-street branches and their staff, its most recent advertisements chastise its competitors for doing just the same things.

but also to telephone enquiries and other computer-mediated communications (CMCs). There were attempts to standardize interactions between bank staff and customers through the provision of 'scripts' for use on the telephone. However, rarely could these be literally followed as the script dictated, but were instead used as a resource for framing appropriate questions as and when the interaction allowed.

One of our specific concerns on the theme of standardization related to the practical realization of customer representations within the computer system, what we termed 'virtual customers', and the utilization of such representations in interaction. Increasingly, the different representations of customers within the machine became a resource for 'forecasting' and marketing activities. One bank project expressly concerned with developing such codified representations of customers was 'Managing Local Markets' (MLM), a set of categorizations upon which to base marketing and lending decisions. The aim was to embed local knowledge 'in the machine' and to replace its highly nuanced character with something ultimately codifiable and therefore more open to further transformation and prediction.

In the initial phase of this project all staff underwent an exercise aimed at gaining some understanding of what they needed to know about customers. This involved going out and finding what lay 'beyond the walls' of the bank. Employees went out onto the streets on walkabouts and drivearounds, collected newspaper cuttings, advertisements of house sales, and so on, trying to assess the character of their particular area and gain some measure of the competition. At the point of application MLM was computer driven. Customers were categorized into five basic categories—A +, A, B, C, and D—the A + s being the 'super accounts' and the Ds the ones that 'cost money to run'. These categories were based upon a thorough knowledge of the customer's dealings with the bank, the nature of their credit balances, the running of their account, credit cards, investments, mortgages, insurance, and so on. In practice, large numbers in the B and C categories necessitated further classifications. Customers were variously listed as being: 'Retireds'; FIYAs (Financially Independent Young Adults); YSs (Young Singles); and Mid-Markets, BOFs (Better Off Financially), and WOEs (Well-Off Establisheds), who were all aged 31 to 50 with the classification being based on the amount of money that passed through their accounts. This process of categorization could then be refined even further, as the following fieldwork extract reveals where a manager is elaborating further about MLM:

. . . what we intend to do is to literally look at these very narrow groups so we may actually go to the computer . . . where we may actually be able to say 'Right what we want to have a look at, we want to have a look at those customers which are classified as Mid-Market, that are aged between 31 and 33, that's this little group, that have a risk grade of one to five on their account so that we know they're good accounts, and that perhaps live in a particular area . . . And that should produce a target group of something in the region of say fifty accounts.

However, it was evident from the fieldwork that regular tensions arose between such systems and the actual, situated work that managers do, where reliance on local knowledge and 'gut feeling' is as prominent as ever. When managers engage with customers on the telephone and in customer interviews, they orient to 'virtual customers' in the same ways as they do to other bodies of information—namely, in terms of the situated concerns and understandings that emerge out of the interaction. Managers, in the first instance, use the customer information on the computer to arrive at some kind of story of how things are from the bank's point of view.

Here, for instance, we have a Business Manager conducting an interview with a proprietor, 'Graham', of a frozen meat products company. The company had been doing business with the bank for a number of years and the Manager, 'Simon', had himself conducted the company's previous Annual Review. However, at that Review Simon had noted a slight downturn in business for which Graham had provided plausible reasons at the time. Simon had looked at the printouts of the company's relationship with the bank over the past year. Having related that to the previous Appraisal Form, he was no longer certain that the reasons Graham had given him the previous year were 'true'. There had continued to be what he termed 'a cash drain on the bank account'. Trying to establish the 'real' cause for this was Simon's chief objective within the interview and it did, indeed, inform a great deal of the discussion that ensued.[5]

SIMON. Right so you can see that...you were sort of creeping up there to 20,000 in May
GRAHAM. Yeah
SIMON. And then it started to go down a bit back up again in October then down again back up again in December, which is when we spoke
GRAHAM. Yeah
SIMON. And it's...almost nothing for a really...period but on the same side...y-your best position was getting higher and higher up to there...it did start to run down...to here but it hasn't run down to the levels it has done in previous years
GRAHAM. Yeah
SIMON. I can show you the limit
GRAHAM. Yeah
SIMON. It started to creep up again now so that y'know...since October the account's not been below ten and its not been below thirteen since...well
GRAHAM. Christmas
SIMON. Yeah
GRAHAM. Christmas
SIMON. If you look back to the previous year...This is exactly the same sort of print-out for the previous year, you can see that there is a much heavier utilization on both sides...That's credit...So during the year [points at document] That last year you were [phone ringing] significantly

---

[5] Since what is required for the purposes of this chapter is a record of what is said rather than conversation analysis we have dispensed with the standard transcription conventions, but unspaced dots represent pauses.

GRAHAM. Big difference

SIMON. Yeah...So there is so what that actually tells me is y'know despite what...your views were in terms of that stock position at Christmas...that seems to tell a slightly different tale whereas

GRAHAM.——

SIMON. Actually over that period there's been an absolute drain on cash on the b- on the bank account

This kind of understanding is arrived at through negotiation with the customer and trying to arrive at a common picture of the state of affairs of the account. Frequently recourse is made to numerical representations to buttress the emerging understanding of 'where things are'.

SIMON. What d'you reckon the background reasons are f- fer that Graham?

GRAHAM. Well the meat jumps

SIMON. Obviously BSE's partly behind that

GRAHAM. Well it's just...They're never leavin' it alone now

SIMON. Mm

GRAHAM. And plus...trade's gone quiet...We've lost Gibson's sausage orders

SIMON. What What...What's the background behind why Gibson's keep changin? Is it purely price?

GRAHAM. No...No...They just... They get these things in their head and they're away like...They get...some off us...They get the frozen sausage off us

SIMON. Mm

GRAHAM. but not the fresh

...

SIMON. Right .. So you reckon you'll get Gibson's back at some stage

GRAHAM. Oh yeah...Fun-...Funny enuff I was only talkin to James Gibson last night...I went deliverin ...

...

SIMON. How much turnover did that reflect then? Gibson's? How much did you do in- in a year?

GRAHAM. In a year?...[sotto voce] four twenty six...It's nearly a hundred thousand

SIMON. That's a lot ain't it?

GRAHAM. Yeah

Time and again this kind of talk became the key resource for decision making. So, when it came to using 'virtual-customer' information as a resource for decision making, managers regularly relied upon the 'gut feeling' born out of conversations such as the above. Decision making is anything but process driven. Rather, judgements are formed about the customer on the basis of highly informal and contingent factors.

Yet somehow conventional attention to matters of standard 'best practice' must be displayed to the bank itself. This was achieved by rendering decisions and judgements as part of a routinely appropriate account; developing a recipient designed story that could rationalize prior action in ways that were manifestly 'sensible' in terms of organizational objectives (Bittner 1965). Nowhere was this more visible than in the completion of post-interview documentation such as Appraisal Forms. Here, for instance, is part of the previously mentioned manager's documentation of his interview with Graham:

[Goes to 'Proposition' section—Shifting cursor over text as he scans for details to alter— Highlights a section and deletes—Entering new comments]

'in so far as business is concerned we are simply asked to mark forward at current levels...'

'Graham Croft recognizes the reasons he proffered last year were only partly true as evidenced by higher borrowing'

Causal factor listed as 'reduced turnover'

Noting 'position is stable'

Suggests with actions they have taken 'they are confident that cash retentions will be seen in the current year...'

It is in their displayed attention to the objectives of the strategic plan commonsensically perceived that managers effectively became a locus between the ideal of the virtual organization and work that is manifestly more 'real'. All the managers were oriented to the fact that relationships are not between abstract entities but between concrete individuals who bring their own specific sets of relevances that have to be recognized and taken into account. This is at the root of effective managerial work, and it is through this ordinary, orderly, everyday kind of work on the part of managers that virtual-organizational ideals are ultimately given sense in working practices.

There is a standard expectation in the literature on virtual organizations that there will be a need for radically new skills and working practices for the achievement of distributed working, particularly with customers. However, when working with customers the prime orientation observably displayed is towards preserving the 'normality' of the interaction and maintaining customer confidence, rather than with revising how these relationships should be conducted. This can, however, be a challenge in customer-facing work when the use of customer representations in the system becomes a matter of displaying one's routine competence by 'seamlessly' weaving the technology into the interaction. In such circumstances it is an accountable matter of competence to make the technology wholly at home within existing work practices.

Competence needs to be displayed, for instance, whilst simultaneously interacting with customers and using information screens. In using such technology the cashiers' interaction with the technology and with their customers must ideally render the technology 'invisible'.[6] However, navigating through screens and reading the information they contain is time consuming, leading to difficulties in conducting smoothly flowing conversations with clients. Problems incurred when interrogating the database and deciphering information can erode customer confidence. Related to this, the fundamental problem of information

---

[6] In particular, it might be noted, the technology is used in such a way that it sits alongside, rather than replacing, existing modes of cashier–client interaction. Cf. the third rule of virtuality: virtual systems supplement rather than substitute for real activities (Woolgar, this volume).

screens is that the information they convey is typically structured according to the flow of transactions, not to the flow of enquiries. A customer's orientation to a given enquiry, however, will be driven by the customer's interests rather than by the structure embodied in the system. It is the absence of context sensitivity that creates difficulties in interrogation of screens. This in turn disrupts the flow of visibly competent work. Whilst customer satisfaction remains an issue, operatives, whether on the telephone, or using video-conferencing systems, will still have to contend with various sources of unpredictability. Hence efficient use of the technology and interaction with customers has to be successfully managed simultaneously. In the act of processing transactions, the competent operative must routinely 'weave' use of the technology into the flow of interaction with customers such that the relevant expertise and skill is made visible.

An example of this issue relates to use of the teleconferencing kit (a commercial, ISDN-based, desktop video-conferencing system, with dedicated database and communication software) that had been installed in the 'Telehelp' section of the insurance division of the bank. The role of the Telehelp team was to give insurance advice to customers. One highly visible feature of the work with the videolink was the extent to which staff were required to 'talk through the technology', both to alert the customer to what was going to happen next— 'the screen will go fuzzy', 'it will take a couple of seconds for this information to be transferred to you', and so on—and to explain the everyday meaning of technical insurance terms. This process is illustrated in the following abbreviated observation of the videolink in use:

1. Preparing PC1 for use—in response to call from branch...2. Call through on link— 'what can I do for you?'...3. Branch intros customer...4. Takes customer details—using screen—filling in form on screen—surname, initials, postcode, house number... 5. Transferring info—explains about picture 'going fuzzy'...6. Buildings insurance— asking questions—rebuilding costs etc....7. Transferring info—explains about screen 'going fuzzy' again—talks about 'features and benefits'—additional insurance. freezer food; 2 million owner liability etc.—makes postman and slate 'joke'.

Apart from preparing the customer for the screen 'going fuzzy', the operator also deploys one of the standard 'jokes' for explaining the importance of a £2 million owner liability feature in the policy in order to mediate between the legal language of 'owner liability' and the everyday world. This is done through the device of 'what would happen if one of your slates fell on the postman's head when he was delivering?' Of course this issue of 'translation' and of coping simultaneously with both the technology and the customer happens with other technologies and in other contexts, but the difficulties that ensue should not be underestimated. Observations document the sheer frequency and regularity of this kind of work. Accomplished use of the technology necessitates operators spending a great deal of their time reassuring customers and navigating them through the technology as part of actually doing the work itself. Thus, as Sacks (1992) once famously remarked, technology is routinely 'made at home in a pre-existing world' rather than serving to refashion that world in new and radical ways.

STANDARDIZATION AND WORKING PRACTICE

A primary everyday activity that proved to be one of the key elements in the pursuit of standardization in the bank was process modelling. Here the specification of tasks can be seen as an attempt to actualize rationalization and standardization. The diagrammatic representations of workflow embedded in process maps were intended to provide a definitive version of the division of labour and in this way achieve a more predictable and clear specification of the work processes in the bank.

Whilst process modelling may be seen as a key way of designing work processes, it is by no means straightforward and regularly had implications beyond the process being modelled, which also had a bearing upon the resultant model itself. In one particular instance, the manager of the sanctioning floor of a brand new lending centre was overseeing the production of a process map by two of his staff. The process in question was a complex one, regarding how to eliminate or reduce the level of 'hard-core' debt run up by customers using a certain kind of credit card, while simultaneously turning it into an opportunity for what was effectively 'a sale' by offering the customers loans to clear the debt. In the course of the modelling, the manager in question had to visit the managers of both the phones floor and the monitoring and control (MAC) floor to discuss the best way forward.

Clive goes upstairs to MAC and waits while Steve is talking to Mel
Clive gets chair then sits and explains to Steve about the Monday 'process map' meeting, and shows Steve a rough copy from the whiteboard—Then he gives Steve the Stage 1 sheet
Steve looks it through and Clive explains as he adjusts his chair
CLIVE. What they've done is they've come up with a three stage process map... but I don't think it's quite there yet... errm... so there's... that's what they're lookin after Stage one... being... in   MAC... but   there   isn-... that-   er   i-... it's   not   quite   right that... [cough]... coz the one- the thing that I tried to get them to do just to say well... what are yer e- what are yer expectations of... of your people... y'know and at least start off... y'know (.) the process
STEVE. Mm
[long pause]
STEVE. So?

An immediate thing to observe about this is that Clive's first stab at conveying what the problem is is a signal failure, as the long pause and Steve's 'So?' make evident. Under the circumstances Clive has to do some more work to get Steve to engage with the activity. This he does by specifically relevancing aspects of the first sheet of the rough draft of the process map (Fig. 14.1) that he has given Steve.

CLIVE. Yeah... Theirs... to me .. u... you look at that [points to end box that says 'YES'] and you think... right okay well... now need to follow on
STEVE. Mm
CLIVE. Er and... when I follow on here I think... things will be a lot... simpler

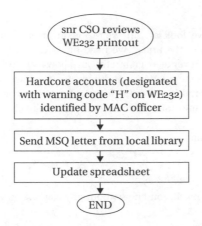

Fig. 14.1. Draft process map.

STEVE. Right
CLIVE. But
STEVE. The only thing I think is what you've got on that...
CLIVE. Yeah
STEVE. as far as I'm concerned... I get there (points out box with no parameter)... there's no parameters inside this hardcore... any risk grade[7]... any amount

From this point onwards the various sheets that make up the draft version of the process map have implications for a whole range of disparate activities. They engender heated discussion about just what the process really does entail, much of which is heavily informed by wholly parochial considerations, such as 'if I buy into this, are my staff going to have to do more work?' and 'if they do, are they going to get any sort of allowance for it so that it doesn't undermine our performance figures?' Much of this revolves around the pros and cons of using a particular print-out, called a WE017, which was a standard diary print-out used to throw up certain kinds of recurrent activities for attention. Clive, while adamant that he would not get any kind of allowance for using that print-out because it was not a process allocated to the sanctioning floor, felt sure that if Steve used it he would get an allowance. The point here for Clive was that if someone was doing this work then they should be getting an allowance of some kind for it so that it did not simply add up to so much lost time and undermine the performance figures for the centre as a whole. Steve, however, was not convinced he would get any allowance for using it and was, in any case, reluctant to devote any time to the process:

STEVE. I'm being selfish here [Looks at Clive]
CLIVE. Yeah [leans back in chair to listen]
STEVE. I will not diary it on a Seventeen... I do not have to have a response (2.0)
CLIVE. Sorry... say again

---

[7] Each customer was allocated a certain risk grade by the system based on a number of variables that together might indicate the potential 'risk' of lending to them.

...

CLIVE. But...if we—If we look at...If we're lookin at er improvin the efficienc.. the operational efficiency of the unit...we need the...We Oh Seventeen...t come in... because the We Oh Seventeen generates an allowance for an activity which is... diarizing for a response to a letter...and if we don't...if we don't bring in the We Oh Seventeen we're undertakin a process for which we're not gettin a measurement

STEVE. Look...write this information down that you've already got

CLIVE. Yeah

STEVE. You set the loan up

CLIVE. Mmmm

STEVE. Yeah?

CLIVE. Yeah

STEVE. And give you the result you know about any way...Coz you've dun it ...

CLIVE. Yeah

STEVE. So that...isn't effective ...

CLIVE. But...what you're asking me to do isn't effective...coz I'm not gettin an allowance for it but by using the We Oh Seventeen....hh you're get- you're goin to get an allowance for the activity that you're undertakin...whereas I'm not goin to get any allowance...but you will

The sheets also implicate a great deal of physical experimentation, drawing bits in, and crossing other bits out, along with verbal projections and collaborative 'imaginings' of scenarios in order to 'see' what might work.

CLIVE. We're still having to go into the sys- into the system

STEVE. But...

CLIVE. To find out...who has responded...on a...on a negative basis [said 'no']

STEVE. Yeah so yo- you're list then i- is partly completed en't it?...Partly

CLIVE. Yeah...So?

STEVE. The one- So you start off with ten [customers] [Demonstrates numbers and divisions with hands on desk]

CLIVE. Yeah

STEVE. Four have responded

CLIVE. Yeah...yeah

STEVE. And you've got those there's six left

...

CLIVE. Right...Okay?...So...Let's see what we need to do here now MAC [appends box and oval on stage 1 document]...so then what we then [crosses out YES/NO]...send them M S Qs and then blah blah blah [scribbles over end ovals and draws fresh lines]

STEVE. Yeah

CLIVE. And i-...all that there then s down to...an action en't it?

STEVE. Mm

CLIVE. Mark yer log...update .... spreadsheet...and...

STEVE. Mm...In a way that lines up wi-...with all the bits to do fer sales

CLIVE. Yeah

STEVE. Then...can I put this in here? [appends further box][8]

CLIVE. Yeah...Right...Okay

[8] See Fig. 14.1 for the outcome of all these changes.

An interesting point is the way that hugely informal representational activities are used here. The scribbling motions, circles, lines, and frequent movements, over the sheets to indicate specific notions but that leave no mark behind are all wholly local and contingent and often abstract to the extent that they have no connection to any external phenomena beyond the nominal connection that is in operation here and now. Ultimately the sheets containing the process maps came to serve as a resource through which the managers found themselves able to negotiate a model they felt they could both 'live with'. They also resolved the problem of the WE017 by adopting Clive's suggestion that they use a screen-based log using shared Excel spreadsheets as the most appropriate and, more specifically, workable (in terms of its both production and use) 'representation' of the current status of customer responses:

STEVE. On here it said...You've sanctioned it...note it on the...Managed Rate Log Pro Forma located on the Gold Card desk...so he's got it in...on a number of places in his process

CLIVE. Right...[takes Stage 1 document] Well we don't...w- we'll change that...we'll work on a spreadsheet...so we'll come up wi a spreadsheet...we'll probably end up...puttin it in customer...put it on Excel

STEVE. It's got to be available t everybody

CLIVE. Yeah...Put it on Excel...and then in sorta Customer Keep [one of the shared server locations for the whole centre] ...

STEVE. Mm

CLIVE. Er...errm...your guys could instead o doin a...coz the thing is the only thing that they're goin to be puttin in there...is

STEVE. Details

CLIVE. Sorta...like...sorta like the date [appends Date Column]...t- t- the date of...er the letter...the account number...and the sort code...so that's your inputs... yeah?...and then it's over to us

STEVE. Mm

CLIVE. As opposed t manual- manual bits o paper...Happy wi that? ...

STEVE. Yeah I mean as I say there's two options you can run

CLIVE. Yeah

STEVE. And it's either manual log...or somethin on there [gestures to Workstation]

Underlying much of the above work is the notion that to achieve the prescription of a task everything must somehow be rendered uniform and predictable. This pursuit of uniformity manifested itself in numerous ways. One was the endeavour to standardize the format and methods for entering details into computer records so that the 'meaning' of such records could be rendered 'transparent', a goal visible in moves towards computer-based knowledge management. The problem, then, became effectively one of how to go about standardizing knowledge so that it could have a general applicability. Yet the above exposition of process modelling work makes it clear that any attempt to see expert knowledge as procedural is wholly unwarranted. Furthermore, a prime conception at play in this kind of process modelling is that it will ultimately prescribe a sequence of tasks that together make up a definitive version of 'best practice'. However, the actual achievement of any process map makes it clear that all versions of 'best practice' are negotiated products. The formulation of 'best practice' is a situated affair—and process maps are, at heart, locally sensible versions of best practice. This is not to be read as any kind of criticism of the efficacy of such maps. Where they are both developed and used in the same sets of local conditions, many affordances may well accrue to such use. It is our contention, however, that problems may arise where such locally sensible versions are exported throughout an organization to other settings where other relevances may apply.

The most significant finding here, however, is that process maps are not systematic, rational, scientific deductions of the most efficient process. Rather they are contingent objects of negotiation and experimentation amongst members who primarily attend to local, situated concerns, and understandings that may well go beyond the narrow and abstracted conceptions of the task itself. In this way it became apparent that, not only does following a process map involve arriving at the situated 'sense within the plan' (Suchman 1987), but the making of such plans is an equally situated accomplishment. This is of significance for the realization of a range of planning activities throughout organizational life.

THE DEVELOPMENT OF MANAGEMENT INFORMATION

Perhaps the most explicit pursuit of standardization in the bank was the development of Management Information (MI) and its attendant metrics. Here tasks were timed and measured and 'Reasonable Expectancies' of time taken to realize some task specified. These metrics were applied in the allocation and monitoring of work. However, the use of such information drew on common-sense understandings and knowledge to arrive at an appropriate and meaningful numerical depiction. Here, for instance, we can see a manager working to achieve a numerical depiction of what were known as 'backlogs':

Clive sorting through MI papers—Looks at the calendar under his keyboard and writes 'P/E 27/2' [Period Ending 27/2] on 4-Weekly Total printout
He then continues to write on a sheet from his notepad:

P/E 27/2 P/E 27/3
ASH %   HE ASH %[9]

He enters the total from the 4-Weekly Total sheet for Non-Personal, then does the same for the others
Clive draws a line down to split up the 'P/E 27/2' group, then shifts the other 4-Weekly Total Sheet in front of himself and notes the figures similarly for the 'P/E 27/3' group
Clive draws a line at the right hand side to separate the figures and percentages—He

[9] ASH = Actual Staff Hours, HE = Hours Earned. The distinction here recognizes the way that the work measurement system in the bank provides a particular allowance for certain activities, but these do not necessarily tally precisely with the actual hours worked.

does the same for the 'Backlogs'—He writes the 'Backlogs' as a total, then puts the P/Es, then notes the figures from the sheets (averages for the 4 week period)

Clive comments that the figures for the backlogs don't relate to any specific allowance—He needs to see if they are retaining the backlogs at a 'manageable level'—He admits it's 'not rocket science'—He is just using it to give him an idea.

We can see then how the development and use of MI can be seen to turn upon achieving a practical 'fit' between the information and the activity to which it is applied (monitoring the backlogs); understanding what an appropriate description might amount to (depicting backlogs in terms of an anticipated number of hours of work to complete them); and necessitating a common-sense understanding of the organization (for instance, what body of work might appropriately be characterized as a backlog).

The development of information of this kind offers particular affordances in relation to standardization. It means seeing all work as ultimately reducible to figures and a meaningful way of representing the work of individuals. In this way it is possible to mathematize, render predictable, and open up to further transformation the inherently unpredictable contingencies of everyday work (Lynch 1990). With the above example, for instance, a variable body of work is transformed into a potential number of hours of actual work through the application of a 'standard' expectation of how long such work might reasonably be expected to take, and having an impact upon subsequent work allocation and staffing.

It is hard to overstress the significance of the bank's drive towards standardization as an essential part of its move towards distributed work activities, and this has clearly had an effect on the actual doing of everyday work. However, the efficacy and very sense of how to use and understand some standard appropriately are intimately bound up with 'local' understandings and relevances rather than 'global' ones.[10] This questions the very perception of 'a standard' as some rigorous and uniform prescription.

CONCLUSION

In this chapter we have presented a discussion of some of the ways in which standardization has been pursued as part of major changes in the organization and working culture of a retail bank. We have tried to show how such attempts continue to depend upon local knowledge, local loyalties, and constellations of assistance, not to mention the ordinary affordances provided by the co-presence of the organization's staff.

This emphasis on standardization was made manifest in a wide variety of the bank's activities, including process modelling, checking, the creation of

[10] In other words, 'the more global, the more local'—the fifth rule of virtuality (Woolgar, this volume).

Management Information, and the attempt to routinize and standardize decision making. An important point to recognize about all of these work activities is the extent to which they rely upon mundane representational practices. A whole range of things—assessment of performance, work allocation, staffing on a day-to-day basis, the development of strategies, the setting of targets—turn upon what prove to be wholly ordinary, orderly ways of representing real-world activities.

Examination of the work of building the virtual organization, its impact on everyday work, and the instantiation of a strategic plan does not, then—however radical the plan—result in a total rewriting of everything. Rather, the very process of change and the other things it brings with it such as rapid technological innovation has to be made 'at home' in a pre-existing world (Sacks 1992). So, for instance, an orientation to organizational objectives and the instantiation of strategic plans is most visible in *post-hoc* rationalization of decisions and actions undertaken on the basis of ordinary local and contingent encounters. This in no sense undermines claims about the changing 'content' of the working world. We have already noted Suchman's astute recognition that the particular sense of any plan can only be achieved in the following of it (Suchman 1987). Large-scale, far-reaching strategic plans with the potential to impact on numerous lives are no less plans despite the scale of their ambition. And it is no less true of their pretensions that the sense of these pretensions necessarily has to be realized in the following of them as situated actions. In that case the inability of such radical aims to rewrite fundamental practices is hardly surprising.

Most of the above observations are implicitly bound up with the realities of achieving distributed and flexible working practices, especially with regard to the work of 'virtual teams'. We have also noted the ways in which co-presence is a routine resource for the achievement of certain kinds of working practice and there is often some measure of neglect in considering how to support distributed work in the absence of such a resource. This omission is a direct consequence of attending to theoretical abstractions and formal accounts of the work rather than inspecting the actual ways in which work gets done, hence our heavy emphasis upon the observation of 'real-world, real-time' work.

If we attend to how IT is used to facilitate 'virtual' teamwork, it becomes clear that there are a number of technological resources that are routinely drawn upon. Two of the most frequently 'to-hand' resources provided by IT are the standard accounting package and a relational database. Screens from these two packages are regularly used to acquire a 'picture' of 'how things stand'. The point of interest here is the extent to which the actual 'sense' of what is on the screens, the relevance of the information, is a product of interactional work between staff, customers, and colleagues. Whilst non-co-located teams may be desirable, and in many cases necessary, there is a clear efficacy to co-present teamwork when it comes to the realization of certain kinds of activity, such as the negotiation of the significance of account entries.

In consideration of what kinds of new practices are necessitated by distributed working and the operation of virtual teams, it is clear that most working practices are relatively unchanged. Where the impact is of most significance is where members would routinely resort to the affordances of co-presence to achieve activities but where, as a result of non-co-location, other kinds of interaction have to be pursued. It is in these kinds of circumstances that representational practices come to have the most significance. A primary concern is the 'exportability' of information, and this, as we saw with process modelling, management information, and knowledge management, involves specification, proceduralization, and mathematization. Whilst these practices offer certain affordances for distributed working, they result in bodies of information that still require re-embedding in locally relevant practices. It is also clear that, in some cases, the kinds of appropriate practices to replace those conventionally available through co-presence are as yet unclear.

One of the largest problems with highly distributed divisions of labour is how to maintain an awareness of others' work. The tight prescription of task implied in process models is intended to obviate the need for this kind of concern. One problem, however, with formal models is that nowhere is any allowance made for the actual work involved in arriving at some sense of 'what the work is about'. Members tacitly orient to common understandings, yet it is exactly this kind of orientation that remains unexplicated by formal accounts of the work process. Hence a great deal of the coordination work revolves around common-sense understandings of the work and how appropriately to make information available. Yet this figures nowhere in formal representations of work. It is hardly surprising, therefore, that an emphasis remains upon local loyalties while other, non-co-located individuals, teams, and units are subject to blame and criticism (Hughes *et al.* 1996*b*). This prevalence of local loyalties problematizes some of the more sanguine hopes expressed within the virtual-organizational literature and is of considerable significance for the practical viability of virtual teamwork. Whilst there is an ever-increasing use of IT to support work across the organizational divide, the daily orientation to the notion of 'the team' is still local and built upon the affordances of co-presence. Consequently, however feasible the notion of a virtual team, the notion of virtual teamwork is altogether more questionable.

15

Cotton to Computers: From Industrial to Information Revolutions

Jon Agar, Sarah Green, and Penny Harvey

INTRODUCTION

In the summer of 1998, Manchester City Council coordinated a series of cele-bratory events in and around the city centre, to honour (and generate) the memory of a machine: to be specific, a computer dubbed 'the Baby'. This was the first electronic computer to be built with a working stored program, and it was fifty years since it had been persuaded finally to calculate something by its designers, who were based at the Victoria University of Manchester. The cele-brations included building a precise replica of the machine, at a cost of over 1 million pounds, as well as a full programme of artistic and museum displays, theatre performances, exhibitions, conferences, and parties, all focusing on the theme of information technologies. A range of Manchester's more established institutions—universities, museums, media organizations, and the electronics manufacturer ICL—all committed resources and organized events.

The computer in question was rarely called 'the Baby' in 1948; the name evoked a sense of historical 'natural' origins intended by the coordinators of the 1998 celebrations.[1] The underlying point from the city's perspective was explicitly the promotion of an image of Manchester as a key player at the birth of the current Information Revolution, just as it had been a key player in the origins of the Industrial Revolution.[2] History was being mobilized by the city's institutional

[1] Interestingly, this habit of seeing early versions of computers as 'babies' has not been restricted to Manchester and the stored-program computer. See, for example, Downey's account of the historiography of CAD/CAM technology, in a section entitled 'Birth History' (Downey 1998: 212–14). Downey traces how ideas of origins, genealogy, and ancestry are all involved in this imagery.

[2] The historiographical irony is that some historians understand innovation in information technologies as being a *development* of industrialization—for example Beniger's cycle (1986) of industrialization–crisis of control–control technology innovation.

elite in a deliberate act of connection: building on school history knowledge of industrialization and then associating it with today's computer-based developments, the city attempted to justify Manchester's claims to having been one of the places, even *the* place, where the machine that pervades our lives today was first developed.

These connections and histories had to be actively drawn out, detached from alternative understandings of the past, and given precedence. There is, in fact, no necessary link between Manchester's industrial past and its contemporary involvement in information and communications technologies (ICTs). The connection had to be made, and the 1998 celebrations were a part of that effort. Why then were the city's institutional elites interested in promoting this particular claim? How did they go about establishing it? And what were the effects of their activities?

The answers to these questions, which required both archival history and contemporary ethnography, produced a story that, in one sense, is particular to Manchester. However, the aim of this chapter goes beyond description of this city's encounter with ICTs. The study provides an example of the difference it makes to look in detail at the actual circumstances and experiences of ICT developments;[3] in line with others in this volume, we have approached the issue of the 'impacts' of new technologies on the social fabric of the city through detailed analysis of the discourses and practices in which these technologies are embedded. That in itself suggested that 'impacts' is something of a misnomer, implying as it does that technologies are separate from the contexts that constitute them.[4] Evidently, the details of the case relate to the circumstances of Manchester; but the study has wider implications, two of which should be flagged up from the start. The experience of the city cannot be understood without an appreciation of ideas—of motivations, possibilities, interpretations—that have far wider cultural purchase. The people and institutions we describe were deploying ideas drawn from communicational networks going far beyond those operating within Manchester. On one level then, our work identifies key cultural tropes surrounding ICTs (the importance of continual innovation, the imperative to connect, the salience of the technical fix, the promise of virtuality itself) and shows how such ideas are grounded in specific and particular relationships (both personal and institutional) when actually deployed by people in practice. Methodologically, this cultural analysis itself has 'impacts', as it recasts the notion of the 'local social context'. The Manchester case reveals how 'context' is a highly dynamic, a contested and emergent field of social relations from which the technical can never be disengaged. One of the persistent problems with 'impact' studies is that questions about the significance of local context tend to

---

[3] This is a point also emphasized by Cooper *et al.* (this volume).

[4] In their social psychological study of social interaction on the internet, Watt *et al.* (this volume) also note that social context is crucial to the kinds of social interaction that occur within computer-mediated communication (CMC).

the teleological. Causal relationships are projected back into the past. Our work seeks to reverse this approach by looking instead at how people actively fashion historical significance in the present, mobilizing cultural (historically established) representations and practices as they do so.[5] Thus, by paying close attention to the ways in which Manchester (as 'context') has been fashioned over time in relation to cultural ideas about technical innovation (both contemporary and historical), we have attempted to provide an example of how to understand the possibilities and limits of the latest technological innovations for urban regeneration.[6]

Our argument is that, in advocating the transformative possibilities of ICTs, contemporary Manchester institutional elites are continuing an established—indeed, institutionalized—recourse to the 'technical fix', a habit that is deeply embedded both locally and within modernist conceptions of the world in Western cultures.[7] The offering of technical solutions for social problems is both popularly comprehensible in this context and politically expedient.[8] The promises made resonate with understandings of what technologies are and what they can achieve. We will describe these understandings as they were played out in the Manchester case and show how contemporary 'technical fixes' relate to appeals to technology that have been made in the past. This relationship is crucial for understanding how the 'technical fix' is operationalized. City elites have created a particular kind of urban history, a history that selectively connects (and creates) the Information and Industrial revolutions. We argue that the repetitive mobilization of the past to justify and give meaning to new urban technology was institutionalized in Manchester by the late nineteenth century, cementing the image of *the* (original) industrial city. This had important consequences for twentieth-century civic policy, public image, and urban memory.

[5] A parallel argument is made about organizational memory by Brown and Lightfoot (this volume).

[6] The relationship between information technologies and contemporary urban change came under intense scholarly scrutiny in the last years of the twentieth century, mostly from sociologists, geographers, and urban planners. See e.g. Castells (1989) and Hall (1996: esp. 402–22). It can no longer be stated, as do Graham and Marvin in their excellent monograph from 1996, that the subject is 'poorly understood' (Graham and Marvin 1996: p. xiii). An explanation of the centrality of this topic in recent years should be found in disciplinary dynamics, changing funding regimes and political contexts within which the novelty of information technology has been highly valorized. This paper—written by two anthropologists and a historian—can be read as an extension and a critique of such work.

[7] See Latour (1993, 1996) for an account of the relationship between Western culture and technology; see Downey (1998: ch. 1) for a summary of the development of the idea of technology as a 'fix', and Bijker *et al.* (1987) for a discussion of the socially constructed character of technology.

[8] Swann and Watts (this volume) have identified this popular comprehensibility of 'innovation' as a key factor in whether or not new products will 'take off'. The existence of a 'paradigm' through which new technologies can be understood is, they suggest, important in building this 'common language'.

As the ethnographic sections of this chapter make clear, ICTs became embedded within social, historical, and political contexts in ways that ran counter to the supposed characteristics of the technologies themselves: space defying, boundary crossing, ubiquitously linking.[9] Our argument is that, despite all the claims to 'dislocation', or freedom from spatial location that these technologies offer, what happened in practice in this case was a process of 'relocation'.[10] Far from removing the relevance of place, the technologies have been used to shore up the idea and presence of 'Manchester' as part of a deliberate policy to promote a particular image of the city: the 'city of glass connections' that is put forward as the successor to the centre of industrial production.[11]

We start with the story of the Manchester Host, a publicly owned file server that was set up in Manchester in 1990. It was this project that involved several Manchester organizations in attempts to provide the city as a whole with public networked computing. As such, it provided a framework—both an 'origin myth' and links between groups both within and beyond the city—upon which future developments have built. Despite it being a very recent story, it has already been written up several times.[12] The people involved, many of whom are still in Manchester and still involved in telematics in the city, strongly felt at the time that they were doing something revolutionary, that they were amongst the first to recognize the potential of telematics and actually to do something about it. It is important, therefore, to say a little about what these key individuals felt that telematics could be used for, and what they believed they were involved in doing.

We then move on to look at how the story of Manchester's relationship with public telematics was actively connected to previous technical projects. This raises the issue of how and why people make historical connections. Urban history unfortunately, and surprisingly, rarely asks whether there is in fact a necessary connection between two periods, let alone how that connection has been constructed: it is not self-evident that simply because Manchester is the place where certain events occurred in two different periods that the earlier events influenced the later ones. Urban history is a product of cities not a description. Even if influence across periods appears to occur, the form it takes and the reasons for that connection being created need to be analysed. In this case, a strategy previously used (the 'technical fix') was repeated and attention

---

[9] See e.g. Mitchell (1995) for an explicit expression of this view in relation to cities; and Springer (1996) and Hayles (1999) for examples of how the 'space-defying' characteristics of ICTs entirely alter our understanding of our bodily selves and location. See also Augé (1999) for an example of the argument that ICTs 'dislocate' people socially and culturally.

[10] In a parallel point, Cooper et al. (this volume) also note that ICTs are actively located by users.

[11] As Wittel et al. argue (this volume), the new economy increases the importance of face-to-face sociality as the ability to create and demonstrate connectivity becomes ever more important. In this sense location is integral to networked sociality. See also Liff et al. (this volume), who suggest that place does indeed continue to matter in the notion of the 'virtual'.

[12] See e.g. Graham and Marvin (1996: 363), which draws on Manchester City Council (1991).

was drawn to the repetition, and *that* made history: it formed part of what Manchester was and is imagined to be, in its essence.[13]

Finally, we turn to the ethnographic account and compare three connected telematics initiatives, those of the Greater Manchester Information Network Group (G-MING), a consortium set up to install and run high-speed connections between the computers of several institutions within the city; the Museum of Science and Industry in Manchester (MSIM), which attempted to make use of the G-MING network in setting up a museum project associated with ICTs; and the Manchester Communities Information Network (MCIN), a community computing project, which became involved in a European-funded ICT programme led by the City Council, through which it was charged with setting up public access 'kiosks' in Manchester. These provide examples of the now oft-observed fact that technology is not separate from the social conditions in which it exists.[14] But, more than that, we suggest that technologies are not separate from the *spatial* conditions in which they exist either, something that is particularly significant in the case of ICTs, which are supposed somehow to erase the relevance of space and place.[15] In each case, a combination of understanding of these technologies, pre-existing relationships between those involved, and the context of Manchester itself deeply informed how the introduction and use of ICTs was experienced in practice. If anything, the use of ICTs reiterated spatial divisions and distinctiveness rather than assisting in ameliorating them.

To that extent, the technologies were used both to shore up an idea of what 'Manchester' was supposed to be and to reinforce pre-existing distinctions and divisions within the city. However, and this is important, that is *not* the same as saying that ICTs failed to change anything. Rather, it is to say that what changed was not due to the 'impact' of these technologies, but more to do with the kinds of connections people and organizations forged between themselves, the constructed past and imagined future, their spatial location *and* the technologies.[16] Making such underlying processes visible is one aim of this chapter, so that changes that do occur along with the introduction of ICTs are understood in their historical and spatial context, rather than described in terms that simply

---

[13] In Gourgouris's terms (1996: 15–16), this process is similar to the generation of the idea of 'nation'; the 'technical fix' becomes part of what was always already true about Manchester, a timeless truth about the way Manchester 'is', as a place.

[14] See e.g. MacKenzie and Wajcman (1985) and Downey and Dumit (1997). Studies that imply such a separation include most 'impact studies'—e.g. Mitchell (1999) and Slouka (1996).

[15] See Smith and Agar (1998) for further discussion of science, technology, and location.

[16] This appears to be somewhat similar to Downey's comment (1998: 21) that 'impact studies' ignore 'the process of technology development itself, including the so-called "knowledge contents" of the technology. They keep hidden the complex activities of technological development, leaving decision makers both invisible and in control.' However, our argument goes beyond this point, in that it focuses on the relevance of *place and location* in these 'invisible' processes; Downey's point relates to the experience of machine–person interactions, and to that extent has no need of the history or location of such interactions.

reiterate cultural rhetoric about technology and its effects. One element of such rhetoric, related to notions of novelty and innovation ('there has been nothing like it under the sun before'), precisely generates ICTs as somehow history resistant and context resistant.[17] This chapter, by analysing the histories and contexts of the introduction of ICTs in Manchester, attempts to reach underneath such rhetoric.

And what of virtuality?[18] Ironically, if anything was 'virtual' in this research, it was the idea of Manchester itself. Indeed, as new possibilities for the social organization of the city were debated in relation to the potential impacts of ICTs, the 'city' itself emerged as a highly contested location,[19] particularly in relation to how the city was represented in bids for development funding. Attempts to fashion Manchester as an 'information city' highlighted the competing versions of both contemporary Manchester and the relevant historical Manchesters through which such versions sought to legitimate themselves.

THE ORIGIN MYTH: THE MANCHESTER HOST STORY

The Manchester Host story begins, according to most accounts, in the late 1970s/early 1980s at the University of Sussex, where a group of students who had come to know each other through their involvement in socialist politics shared an interest in the potential of networked computing for the international labour movement.[20] In 1983, some of these friends founded a company in London called Soft Solutions Ltd, a worker's cooperative, which developed software, but also came up with the idea of an alternative to Prestel, which had been launched by the Post Office in 1979.[21] Others of the group, and two in particular, left the south and moved up to Manchester, where they began to become involved in both city council politics and the trade-union movement. Meanwhile, Soft Solutions approached the then left-wing Greater London Council, proposing an alternative to Prestel; eventually, a grant was awarded. The new service, Poptel,

[17] This kind of notion is not a view that is held so much as an assumption from which various culture-specific views are formed. See e.g. Shawn Wilbur's exploration of this issue (Wilbur 2000).

[18] We refer here to the representational and referential notion of virtual reality in which there is 'an attempt to match experience with a series of representations, to copy the shapes of external realities, and to make participants live these copies as if they are real or actual' (Kapferer 1997: 181).

[19] At one point there were two entirely independent and quite distinct 'virtual Manchesters' on the Web.

[20] We are grateful to Steve Walker for adding corrections to an earlier version of this chapter on this point. Walker was one of the students in question.

[21] Prestel was the Post Office's viewdata service. Further, the French Minitel experiment, which had its user trial between 1981 and 1982, provided an example of a more interactive and popular provision of electronic services. See Cohen and Walsh (1995) for details of the Minitel experience.

began by selling an e-mail facility, mostly to trade unions, and by 1989, the turnover from this was as high as Soft Solution's software business. Poptel acted as the UK agents for GeoNet—a PC-and-modem system for electronic mail and databases (Lane 1990: 40).[22]

Several members of the original group had by this time secured jobs in Manchester, at the City Council and at what is now Manchester Metropolitan University (MMU), where the Manchester Employment Research Group, later renamed the Centre for Employment Research (CER), was housed. CER was asked by one of the group who now worked for the council to do a feasibility study for setting up a public e-mail service in Manchester. The underlying motivation for the public e-mail service, which was supported by CER, was (in contrast to, say, the alternative of business-focused Teleports) to help forge links within the international labour movement.[23] But another formal aim was added at this point, as Manchester City Council was now involved as a sponsor of putting the project into practice. The e-mail service was going to have to serve Manchester's public, whatever it may or may not do for the international labour movement. The council also made support conditional on Poptel moving to Manchester. Thus the Manchester Host, run by Poptel and sponsored by the council, started with at least two (different) underlying aims, neither of which concerned commercial profit.

CER's feasibility study for the council suggested that Poptel's service could borrow the idea of setting up 'electronic village halls' from Scandinavian countries—that is, providing local communities with access to telematics via a community centre housing a cluster of computers with modems. Following a call for tenders, three bids were accepted, and subsequently Bangladesh House, built up from a pre-existing Asian community centre, Chorlton Workshop, built up from a pre-existing Chorlton community centre, and the Women's Electronic Village Hall (WEVH), an entirely new venture, were founded to serve their respective 'communities'. All three were initially located in the same area of south Manchester, although the WEVH later moved to a more central location.

---

[22] Lane shared many of the ideals of Poptel, especially an interest in getting non-commercial and non-governmental organizations online.

GeoNet Mailbox Systems GmbH was founded in 1981 by the Brunswick-born Guenther Leue, who had worked since 1953 for a large American computer manufacturer. GeoNet's strategy was based on 'distributed processing' to share systems across a network. This meant relatively cheap services, which in turn meant that, even though GeoNet was a private company, it was one of the first companies that could sell its e-mail services to cash-poor organizations, in particular small to medium-sized enterprises (SMEs) and political groups. By 1994 GeoNet had grown to include many 'hosts' from America to Siberia.

[23] Note the contrast between these developments and those only thirty miles distant in Sheffield, described by Hakken (1991), where 'computerization was used by public officials ... to justify the view that traditional forms of trade union struggle were an anachronism in an information age. These public officials simultaneously pushed legislation that undercut the powers of trade unions'.

The underlying political project of linking the international labour movement together through the Host initiative did not initially fade from view.[24] However, the Host did not achieve that goal, and by 2000 no longer existed, having been funded for only five years and not subsequently refunded. Not much is now said about the international trade-union movement, as Poptel soon moved away from its earlier political ideals (a source of tension within Soft Solutions) and now, like Prestel, is a small internet service provider.[25]

However, the international focus provided by pre-existing links with international labour organizations did have some consequences. Once the initial funding was provided, telematics links were rapidly made with groups in Bulgaria and St Petersburg, with which Manchester is twinned, but also in European Union member states. The connections to the EU were later used to great effect to attract European funding for further projects.[26] In 1994, Manchester became a key member of Telecities, a consortium of over fifty European cities involved in developing telematics strategies and links throughout Europe (Carter 1997). Three years later, the city helped to initiate Infocities, a consortium of seven cities that were provided with funding to experiment with and share information about high bandwidth applications across their networks; and the existence of the Host project has been acknowledged to have influenced Brussels's view of Manchester's 'advanced' position in telematics, which has apparently helped a range of projects, including the G-MING project, to be funded with European money.[27]

In short, gaining a reputation for being an 'information city', however successful or unsuccessful the Host project was in retrospect, has opened a fairly substantial avenue into European funding. In that respect, the presentation of Manchester as being (once again) on the 'cutting edge' of a technological revolution has most certainly paid off. Under such circumstances, we can begin to see how and why so much money was spent resurrecting 'the Baby' in 1998.

Finally, the Host project shaped alliances and divisions within the city, alliances and divisions that were central to the way public telematics was introduced, and that remain active. The importance of this point is related to the way funded projects such as Infocities relate to different parts of the city. The Manchester Host, not having been initially motivated by the dynamics of the city itself but by the international labour movement, later being incorporated into the city via council funding, but rapidly moving on to being funded by Europe and consolidating its links with MMU, led to a very particular kind of location within the city. It was one that was markedly based on the rapidly 'urban regenerating'

---

[24] See e.g. On-Line News, 4 (Winter 1994), 4. On-Line News was the Host's users' newsletter.

[25] Steve Walker, personal communication, 23 Feb. 2000.

[26] Indeed, some of the founders of the Host, who subsequently left, said that this development was one of the reasons that they left: the Host appeared to have become an effective vehicle for raising European funds, and became rather distant from its original aims as a result. Steve Walker, personal communication.

[27] Dave Carter, interview with Penny Harvey and Sarah Green, 1998.

city centre and, more recently, on the arts and music industries based in that area. It was not focused on the more economically deprived areas such as Moston in north Manchester, where MCIN, discussed below, was based.

This sketch of the more recent origins of Manchester's relationship with public telematics illustrates a fairly straightforward point: that ICTs do not simply 'appear' in a place. They are made to appear, and much work had to go into accomplishing that impression. This inevitably means that how they appear will be associated with the motivations and perceptions of those who work to put them in place, which also means they will be located and perceived as being connected to particular people, organizations, interests, and so on. And, as the City Council has played such a key part in this story, we now turn to the municipal mobilization of history, the way in which Manchester has repeatedly constructed itself as a city of 'technology'. Such associations make it appear 'natural' that Manchester should embrace ICTs; but, again, much work had to go into creating that impression.

MAKING HISTORICAL CONNECTIONS

A brief sketch of the history of Manchester will enable several important points to be made. The first industrial 'shock city' rapidly expanded from the mid-eighteenth century in conditions that many authors have noticed as being relatively unregulated (although other more regulated cities also grew). Historians have cited this lack of regulation, environmental advantages, and early special-ization in cotton as reasons for Manchester's growth (Briggs 1968; Kidd 1996: 21–36). By 1838 liberal agitation had achieved a measure of political indepen-dence for the city, and the Manchester Corporation was set up as a local gov-ernment body to run the city's own affairs. At this point, free-trade liberalism was in the political ascendant, and the corporation acted to protect the city's businesses from too much regulation. However, in the later nineteenth century a quiet revolution occurred, with the corporation taking on more and more roles, in particular providing more services and building very large technolo-gical projects requiring massive quantities of capital. As Kidd (1996: 154) asks: 'how and why did the living symbol of free trade succumb to corporate pro-vision on such a scale?' Why, in other words, did the city renowned for free trade become dominated by a centralized and powerful local government? The solutions he gives to this paradox are only partially satisfying: the practical advantages of good utilities overcame liberal doubts, an argument that civic responsibilities gained 'a momentum of their own', and an acceptance that the city's public institutions, rather than industry, should provide technical and further education.

During the nineteenth century, Manchester's corporate growth is well des-cribed as 'imperial', both in its relations with the world (the city was a centre of trade links that stretched in the case of cotton from the southern USA, the Caribbean, and the Levant for raw cotton, to worldwide markets such as India) and with neighbouring authorities since the corporation absorbed a succession of smaller townships (Redford and Russell 1940; Rose 1996). In the early to mid-twentieth century, corporation activities were marked by the extension (and professionalization) of 'planning', best illustrated by the new 'garden suburb' of Wythenshawe and the first industrial estate, Trafford Park, and by public celebrations of municipalism. Post-war Manchester saw decline, in the cotton industry particularly. However, new urban technological systems were still significant, especially the expansion of the airport and road systems, such as the peripheral motorways that eventually encircled the city, and inner-city 'fly-overs' such as the Mancunian Way opened by Harold Wilson to gushing praise in the press announcing Manchester as the 'super space city'.

The history of Mancunian technological systems forms the basis for a series of claims. First, public bodies in Manchester have been the most significant local agent of technological systems growth. For example, Manchester is quite unusual in that the gas supply was publicly owned, after great struggle, from the early nineteenth century. Revenue from this municipal monopoly was used to bankroll other projects, including new technological systems (Turner 1994). The corporation developed water supply systems on a massive and politically sensitive scale: urban control stretching out to reservoirs built eighteen miles east in Longdendale in mid-nineteenth century, and 100 miles north to Thirlmere in the Lake District by the late nineteenth century (Redford and Russell 1940: ii. 171–204, 333–52). Sewerage, and connected public health systems, were publicly run. The greatest of all the city's technological projects, the Manchester Ship Canal, which connected inland Manchester to the Irish Sea, thus cutting out Liverpool dock charges, started as a private initiative but finished in 1894 as a public project (Farnie 1980; Owen 1983; Harford 1994). These nineteenth- and twentieth-century schemes contrast sharply with older projects, such as the Bridgewater Canal, built in the eighteenth century, and the first modern canal, which were private ventures.

Second, during Manchester's period of imperial growth, technology was a crucial tool in inter-authority politics. Access to gas, for example, was used as a lever for persuading smaller local authorities to merge with the corporation. If a technological system necessarily passed through another authority (for example, clean water from the Lake District, or the Ship Canal through Salford or Cheshire), the process of negotiating agreement over access tied neighbouring authorities to Manchester. This technological strategy in inter-local authority politics developed early compared to other UK cities.

Third, while the major historiographical theorization of technological system growth, the model put forward in *Networks of Power* by Thomas Parke Hughes, stresses the work of private inventor-entrepreneurs in the early phases, in Manchester, in a way that would be entirely alien to Hughes's private entrepreneurs, technology was closely bound to strong local commitments to 'self-government', and therefore public bodies (T. P. Hughes 1983: 14). The liberal free-trade economic philosophy that was espoused by the Manchester political elite celebrated 'self-government', to which Alfred Waterhouse's gothic Town Hall of the 1870s is a monument. Publicly developed and owned technological systems were not seen as inimical to the creed; *indeed for the elite they embodied it*. For example, gas revenue gave them 'freedom' to pursue their projects in the city, whereas the ship canal was a bid for 'freedom' from Liverpool dock rates (in Hughes's terminology these were 'reverse salients').[28] In this way we can resolve Kidd's paradox: the reason that the city of free trade had succumbed to corporate provision on a large scale was because technological systems became the physical representation, the embodiment, of the city elite's liberal virtues of self-government—there was, for them, no contradiction.

Finally, there was a curious feedback effect. Self-governance might have become embodied in technological systems, but incorporating the management of these systems also altered the administration. Redford, for example, argues that

in the early [1870s] some members of the City Council and some officials of the Corporation realized the complexity of the problems which they had to face. The civic machinery was beginning to be reorganized in such a fashion as to centralise the general control of administration, while leaving the separate departments adequate freedom in the organisation of specialised work. (Redford and Russell 1940: ii. 294)

Thus as governance and technological systems became entwined, local bureaucracy grew, a trend deepened by legislation such as the Local Government Act (1888), which placed more responsibilities on the shoulders of the corporation. The organization of the city was also subject to extensive external criticism—for example, from Beatrice Webb and the journalist Joseph Scott—which hastened change.[29] Intermeshed with these factors was the growth in the city's population, growth encouraged by the attention to infrastructure paid by the corporation. Overall, bureaucratic centralized power in Manchester grew, and at the heart of the transformation was an identification of technological systems as a source and tool of local power, and a symbol and example of urban order.

The consequence of these developments was that technological systems became highly significant for the image of Manchester. This argument differs from the usual explanation that Manchester was the first industrial city, and

---

[28] M. J. Turner (1994) is right to stress that the struggle over gas ownership was a conflict over governance; our point is that governance and the technological systems are intimately connected.

[29] Redford and Russell (1940: ii. 430–1, 443). Another example is Horsfall in 'The Government of Manchester' (1895): 'A very imperfectly governed town' which 'expressed only the worst qualities of our race, our disbelief in the need of a system, our belief that the most difficult work can be well done by untrained people.' The tide of criticism led to the publication of the *Manchester Municipal Code*, six massive volumes by 1901 and five supplementary volumes by 1932. Agar has argued elsewhere that the process of making rules explicit, especially in government, is often connected to mechanization. See Agar (forthcoming).

therefore it was identified with industrial machinery: the public image of Manchester had to be fashioned by public bodies, and public bodies had to have a good reason for doing so. The good reason here was the way in which it could be used in local politics, in particular as cause and effect of the city's elite's liberal values of self-government. From the late nineteenth century onwards, this technological representation of Manchester was recycled and mobilized for the purpose of justifying further projects: the Manchester Ship Canal, for example, was portrayed as a means of *restoring* commercial prestige, by doing something old—building canals—now new. At a time of perceived competitive slippage, Manchester's planners turned to a very expensive technological fix and over time this reaction came to be seen as inevitable, as part of the substance and inherent character of Manchester: it came to be institutionalized. In the process the role of technology also had to be historicized. It is not entirely unconnected that the Industrial Revolution as a historical event rather than as a tag for contemporary radical change was an invention of the late nineteenth century.[30]

The institutionalized technological fix has survived in Manchester's public institutions. Some more recent examples are the high priority given to the airport in the post-war period in another period of perceived local economic decline, or the optimistic rhetoric of the 'second industrial revolution' of the 1960s (the public promotion of private businesses, such as MetroVicks, Ferranti, ICI, Courtaulds).[31] The G-MING project, discussed below, was justified by rhetorically connecting to past systems: like the Ship Canal, it would supposedly 'pipe prosperity' back into Manchester. With the 'Birth of the Baby' this historicizing process has been taken to another level.[32] The remarkable project to rebuild an identical replica of the first stored-program computer marks the *absence* of a thriving computer industry in the area, while expressing a hope for future prosperity—either for computing (the University of Manchester's interest) or more likely cultural heritage (the City Council's and the MSIM's interest). It is, therefore, a cargo cult, an attempt to create something out of nothing through the belief that the assertion of the possibility is key to a successful outcome.[33] And resources continue to flow into Manchester: in 1999, a year after the well-publicized celebrations, a Cray T3E-1200E, financed through a public–private consortium and then the fourth fastest supercomputer in the world, was installed at the University of Manchester.

There has thus been continuity in the connection between Manchester and technology, a connection made for a particular reason. This continuity justifies

[30] In Britain, Industrial Revolution as a past historical event, lasting between 1760 and 1840, was promulgated by Arnold Toynbee in 1884 in his *Lectures on the Industrial Revolution in England*. See Hudson (1992: 11).

[31] For the 'second industrial revolution', see Kidd (1996: 189).

[32] Discussed in greater detail in Agar (1998).

[33] The use of the phrase 'cargo cult' is here used in its popular understanding, rather than its more complex anthropological meaning. See e.g. Kulick and Stroud (1990).

the study of urban history when thinking about recent or contemporary change. However, it is important to stress that the continuity exists because historicity is built into contemporary understandings both of the city and of the technologies, which would otherwise be stratigraphically unconnected. The process has been selective, remembering certain past events (the Ship Canal) but not others (Peterloo), but the creation of historicity was crucial to the actions of local institutions.

This historical account has demonstrated the particularities of, and the justification for, making connections between the city and the Information Revolution. The question that remains to be considered is the *content* of the concept of the 'technical fix' in contemporary Manchester: what happens in practice, within social networks and across different groups in the city, when the new information technologies are actually introduced? In order to get at this issue, three examples from the ethnographic research will be introduced here. The first, concerning G-MING, continues the story where the Host left off, and looks at the conditions that led G-MING to have to confront the (non-technical) issue of 'users'; the second, about the MSIM, looks at the way much wider cultural understandings of the 'technical', particularly the idea of technology being 'autonomous' or 'neutral' with respect to the social context in which it is applied, confronts the practicalities of having to be *somewhere* and for *someone*; and the third example involving the MCIN, considers what happens when you are located in the 'wrong' place.

G-MING: TECHNICAL FIX MEETS SOCIAL LOCATION

The G-MING network was funded in 1994 under the EU's 4th Framework to the tune of 2.9 million Ecus, with Manchester securing one of only four such funded networks.[34] It 'went live' in 1995, and was conceived as an academic fibre-optic network that would gradually grow to become a Metropolitan Area Network 'serving a wide range of non-commercial uses, covering schools, colleges, libraries, advice centres, hospitals, health centres and residential homes'.[35]

As a project, G-MING was not presented by anybody as ground-breaking or innovative in the way the Host was, but it did enable Manchester to build new projects (and acquire new funding), particularly in the fields of telematics and cultural heritage. The initial funding was acquired because of Manchester's

[34] This was related to an overall European strategy to develop an 'Information Society' in Europe. See CEC (1993) and the Bangemann Report (Bangemann 1994).

[35] Carter (1997: 150). Ironically, given the later tensions that we discuss, Carter expressed hope that G-MING would serve to connect: 'the challenge here is not the profit motive of multinational corporate decision-making but rather an inherent conservatism and elitism within higher education institutions that sees developments such as this as enhancements to internal systems rather than an essential element of wider urban and regional development.'

established reputation as a city that could and would 'grow' the uses for such technologies, a potential that certain people in the council were quick to exploit when the opportunity arose. The rationales that were mobilized for the location of this network in Manchester were the issues that preoccupied all the Telecities partners—that is, how to regenerate the urban centres of post-industrial cities. The G-MING funding thus brought with it an implicit connection to the Telecities agenda to harness telematics to the cause of promoting 'cities' as attractive places to live, to try to get people to use the city 'in more flexible ways', and to repopulate the city, treating city centres as new suburbs. For Telecities, in order to do this it was very important to build networks, to put in the physical connections, to invest in real infrastructure. Furthermore, this was a grant that required matched funding. The key partner who came in with this funding was Norweb, the local electrical services provider. Finding its core business heavily regulated, post-privatization, the company was looking for alternative sources of income and was quick to use its established name as a reliable, local service provider to move into the growth market for telecommunications. Norweb was particularly interested to develop a market lead in carrying high-bandwidth applications. The company's key interest in its involvement with G-MING thus seems to have been the hope that, through G-MING, it would, first, boost its image as a high bandwidth telecommunications provider in the north-west and, secondly, learn more about the kinds of applications that people might want to use these networks for in order to expand its customer base. G-MING's 'customers' were limited to their funded commitments to various public-sector institutions—initially the universities, then the City Councils of Manchester and Salford, the MSIM—and more recently hospitals.

G-MING as an organization formed around people with strong engineering and computer science backgrounds, unlike the charismatic and politically motivated creators of the Host. In 1998–9, it was presented in public for what the network offered in terms of speed and bandwidth: 155 million bits per second, 5,000 times faster than a standard modem dial-up connection. They emphasized that they had the infrastructure to cope with huge numbers of users and with applications that needed speed. G-MING, like Norweb, was less sure about how these capacities might be required by genuine commercial users, and it tended to discuss applications in terms of generic services rather than specific uses: video conferencing, real-time video, desk-top conferencing, web caching. And, while committed to the premiss that the most important thing was to find 'users', as users directly represented the ongoing funding base for such technological projects, there was also a strong sense that 'you have to know there is a solution as well as a problem', and in that sense the technological 'solutions' came first.

Despite this overt technological focus, there was also a sense that G-MING was a located service, operating for the people of the north-west. In demonstrations of their work, representatives of G-MING always represented themselves as north-western, and the name itself (Greater Manchester Information

Network Group) was a reminder of that. The local benefits were seen as threefold. In the first place, there was an explicit recognition that the existence of an area network could help produce a regional base to extract public money in a European context, where metropolitan regions are seen as a key focus of expenditure. Second, one of the reasons why money went to money in this way was because the network represented a concentration of technological expertise, both in running the network and in being able to advise others in terms of equipment, installation, and programming. Finally, Manchester users could, through this network, should they so wish, get more information at 'reasonable' access speeds.

It was not long before G-MING was used to draw more money into the city from Europe. The Infocities project, which began early in 1997 and involved a consortium of seven European cities (a subgroup of Telecities), was jointly managed, for Manchester, by G-MING and the City Council. Manchester was the lead city for 'Culture'—developing and testing applications—one of which was located in the MSIM. The link seemed very promising in the cargo cult atmosphere that we described above: the coupling of computing and cultural heritage seemed set to deliver new users, both to the MSIM and to G-MING. However, the relationship between the museum and G-MING was problematic and provides us with a clear example of how technologies become embedded within social, historical, and political contexts, often despite the technologists' best efforts.

THE DISPUTED SOCIALITY OF TECHNICAL NETWORKS

The Museum of Science and Industry in Manchester (MSIM) is an unusual organization. It grew out of an earlier foundation, established at UMIST in 1969, with a strong academic bias and a mission to use its collections of industrial artefacts to educate visitors. The MSIM in its current form dates from 1983 and in more recent years it has worked to embrace a more communicative approach. Operating since 2000 as a charitable foundation, it aims to integrate itself into the fabric of the city, to become part of the city, a resource for more general public use.

In 1998 there were still tensions within the museum between the older idea of the museum visitor as passive consumer of expert knowledge, and the visitor as a person who brings his or her own experience (and expertise) to what is conceptualized as an interpretative and interactive process. Backed by extensive visitor research, the new approach within the museum had the upper hand, and visitors were encouraged to touch and feel, to get personally involved in science, thoroughly to mix the social and the scientific, and to produce new unexpected artefacts from the fragments of past industrial production. ICTs have in many ways worked as catalysts in enabling a conceptual move away from the idea of museums as places where objects are (re)-stored, held, and displayed—to places where the relationships between people and objects are brought out and explored. And, as in many contemporary museums and science centres, visitors are encouraged to think of knowledge as experiential, the machines as expressive and communicative (P. Harvey, forthcoming).

In June 1998, the museum opened 'Futures', a new gallery, which traces the history of communications from the railway, through telephony, the birth of the computer with stored memory to the contemporary networked society. In fact, the entirety of the Futures gallery was based around 'the birth of the Baby', which, after it had been rebuilt at the University of Manchester, was to be permanently located at the museum. The progression from the Baby to the contemporary 'networked' world is represented in various ways, but includes a suite of networked PCs for public use. G-MING, through the Infocities connection, installed the network.

However, there were problems: most importantly, it did not work. At one time, every time the machines were switched on at the museum they were rebooting the whole of the University of Manchester. The server was continually crashing. Museum staff were very frustrated that their new exhibit was basically 'out of order' before it had even opened. A tense but interesting relationship developed between G-MING and the museum, for what emerged in the dispute was a clash over fundamentally divergent ideas about responsibility, about the nature of networks, and about the way in which the user–provider relationship was conceptualized. It is this lack of fit to which we wish to draw attention.

The museum staff understood G-MING to be the provider of a service. They expected G-MING to communicate with them about their needs and constraints, to understand how they wanted to use the network, and to take the technical decisions accordingly. G-MING did not see it in the same way. The G-MING staff saw themselves in this context as technologists; when the network failed, their analysis of the situation was based on two related ideas: that human beings cause problems through lack of understanding and interference, and technologies offer solutions to problems.[36] Thus, while G-MING was able to acknowledge that the problem might well be a human one, the solution would be technical. Within this scenario, there were various possibilities: had the museum purchased the wrong 'switches', or had these 'switches' been configured wrongly? Alternatively, the problem might well have been technical: was there something in the way that these 'switches' operated that caused an automatic and unsustainable volume of 'traffic' over the network, such that the system crashed each time anyone tried to use it? In any event, it was clear that, as far as G-MING was concerned, there was no need to consult with the museum over the solutions, although it seemed likely to G-MING staff that the lack of technical expertise within the museum was largely to blame for the wrong

---

[36] See Downey (1998) for an excellent ethnographic study of this approach towards technology; and see also Traweek (1988) for a study of technologists' habit of giving sociality to their machines, rather than to the people for whom the machines are theoretically built.

configurations that were causing the problems. Within this more technical framing of the situation, the relationship between user and provider is more hierarchical and one way. The provider offers a technical solution to an ultimately passive user, for the user is not required to take an active role for the solution to work. In this scenario a user has 'needs' that the technologists then respond to, and those 'needs' are understood in very abstract terms, as something generic, which manifest themselves in use. In this idiom, the technical fix can in fact produce prior needs, via a kind of functional teleology.

Not surprisingly, real 'users' saw things rather differently. Museum staff saw G-MING as having emerged from the social agendas of the EU, and furthermore as having been paid for locally out of the Infocities budget. They were expecting a far more personalized service than G-MING was in fact offering. They saw themselves as an example of the kinds of 'users' who had motivated the technical development, and were inclined to test the efficacy of that technology in terms of how effectively it worked for them, to what extent it met their specific needs. It was thus axiomatic to them that they would be involved in all discussions over the problems that they were having, as only they, as users, could know when they had got what they wanted.

It became clear that the museum and G-MING had different understandings of what the information technologies were ultimately for. The museum staff's interest was in the 'communicative' potentials of these technologies; their understanding of a network was of a linkage of persons and machine, of distributed responsibilities and dynamic outcomes. G-MING's interest was in providing the hardware for other people to do things with; what other people did was largely up to them. The G-MING staff did not pretend to understand that, nor were they particularly interested, beyond their need to identify users in order to find new markets for the network. In a forum for users from the cultural sectors of the city, one of the G-MING managers presented the Manchester Area Network (MAN) as 'a Manchester MAN for all reasons'. He added that this allusion to the nineteenth-century stock literary figure, the 'Manchester Man', would be all that he had to say about culture.[37]

In the G-MING concept the agency of the technologists (or the machines), and the agency of the users are not of a kind. The technologists have knowledge and expertise and are thus able to construct and link machines, which in turn are able to perform certain kinds of machinic activities. Users can take advantage of these machines to do whatever they might want to do. G-MING can thus be seen as fulfilling its project of using technologies to stimulate change, while perpetuating integral and mutually exclusive human and machinic agencies.[38]

[37] For 'Manchester Man', see Kidd (1996: 72–3). The contrast was between the 'Liverpool Gentleman' and the coarse self-made 'Manchester Man'. Examples are Dickens's Josiah Bounderby and Thomas Gradgrind in *Hard Times*, and, far more sympathetically, G. Linnaeus Banks's eponymous hero. The G-MING manager's self-deprecating joke is an insightful one.
[38] The question of how G-MING employees regarded *themselves* and their agency with respect to the machines is another matter, and one that is not touched upon by this chapter. Again, see

The museum, on the other hand, was working with a very different understanding of 'network', one that links humans and machines in mutually constitutive relationships of possibility, in which science and politics are thoroughly entangled, and in which agency depends on exchanges of information and expertise.

This example has drawn out the way in which different notions of the technical confronted those of practical application; it remains to consider how the way in which ICTs were 'located' in Manchester resulted in an inability for those technologies to do what they apparently do best: connect across a distance.

THE DISPUTED POLITICS OF TECHNICAL NETWORKS

The Manchester Community Information Network (MCIN) was founded in 1993, only a few years after the Manchester Host, and on the surface, it appeared to be doing what the formal intentions of the Host project had in mind. MCIN had the official aim of bringing together 'community information' from diverse places, to reduce duplication of this information and to make it as widely and as transparently publicly available as possible, both on the internet and via a network of public access points in places such as libraries, Asda supermarkets, and the Manchester office of the *Big Issue*. The underlying idea was to make public information accessible to people who would be highly unlikely to own a computer, or even have any interest in doing so.

What brought MCIN into conflict with the Infocities project were not these formal aims, but the organization's history and involvement in one particular part of Manchester. Before its involvement in ICTs, MCIN had a previous life as a community mental health services project in Moston, one of the more economically deprived areas of the city in north Manchester. MCIN remains strongly based in north Manchester, where its offices and most of its public access points are located, despite its public aim to serve the whole of Manchester. This places the centre of MCIN's activities outside the 'urban regeneration' area of the city centre, where the post-Host projects are focused, and its history also places it outside the 'centre of gravity' of the council's telematics strategy, born of the Host experience combined with the influence of EU strategies.

An IT consultant company, Sema, first involved MCIN in Infocities. Sema had been given a small contract by the council to set up six multimedia kiosks in Manchester, and six in Barcelona. The company then contracted MCIN to develop the content for the six machines in Manchester, and this project was included under the Infocities umbrella. So, in fact, MCIN never did have an

Downey (1998) for a thorough ethnographic treatment of the idea of agency with relation to machines and those who use them (in that case, computer-aided design systems).

unmediated relationship with Infocities. The project's manager and her only co-worker, who fixed bugs in the software, repaired the machines, and developed the web site, regarded it as a fundamental responsibility of the council to make the advantages of new information technologies accessible to everyone in Manchester. The manager was keen on involving 'members of the community' themselves in designing what kind of information should be provided, and, for her, this meant going out to meet people and becoming a part of the community. Her perspective on ICTs was that they provided an improved way to get information that members of a community wanted anyway, and as such they would serve to support the continued viability of local communities. This approach explains MCIN's continued strong link to Moston: it requires the public information service to be a part of a spatially located community.

At the same time as seeing the advantages of networked computing, MCIN's manager was deeply suspicious of technophiles, and was exasperated by the regularity with which the software crashed and the machines broke down. She put this tendency down to the computer industry's habit of constantly altering and expanding the size of software, which, apart from making it unstable, meant people with small machines had no access to it, or did not understand how to use it. In fact, people running a variety of community ICT projects in Manchester often expressed the opinion that people and their computers were being over-fed with stuff that was also fairly indigestible.

There was a distinct difference between this perspective and those expressed by people involved in the Host project and later involved in designing Infocities. While the founders of the Host were concerned about providing access to the technology for all, their commitment was also fundamentally to the technology, and to the prospect that the technology could potentially provide a whole range of 'fixes', once the barriers of training and cost were overcome. The MCIN manager, in contrast, felt that only so much of the technology as was necessary to enhance what local communities were doing anyway ought to be used. As a result, her worries about the excesses of the computer hardware and software industries, and her geographical location within the city, gave her a somewhat marginal position within the Infocities group. When she turned up at meetings, she often said little and looked distinctly uncomfortable; when she did speak, it was in a conscious effort to remind the group of their public access responsibilities, or simply to remind them of the existence of MCIN. There was a tendency in Infocities meetings not to mention MCIN at all if she was not present. The monthly Infocities coordination meeting was held only once at the MCIN offices. People who were quite happy to fly around Europe for a meeting expressed dismay at the idea of going to Moston and had to be tempted out of the city centre on that one occasion with promises of an excellent lunch.

Things came to a head during the summer of 1998 celebrations marking the 'birth of the Baby' and Manchester's position as an 'information city'. During these events, there were to be several opportunities to display public access kiosks. Unbeknown to MCIN, the council, in partnership with the Multimedia

Centre at MMU, had entered into negotiations with an international computer company to develop a new public kiosk project. The MCIN manager discovered several days before an exhibition to be held at the Town Hall that the computer company was going to be exhibiting its kiosks, and nobody had thought to ask MCIN to do the same. At the last minute, MCIN secured agreement from the council to exhibit its machines, but this did not assuage the manager's fury about the council's failure to consult her about the bid with the computer company, which appeared to be excluding MCIN altogether.

In this example, the problems of linking MCIN's community-based approach with the dynamics of Infocities and the council led to a serious rupture, which in the end was irresolvable. In this case, the rupture had to do with fundamental disagreements about the purpose, nature, and, in a sense, *location*, of public information. The history of MCIN made it committed to a sector of the population and an area of Manchester that was increasingly invisible in both the City Council's and the EU's rhetoric about urban regeneration and ICTs. Most of the organizations we have studied experienced similar kinds of conflicts, but either had different histories that linked them to Manchester and their telematics projects in ways that were not quite as incompatible, or had shifted their ground somewhat, at least publicly, to secure the funding base needed to continue.[39]

CONCLUSIONS

If there is one overall conclusion from the historical and ethnographic examples in this chapter, it is that ICTs are always and everywhere *actively* embedded within the social networks through which place is constituted and histories made relevant. In the case of Manchester, an assertion of what the place represented (its 'ancestry') was interwoven into the introduction of these technologies to the city. The originators of the Host did not initially imagine it as being 'located', but, through its being sponsored by the City Council, it was located and associated with Manchester from the beginning. And that intimacy of association between technology and the city turns out to be an old habit, one expressed in practice through an institutionalized predilection for the 'technical fix', which itself was made to *appear* axiomatic through a particular construction of the city's past. The historiography of Manchester as having been built upon large technical projects and technological innovation (a story that goes

---

[39] MCIN did in fact survive and has even expanded. It has since secured a substantial amount of Lottery funding, and has aligned itself with WEVH in Manchester, rather than the City Council. WEVH explicitly aimed to exist independently of the types of connections and links provided by the council early on in its history. It consciously worked towards generating links between them that suited the broadly feminist aims of the organization. WEVH has, therefore, generated its own 'location' in the city, with which MCIN has been able to align itself much more easily than it did with the council.

AGAR, GREEN, AND HARVEY

back to even before the Manchester Corporation's activities, and the practices of particular elites) resulted in technical solutions seeming to be 'natural' for the city, and a depiction of the city's political authority as being the 'natural' manager and instigator of such solutions.

Moreover, the city's more recent pursuit of 'urban regeneration', of which the promotion of Manchester as an 'information city' was a part, has been nostalgically oriented, aiming to reconstruct the city centre as the 'cultural heritage' of the Industrial Revolution. To do this with the tools provided by the new 'revolution', the Information Revolution, closes the circle, and allows the future to be firmly constructed within the past. The 'birth of the Baby' finally gives flesh to this history, embodies it, and invites one to look backwards towards the future.

It has also been seen that none of this was inevitable: a great deal of effort and work went into constructing ICTs as technologies that 'belong' to Manchester, work that could be realized only through the mobilization of existing alliances, networks, and, of course, ideas. Those kinds of connections importantly also entailed *disconnections*, from places and organizations that did not, for one reason or another, fit the image and understanding of these technologies and their location in Manchester. MCIN was an example of that; but so too were some of the founders of the Host, who began to experience the images surrounding *their* 'Baby' drifting in a direction that went beyond their own interests in international labour organization, and, quietly, they left.

For those who remained engaged in the city's projects, such as the MSIM and G-MING, there were drawn-out confrontations between diverse understandings of what ICTs *are*, exactly. This eventually led to experiencing the practical impossibility of maintaining a separation between the agency of technologies and the agency of persons. Members of G-MING found that the use of deeply held notions of 'technology' as an autonomous and neutral object in the field of sociality did not hold up in practice, and that created continual problems in actually implementing proposed projects.[40]

Beyond the city, ICTs were also used to forge and consolidate links to other European cities; but, while ICTs provided a vehicle for these connections, they were not created by the technologies themselves. In some cases they pre-existed the ICT initiatives (the twin-city connection to St Petersburg is a particularly good example of contingency); in other cases, they were created by funding opportunities, opportunities that were not dependent on ICT innovations, but controlled by, for example, EU aims to generate links between regions

---

[40] These kinds of notions are, of course, stereotypical, but they are powerful tropes that strongly inform the way technologies become embedded in social life. See Dumit (1997) for an exploration of how this kind of idea has the effect of constituting people's understandings of the world and themselves in relation to ideas about technologies, and see also Traweek (1988) and Haraway (1997) for other analyses of the consequences of these kinds of cultural constructions of technologies.

across member states and to build up effective competition with North America in the area of ICTs.

Finally, if there was anything 'virtual' in the transition from cotton to computers in Manchester, it was not the product of ICTs' technical capacities, but the creation of the place itself, in finding and making a location for those technologies. Global connections are clearly always located in practice. However, in this chapter we have argued that 'place' cannot simply be added as a further variable when formulating policy for the introduction of ICTs. It is the social *process* of location, as an active engagement with both past and future, that needs to be considered. Whatever the potential for social change, people apprehend novelty in relation to existing social knowledges. Technological innovation is thus always embedded in historical representations and practices. The Manchester study exemplifies this process. The institutional predilection for the 'technical fix' emerged as a key feature of the social contexts of virtual Manchester, effecting how, for better or worse, institutions have, over time, conceptualized social problems and the ways in which answers are sought in technical solutions.

16

Mobile Society? Technology, Distance, and Presence

Geoff Cooper, Nicola Green, Ged M. Murtagh,
and Richard Harper

INTRODUCTION: THE VIRTUAL AND THE MOBILE

There are many reasons—theoretical, epistemological, practical, political—for sustaining a critical or sceptical stance towards confident assertions that particular technologies, of themselves, usher in new forms of social behaviour that warrant the use of new descriptors such as 'virtual society'. For example, much recent social-scientific investigation of new information and communications technologies (ICTs) has an implicitly critical orientation to totalizing theoretical terms such as the 'information age' or 'virtual society', detailing the problematic assumptions underlying such rhetoric, and asking questions about the technological determinism implied. It is argued that any assessment of the adequacy of these terms must be derived, at least in part, from the study and consideration of the situated social and material uses of technologies in everyday life.[1]

In part, this suggests both the need for vigilance with regard to 'cyberbole', and an affirmation of the value of deflating it where appropriate.[2] However, it also invokes a particular relation: a technology may have, or be conceptualized as having, particular potentialities, but the latter's realization—or reconfiguration,

---

[1] On the theory and rhetoric of the information society, see Webster (1995). For critiques of determinism, see Grint and Woolgar (1997) and MacKenzie and Wacjman (1999) and, in relation to communications technologies, Winston (1998). See Suchman (1987) on the value of studying technology use *in situ*.

[2] See Woolgar (this volume). This task is complicated by Pollner's argument that social-scientific concepts are themselves subject to analytic deflation by their objects of analysis in certain domains, such as the 'I/I junction' (Pollner, this volume).

or subversion—takes place in and through, and thus depends on, actual situated everyday practice.[3] In fact, the opposition potential/actual forms part of a cluster of closely related, in some ways intertwined, conceptual distinctions that can usefully be teased out a little. For example, 'potential' is equivalent to one of the meanings of 'virtual'. A virtual society would, according to this sense of the term, be one that was not (yet) fully realized: almost a society, with the possibility of becoming a society. Indeed, criticism of those who endorse the existence of a virtual society could be posed in reflexive terms: that their descriptions are located at the virtual level, that they mistake technical potentiality for socio-technical actuality.

The formulation of a virtual society can also imply both the viability of a degree of conceptual separation from wider society, and confidence in the given, and completed, reality of the latter. Potentiality however, as Agamben (2000) has argued, is anything but a simple concept. Part of its difficulty derives from the fact that, in its pure form, it negates itself: as Derrida (1987: 178) puts it, 'if it's too potential, it's nothing'. A purely virtual society would by this logic be entirely chimerical, and a (non-virtual) society solid and self-evident.

Stated in this pure form, the opposition between virtual and real appears somewhat problematic, and we would wish to argue for the necessity of some mutual contamination of conceptual categories. However, the fact of its articulation with a number of other oppositions suggests that there may be further implications for how socio-technical phenomena might be approached. This articulation might be expressed as follows: on the one hand, technical/potential/virtual/theoretical, and, on the other, social/actual/real/empirical. Thus, whilst sceptics may argue that claims for the existence of a radically new, technologically derived, epoch or social formation rest on a valorization of technical possibilities and exhibit a tendency to operate at a speculative theoretical level, one may also suggest that the sceptical position itself risks staying within the same terms of reference, through its privileging of social realization and empirical study.

Our strategy in this chapter is informed by these considerations. Whilst endorsing the need for and drawing upon empirical studies of situated action, and indicating the limits of certain theoretical approaches that stay at the virtual level, we neither eschew theory nor are primarily concerned either to endorse or to debunk the notion of a virtual society. Rather, we address the question of virtuality in a more oblique manner. This chapter is based on studies of the everyday use of mobile telecommunications, highly dynamic technologies that pose particular analytical challenges that may have general significance for thinking about virtuality. Based on ethnographic research, we examine the situated use of mobile devices, and consider the coexistence and management of distant and co-present communication in public and private spaces. By focusing on the highly dynamic and fluid contexts of use for mobile

[3] On the subversive nature of everyday practice, see Certeau (1984).

technologies in everyday life, and by bringing this into dialogue with some suggestive ideas within social theory, we attempt to interrogate the complex and possibly changing relationship between distance and presence, and its implications for a number of associated concepts, such as the private and the public.

The evolving form of the mobile would certainly permit consideration of whether the proliferation of certain practices, text messaging being the obvious example, should be thought of as constituting new forms of association or community, forms that might be contrasted with face-to-face social interaction: our focus, however, is on the ways in which such forms of practice are (becoming) embedded within the latter. The mobile's strategic value for thinking about new forms of association is precisely that whilst it is, in technological terms, a device that would appear to render location insignificant, allowing undifferentiated access to a worldwide network of satellite-enabled communication, it must always be used within a particular local context. Indeed, its capacity to be used in many local contexts highlights the significance of situational proprieties in a particularly striking manner: as Woolgar (this volume) argues, 'the more global, the more local'.

CONCEPTUALIZING THE MOBILE

In comparison with other technologies, the mobile has a somewhat equivocal status, and is difficult to conceptualize. It seems to belong to the category of 'new media', but much of that literature is not pertinent, for the mobile, resembling in part its ancestor the fixed-line phone, seems relatively transparent, at least at an intuitive or phenomenological level: speaking on the phone appears so natural that the mediating technology is often forgotten (see G. Cooper 2001). Similarly, terms such as 'cyberspace' do not seem to fit, at least not yet. When we think about the empirical phenomena of mobile phone/ device use in everyday life, we find that sociology and philosophy contain a number of terms which seem apt, but have or have had somewhat different referents: for example, social mobility, the problematizing of the public/private distinction, the structural transformation of the public sphere, the metaphysics of presence, phonocentrism, and, of course, the immutable mobile.[4] They are relevant concepts, but to 'apply' them to the study of the mobile is, often, to give them an interestingly literal twist.

Part of this theoretical hesitation derives from the mobile's relation to an older and more routine and mundane technology, and part of it from its current

---

[4] See Urry (2000) for a discussion of sociology and mobility; Weintraub and Kumar (1997) on the public/private distinction; Habermas (1989) on the public sphere; Derrida (1976) on the metaphysics of presence and phonocentrism; and Latour (1986) on the immutable mobile.

state: it is said to be in the process of 'convergence', which, limiting ourselves to consideration of technical capacity for the moment, will result in a device that will allow access to a wide range of information and services from any point in physical space. What is projected is an unprecedented level of integration of what might be called virtual and everyday life. However, the precise form that this brave new socio-technical world might take will depend on a whole range of factors including: the practicalities of the production process, the relations between the different players (manufacturers, operators, service and content providers), the economic and regulatory context, the usability of devices, the cultural and symbolic meanings that they acquire in different social contexts, the possible social disadvantage of non-ownership, and the emerging norms of acceptable use and social obligation.

The project on which the authors, and others, are working addresses all these issues, but the focus in this chapter is on the fact that, even in its current form, the mobile constitutes, perhaps more than any other technology, a striking conjunction of remote and co-present communication.[5] We consider how people manage the (often simultaneous) demands of these forms of communication, and what this can tell us about the social worlds in which the technology is (becoming) embedded. These observations are based on or informed by observational studies and interviews. We then focus on what might be called the component categories of mobility, space, and time, and consider mobile use in relation to theoretical and historical arguments about social transformation. Finally, we return to the articulation of technical/potential/virtual/theoretical outlined above, and address the question of how and where the mobile, and its empirical study, can be located.

THE PUBLIC AND THE PRIVATE

Co-Presence and Modernity

Simmel, writing a century ago about the shock of the experience of modernity in the metropolis, commented thus:

Interpersonal relationships in big cities are distinguished by a marked preponderance of the activity of the eye over the activity of the ear. The main reason for this is the public means of transportation. Before the development of buses, railroads, and trams in the nineteenth century, people had never been in a position of having to look at one another for long minutes or even hours without speaking to one another.   (cited in Benjamin 1983: 38)

[5] The project, 'The Socio-Technical Shaping of Mobile Multimedia Personal Communications (STEMPEC)', was funded by the ESRC (L487 25 4002) and Vodafone, One2One, Orange, BTCellnet, and Granada Media Group, as part of the Foresight Link Programme.

Since one of the most notable features of the mobile, if we are to judge by the level of attention it receives in everyday discourse, is its use in the confined public places that Simmel describes, it is worth considering whether this represents a kind of accentuation of the experience of modernity.

Simmel's analysis of the metropolitan experience places emphasis on the conflict of private—conceptualized, perhaps problematically given subsequent theoretical developments, as inner subjectivity—and public. He suggests, for example, that one way in which the individual can deal with the shocks of modernity is through the securing of 'an island of subjectivity, a secret, closed-off sphere of privacy' (Frisby 1985: 105); thus, the individual can handle the apparent horrors of inflicted co-presence and other disorientating phenomena. The predominance of the eye over the ear is manifested in the possibility of, or preference for, silence. There is a strong sense here that the emerging form of public life is based on an aggregation of individuals with their own private, possibly incompatible lives. Benjamin (1983: 250) makes a similar point, arguing that public gatherings of certain kinds 'have only a statistical existence' and are 'abstract' even 'monstrous' since individuals' interests (including class interests) are radically different.

It can be argued that use of the mobile in certain public spaces makes the relation of private and public more concrete, for it brings a normally private activity (talking on the landline) into the public sphere. Moreover, it may be seen to disturb what is normally a preference for silence in certain public settings. No longer is the private conceivable as what goes on, discreetly, in the life of the individual away from the public domain, or as subsequently represented in individual consciousness; although it may still be the case that the co-present tend not to speak to each other, they *can* now have conversations with remote others that are (half) audible to all. The coexistence of, and potential friction between, public and private are in this respect material and observable phenomena, even if still subject to the uncertainties of interpretation; furthermore, their mutual articulation provides the analyst with an opportunity to investigate the 'discoverable logic which marks segments of interaction' (Birdwhistell 1971: 233).

Goffman (1971) develops Simmel's interest in public behaviour and its normative dimensions, as it is experienced through communication and interaction. On this basis his work provides some useful resources for thinking about and analysing mobile phone use in public space. Simmel's observation of the marked preponderance of the activity of the eye over the activity of the ear is developed in Goffman's work through his concept of civil inattention. Civil inattention, as Goffman describes, is the practice of averting the gaze from others present so as not to draw particular attention to oneself. In public settings, Goffman argues, a state of mutual gaze is avoided. The normative aspects of this requirement are particularly noticeable in relatively confined spaces where active avoidance is necessary: lifts, for example.

The use of the mobile in a public space may have a number of possible implications for these normatively sanctioned forms of behaviour. Its use can draw attention to the user. It may perhaps transform civil inattention, in that it can mark a shift from (what Goffman refers to as) unfocused to focused interaction. This can be observed in so far as the user and co-present others display their activities and responses to phone use in a public setting. Or, to put this differently again, the use of a mobile creates a situation in which, unlike landline use, the likelihood is that the co-present other is a stranger to whom one's obligations are more uncertain.[6] Empirical study can tell us about how in practice normative obligations are constructed, destroyed, or more generally managed, and can raise questions about the level and scope of perceived mutual involvement of speakers and involuntary listeners. These practices may be provisionally thought of in terms of resources for achieving a form of privacy that make manifest a form of interactional orientation to the co-present other.

To illustrate these points, we return to Simmel's public transport, and discuss some of our observations of mobile-related behaviour in train carriages, which serve as useful exemplars of Goffman's unfocused occasion. Responses to phone use within this setting can be evidenced in the naturally occurring socially organized movements of gaze and gesture.

Resources for Privacy: Gaze

Throughout our research in this setting, the use of gaze remained one of the most noticeable features of social behaviour where mobile phones were used in the presence of others. Phone users were seen to avert their gaze from co-present others in a variety of different ways. For example, some were observed averting their eyes towards the window, particularly if they were sat next to one; other users were observed initiating a downward head movement whilst simultaneously raising the phone to the ear. Eye movement and adjustment of gaze direction were also observable features of the initial responses of co-present others. We suggest that gaze emerges as one of the resources for managing the simultaneous demands of remote and co-present communication, and as such is demonstrative of their social organization.

The key factor here is the direction of gaze and how that is used to display an activity or a response to that activity. Phone users regularly displayed marked instances of a change in gaze direction when using the phone. This can be seen as one of the ways in which participants mark out or display the interactional boundaries between the public and the private. Typically, phone users would avert their gaze from the immediate surrounding environment. When initiating phone use, gaze direction would shift towards to a neutral space—for example,

---

[6] This uncertainty may be historically specific—that is to say, derived from the temporary tension that accompanies the introduction of a new communications technology into an existing pattern of social behaviour based on other modalities (see Marvin 1988).

towards the window or the aisle. In so doing phone users display what Heath (1986) has referred to as a 'middle distance orientation' to manage the contingencies of the interaction. One of the reasons Goffman offers for the avoidance of mutual gaze in public is that mutual gaze is one of the primary means through which participants display openness to communication. Thus what is at issue here for the phone user is a concern not just with establishing a public/private boundary but also with establishing the parameters of participation status within that same setting.

Non-users would typically display the 'civil inattention' that Goffman describes. Frequently, they would glance at the phone user but then return to their own activities or lines of concern. However, civil inattention could be disrupted. In the relatively few cases of manifest irritation that we observed, duration and topic of call appeared to be relevant factors. The most common source of the disruption of civil inattention was the unanswered phone. The ringing of a phone would often generate a response from others, if only a glance, but thereafter the conversation was ignored, much like a face-to-face conversation between two fellow passengers. However, in several cases where a phone remained unanswered, gaze was used as a means of organized response to the event. In these instances the initial glance when the phone rang would be extended to a gaze or a stare. This response is suggestive of a normal expectation concerning the length of time of a ringing phone deemed appropriate by others.

Kendon (1967), who suggests that gaze acts as a unique form of social control, provides a useful insight into this response. He suggests that the use of gaze enables us to monitor and regulate the behaviour of others. In his pioneering study of gaze in social interaction he identifies two functional aspects of gaze. First, he suggests gaze provides a function whereby parties in interaction can monitor one another's behaviour. Indeed, by looking or not looking one can control the degree of monitoring. Secondly, gaze serves a regulatory function, enabling persons in interaction to regulate each other's behaviour. In the instance of phone use, gaze is simultaneously available to phone user and co-present others to organize technology use, distance, and co-presence.

It is worth noting that the mobile itself, as a technology with both audio and visual functionality, can provide a resource for the avoidance of mutual gaze. The following extract from field notes provides a useful illustration:

On the Bristol–London journey one young woman (white, early twenties) is facing towards my direction in a booth of four, one seat away. She gets a call (on a neon pink phone). Did a location talk/reply. She seems to be having some kind of emotional hard time. As she's making replies to the caller which describe her current emotional state—it seems she is a student, as she describes going to a lecture during the day and bursting into tears. She thanks the caller for her support, and they chat about when they are next going to get together—talking about a common friend in the process.

After she finishes talking, she continues to play the phone for around 10 minutes. It looks as if she's messaging, as she is playing with the number pad, but not talking (but then again, she could be using the calculator, phone book, or something). She looks as if she's re-creating a private space by using messaging.

Here, a potentially embarrassing display of emotion appears to be handled by a systematic avoidance of engagement with co-present others, and achieved by a control of gaze and continued engagement with the mobile after the conversation has ended. The mobile here serves as a visual resource for the avoidance of co-present social interaction.

Resources for Privacy: Gesture and Bodily Movement

One observable behaviour, though a relatively rare one, is movement to the space that joins the carriages in order to use the phone; or, on one occasion, leaning out of the train window in order to conduct a less audible conversation.[7] More common is the use of posture to achieve a form of privacy. Posture can be conceptualized as bodily gesture, and seen as an integral part of phone use. Generally speaking these gestures were exhibited more frequently by phone users than co-present others. Typically this involved movements of the head and upper body, in most instances in conjunction with a change in gaze direction. Thus the most common behavioural pattern observed was the turning of the head, or head and upper body, towards a neutral space—for example, the window or the aisle. These gestures and movements tend to correspond with the opening and closure of the remote/co-present encounter.

Such gestures were even more marked when personal information was being discussed. In several instances of personal, and thus potentially embarrassing, information exchange on the phone (such as the one noted above) participants were able to manage the situation by a systematic avoidance of engagement with co-present others. Whilst avoidance of gaze is central to this, the use of the body as a communicative channel—body idiom in Goffman's terms (1963)—can also be significant. Gesture can display to others the parameters of social encounters. More specifically, Goffman (1971) explains that appearance and gestures can serve as a 'gloss' to describe one's situation. A 'body gloss' is something like a non-verbal explanation that is offered, by the individual, to account for his or her interactional positioning. Similarly, Scheflen has argued that a change in the mode of participation status is usually accompanied by a change in posture to mark the boundary of this change (reported in Kendon 1990). Head and upper body movements are routinely employed to organize social interaction. Such gestural work is an observable feature of the social organization of phone use.

For example, on one occasion a man, sitting in the aisle seat of two, received a call. He pulled his phone out, and as he started speaking, hunched himself

7 The train was stationary at the time.

over, leaning down over the spare seat beside him so that his head was below the level of the seat backs. His back was now facing the more public space of the aisle, his face towards the wall of the carriage. He seemed to be attempting to create privacy by using the space available to him in the double seat space. This manœuvre did not affect the volume of the conversation, which could still be heard relatively clearly from the researcher's position one seat back on the opposite side of the aisle; but, in line with Goodwin's argument (1981: 96), it did serve to indicate 'participation status' in terms of levels of engagement/disengagement and, in particular, marked a boundary between those physically present and those relevantly present.

Thus we might summarize the above by saying that the management of gaze and gesture in public becomes one of the ways in which the boundary between public and private is negotiated; but also, that the constitution of this boundary, and of the normative framework that it implies, is the ongoing and situated accomplishment of social members themselves. As Goffman (1967: 105) points out, 'given their social identities and the setting, the participants will sense what sort of conduct *ought* to be maintained as the appropriate thing, however much they despair of its actually occurring'. With respect to this particular and still relatively new technology, the normative expectations and obligations are not entirely predictable and, like the technology, still evolving (see n. 6). One notable feature of this evolution is the increasing prevalence of explicitly stated norms, as evident in notices in public places, and advice from mobile operators about appropriate forms of behaviour within advertising; however, such statements give only an approximate indication of the operation of normative frameworks in practice.

Rethinking 'Public' and 'Private'?

'Private' and 'public', however, have only provisional analytic value here. At a theoretical level, to look at the phenomenon in these terms is to presume certain traditional (humanist) conceptions, notably of community and stranger, that some see as problematic and that certainly merit further interrogation. One might suggest, loosely following Derrida, that there is a conflation of community and (co-)presence that needs deconstructing. Maffesoli (1996) argues that contemporary life is organized not around a rooted sense of community, but around multiple, loose, and shifting forms of association and affiliation, which he calls tribes. At an empirical level, we might ask whether there is such an affiliation between mobile users: whether, for example, the experience of having undergone embarrassment at receiving a call in an awkward situation creates a degree of empathy for others in a similar situation, as some claim, or whether, in terms of consumption and identity, there are forms of brand awareness with style connotations that lead to mutual identification.

At another level, it can be argued that the personalization of mobile devices—their attachment to an individual body rather than to specific locations, the personalized nature of the technologies, and the attendant atomization of communications—fundamentally decentralizes both 'public' and 'private' communication activities, collapsing each into the other. The decentralization of work activities, and the practices of 'assembling the mobile office' on the part of 'nomadic workers' (Laurier 1999) entails the simultaneous management of private activities, as when mobile teleworkers coordinate their work life from/at home. 'Public' work activities may be drawn into 'private' spaces, with a variety of effects on an individual's home and family life (both positive and negative). Concomitantly, the decentralization of private communications entails their appearance in public space in new ways. In those European cities with a wide uptake of mobile communication devices, individuals now maintain constant connection with their interpersonal others in public spaces through a variety of communication forms—text messaging being the most significant recent addition—rather than relying on intermittent home-based communications to arrange co-present meetings.

The logic of this argument would suggest that a reconfiguration of space and time is taking place, a reconfiguration that implies that the form and purpose of the communication is what comes to describe 'public' and 'private', rather than the space in which that communication is carried out. Let us consider this reconfiguration in a little more detail.

MOBILITY: SPACE AND TIME

Spatial Technologies

Technologies such as the telephone are specifically spatial: their function is to support social communication at a distance, and their ability to collapse distance has made possible many spatial features of contemporary urban life—the office tower being a case in point (Pool 1977).

Some have argued that the construction of the modern city, by concentrating population and allowing for dense co-present and tele-present interactions amongst centralized infrastructures, has contributed to a fragmented experience of modern life.[8] Centralizing interactions in modernity created an experience of the urban metropolis that is disconnected—dividing previously continuous and durable spaces, separating the private from the public, and instituting locations/places that had little connection with each other. Public social life therefore

---

[8] On fragmentation as a feature of the postmodern urban environment, see Harvey (1990); on the role of telecommunications within this and other processes, see Graham and Marvin (1996).

became an experience of spatial fragmentation and discontinuity, where activities became compartmentalized in a series of fleeting encounters and impressions of little duration (Simmel 1997). Private space, by contrast, becomes that of co-presence, continuity, and proximity, instituting a divide between geographically defined public and private spaces.

According to some researchers, however, mobile devices again reconfigure the spaces of urban social life, or are part of such a reconfiguration (Townsend 2001). The introduction of communication technologies that no longer require connection at a fixed location has prompted a re-examination of what is meant by proximity, distance, and mobility.

Conceptions of Mobility

On the one hand, the notion of 'mobility' is commonly one that has come to denote an individual body's movement in fundamentally geographical space, and between locations (which includes the space 'in between' while moving). The insinuation of public into private geography (and vice versa) through mobile technologies is evidenced in shifting cultural notions of geographical space presented by advertising. Mobile technologies are sold on the basis that they provide 'anytime, anywhere' connection, whether that connection is via voice or data connectivity. Advertising presents mobile technologies as devices to transcend the 'limitations' of geography and distance, including those posed by geographical differences in the location of work and home activities. The advertisements such as the one in which a mother working in another city tells her son a bedtime story, emphasize the devices as tools to engage simultaneously in work and home relationships despite distance or location. On the other, as already noted, the categories public and private become problematized, and the notion of mobility becomes extended. A distinction is made, by some mobile operators, for instance, between three kinds of mobility, which find their expression in the mobile phone/device: mobility of the user; mobility of the device; and, since they can be accessed from any point, mobility of services.

Some theorists, such as Virilio (2000: 20), see a shift from movement in physical space to relative stasis in which, thanks to electronic mediation 'everything arrives without any need to depart'. Others might conceptualize a separate domain through which we move. The mobile, in its emerging third-generation mobile (3GM) form, would then offer the possibility of movement in both these physical and virtual domains.[9] There are, of course, good reasons to question this quasi-spatial metaphor for the use of electronic information, leaving aside

[9] 3GM (third-generation mobile) denotes one key stage in the envisaged technical development of telecommunications: for an accessible account, see Office of Science and Technology (1998).

the in some ways indeterminate current state of the mobile. Moreover, the constraints of practical action will have a bearing on such a notion of simultaneous movement: in many settings, for example, pedestrians can be observed coming to a standstill in this world in order to use some of the functions on their mobile.

TEMPORAL TECHNOLOGIES

It can be claimed that such a decentralization of communications also entails a reconfiguration of time, and an individualization in the experience of time. Whereas lives remain, at least in part, structured through formal or clock time (including the practice and regulation of work time into compartments of daily and weekly duration, especially as they are associated with fixed location in geographical space), decentralization of both work and home life prompts flexibility and individualized scheduling. The mobile phone interrupts the time-based coordination of communication and information activities required for scheduling from fixed locations. Individuals may organize their 'work' and 'home' activities around flexible compartments of time rather than compartments of time associated with particular geographical spaces.

According to Townsend (2001: 70),

time becomes a commodity that is bought, sold and traded over the phone. The old schedule of minutes, hours, days, and weeks becomes shattered into a constant stream of negotiations, reconfigurations, and rescheduling. One can be interrupted or interrupt friends and colleagues at any time. Individuals live in this phonespace—they can never let it go, because it is their primary link to the temporally, spatially fragmented network of friends and colleagues they have constructed for themselves. It has become their new umbilical cord.

Some have argued that this entails a greater 'speed' in the pace of life, an intensification of more and different activities of a shorter duration in the subjective experience of time. The decentralization of communication creates new webs of potential interaction between atomized individuals, which on the one hand increase the communication activities carried out, while at the same time fragmenting that communication into more numerous communications of shorter duration. Townsend (2001: 66) argues that this is 'dramatically speeding the metabolism of urban systems, increasing capacity and efficiency. The "real-time city", in which system conditions can be monitored and reacted to instantaneously, has arrived'.

The notion that the prevailing technology of a particular era can play a key role in modifying its sense of time is a well-established theme in social thought. Anderson (1983), for example, documents the relationship between print technology, conceptions of nationality, and the emergence of a 'modern' (secular) conception of time as linear, homogenous, and progressive in place of time as decay, as fall from grace. The printed word helped create a sense of community with others (whom one would never meet) as occupants of a common territory, located in the same empty temporal parameters.[10]

Many argue that we are in the process of another such transformation, begun in the early twentieth century but undergoing a further accentuation and radicalization: what Nowotny in 1994 called 'the illusion of simultaneity' (Roberts 1998: 120) has replaced linear time. This means the replacement of one time by a series of overlapping times, and a corresponding intensification of the demands made upon people. The mobile might then be a classic example of a device that both facilitates the demand and makes it possible to meet it. However, its status as one component in an assemblage of social, economic, and technological practices, developments, and artefacts is crucial. Only within such a configuration is its efficacy conceivable.

AVAILABILITY: ANY TIME, ANY PLACE

To state the relation between the technology and social practice in terms of 'demand' is to presuppose a great deal, and to gesture towards a particularly unequivocal—and bleak—conception of the nature and significance of technological development (see, in particular, Heidegger 1977). On this view, the mobile would simply exacerbate the problems of living in a culture of simultaneity in which, as Nowotny argues, the challenge for modern citizens is to find time for themselves (Roberts 1998). The fact that time spent getting to and from work, for example, can now be reconfigured as potentially productive time might be read as simple evidence of the spread of a form of instrumental rationality that is difficult to resist. Or again, in spatial terms, the fact that the mobile allows people to be reached anywhere can, paradoxically, contribute to a kind of stasis of identity for practical purposes; retention of the same mobile number means that moving office or house, being stationary or on the move, are not significant from the perspective of the caller. We must be perpetually on call (see Ronell 1989).[11]

We suggest that the role of the mobile is not determinate in this sense. For example, careful study, such as Laurier (1999), suggests that using the technology to its full potential can help to *control* time. More generally, people develop different strategies to maintain boundaries (work and leisure, for example) that

[10] Developments in technologies for measuring time have been no less significant: see Stengers and Gille (1997) on the technical standardization of time and timepieces.

[11] 'Demand' may be considered on another level. The fixed-line phone assumes a form of priority over face-to-face interaction in many settings: the phone may be ignored, with difficulty, but it cannot be kept waiting, unlike the co-present other who may be mollified with sympathetic gestures during the call (see Goffman 1971). Responses to the unanswered mobile, as detailed above, suggest at least some commonality of normative expectation.

are important to them, notwithstanding the technical capacity of a particular device for erasing them. Popular discourse, advertising for instance, is instructive in this regard. A 1999 UK radio advert aimed at the mobile professional, for example, concluded by acknowledging that perpetual contact can be bad news for some with the words 'You can run but you can't hide'. Availability here can be both an advantage and a possible liability.[12] The mobile's status as inherently demanding is at best ambivalent.[13]

CONCLUSION: THE MOBILE AND THE VIRTUAL

In relation to questions about the status and significance of the virtual, the analytic value of looking, empirically, at mobiles can be shown by considering two claims of Paul Virilio's. First, he asserts that we are becoming disconnected from our physical environment. The availability and increasing priority of remote communication and information are seen as effecting a kind of spatial detachment from our immediate surroundings (and more): 'closer to what is far away than to what is just beside us, we are becoming progressively detached from *ourselves*' (Virilio 2000: 83; emphasis added).[14] Leaving aside the question of how, in any case, such a claim might be assessed, it is possible to read in(to) this an image of a solitary user in front of his or her PC. When looking at remote communication on the move, such a claim would have to be highly qualified by a number of practical, cultural, and ethical considerations. For example, one grossly observable feature of the content of mobile phone conversations in public spaces is the frequent recourse to explicit contextualization as a feature of talk. Here we see that, whilst the mobile may provide the technical capacity to converse from any location or situation, contextual sensitivities that are at the heart of communicative action still prevail: thus, users often feel obliged to provide each other with explicit information in order that, for example, situational proprieties may be taken into account. 'Hello I'm on the train' is the most obvious example of this, and the fact that it has become both a joke and a cliché

---

[12] Some advertising can appear a good deal less reflexive about negative connotations than this. Another UK advert, in which a group of friends watch a young woman in a variety of locations as she goes about her everyday life, and communicate her activities to one of them via their mobile phones, tells a story that in other contexts (and for some in this one as well) might be seen as disturbing.

[13] To the extent that this technology might be granted to be in some sense 'demanding', there are also questions to be explored on the nature of this demand (Cooper 2001). On the problems of Heidegger's unequivocal view of technology, see Derrida (1994).

[14] This would be an interesting reinflection of Benjamin's notion of 'aura' in which certain things that are immediately present (such as works of art) retain a kind of remoteness, mystery, and distance, thus marking, as Samuel Weber (1996) argues, the separation that is an irreducible feature of presence. Here, by contrast, the remote becomes present, and the present becomes not mysterious but secondary or a matter of relative indifference.

in the UK demonstrates its necessity. (Its very ubiquity causes further dilemmas for the user, as evidenced in the following overheard exchange: 'I'm on the train...I know, isn't it awful!', an utterance that acknowledges and thereby deals with the difficulty.)

Secondly, Virilio sees the growing availability of information on demand as leading to, not a frenzy of simultaneity, but a form of inertia: we will change from the 'unbridled nomadism' of modernity to 'the definitive inertia or sedentariness of whole societies' (Virilio 2000: 20). The instant availability of all kinds of information at any time or place means that there will be no need for physical motion. If we are to accept this as a plausible vision, the 3GM device is placed in an interesting and paradoxical position: at the juncture of virtual and physical mobility, it makes use of the electronic resources that would make the latter unnecessary.

However, people have other reasons for continuing to travel, dwell, or gather that deserve some consideration. There seems to be here an underlying assumption in which communication is seen as significant in purely functional terms as information exchange. Such an assumption can be traced through a variety of contexts in which it takes on a variety of inflections; for instance, normative ones in those disciplines (not just engineering disciplines) that regard the construction of more effective and more efficient communication that can operate regardless of the constraints of the physical environment as an unquestioned goal. Deborah Cameron's *Good to Talk?* (2000) ably documents the spread of a certain orientation towards the inherent value of effective communication *per se*. The relation between this model of communication (information exchange), normative assumptions about the value of communication as discussed by Cameron, and perhaps the perceived need to be 'in touch' requires further elaboration.

At the very least, the study of the emerging (socio-technical) form of the mobile device—and in particular of its use in specific contexts—raises questions about such purely functional models of communication, and adds further complications and dimensions to discussions of virtuality. Indeed, if context is the *sine qua non* of studies of situated practical action, then a definitively portable technology might be said to have a particular strategic value for deconstructing ungrounded assertions about virtuality—not to mention mobility— and, as such, imply the need for extensive multi-sited empirical study. However, it would be a mistake simply to equate the virtual (or remote) with the theoretical, and the real (or materially co-present) with the empirical, and thereby to dismiss the theoretical as idle speculation. As we have stated or implied throughout, not only is co-presence itself subject to interpretation and thus neither given nor, in a philosophical sense, present; but also, as is the case with other recent technologies (Hine 2000), the mobile device invites questions about what constitutes the empirical, and what is the most appropriate unit of analysis (Cooper 2001). Answers to these questions cannot be simply derived from the empirical. Just as the emerging shape of mobile usage takes place within the force field between production and everyday practice, so an adequate understanding of its social significance will emerge from the interplay of, and tensions between, theoretical reflection and empirical study: correspondingly, the virtual might be mapped in terms of the motion between these points of orientation, rather than placed on one side or another.

17

Abstraction and Decontextualization: An Anthropological Comment

Marilyn Strathern

> Short of becoming anthropologists [ethnographers] of their own institutions, its members can no longer know each other.
>
> (Ron Barnett (2000: 94) on the dispersed nature of the 'virtual' university)

Many of the findings in this book, writes the editor, are counter-intuitive. This is itself a finding, one reached early on in the 'Virtual Society?' programme on which these contributions are based, and it has remained importantly true. The ethnographic reach of the diverse studies brought together here underpins it. But to know that as a finding then makes it part of the study. This chapter reflects on the process of study.

One question running through the 'Virtual Society?' programme is to do with the overenthusiastic claims made in the name of virtual technologies. If ideas about virtual systems have raced ahead of their actualization, then it has to be other ideas and other systems, ones already in place, that speed them on their way. Certain well-established processes of 'abstraction' and 'decontextualization' are suggestive here. It is arguable that, for as often as abstraction may be regarded as taking content out of human interactions, it is also inherent to the imagination of social relations; and, for as often as observers seek to restore context as an aid to interpretation, the capacity to cross domains is inherent in social understanding. This chapter sets out to render these thoughts concrete

This is based on a talk given to the concluding conference of the 'Virtual Society?' programme. The text of the talk is published in *Cambridge Anthropology*, 22 (2001). I am most grateful to Steve Woolgar for the invitation, which enabled me to learn about the programme at first hand. My closest acquaintance with individual projects has been with 'Social Contexts of Virtual Manchester' (Penny Harvey, Sarah Green, and Jon Agar), and the stimulus of that work on several levels will be very evident here. Many thanks to the anonymous reader who prompted me to re-situate this argument.

by the social anthropological use of comparative material. This will include material drawn from practices of audit, particularly in higher education. Here information and communications technology (ICT) carries a heavy symbolic role, but is otherwise ancillary to procedures that have a long history in financial accounting and management systems. But, if recently auditees appear to have become a new kind of consumer, then what is added, and what is taken away, by thinking of them as virtual consumers?

Bruno Latour (1998) made a telling half-joke at the end of his lecture inaugurating the Programme, with a pun on virtual and virtuous. Can the virtual society produce new virtues, he asks? Virtuous is not a word we care to use much these days, but I shall try to show how it might apply to the future of higher education and indeed to the future of research activities, for there is an important and complex relationship between the research process and the subject of the research that the 'Virtual Society?' programme mapped out. As Woolgar's (this volume) conclusion about counter-intuitive findings indicates, there are some surprises in that relationship.

THE MULTIPLICATION OF CONTEXTS

Social-science research, and especially anthropological research, is often justified by the need to 'put things into context', especially where that context is understood as society or culture.[1] Contexts are regarded as piling on layers of understanding, which should thus become deeper, richer; one tool of this deepening process is research through ethnography. This is not, however, quite the straightforward project of enhancement one might presume.

It is two anthropologists, Schlecker and Hirsch (2001), who pinpoint the phenomenon of diminishing returns. The turn to ethnography in media and science studies, they argue, has not yielded the overview that might have been expected. Instead of allowing one to specify (garner more knowledge about) relational contexts, the more ethnographically local studies became, the more new contexts (and new areas of ignorance) were opened up; every new perspective meant loss of others. This is partly because of a failure, they argue, to understand the multiplication and displacements effects of that mode of study, one that supposed that the contexts themselves added knowledge. Of course they do; but, in so far as they produce fresh (exogenous) data, they simultaneously point to yet more possibilities for contextualization. There is seemingly no stopping this 'fractal unfolding of complexity' (Schlecker and Hirsch 2001: 76). In fact they conclude on a positive note about ethnography, but as an intensive rather than an extensive exercise. The problem was ever to think that a context or 'field' could be encompassing (as suggested by the happy metaphor of putting something 'in' it).

[1] For an excellent anthropological discussion, see Dilley (1999).

The 'Virtual Society?' programme as represented by the chapters in this volume offers one kind of stopping point. And that is because its problematic was from the outset conceived as decontextualization. If the programme seeks to provide contextualization in order to understand the 'social and human dimensions' of the new technologies, it has to be because the electronic technologies themselves are already depicted as 'decontextualized'.[2] In other words, they are imagined as having the power to communicate and convey information stripped of the encumbrances of social relations, as well as of physical limitation on travel. This, as Carrier (1998: 2; cf. Riles 1999) reminds us, was Polyani's original analysis of abstraction in economics, a dis-embedding process, 'the removal of economic activities from the social and other relationships in which they had occurred, and carrying them out in a context in which the only important relationships are those defined by the economic activity itself'. The notion of a decontextualized process already implies or points to the wider context from which it has been carved out. This affords a vantage point of tremendous interest.

If one is dealing with a phenomenon whose distinctiveness is the very characteristic of decontextualization (hence its 'virtual' nature), there is an obvious alternative to the kind of contextualization process that by adding ever more fields of possible relevance increases rather than satisfies the need for context. We can consider instead how it is that virtual phenomena are regarded as 'out of context' in the first place. That is, what phenomena do the purveyors of virtual realities themselves regard as exogenous? What 'missing' realities are already contained within the way people think about virtual reality? We can use ethnographic methods to find out. But the result will be, so to speak, a description that is *inside* virtual reality rather than outside it. In this regard we would meet Schlecker and Hirsch's advocacy for an intensive rather than an extensive ethnographic move.

But this does not mean that the ethnographer is bound only by assumptions people make explicit to themselves. Rather it is a question of taking whatever one finds inside virtual reality as part of that phenomenon; this is distinct from knowing that there is no end to the discovery that it can also be part of something else (no end to the number of extraneous contexts it is possible to summon). What interests me is that part of the inside of virtual reality resonates with another phenomenon altogether, audit. It is not trivial that audit also interested Woolgar (1997), and that he dubs it one of the technologies of

---

[2] Woolgar pinpointed this from the outset. In the ESRC 'Virtual Society?' Programme (2000) he notes that 'UK and European White Papers on Growth and Competitiveness, and users in industry, have ... identified *the social context* in which technologies are actually used as a key area which is poorly understood' (emphasis added). The 'Virtual Society?' programme sought to put electronic technologies 'into' a social context: it opened up diverse channels of enquiry and spread over several domains, with multiple themes and cross-cutting vantage points. Indeed it invites one to venture into a huge and sprawling field, not unlike that of an anthropological ethnographer.

accountability. It offers a perspective that is at once part of and not part of a field in which one might put ICT. But, before introducing audit, a short comment on an initial displacement of contexts is in order.

CIRCUMSCRIBING THE VIRTUAL

In his address, Latour pointed to diverse antecedents for decontextualization in the form of reduction or abstraction—maps and plans, scale models, spirit houses as the microcosm of society. So what does the contemporary idea of 'the virtual' add? Perhaps it adds the capacity of something to point to its own effects. The power of communication is communication. This is not as absurd as it sounds; indeed, it has the virtue of resonating at once with virtual's original meaning *and* with the subsequent devolution of that meaning.

The term 'virtual' has undergone an intriguing metamorphosis from the concrete to the abstract.[3] In this displacement of contexts, we see how the notion of abstractness came to be formed as a defining feature. Very briefly, 'virtual' started off as a reference to the physical qualities (or virtues) that things have, and to the effects of these qualities, like the virtual heat of wine or of sunshine. It then came to describe the state of being effective or potent. Not until the seventeenth century was the term first used for the essence or effect of qualities by themselves, so that things could be called virtual—as one might refer to a ruler who was a virtual sovereign—in reference to qualities that were not endowed in formal or 'actual' terms. The point is that virtual entities point to their own potency: the virtual sovereign did not need to be crowned. Such efficacy appears not to need the props of human social relations or wider contexts of activity.

Technology often appears to have such internal efficacy. And a technology that doubles up with the capacity to communicate, which Euro-Americans take as itself a process of abstraction, seems irresistible. Indeed this book probes the hype that presents ICT as offering communication and information networks free of the labour of other forms of interaction. However, there are also *social* precursors to imagined technologies in this auto-enabling sense: systems (or closed system (cf. Dilley 1999: 21)) that generate their own rationales for existence. Here the self-describing practices of institutions and organizations that represent themselves *as* instutitions or organizations become interesting. Audit is one such.

We can think of audit as a set of institutional practices deeply committed to a certain form of description—namely, to eliciting from auditees their descriptions of themselves. Perhaps no surprise, then, that the epithet 'virtual' has been applied to it. Indeed, audit is quite usefully thought of as a producer of virtual realities, for self-description meets the criterion of auto-enabling efficacy—it

---

[3] A progression often taken literally to characterize huge historical sweeps as well (see Carrier 1998).

effects what it points to. Yet speaking of audit in these terms prompts one to acknowledge a divergence. Ethnographic description is the very opposite of self-description, and means nothing—has no efficacy—unless one knows the conditions of its compilation or its theoretical underpinnings; it cannot be made abstract in this sense.

AUDIT

It is Miller (1998) who calls audit a manifestation of virtualism.[4] Activities are decontextualized for the purposes of quantification, output disembedded from the complexity of organizational life. He puts this in the larger context of political and economic shifts, where, he argues, the consumer is silently transformed into a virtual consumer.

The paradox is that, while consumption is the pivot upon which these developments in history spin, the concern is not the costs and benefits of actual consumers, but of what we might call virtual consumers, which are generated by management theory and models... [And] the rise of auditing in Britain [is thus] symptomatic not of capitalism, but of a new form of abstraction that is emerging, a form more abstract than the capitalism of firms dealing with commodities.   (Miller 1998: 204–5)

As we have seen, alongside abstraction as such the perception of auto-enablement or efficacy also has a decontextualizing effect ('communication communicates'). Audit enrols various social mechanisms that confirm its internal efficacy; thus it can evaluate the results of social processes without having to deal with the processes themselves. One can get straight to the end-result to the extent that it is possible to *bypass* these other processes. Let me show you how this works.

In the expanded sense that it has recently acquired (Power 1994, 1997), audit has come to be used for almost any investigation involving analysis ('reckoning' or 'accounting'). One of the Cambridge colleges was visited last year by managers from a well-known plc on an MBA course at a well-known university who wanted to do a study of an organization different from their own: they spent the day asking people questions and looking at documents. They had already decided that what was going to differ was the culture, and the operation was called 'cultural audit'. They also knew the graphic form in which their results would be presented: 'a detailed Cultural Web'. That indeed is the nub of audit, at least as it operates through quality assessment regimes (such as the Research Assessment Exercises (RAE) and the former Teaching Quality Assessment (TQA)[5]) in British higher education (HE). The form in which the outcome is to be

---

[4] Perhaps a more satisfactory way of putting it than focusing on audit's 'reflexive' potential (cf. Strathern 1997; Shore and Wright 2000).
[5] The four-yearly RAE are organized by the Higher Education Funding Councils. The TQA was a precursor to the Quality Assurance Agency's (QAA) new review of teaching in higher education.

described is *known in advance*. You bypass having to construct the form from the investigations themselves. The investigation—the research if you will—is in that sense retrospective; that is, it works backwards from the bottom line up, from the categories by which accountability (say) can be ascertained to the evidence for it. The outcome of the audit report is a report on the outcome of the institution under scrutiny. In looking at outcome as output, audit looks at the *effect* of productive processes. It may or may not be interested in the processes themselves, and usually only in order to verify the bottom line.[6] In short, audit produces its own effect in so far as the report on outcome/output takes a form it itself creates.

Interest in outcome leads to management accounting or policy-directed audit (see Harper 2000: 37).[7] That is, you measure the accomplishments (output) in the hope that you can improve the system. And here there is an inbuilt little gadget that gets over the time problem, the fact that academics in higher education traditionally accounted for their output in terms of (student) generations—the reputation books acquired over decades or the successes of former pupils in their middle years of life. The gadget means that you do not have to wait a generation or two. You can speed up the process. It is very simple: you turn the system of measurement into a device that also sets the ideal levels of attainment. In short, audit measures become targets (Hoskin 1996; Macintyre 2000). They collapse the 'is' and the 'ought', continuing a long process that began when examination results became aims—when a high score is not simply how you measure up but is a level you have aimed and striven for.

And how, in turn, is that device created? The mechanism is already there in the focus on outcome; this is a highly effective procedure of abstraction, for it restricts the output (results) of observation to data suitable for constructing measures of it. So in teaching, for example, you do not have to wait for the results years hence but can create a simulacrum of what the classroom *should be* producing (what its outcome or effect should be) through a virtual model, a map or plan, a kind of spirit house, in the form of indicators.

This decontextualization leads to another: indicators come in turn to have a life or efficacy of their own, and it is no surprise that there is much complaint about their arbitrariness. Tsoukas (1994: 4) describes the self-defeating specification of performance indicators as it might apply in the sphere of local government.[8] In 1993 new regulations meant that local authorities in the UK had to publish indicators of output, no fewer than 152 of them. The idea was, he

---

[6] See the recent discussion in Velody (1999) and Scott (2000), and, in a policy context, Kogan and Henkel (1998).

[7] Thus it was with approval that the cover story in the UK magazine called *Managing Higher Education* (intended 'for decision-makers in higher education') opines that surviving the RAE has entailed higher education institutions trying to influence or anticipate changes in national strategy, 'adapting institutional policy to maximise achievement under the Exercise' (Muckersie 1996: 15).

[8] For another context for this commentary, see Strathern (2000).

reports, to make councils' performance transparent and thus give them an incentive to improve their services. So, even though elderly people might want a deep freeze and microwave rather than food delivered by home helps, if the number of home helps is the indicator for helping the elderly with their meals, then an authority could improve its recognized performance of help only by providing the elderly with the very service they wanted less of—namely, more home helps.[9] Local authorities would be aiming for high scores, and the language of indicators takes over the language of service.[10]

As it turns out, ICT is a highly visible ally of audit practices. Its speeding-up of the performance of office equipment does not just facilitate the production of the audit reports and so forth, but as an entity in itself (*as* ICT), it can be used as an indicator of performance.[11] HE audit visits frequently exhort the use of office-like technology while also managing to suggest that knowledge itself is at stake: it is all contained in the phrase 'information technology'. My point is not the benefits (or otherwise) here, but the obvious symbolic status of ICT. Using ICT in teaching has been a criterion in the TQA's evaluation procedures; this is how teaching in the discipline of anthropology was chastised:

The overview report [on anthropology] highlights some areas for further attention of the institutions and of anthropologists. Whilst information technology (IT) provision is generally adequate to meet current needs, there is significant variation in the use made of IT and a lack of emphasis on IT skills development.   (Glasner 1996: 8)

Suggestions for useful improvement and proof (measures) of improvement merge. As a self-evidently useful technology, ICT points to itself. In the same way, the self-evidently good practice of auditing emerges as a virtual activity pointing to its own effects, captured by Power in his reference to the auditing loop that creates auditees.[12]

'Loop' is apposite. As a descriptive practice, audit cannot afford to tolerate loose ends, unpredictability, or disconnections. It carves out its own domain of what is going to count as 'description'. This means that what may be brilliant

---

[9] Quoting the vice-chairman of the Association of Metropolitan Authorities, Margaret Hodge (*Independent*, 11 Sept. 1992).

[10] A student pointed out to me apropos the Cambridge University mission statement that its opening assertion, 'to foster and develop academic excellence across a wide range of subjects', immediately gives as its rationale 'and thereby to *enhance its position* as one of the world leading universities', that is, its league table position.

[11] Ideologically speaking, and this is one of the targets of the 'Virtual Society?' programme. Since ICT's effectiveness in enhancing existing practices is taken for granted, ICT itself may well get off audit-free (no examination of whether it really does enhance).

[12] Audit systems miniaturize real-world complexities. What is often subject to inspection is the auditees' own auditing methods; in this context, Power (1994: 36–7) observes: 'What is audited is whether there is a system which embodies standards and the standards of performance themselves are shaped by the need to be auditable... audit becomes a formal "loop" by which the system observes itself.' Audit makes sense of an institution *as* an organization, and requires that it 'perform' *being* an organization, focusing on those parts that indicate performance. Here is a second loop: administrative audits literally embody organizational ideals: it is smooth running that is under scrutiny.

accounting is bound to be poor sociology, and—very obviously—different from an ethnography of an institution or organization, or of society for that matter. But what lies behind this distinction?

Itself a system, audit elicits a view of an institution or organization as a system—as system, not as a 'society'. Ethnographic practice, on the other hand, elicits the open-endedness of institutions and organizations *as* 'society'. What characterizes people's behaviour in 'society' is precisely their capacity to tolerate loose ends, to deal with unpredictability, and to revel in the disconnections that mean that they live in multiple worlds and traverse different domains. This is where intensive ethnography comes into its own. It is a matter for investigation what worlds people pack into one another, the contexts they think they have abstracted themselves from and that fuel their own sense of efficacy. Investigation has to be open-minded in the matter.

ETHNOGRAPHIC DESCRIPTION AND THE COUNTER-INTUITIVE

Ethnography does not measure accomplishments in the hopes of improving the system.[13] More to the point, its open-minded and open-ended procedures refer *both* to the manner in which observations are made *and* to the process of compiling a description. Far from truncating description, it has its own search engine in the form of a question: what connections are going to be useful? That is simply because one cannot always tell in advance; more strongly, it puts one into the situation of not wanting to tell in advance.

Indeed, ethnography throws up the unplanned, the counter-intuitive, the unpredictable. It tolerates disconnections. You do not have to tie up all the loose ends; on the contrary, there may be data that will become a resource only from some vantage point in the future. But how does it create this situation? The device is that of crossing contexts. In an extensive mode, this precipitates potentially infinite differences 'between' contexts. In an intensive mode, it tracks people's activities and narratives as *they* cross domains, and thereby unpacks the heterogeneous social worlds people pile up for themselves. If worlds are stacked inside one another, their compatibility may or may not be an issue.

Let me refer to a specific project where it was not. Jon Agar, Sarah Green, and Penny Harvey's account (this volume) of people setting up an inter-system network of communications in order to turn Manchester into a virtual city describes a significant and absolute requirement of electronic technological systems: they must be compatible (made into a single system, inhabit the same circuit/domain) before they interact. Interaction is an outcome or effect of their compatibility. Society, to the contrary, effects interactions between people that

---

[13] That does not mean that it cannot be pressed into that service.

may, but may not, lead to compatibility. In other words, compatibility may be an outcome; but many other states of being could be the outcome too. Social interactions are thus inherently open-ended—can encompass diverse aims and intentions—because communication between persons does not require compatibility between them in advance. From this comes much of the creativity and energy of social life.[14] Predictability and unpredictability go hand in hand.

It follows that any one interaction may represent as much a potential divergence as a convergence of people's trajectories. It also follows that ethnographers cannot possibly englobe data within a single context, make it all compatible, but must instead be explicit about their own preconditions of context production, whether they think of themselves as crossing domains or recovering the dimensions of decontextualization. We come to another device. The little social engine that makes either route possible is *relations*. By this I refer doubly to the conceptual relations that link data and to the living relations people have with one another.

RELATIONS VIRTUAL AND VIRTUOUS

I return yet again to the address that Latour gave at the start of the 'Virtual Society?' programme, his evocation of the long history of virtual artefacts as bureaucratic procedures, plans, representations, as in the Papua New Guinean spirit house that lays out a map of social groupings. Evidently, making plans of what is imagined to be 'society' is not the same order of phenomenon as society as such. It is not just that plans never exhaust all there is to know but that they never replicate how people activate society on the ground, as they do through the relations and connections they sustain.

Connections and relations, like society itself, require imagining (Battaglia 1994) and may be (virtually) imagined *as* virtual as well as (imagined as) actualized in interpersonal relationships. Indeed, historically speaking, the very term 'relation' referred to abstract concepts before it referred to connections between persons (Strathern 1995). Latour emphasized the way in which ICT materializes 'society' by making its contours visible, although any of a number of technologies or practices can do this.[15] What is distinctive about ICT is the fact that it mobilizes society in a particular mode, not just as a network of communications but as *the network of connections or relations* that carries

[14] Cf. Tsoukas (1994: 15–16): 'it is impossible to know in advance the entire range of responses an individual is capable of', a truism that can be startling in the context of certain management theories.

[15] The ubiquity of 'connection' and its capacity to animate networks that constantly reconfigure their internal relations is specifically but not exclusively discussed in Green and Harvey (1999) and Riles (2000). On the originating capacity of 'the relation' to do just this, see Strathern (1995).

communications (Riles 2000). Here the hype and rhetoric surrounding ICT is an important part of the technology itself. The fact that the rhetoric then comes adrift against 'actual' social relations is beside the point: it has already provided a measure of sorts for them. ICT points to the connecting power of connections. That is its virtue.

What we choose to describe as virtual and choose to describe as actual will depend on the purposes of the moment. But those two terms harness certain qualities about social life that we know must always work in tandem. The point is that in the popular imagination ICT stands for the possibility of actualizing connections otherwise beyond reach except in a virtual state. All kinds of attributions of power come in the wake of this, and with it the deflations that attend its actual actualization. But, then, 'Realising Virtuality [could never be] actualizing potential, because what is in the realization of Virtuality is unpredictable' (Latour 1998: 6).

If one were looking for a methodology to grasp this interplay between imagination and the unpredictable outcomes of lived social relations,[16] one could do worse than ethnography. Ethnography does in particular what social science does in general: its points to the dimensionality of phenomena and thus refuses claims to self-sufficiency. It introduces, in the simplest way, numerical complexity of the most significant kind (Macintyre 2000): there is (always) more than 'one' thing to consider (and cf. Battaglia 1999; Riles 1999). What is painfully obvious as a truism about knowledge, as a truism about society, also contains a truth. The activity of description reminds us that we live in a world full of people's descriptions of what they do. And these multiply the unpredictability, quite as much as the predictability, of outcomes. This awareness I take also as something approaching a virtue—although we could translate its implementation into the more humdrum language of skills.

Knowing how to deal with unpredictability—that is, with the effects of the unforeseen, the added elements we never thought of—is a skill that university academics, as well as citizens, are going to need in the future—if, that is, we follow Ron Barnett's at once chilling and stimulating vision (2000: 62) for realizing the university in an age of supercomplexity. This gives me an opportunity. Rather than summarizing the argument of this chapter, I recontextualize it.

Complexity Barnett defines as a condition brought about by the surfeit of information, supercomplexity as that surfeit stacked and multiplied through a surfeit of frameworks for processing the information. Indeed, he invites us to think of a world changing so fast it is radically unknowable. He invokes a constellation of concepts—uncertainty, unpredictability, challengeabilty, and contestability—that renders all frameworks fragile. Or, we could say, all procedures (frameworks) for abstraction and decontextualization become visibly contingent. Theoretical frameworks, like other models, can be thought of as virtual systems. Their effects are perceived in their own terms (how far does the

---

[16] Strathern (1999b) unpacks this to some extent.

data fit into the framework?). Yet such self-realization can be only momentary. We might, to the contrary, say that we encounter effects only when they are already realized (contextualized) and thus translated, as Latour noted, into something else by the contingencies and unpredictabilities of their materialization. Research replays the essential disjunction between any imagining of our condition and social life as a fabrication of divergences and of events quite unforeseen. The research process itself introduces disconnections of its own.

It is just this kind of interplay that I think Barnett is after in defining how the university of the future might realize itself.

The university is an institution that (i) contributes to our uncertainty in the world (through its research and consultancy); (ii) helps us to monitor and evaluate that uncertainty (through its work as a centre of critique); and (iii) enables us to live with that uncertainty, through both the operational capacities and the existential capacities it promotes (in its pedagogical activities).   (R. Barnett 2000: 69)

Research and teaching have to cut loose from the axiomatic authority of knowledge and embed themselves (he more or less says) in a real world of uncertainties. At the same time, the university has a role in promoting certain virtues (not his term): to set the informed apart from the uninformed, to distinguish enlightenment from ideology, and to monitor the kinds of accounts we give. Indeed, Barnett argues that the university is uniquely placed to help the world address the condition of supercomplexity. A condition the universities have helped create is one they can also help us to live with.[17] This is not a condition to be remedied but it is one that has to be confronted. The university is 'realized' in the kinds of intellectual responsibilities (this is his term) it takes on.[18]

I do not follow his line entirely. For instance, I would take complexity not as adding more of the same (adding uncertainty to uncertainty) but as the intermeshing of different orders of phenomena, having to take certainties and uncertainties together. But his argument does delineate a difference between accountability, rendering an account to those to whom one is accountable, manifest in the self-evident efficacy of audit, and responsibility, which is discharged to those in one's care, whether students or colleagues or the wider

---

[17] Ron Barnett (2000: 93) refers to the postmodern university as the *virtual university*, by which he means to point to its dispersed field—dispersed in terms of the networks of individuals that belong to it, the intellectual capital on which it draws, the multiple audiences with which it engages, and its general 'loss of a defining centre'. It is simply, he says, a set of possibilities to be realized. Every point of realization is of course a recontextualization.

[18] The responsibility of academics as scholars is to attend to supercomplexity as a condition of the way the world is, and thereby to hold up to society new frames of understanding and ways of living effectively with it (R. Barnett 2000: 168–9). The university is unique here: no other social institution, he argues, holds quite these responsibilities. He explicitly takes issue with performance indicators and the bottom line balance sheet as criteria by which to measure the university's (civic) role in society (R. Barnett 2000: 171).

public.[19] What the 'Virtual Society?' programme yielded is insight into some of our choices in how to describe these dimensions. If one describes them as the difference between 'virtual' and 'social' duties, then one is taking virtualism's viewpoint; if one describes them as equally the outcomes of social process, equally socially produced, then one is taking society's viewpoint.

[19] Needless to say, Total Quality Management already has 'responsibilization' in its arsenal (Shore and Wright 2000: 69).

REFERENCES

Abbey, J. A. (1996). 'Fools and their Money', *TIME Magazine*, 17 June.

Abolafia, M. Y. (1996). *Making Markets: Opportunism and Restraint on Wall Street*. Cambridge, MA: Harvard University Press.

Adler, P. A., and Adler, P. (1984). *The Social Dynamics of Financial Markets*. Greenwhich, CT: JAI Press.

Agamben, G. (2000). *Potentialities*. Stanford, CA: Stanford University Press.

Agar, J. (1998). 'Digital Patina: Texts, Spirit and the First Computer'. *History and Technology*, 15: 121–35.

—— (forthcoming). *The Government Machine*. Cambridge, MA: MIT Press.

Aldrich, H., and Herker, D. (1977). 'Boundary Spanning Roles and Organisational Structure'. *Academy of Management Review* (Apr.), 217–30.

Anderson, B. (1983). *Imagined Communities*. London: Verso.

Armstrong, G., and Norris, C. (1999). *The Maximum Surveillance Society*. Aldershot: Ashgate.

Ashmore, M., Edwards, D., and Potter, J. (1994). 'The Bottom Line: The Rhetoric of Reality Demonstrations'. *Configurations*, 2/1: 1–14.

Augé, M. (1999). *The War of Dreams: Studies in Ethno Fiction*. London: Pluto Press.

Bacharach, M. (1991). 'Commodities, Language and Desire'. *Journal of Philosophy*, 87/7: 346–86.

Bangemann, M. (1994). *Europe and the Global Information Society: Recommendations to the European Council*. Brussels: European Council.

Barnett, A. (2000). 'The End of Privacy'. *Observer*, 30 July.

Barnett, R. (2000). *Realizing the University in an Age of Supercomplexity*. Buckingham: Society for Research into Higher Education and Open University Press.

Bass, D. M., McKee, M., Flatley-Brennan, P., and McCarthy, C. (1998). 'The Buffering Effect of a Computer Support Network on Caregiver Strain'. *Journal of Aging and Health*, 10/1: 20–43.

Battaglia, D. (1994). 'Retaining Reality: Some Practical Problems with Objects as Property'. *Man*, 29: 631–44.

—— (1999). 'Towards an Ethics of the Open Subject: Writing Culture in Good Conscience' in H. Moore (ed.), *Anthropological Theory Today*. Cambridge: Polity.

Bauer, M. (1995). *Resistance to New Technology: Nuclear Power, Information Technology and Biotechnology*. Cambridge: Cambridge University Press.

Baym, N. (1998). 'The Emergence of On-Line Community', in S. G. Jones (ed.), *Cybersociety 2.0: Revisiting Computer-Mediated Communication and Community*. London: Sage.

Becattini, G. (1990). 'The Mashallian Industrial District as a Socio-Economic Notion', in F. Pyke (ed.), *Industrial Districts and Inter-Firm Co-operation in Italy*: Geneva: International Institute for Labour Studies.

Beck, U. (1998). 'The Cosmopolitan Manifesto', *New Statesman*, 20 Mar.

——Giddens, A., and Lash, S. (1994). *Reflexive Modernisation: Politics Tradition and Aesthetics in the Modern Social Order*. Cambridge: Polity.

Bell, C., and Newby, H. (1971). *Community Studies: An Introduction to the Sociology of the Local Community*. London: Allen & Unwin.

Beniger, J. R. (1986). *The Control Revolution: Technological and Economic Origins of the Information Society*. Cambridge, MA: Harvard University Press.

Benjamin, W. (1983). *Charles Baudelaire*. London: Verso.

Berg, M. (1997). *Rationalizing Medical Work: Decision Support Techniques and Medical Practices*. Cambridge, MA: MIT Press.

Bergham, J. (1995). 'Social Exclusion in Europe: Policy Context and Analytical Framework', in G. Room (ed.), *Beyond the Threshold: The Measurement and Analysis of Social Exclusion*. Bristol: Policy Press.

Bijker, W. E., Hughes, T. P., and Pinch, T. J. (1987) (eds.), *The Social Construction of Technological Systems: New Directions in the Sociology and History of Technology*. Cambridge, MA: MIT Press.

Bingham, N. (1999). 'Unthinkable Complexity? Cyberspace Otherwise', in M. Crang, P. Crang, and J. May (eds.), *Virtual Geographies: Bodies, Space and Relations*. London: Routledge.

Biocca, F., Kim, T., and Levy, M. R. (1995). 'The Vision of Virtual Reality', in F. Biocca and M. R. Levy (eds.), *Communication in the Age of Virtual Reality*. Hillsdale, NJ: Lawrence Erlbaum Associates.

Birdwhistell, R. (1971). *Kinesics and Context: Essays on Body-Motion Communication*. Harmondsworth: Penguin.

Bittner, E. (1965). 'The Concept of Organisation'. *Social Research*, 23: 239–55.

Bliss, J., Light, P., and Saljo, R. (1999). *Learning Sites*. Oxford: Elsevier Science.

Bloomfield, B. P. (1998). 'In the Right Place at the Right Time: Electronic Tagging and Problems of Social Order/Disorder'. Paper presented at the European Association for the Study of Science and Technology Conference, Lisbon, 1–3 Oct.

——and Vurdubakis, T. (1997). 'The Revenge of the Object? Artificial Intelligence as a Cultural Enterprise'. *Social Analysis*, 4/11: 29–45.

——(1999). 'IBM's Chess Players'. Paper presented at conference on 'Sociality/Materiality: The Status of the Object in Social Science', Brunel University.

——(2001). 'The Vision Thing: Constructions of Time and Technology in Management Advice', in T. Clark and R. Fincham (eds.), *Critical Consulting: Perspectives on the Management Advice Industry*. Oxford: Blackwell.

——(forthcoming). 'What a Performance! On Management Consultancy and its Discontents'. Unpublished typescript.

Blustein, H., Goldstein, P., and Lozier, G. (1999). 'Assessing the New Competitive Landscape?', in R. Katz (ed.), *Dancing with the Devil: Information Technology and the New Competition in Higher Education*. San Francisco: Jossey-Bass.

Boberg, E. W., Gustafson, D. H., Hawkins, R. P., Chan, C. L., Bricker, E., Pingree, S., Berhe, H., and Peressini, A. (1995). 'Development, Acceptance and Use Patterns of a Computer Based

Education and Social Support System for People Living with AIDS/HIV Infection'. *Computers in Human Behaviour*, 11/2: 289–311.

Boden, D. (1990). 'People are Talking: Conversation Analysis and Symbolic Interaction', in H. S. Becker and M. M. McCall (eds.), *Symbolic Interaction and Cultural Studies*. Chicago: University of Chicago Press.

Booz, Allen & Hamilton (2000). 'Achieving Universal Access', London: Booz, Allen & Hamilton.

Bradbury, D. (1999). 'Internet Web Retailing Still Means Manual Labour'. *Computer Weekly*, 36, 6 May.

Bresler, F. (2000). 'Human Rights at Work'. *The Times*, 15 Nov.

Briggs, A. (1968). *Victorian Cities*. Harmondsworth: Penguin.

Brigham, M., and Corbett, J. M. (1997). 'E-mail, Power and the Constitution of Organisational Reality'. *New Technology, Work and Employment*, 12/1: 25–35.

Brown, S. D., and Lightfoot, G. (1998). 'Insistent Emplacement: Heidegger on the Technologies of Informing'. *Information Technology & People*, 11/4: 290–304.

—— and Middleton, D. (2002). 'Words and Things: Discursive and Non-Discursive Ordering in a Networked Organization'. Mimeo, Department of Human Sciences, Loughborough University. Available at http: //devpsy.iboro.ac.uk/psygroup/sb/talking.htm.

—— —— and Lightfoot, G. (2001). 'Performing the Past in Electronic Archives: Interdependencies in the Discursive and Non-Discursive Organization of Institutional Rememberings'. *Culture and Psychology*, 7/2: 123–44.

Buchanan, K., and Middleton, D. (1995). 'Voices of Experience: Talk and Identity in Reminiscence Groups'. *Ageing and Society*, 15: 457–91.

Burchardt, T., Le Grand, J., and Piachaud, D. (1999). 'Social Exclusion in Britain 1991–1995'. *Social Policy and Administration*, 33/3: 227–44.

Burrows, R. (1997). 'Virtual Culture, Urban Polarisation and Social Science Fiction', in B. Loader (ed.), *The Governance of Cyberspace*. London: Routledge.

—— and Nettleton, S. (2002). 'Reflexive Modernization and the Emergence of Wired Self Help', in K. A. Renninger and W. Shumar (eds.), *Building Virtual Communities: Learning and Change in Cyberspace*. New York: Cambridge University Press.

—— Loader, B., Pleace, N., Nettleton, S., and Muncer, S. (2000). 'Virtual Community Care? Social Policy and the Emergence of Computer Mediated Social Support'. *Information, Communication and Society*, 3/1: 95–121.

Button, G., Mason, D., and Sharrock, W. (forthcoming). 'Disempowerment and Resistance in the Print Industry? Reactions to Surveillance-Capable Technology'. *New Technology, Work and Organisations*, 18/1.

Byrne, D. (1999). *Social Exclusion*. Buckingham: Open University Press.

Cairncross, F. (1998). *The Death of Distance: How the Communications Revolution will Change our Lives*. London: Orion Business Books.

Callaghan, P., and Morrissey, J. (1993). 'Social Support and Health: A Review'. *Journal of Advanced Nursing*, 18: 203–13.

Cameron, D. (2000). *Good to Talk?* London: Sage.

Carrier, J. (1998). Introduction to D. Miller and J. Carrier (eds.) *Virtualism: A New Political Economy*. Oxford: Berg.

Carter, D. (1997). ' "Democracy" Digital or "information aristocracy"? Economic Regeneration and the Information Economy', *The Governance of Cyberspace: Politics, Technology and Global Restructuring*. London: Routledge.

Casey, C. (1995). *Work, Self and Society after Industrialism*. London: Routledge.

Castells, M. (1989). *The Informational City: Information Technology, Economic Restructuring, and the Urban–Regional Process*. Oxford: Blackwell.

—— (1996). *The Rise of the Network Society*. Cambridge, MA: Blackwell.

—— (2000a). 'The Institutions of the New Economy'. Paper presented at the Virtual Society? Programme Conference, 'Delivering the Virtual Promise', London, 19 June.

—— (2000b). 'Materials for an Exploratory Theory of the Network Society'. *British Journal of Sociology*, 51/1: 5–24.

—— (2001). *The Internet Galaxy: Reflections on the Internet, Business and Society*. Oxford: Oxford University Press.

CEC (1993): Commission of the European Communities, 'Growth, Competitiveness, Employment: The Challenges and Ways Forward into the 21st Century (white paper)'. *Bulletin of the European Communities*, suppl. 6/93. Brussels: CEC.

—— (2000). *eEurope: An Information Society for All: Progress Report*, COM, Vol. 130 Final. Brussels: CEC.

Central Office of Information (1999). *Our Information Age: The Government's Vision*, vol. INDY J98-2429 URN 98/677 4/98. London: Central Office of Information.

Certeau, M. de (1984). *The Practice of Everyday Life*. Berkeley and Los Angeles: University of California Press.

CITU (1998): Central Information Technology Unit, *View from the Queue*. London: Cabinet Office.

Cochrane, P. (2001). 'Hard Drive'. *dotcomelegraph*, 18 Jan.

Cohen, C., and Walsh, V. (1995). 'Networks and Alliances in the Design and Innovation Process: The case of Minitel', in D. Bennet and F. Steward (eds.), *Technological Innovation and Global Challenges*. Birmingham: Aston University.

Cohen, S. (1985). *Visions of Social Control: Crime, Punishment and Classification*. Cambridge: Polity.

—— and Wills, T. (1985). 'Stress, Social Support and the Buffering Hypothesis'. *Psychological Bulletin*, 98: 310–57.

Cohen, W. M., and Levinthal, D. A. (1989). 'Innovation and Learning: The Two Faces of R&D'. *Economic Journal*, 99: 569–96.

Cole, M. (1996). *Cultural Psychology*. Cambridge: Cambridge University Press.

Coleman, A. (1985). *Utopia on Trial: Vision and Reality in Planned Housing*. London: Hilary Shipman.

Collie, J. (1997). 'Net Profit'. *Internet Business*, 2 Mar., 40–3.

Comaroff, J., and Comaroff, J. (1992). *Ethnography and the Historical Imagination*. Boulder, CO: Westview Press.

Constant, D., Sproull, L., and Kiesler, S. (1996). 'The Kindness of Strangers: The Usefulness of Electronic Weak Ties for technical Advice'. *Organization Science*, 7: 119–35.

Conway, S., and Steward, F. (1998). 'Mapping Innovation Networks'. *International Journal of Innovation Management*, 2/2: 223–54.

Cooper, G. (2001). 'The Mutable Mobile: Social Theory in the Wireless World', in B. Brown, N. Green, and R. Harper (eds.), *Wireless World: Social and Interactional Aspects of the Mobile Age*. London: Springer-Verlag.

—— and Woolgar, S. (1992). 'Software Quality as Community Performance'. Discussion paper, CRICT, Brunel University.

Cooper, H., Arber, S., Fee, L., and Gin, J. (1999). *The Influence of Social Support and Social Capital on Health: A Review and Analysis of British Data.* London: Health Education Authority.

Corrigan, L. (1996). 'The Rogue Media and Technology, The Motley Fool'; www.fool.com.

Coutard, O. (1999). *The Governance of Large Technical Systems.* London: Routledge.

Crang, M., Crang, P., and May, J. (1999) (eds.). *Virtual Geographies: Bodies, Space and relations.* London: Routledge.

Crook, C. K. (1988). 'Electronic Media for Communications in an Undergraduate Teaching Department', in D. Smith (ed.), *New Technologies and Professional Communications in Education.* London: National Council for Educational Technology.

—— (1994). *Computers and the Collaborative Experience of Learning.* London: Routledge.

—— (1997). 'Making Hypertext Lecture Notes More Interactive: Undergraduate Reactions'. *Journal of Computer Assisted Learning,* 13: 236–44.

—— (2000). 'Motivation and the Ecology of Collaborative Learning', in R. Joiner (ed.), *Rethinking Collaboration.* London: Routledge.

—— (2001). 'The Campus Experience of Networked Learning', in C. Steeples and C. Jones (eds.), *Networked Learning in Higher Education.* London: Springer, 293–308.

—— and Barrowcliff, D. (2001). 'Ubiquitous Computing on Campus: Patterns of Engagement by University Students', *International Journal of Human–Computer Interaction,* 13/2: 245–58.

—— and Webster, D. S. (1997). 'Designing for Informal Undergraduate Computer Mediated Communication'. *Active Learning,* 7: 47–51.

CTCNet Research and Evaluation Team (1998). 'Impact of CTCNet Affiliates: Findings from a National Survey of Users of Community Technology Centres'; www.ctcnet.org/impact98.htm.

Culnan, M. J., and Markus, M. L. (1987). 'Information Technologies', in F. M. Jablin, L. L. Putnam, K. H. Roberts, and L. W. Porter (eds.), *Handbook of Organizational Communication: An Interdisciplinary Perspective.* London: Sage.

Cyber Dialogue (2000). 'Cyber Dialogue Study Shows US Internet Audience Growth Slowing'; www.cyberdialogue.com.

Cydata (2000). 'UK Business Potential for Virtual Reality'. *DTI Information Society Initiative*; www.ukvrforum.org.uk/resources/mr2report.pdf.

Daft, R. L., and Lengel, R. H. (1984). 'Information Richness: A New Approach to Managerial Behavior and Organizational Design'. *Research in Organizational Behaviour,* 6: 191–233.

—— (1986). 'Organisational Information Requirements, Media Richness and Structural Design', *Management Science,* 32: 554–71.

Dalby, A. (1998). *Dictionary of Languages.* London: Bloomsbury.

D'Ambra, J., Rice, R. E., and O'Connor, M. (1998). 'Computer-Mediated Communication and Media Preference: An Investigation of the Dimensionality of Perceived Task Equivocality and Media Richness'. *Behaviour and Information Technology,* 17: 164–74

Daunton, M. (1983). 'Public Place and Private Space: The Victorian City and the Working Class Household', in D. Fraser and A. Sutcliffe (eds.), *The Pursuit of Urban History* London: Edward Arnold.

David, P. A. (1985). 'Clio and the Economics of QWERTY'. *American Economic Review Proceedings,* 75/2: 332–36.

—— (1997). 'Path Dependence and the Quest for Historical Economics: One More Chorus of the Ballad of QWERTY'. Discussion Paper in Economic and Social History, University of Oxford.

Davis, M. (1991). *City of Quartz: Excavating the Future of Los Angeles*. London: Vintage.

—— (1992). *Beyond Blade Runner: URan Control—The Ecology of Fear*, Westfield, NJ: New Press.

Davis, M. S. (1971). 'That's Interesting! Towards a Phenomenology of Sociology and a Sociology of Phenomenology'. *Philosophy of Social Science*, 1: 309–44.

Day, R. E. (2001). *The Modern Invention of Information: Discourse, History and Power*. Carbondale, IL: Southern Illinois University Press.

DCMS (1998): Department for Culture, Media, and Sport, *'New Library: The People's Network': The Government's Response*. London: DCMS.

—— (1999). *Libraries for All: Social Inclusion in Public Libraries*. London: DMCS.

De Kare-Silver, M. (2000). *e-shock 2000: The Electronic Shopping Revolution Strategies for Retailers and Manufacturers*. London: Macmillan Business Press.

Dean, K., Holst, E., Kriener, S., Schoenborn, C., and Wilson, R. (1994). 'Measurement Issues in Research on Social Support and Health'. *Journal of Epidemiology and Community Health*, 48/2: 201–6.

Delacour, J. (2001). 'Proust's Contribution to the Psychology of Memory: The Reminiscences from the Standpoint of Cognitive Science'. *Theory and Psychology*, 11/2: 255–71.

Delbridge, R. (1995). 'Surviving JIT: Control and Resistance in a Japanese Transplant'. *Journal of Management Studies*, 32: 803–17.

Denzin, N. (1998). 'In Search of the Inner Child: Co-Dependency and Gender in a Cyberspace Community', in G. Bendelow and S. Williams (eds.), *Emotions in Social Life*. London: Routledge.

Derrida, J. (1976). *Of Grammatology*. Baltimore: Johns Hopkins University Press.

—— (1987). 'On Reading Heidegger'. *Research in Phenomenology*, 17: 171–85.

—— (1994). 'Nietzsche and the Machine'. *Journal of Nietzsche Studies*, 7: 3–66.

—— (1997). *Archive Fever: A Freudian Impression*. Chicago: University of Chicago Press.

DfEE (1999): Department for Education and Employment, 'Learning Centres will Bridge Gap between Computer Haves and Have-Nots'; http://213.38.88.195/coi/coipress.nsf.

—— (2001). 'What will a UK Online Centre Do for Me?'; www.dfee.gov.uk/ukonline-centres/whatwill/default.ctm.

Dibbell, J. (1983). 'A Rape in Cyberspace'; http://www.levity.com/julian/bungle.html.

Diener, E. (1976). 'Effects of Prior Destructive Behavior, Anonymity, and Group Presence on Deindividuation and Aggression'. *Journal of Personality and Social Psychology*. 33: 497–507.

Dilley, R. (1999). *The Problem of Context*. Oxford: Berghahn Books.

DOE (1988): Department of Environment, *A Better Reception: The Development of Concierge Systems*. London: HMSO.

Dosi, G. (1982). 'Technological Paradigms and Technological Trajectories: A Suggested Interpretation of the Determinants and Directions of Technical Change'. *Research Policy*, 12: 147–62.

Douglas, K. M., and McGarty, C. (forthcoming). 'Identifiability and Self-Presentation: Computer-Mediated Communication and Intergroup Interaction'. *European Journal of Personality and Social Psychology*.

Downey, G. L. (1998). *The Machine in Me: An Anthropologist Sits among Computer Engineers*. New York: Routledge.

—— and Dumit, J. (1997) (eds.). *Cyborgs and Citadels: Anthropological Interventions in Emerging Sciences and Technologies*. Santa Fe, N. Mex.: School of American Research Press.

DTI (1999): Department of Trade and Industry, *Is IT for All*? London: DTI.
—— (2000). *Smoke on Water. A Fire in the Sky: Electronic Commerce Task Force.* Report for Consultation. London: DTI.
—— and DCMS (2000): Department of Trade and Industry and Department for Culture, Media, and Sport, *A New Future for Communications.* London: DTI and DCMS.
Du Val Smith, A. (1999). 'Problems of Conflict Management in Virtual Communities', in M. A. Smith and P. Kollock (eds.), *Communities in Cyberspace.* London: Routledge.
Dubrovsky, J., Kiesler, S., and Sethna, B. N. (1991). 'The Equalization Phenomenon: Status Effects in Computer-Mediated and Face-to-Face Decision Making Groups'. *Human-Computer Interaction,* 6: 119–46.
Duderstadt, J. J. (1999). 'Can Colleges and Universities Survive in the Information Age?', in R. Katz (ed.), *Dancing with the Devil: Information Technology and the New Competition in Higher Education.* San Francisco: Jossey-Bass.
Dumas, A. (1994). 'Building Totems: Metaphor-Making in Product Development'. *Design Management Journal* (Winter), 71–82.
Dumit, J. (1997). 'A Digital Image of the Category of the Person: PET Scanning and Objective Self-Fashioning', in G. L. Downey and J. Dumit (eds.), *Cyborgs and Citadels: Anthropological Interventions in Emerging Sciences and Technologies.* Santa Fe, N. Mex.: School of American Research Press.
Dutton, W. H. (1999) (ed.). *Society on the Line: Information Politics in the Digital Age.* Oxford: Oxford University Press.
Dyson, E., Gilder, G., Keyworth, G., and Toffler, A. (1994). 'Cyberspace and the American Dream: A Magna Carta for the Knowledge Age'; www.pff.org/position.html.
The Economist (1999). 'Death by 1,000 clicks', 10 Dec., 23–6.
The Economist (2001). 'The New Economy: What's Left?' 12 May, 99–104.
Edwards, P. K. (1988). 'Patterns of Conflict and Accommodation', in D. Gallie (ed.), *Employment in Britain.* Oxford: Blackwell.
Elstad, J. I. (1998). 'The Psycho-Social Perspective on Social Inequalities in Health', in M. Bartley, D. Blane, and G. Davey-Smith (eds.), *The Sociology of Health Inequality.* Oxford: Blackwell.
Emmett, R. (1981). 'Vnet or gripenet?' *Datamation* (Nov.), 48–58.
Engel, S. (2000). *Context is Everything: The Nature of Memory.* New York: Freeman.
ESCR Virtual Society? Programme (1999). 'Profile 1999'. Report by ESCR Virtual Society? Programme, Brunel University.
—— (2000). 'Profile 2000'. Report by ESCR Virtual Society? Programme, Brunel University.
Eysenbach, G., Ryoung Sa, E., and Diepgen, T. L. (1999). 'Shopping around the Internet Today and Tomorrow: Towards the Millennium of Cybermedicine'. *British Medical Journal,* 319: 1294.
Ezzamel, M. (1994). 'The Emergence of the Accountant in the Institutions of Ancient Egypt'. *Management Accounting Research,* 5: 221–46.
Farnie, D. A. (1980). *The Manchester Ship Canal and the Rise of the Port of Manchester, 1894–1975.* Manchester: Manchester University Press.
Feenberg, A. L., Licht, J. M., Kane, K. P., Moran, K., and Smith, R. A. (1996). 'The Online Patient Meeting'. *Journal of the Neurological Sciences,* 139 (suppl.): 129–31.
Festinger, L., Pepitone, A., and Newcombe, T. (1952). 'Some Consequences of Deindividuation in a Group': *Journal of Social and Abnormal Psychology,* 47: 382–9.
—— Riecken, H., and Schlachter, S. (1964). *When Prophecy Fails.* New York: Harper.

Fincham, R., Fleck, J., Proctor, R., Scarborough, H., Tierney, M., and Williams, R. (1994). *Expertise and Innovation: Information Technology Strategies in the Financial Services Sector*. Oxford: Oxford University Press.

Finn, J. (1999). 'An Exploration of Helping Processes in an Online Self-Help Group Focussing on the Issues of Disability'. *Health and Social Work*, 24/3: 220–31.

Fischer, J. (1996). 'Iomega Corp: A retrospective 5 part series'; www.fool.com/features/1996/sp961203a.htm.

Fleetwood, C. (1996). 'Iomega's Devoted Fans: Foes Declare a Cyber War of Words over its Stock' *Wall Street Journal*, 15 Mar.

Ford, M. (1998). *Surveillance and Privacy at Work*. London: Institute of Employment Rights.

Foucault, M. (1972). *The Archaeology of Knowledge*. London: Tavistock.

—— (1977). *Discipline and Punish: The Birth of the Prison*. London: Allen Lane.

Fox, N., and Roberts, C. (1999). 'GPs in Cyberspace: The Sociology of a "Virtual Community"'. *Sociological Review*, 47: 643–71.

Frank, T. (2000). *Market under God: Extreme Capitalism, Market Populism, and the End of Economic Democracy*. London: Doubleday.

Fraunhofer Institute (1997). www.igd.fhg.de.

Frick, F. C. (1959). 'Information Theory', in S. Koch (ed.), *Psychology: A Study of Science*. London: McGraw-Hill.

Frisby, D. (1985). *Fragments of Modernity*. Cambridge: Polity.

Gadamer, H. G. (1993). *The Relevance of the Beautiful and Other Essays*. Cambridge: Cambridge University Press.

Gannaway, B. (2000). 'Ahead of the Game?' *Grocer*, 22 July, 36.

Gardner, D. (1997). 'Fool Portfolio Report, The Motley Fool'; www.fool.com.

—— and Gardner, T. (1996). *The Motley Fool Investment Guide: How the Fools Beat Wall Street's Wise Men and How You Can Too*. New York: Simon & Schuster.

Garfinkel, H. (1967). *Studies in Ethnomethodology*. Englewood Cliffs, NJ: Prentice-Hall.

Gatz, L. B., and Hirt, J. B. (2000). 'Academic and Social Integration in Cyberspace: Students and E-Mail'. *Review of Higher Education*, 23: 299–318.

Gauntlett, D. (2000) (ed.). *Web.studies*. London: Arnold.

Gaver, W. (1996). 'Situating Action II: Affordances for Interaction: The Social is Material for Design'. *Ecological Psychology*, 8: 111–30.

Geertz, C. (1973). *The Interpretation of Cultures*. New York: Basic Books.

Georghiou, L., Metcalf, J. S., Gibbons, M., Ray, T. and Evans, J. (1986). *Post Innovation Performance: Technological Development and Competition*. London: Macmillan.

Georgia Technical University (1999). 'Internet User Surveys'; www.cc.gatech-edu/gvu/usersurveys.

Gibson, W. (1984). *Neuromancer*. New York: Ace Books.

Giddens, A. (1991). *Modernity and Self Identity*. Cambridge: Polity.

—— (1998). *The Third Way*. Cambridge: Polity.

Girard, M., and Stark, D. (2001). 'Distributed Intelligence and Organization of Diversity in New Media Projects'. Paper presented at International Workshop 'Socio-Economics of Space', University of Bonn.

Glasner, A. (1996). 'Teaching and Learning in Anthropology: The HEFCE Review of Anthropology Provision in England and Northern Ireland'. *Anthropology in Action*, 3: 7–9.

Goffman, E. (1961). *Encounters: Two Studies in the Sociology of Interaction*. Indianapolis: Bobbs-Merrill Educational Publishing.

Goffman, E. (1963). *Behavior in Public Places: Notes on the Social Organization of Gatherings.* New York: Free Press.

——(1967). *Interaction Ritual: Essays on Face-to-Face Behavior.* New York: Pantheon.

——(1971). *Relations in Public.* Harmondsworth: Penguin.

Goodwin, C. (1981). *Conversational Organization: Interaction between Speakers and Hearers.* New York: Academic Press.

Gourgouris, S. (1996). *Dream Nation: Enlightenment, Colonization, and the Institution of Modern Greece.* Stanford, CA: Stanford University Press.

Grabher, G. (2001). 'Ecologies of Creativity: The Village, the Group and the Heterarchic Organisation of the British Advertising Industry'. *Environment and Planning,* A33: 351–74.

——and Stark, D. (1997). 'Organizing Diversity: Evolutionary Theory, Network Analysis and Post-Socialism', in G. Grabher and D. Stark (eds.), *Restructuring Networks in Post-Socialism: Legacies, Linkages and Localities.* Oxford: Oxford University Press.

Graham, S. (1998). 'Towards the Fifth Utility? On the Extension and Normalisation of Public CCTV', in C. Norris, J. Moran, and G. Armstrong (eds.), *Surveillance, Closed Circuit Television and Social Control.* Aldershot: Ashgate.

——and Marvin, S. (1996). *Telecommunications and the City: Electronic Spaces Urban Places.* London: Routledge.

Grande, C. (2000). 'Success of the Latest Unorthodoxy: Managing Online Retailing'. *Financial Times,* 15 Sept.

Granovetter, M. (1973). 'The Strength of Weak Ties'. *American Journal of Sociology,* 78: 1360–80.

Green, S., and Harvey, P. (1999). 'Scaling Place and Networks: An ethnography of ICT "Innovation" in Manchester'. Paper presented at Internet Ethnography Conference, Hull University, 13–14 Dec.

Grint, K., and Woolgar, S. (1992). 'Computers, Guns and Roses: What's Social about Being Shot?'. *Science, Technology and Human Values,* 17: 366–80.

————(1997). *The Machine at Work.* Cambridge: Polity.

Griset, P. (2001). 'From the Delights of Marginality to the Search of [sic] Social Respectability: French Consumers and Citizen Band (1979–1990)'. Paper presented at seminar on the Social Sustainability of Technological Networks, New York.

Guardian (2001). 'Efficiency Drive: Gates Tries to Revive Office Market', 2 June, Finance Section.

Gunn, R. (1988). 'Recognition in Hegel's Phenomenology of Spirit'. *Common Sense,* 4. Edinburgh: Centre for Study of Evolution.

Habermas, J. (1989). *The Structural Transformation of the Public Sphere.* Cambridge: Polity.

Hagel, J., and Armstrong, A. (1998). *Net Gain.* Boston: Harvard Business School Press.

——and Singer, M. (1999). *Net Worth.* Boston: Harvard Business School Press.

Hague, B., and Loader, B. (1999) (eds.). *Digital Democracy: Discourse and Decision Making in the Information Age.* London: Routledge.

Hague, D. (1991). *Beyond Universities.* London: Institute of Economic Affairs.

Hakken, D. (1991). 'Culture-Centred Computing: Social Policy and Development of New Information Technology in England and the United States'. *Human Organization,* 50 406–23.

Hall, P. (1996). *Cities of Tomorrow: An Intellectual History of Urban Planning and Design in the Twentieth Century.* Oxford: Blackwell.

Hamel, G., and Prahalad, C. K. (1994). *Competing for the Future*. Boston: Harvard Business School Press.

Hammer, M., and Champy, J. (1993). *Re-Engineering the Corporation: A Manifesto for Business Revolution*. London: Nicholas Brierley Publishing.

Haraway, D. (1997). 'Mice into Wormholes: A Comment on the Nature of No Nature', in G. L. Downey and J. Dumit (eds.), *Cyborgs and Citadels: Anthropological Interventions in Emerging Sciences and Technologies*. Santa Fe, N. Mex.: School of American Research Press.

Hardingham, A. (1995). *Working in Teams*. London: Institute of Personnel and Development.

Harford, I. (1994). Manchester and its Ship Canal Movement: Class, Work and Politics in Late-Victorian England. Keele! Ryburn Publishing.

Harper, R. (2000). 'The Social Organization of the IMF's Mission Work: An Examination of International Auditing', in M. Strathern (ed.), *Audit Cultures: Anthropological Studies in Accountability, Ethics and the Academy*. London: Routledge.

Harrison, T., and Stephen, T. (1999). 'Researching and Creating Community Networks', in S. Jones (ed.), *Doing Internet Research: Critical Issues and Methods for Examining the Net*. London: Sage.

Harvey, D. (1990). *The Condition of Postmodernity*. Oxford: Blackwell.

Harvey, P. (forthcoming). 'Memorializing the Future: The Museum of Science and Industry in Manchester', in M. Bouquet and N. Porto (eds.), *Science, Magic and Religion: The Museum as a Ritual Site*. Oxford: Berghan.

Hayes, B. (1997). 'The Infrastructure of the Information Infrastructure'. *American Scientist*, 25/3: 214–18.

Hayles, N. K. (1999). *How we Became Posthuman: Virtual Bodies in Cybernetics, Literature, and Informatics*. Chicago: University of Chicago Press.

Heath, C. (1986). *Body Movement and Speech in Medical Interaction*. Cambridge: Cambridge University Press.

Hegel, Georg W. F. (1806/1977). *Phenomenology of Spirit*, trans. A. V. Miller. Oxford: Oxford University Press.

Heidegger, M. (1977). *The Question Concerning Technology and Other Essays*. New York: Harper.

Heller, R., and Spenley, P. (2000). *Riding the Revolution: How Businesses Can and Must Win the E-Wars*. London: HarperCollins.

Hetherington, K. (1997). *The Badlands of Modernity: Heterotopia and Social Ordering*. London: Routledge.

Hillier, B. (1996). *Space is the Machine*. Cambridge: Cambridge University Press.

—— and Hanson, J. (1984). *The Social Logic of Space*. Cambridge: Cambridge University Press.

Hilton, A. (2000). *Internet Banking: A Fragile Flower?* London: Centre for the Study of Financial Innovation.

Hiltz, S. R., Turoff, M., and Johnson, K. (1989). 'Experiments in Group Decision Making, 3: Disinhibition, Deindividuation, and Group Process in Pen Name and Real Name Computer Conferences'. *Decision Support Systems*, 5: 217–32.

Hine, C. (2000). *Virtual Ethnography*. London: Sage.

—— and Woolgar, S. (2000). 'New Technology, New Methodology'. Paper presented at joint meeting of Society for Social Studies of Science (4S) and European Association for the Study of Science and Technology, Vienna.

Hoffman, D. L., and Novak, T. P. (1998). 'Bridging the Digital Divide: The Impact of Race on Computer Access and Internet Use'. Nashville: Vanderbilt University; www2000. ogsm.vanderbilt.edu.

Honneth, A. (1996). *The Struggle for Recognition: The Moral Grammar of Social Conflicts.* Cambridge: Polity.

Horsfall, T. C. (1895). 'The Government of Manchester: . . . a Paper Read to the Manchester Statistical Society, November 13th, 1895, with additions.' Unpublished paper, Manchester Statistical Society.

Hoskin, K. (1996). 'The Awful Idea of Accountability: Inscribing People into the Measurement of Objects', in R. Munro and J. Mouritsen (eds.), *Accountability: Power, Ethos and the Technologies of Managing.* London: Thomson Business Press.

——and Macve, R. (1988). 'The Genesis of Accountability: The West Point Connections'. *Accounting, Organizations and Society,* 13/1: 37–73.

Hounsell, D. (1987). 'Essay Writing and the Quality of Feedback', in J. Richardson, M. Eysenck, and D. Piper (eds.), *Student Learning: Research in Education and Cognitive Psychology.* Milton Keynes: Society for Research into Higher Education and Open University Press.

House of Lords Select Committee on Science and Technology (1996). 'Information Society 5th Report'; www.parliament.the-stationery-office.co.uk/pa/ed199697/ldselect/infor-soc/inforsoc.htm.

Hudson, P. (1992). *The Industrial Revolution.* London: Edward Arnold.

Hughes, J. A., O'Brien, J., Rouncefield, M., Sommerville, I., and Rodden, T. (1995). 'Presenting Ethnography in the Requirements Process'. *Proceedings of RE '95.* York: IEEE Press.

——Kristoffersen, S., O'Brien, J., and Rouncefield, M. (1996a). 'When Mavis Met IRIS: Ending the Love Affair with Organisational Memory', *Gothenburg Studies in Informatics Edition,* 2/8.

——Rodden, T., and Rouncefield, M. (1996b). 'Ethnographic Fieldwork Report: The Lending Process'. SYCOMPT Project Report, Lancaster University.

——O'Brien, J., Rodden, T., Rouncefield, M., and Blyhin, S. (1997). 'Designing with Ethnography: A Presentation Framework for Design'. *Proceedings of the ACM Conference on Designing Interactive Systems: Processes, Practices, Methods, and Techniques.* Amsterdam: ACM Press, 199–209.

————Randall, D., Rouncefield, M., and Tolmie, P. (1999). 'Virtual Organisations and the Customer: How "Virtual Organisations" Deal with "Real" customers: Information Systems—The next Generation'. *Proceedings of the 4th UKAIS Conference.* Maidenhead: McGraw Hill.

———————(2001). 'Some "real" Problems of "virtual" Organisation'. *New Technology, Work and Employment,* 16/1.

Hughes, T. P. (1983). *Networks of Power: Electrification in Western Society, 1880–1930.* Baltimore: Johns Hopkins University Press.

Huizinga, J. (1950). *Homo Ludens: A Study of the Play Element in Culture.* London: Beacon Press.

Huxley, A. (1963). *Literature and Science.* London: Chatto & Windus.

Imken, O. (1999). 'The Convergence of Virtual and Actual in the Global Matrix: Artificial Life, Geo-Economics and Psychogeography'; in M. Crang, P. Crang, and J. May (eds.), *Virtual Geographies: Bodies, Space and Relations.* London: Routledge.

Information Infrastructure Task Force (1993). 'National Information Infrastructure: Agenda for action'. *Federal Regulations*, 58.

Inman, P. (2000). 'Email? You've Got the Elbow'. *Guardian*, 25 Nov.

Introna, L. D. (2000). 'Workplace Surveillance, Privacy and Distributive Justice'. *Computers and Society*, 30/4 33–9.

IPPR (2001): Institute for Public Policy Research, *Digital Society Programme Newsletter*, 1.

Jamieson, P., Fisher, K., Gilding, T., Taylor, P., and Trevitt, A. (2000). 'Place and Space in the Design of New Learning Environments'. *Higher Education Research and Development*, 19: 221–36.

Jessup, L. M., Connolly, T., and Tansik, D. A. (1990). 'Toward a Theory of Automated Group Work: The Deindividuating Effects of Anonymity'. *Small Group Research*, 21: 333–48.

Johnson, R. D., and Downing, L. L. (1979). 'Deindividuation and Valence of Cues: Effects on Prosocial and Antisocial Behaviour'. *Journal of Personality and Social Psychology*, 37: 1532–8.

Jones, S. G. (1998) (ed.). *Cybersociety 2.0: Revisiting Computer-Mediated Communication and Community*. London: Sage.

Jones, T. (2000). 'Chair's Foreword', in *Smoke on Water: A Fire in the Sky. Electronic Commerce Task Force, Report for consultation*. London: DTI.

Jordan, T. (1999). *Cyberpower: The Culture and Politics of Cyberspace and the Internet*. London: Routledge.

——(2001). 'Measuring the Internet: Host Counts versus Business Plans'. *Information, Communication and Society*. 4/1: 34–53.

Kalawsky, R. S. (1993). *The Science of Virtual Reality and Virtual Environments*. Wokingham: Addison Wesley.

Kandola, R., and Fullerton, J. (1998). *Diversity in Action: Managing the Mosaic*. London: Institute of Personnel and Development.

——— and Ahmed, Y. (1995). 'Managing Diversity: Succeeding where Equal Opportunities have Failed'. *Equal Opportunities Review*, 59 (Jan.–Feb.), 31–6.

Kapferer, B. (1997). *The Feast of the Sorcerer: Practices of Consciousness and Power*. Chicago: University of Chicago Press.

Katz, J. E., and Aspden, P. (1998). 'Internet Dropouts in the USA'. *Telecommunications Policy*, 22/4–5: 327–39.

Kelly, M., and Field, D. (1998). 'Conceptualizing Chronic Illness', in D. Field and S. Taylor (eds.), *Sociological Perspectives on Health, Illness and Health Care*. Oxford: Blackwell.

Kendon, A. (1967). 'Some Functions of Gaze Direction in Social Interaction'. *Acta Psychologica*, 26: 22–63.

——(1990). *Conducting Interaction: Studies in the Behaviour of Social Interaction*. Cambridge: Cambridge University Press.

Kerfoot, D., and Knights, D. (1996). ' "The Best is Yet to Come?": Searching for Embodiment in Management', in D. Collinson and J. Hearn (eds.), *Men as Managers, Managers as Men*. London: Sage.

Khoshafian, S., and Buckiewicz, M. (1995). *An Introduction to Groupware, Workflow and Workgroup Computing*. New York: Wiley.

Kidd, A. J. (1996). *Manchester: Town and City Histories*. 2nd edn. Keele: Keele University Press.

Kiesler, S., and Sproull, L. (1992). 'Group Decision Making and Communication Technology'. *Organizational Behaviour and Human Decision Processes*, 52: 96–123.

Kiesler, S., Siegel, J., and McGuire, T. (1984). 'Social Psychological Aspects of Computer-Mediated Communication'. *American Psychologist*, 39: 1123–34.

——Zubrow, D., Moses, A. M., and Geller, V. (1985). 'Affect in Computer-Mediated Communciation: An Experiment in Synchronous Terminal to Terminal Discussion'. *Human Computer Interaction*, 1: 77–104.

Kindleberger, C. P. (1989). *Mania Panics, and Crashes: A History of Financial Crises*. New York: Basic Books.

Kitchen, R. (1998). *Cyberspace*. Chichester: Wiley.

Klemperer, P. (1987). 'The Competitiveness of Markets with Switching Costs'. *RAND Journal of Economics*, 18/1: 138–50.

Kline, R., and Pinch, T. (1996). 'Users as Agents of Technological Change: The Social Construction of the Automobile in the Rural United States'. *Technology and Culture*, 37/4: 763–95.

Kling, R. (1992). 'Audiences' Narratives and Human Values in the Social Studies of Technology'. *Science, Technology and Human Values*, 17: 349–65.

Knights, D., and Noble, F. (1997). 'Networks and Partnerships in the Evolution of Home Banking'. Paper present at 2nd IFIP WG8.6 Working Conference, 'Diffusion, Transfer and Implementation of Information Technology', Ambleside, Lake District, England.

——————Vurdubakis, T., and Willmott, H. (2000a). 'The Great Millennial Bug Hunt: Success and Failure in Information Technology Applications'. Paper presented at the 'Working Together' Conference, University of Keele.

——————(2000b). 'More Money than Sense?' *Financial World* (Aug.), 37–9.

Knorr-Cetina, K., and Bruegger, U. (2000). 'The Market as an Object of Attachment: Exploring Postsocial Relations in Financial Markets'. *Canadian Journal of Sociology*, 25: 141–68.

Koestler, A. (1969). *The Act of Creation*. London: Hutchinson.

Kogan, M., and Henkel, M. (1998). 'Policy Changes and the Academic Profession in England'. *European Review*, 6: 505–23.

Kojève, A. (1969). *Introduction to the Reading of Hegel*. Ithaca, NY: Cornell University Press.

Kolko, B., and Reid, E. (1998). 'Dissolution and Fragmentation: Problems in On-Line Communities', in S. G. Jones (ed.), *Cybersociety 2.0: Revisiting Computer-Mediated Communication and Community*. London: Sage.

Kraut, R., Mukhopadhyay, T., Szezypula, J., Kiesler, S., and Scherlis, W. (1998). 'Communication and Information: Alternative Uses of the Internet in Households' in *Proceedings of the Conference on Computer-Human Interaction CHI98*. New York, ACM.

Kuhn, T. S. (1962). *The Structure of Scientific Revolutions*. Chicago: University of Chicago Press.

Kulick, D., and Stroud, C. (1990). 'Christianity, Cargo and Ideas of Self-Patterns of Literacy in a Papua-New-Guinean Village', *Man*, 25/2: 286–304.

Lane, G. (1990). *Communications for Progress: A Guide to International E-Mail*. London: Catholic Institute for International Relations (CIIR).

Lankshear, G., and Mason, D. (2001). 'Technology and Ethical Dilemmas in a Medical Setting: Privacy, Professional Autonomy, Life and Death', *Ethics and Information Technology*, 3/3: 225–35.

——Cook, P., Mason, D., Coates, S., and Button, G. (2000). 'Call Centre Employees' Responses to Electronic Monitoring: Some Research Findings'. *Work, Employment and Society*, 15/3: 595–605.

Lash, S., and Urry, J. (1987). *The End of Organized Capitalism*. Madison, Wis.: University of Wisconsin Press.

Latham, R. (1995). *The Dictionary of Computer Graphics and Virtual Reality*. New York: Springer-Verlag.

Latour, B. (1986). 'Visualization and Cognition: Thinking with Eyes and Hands'. *Knowledge and Society*, 6: 1–40.

——— (1993). *We Have Never Been Modern*. London: Harvester Wheatsheaf.

——— (1996). *Aramis, or, The Love of Technology*. Cambridge, MA: Harvard University Press.

——— (1998). 'Thought Experiments in Social Science: From the Social Contract to Virtual Society'. *First Virtual Society? Annual Public Lecture*, Brunel University, 1 April.

——— (1999). *Pandora's Hope: Essays on the Reality of Science Studies*. Cambridge, MA: Harvard University Press.

——— and Woolgar, S. (1986). *Laboratory Life: The Construction of Scientific Facts*. 2nd edn. Princeton: Princeton University Press.

Laurel, B. (1992). *Computers as Theatre*. Reading, MA: Addison-Wesley.

Laurier, E. (1999). 'Conversations in the Corridor (M4): Assembling the Mobile Office'. Paper presented at the BSA Conference, Glasgow.

Lave, J. (1988). *Cognition in Practice*. Cambridge: Cambridge University Press.

——— and Wenger, E. (1991). *Situated Learning: Legitimate Peripheral Participation*. Cambridge: Cambridge University Press.

Law, J. (1994). *Organizing Modernity*. Oxford: Blackwell.

Le Bon, G. (1995). *The Crowd: A Study of the Popular Mind*. London: Transaction. Original work published 1895.

Lea, M., and Giordano, R. (1997). 'Representations of the Group and Group Processes in CSCW Research: A Case of Premature Closure?', in G. C. Bowker, S. L. Star, W. Turner, and L. Gasser (eds.), *Social Science, Technical Systems and Cooperative Work: Beyond the Great Divide*. Mahwah, NJ: LEA.

——— and Spears, R. (1991). 'Computer-Mediated communication, De-Individuation and Group Decision-Making'. *International Journal of Man–Machine Studies*, 34: 283–301.

——— ——— (1992). 'Paralanguage and Social Perception in Computer-Mediated Communication'. *Journal of Organizational Computing*, 2: 321–42.

——— ——— (1995). 'Love at first byte? Building Personal Relationships over Computer Networks', in J. T. Wood and S. Duck (eds.), *Understudied Relationships: Off the Beaten Track*. Thousand Oaks, CA: Sage.

——— O'Shea, T., Fung, P., and Spears, R. (1992). '"Flaming" in Computer-Mediated Communication: Normative versus Antinormative Explanations', in M. Lea (ed.), *Contexts of Computer-Mediated Communication*. Hemel-Hempstead: Harvester-Wheatsheaf.

——— Rogers, P., Postmes, T., and Schouten, A. (2000a). 'SIDE-VIEW: A Design to Develop Team Players and Improve Productivity in Internet Collaborative Learning Groups'. Paper presented at International Symposium on Interactive and Collaborative Computing (ICC2000), ICSC Congress on Intelligent Systems and Applications (ISA2000), University of Wollongong, Australia.

——— Spears, R., Watt, S., and Rogers, P. (2000b). 'The InSIDE story: Social Psychological Processes Affecting On-Line Groups', in T. Postmes, R. Spears, M. Lea, and S. D. Reicher (eds.), *SIDE-Issues Centre-Stage: Recent Developments in Studies of De-Individuation in Groups*. Amsterdam: North Holland.

Lea, M., Spears, R., and de Groot, D. (2001). 'Knowing me, Knowing you: Anonymity Effects on Social Identity Processes within Groups'. *Personality and Social Psychology Bulletin*, 27: 526–37.

————— and Rogers, P. (forthcoming). 'Social Processes in Electronic Teamwork: The Central Issue of Identity', in A. Haslam, D. van Knippenberg, M. Platow, and N. Ellemers (eds.), *Social Identity at Work: Developing Theory for Organizational Practice*. Philadelphia: Taylor & Francis.

Leadbeater, C. (2000). *Living on Thin Air: The New Economy*. Harmondsworth: Penguin.

LeBreton, D. (1997). *Du silence*. Paris: Métailié.

Lejeune, R. (1984). 'False Security: Deviance and the Stock Market', in P. A. Adler and P. Adler (eds.), *The Social Dynamics of Financial Markets*. Greenwich, CT: JAI Press.

Leung, L., and Wei, R. (1999). 'Who are the Mobile Phone Have-Nots? Influences and Consequences'. *New Media & Society*, 1/2: 209–26.

Levy, P. (1997). *Collective Intelligence: Mankind's Emerging World in Cyberspace*. New York: Plenum.

———— (1998). *Becoming Virtual: Reality in the Digital Age*. New York: Plenum.

Lie, M., and Sørenson, K. H. (1996) (eds.). *Making Technology our Own? Domesticating Technology into Everyday Life*. Oslo: Scandanavian University Press.

Liff, S., and Steward, F. (2001). 'Community e-Gateways: Locating Networks and Learning for Social Inclusion', *Information, Communication and Society*, 4/3: 317–40.

Light, P., Nesbitt, E., Light, V., and White, S. (2000). 'Variety is the Spice of Life: Student Use of CMC in the Context of Campus Based Study'. *Computers and Education*, 34: 257–67.

Lipnack, J., and Stamps, J. (1997a). 'Virtual Team Web Book'; www.netage.com.VT/VTWebBook/webbktop.html.

———— (1997b). *Virtual Teams: Reaching across Space, Time and Organizations with Technology*. New York: John Wiley & Sons.

Loader, B. (1997) (ed.). *The Governance of Cyberspace*. London: Routledge.

———— (1998) (ed.). *Cyberspace Divide: Equality, Agency and Policy in the Information Society*. London: Routledge.

———— Muncer, S., Burrows, R., Nettleton, S., and Pleace, N. (2001). 'Medicine on the Line? Computer Mediated Social Support and Advice for People with Diabetes', *International Journal of Social Welfare*, 11/1: 53–65.

Loasby, B. J. (1991). *Equilibrium and Evolution: An Exploration of Connecting Principles in Economics*. Manchester: Manchester University Press.

Lomas, J. (1998). 'Social Capital and Health: Implications for Public Health and Epidemiology'. *Social Science and Medicine*, 47/9: 1181–8.

Ludlow, P. (2001). *Crypto Anarchy, Cyberstates and Pirate Utopias*. Cambridge, MA: MIT Press.

Lury, C., and Lash, S. (forthcoming). *The Global Culture Industry: The Mediation of Things*. Cambridge: Polity.

Lyman, P., and Wakeford, N. (1999). 'Analyzing Virtual Societies: New Directions in Methodology'. *American Behavioral Scientist*, special issue, 43/3: 355–492.

Lynch, M. (1990). 'The Externalized Retina', in M. Lynch and S. Woolgar (eds.), *Representation in Scientific Practice*. Cambridge, MA: MIT Press.

———— (1999). 'Archives in Formation: Privileged Spaces, Popular Archives and Paper Trails'. *History of the Human Sciences*, 12/2: 65–87.

—— and Bogen, D. (1996). *The Spectacle of History: Speech, Text and Memory at the Iran-Contra Hearings*. Durham, NC: Duke University Press.

Lyon, D. (1994). *The Electronic Eye: The Rise of Surveillance Society*. Cambridge: Polity.

—— and Zureik, E. (1996) (eds). *Computers, Surveillance, and Privacy*. Minneapolis: University of Minnesota Press.

MacFarlane, A. (1987). *The Culture of Capitalism*. Oxford: Blackwell.

—— (1998). 'Information, Knowledge and Learning'. *Higher Education Quarterly*, 52: 77–92.

McGrail, B. (1998). 'Living in a Cyborg: The Social Contexts of Intelligence-Gathering Networks in Intelligent Buildings'. Paper presented at the European Association for the Study of Science and Technology Conference, Lisbon, 1–3 Oct.

—— (1999*a*). 'Communication Technology and Local Knowledges: The Case of "Peripheralised" High-Rise Housing Estates'. *Urban Geography*, 20/4: 303–33.

—— (1999*b*). *Highly Thought Of? New Electronic Technologies and the Tower Block*. Edinburgh: Open University/ESRC.

McGuire, T. W., Kiesler, S., and Siegel, J. (1987). 'Group and Computer-Mediated Discussion Effects in Risk Decision Making'. *Journal of Personality and Social Psychology*, 52: 917–30.

McIntosh, N. (2001). 'Missing the High Speed Revolution'. *Guardian* (online), 2nd and 3rd edns.

Macintyre, M. (2000). 'Audit, Education and Goodhart's Law, Or, Taking Rigidity Seriously'; www.atm.damtp.cam.ac.uk/people/mem/papers/LTTCE.

McKenna, K. Y. A., and Bargh, J. (1998). 'Coming Out in the Age of the Internet: Identity "Demarginalization" through Virtual Group Participation'. *Journal of Personality and Social Psychology*, 75: 681–94.

—— —— (2000). 'Plan 9 from Cyberspace: The Implications of the Internet for Personality and Social Psychology'. *Personality and Social Psychology Review*, 4: 57–75.

MacKenzie, D. (1990). 'Economic and Sociological Explanations of Technical Change'. Paper presented at the 'Firm Strategy and Technical Change Micro-Economics or Micro-Sociology?' Conference, UMIST, Manchester.

—— and Wajcman, J. (1985) (eds.), *The Social Shaping of Technology: How the Refrigerator Got Its Hum*. Milton Keynes: Open University Press.

—— —— (1999). 'Editor's Preface', in D. MacKenzie and J. Wacjman (eds.), *The Social Shaping of Technology*. 2nd edn. Buckingham: Open University Press.

McLaughlin, I. (1997). 'Babies, Bathwater, Guns and Roses', in I. McLaughlin and M. Harris (eds.), *Innovation, Organizational Change and Technology*. London: International Thompson Press.

McRobbie, A. (1999). *In the Culture Society*. London: Routledge.

Madanipour, A., Cars, G., and Allen, J. (1998) (eds.). *Social Exclusion in European Cities: Processes, Experiences and Responses*. London: Jessica Kingsley Publishers.

Maffesoli, M. (1996). *The Time of the Tribes*. London: Sage.

Manchester City Council (1991). *Manchester: The Information City*. Manchester: Manchester City Council.

Manovich, L. (2001). *The Language of New Media*. Boston: MIT Press.

Mantovani, G. (1994). 'Is Computer-Mediated Communication Intrinsically Apt to Enhance Democracy in Organizations?' *Human Relations*, 47/1: 45–62.

Markus, T. (1982) (ed.). *Order in Space and Society: Architectural Form and its Context in the Scottish Enlightenment*. Edinburgh: Mainstream.

Markus, T. (1994). *Buildings and Power: Freedom and Control in the Origin of Modern Building Types*. London: Routledge.

Marvin, C. (1988). *When Old Technologies Were New*. Oxford: Oxford University Press.

Marx, G. T. (1998). 'An Ethics for the New Surveillance', *Information Society*, 14/3; http://web.net.edu/gtmarx/www/ncolins.html.

Massey, D. (1994). *Space, Place and Gender*. Cambridge: Polity.

Mayntz, R., and Hughes, T. (1988) (eds.). *The Development of Large Technical Systems*. Boulder, CO: Westview Press.

Melnicoff, Richard M. (1999). 'The eEconomy: It's Later than you Think'. *Outlook*; http://www.ac.com/overview/Outlook/6.99/over-economy.html (accessed 29 Sept. 1999).

Melossi, D., and Pavarini, M. (1979). *The Prison and the Factory: Origins of the Penitentiary System*. London: Macmillan.

Merton, R. (1957). *Social Theory and Social Structure*. Glencoe, IL: Free Press.

Mesny, A. (1998). 'The Appropriation of Social Science Knowledge by Lay People: The Development of a Lay Sociological Imagination?' Discussion paper, University of Cambridge.

Metcalfe, J. S., and Boden, M. (1993). 'Paradigms, Strategies and the Evolutionary Basis of Technological Competition', in G. M. P. Swann (ed.), *New Technologies and the Firm*. London: Routledge.

Middleton, D. (1997). 'Conversational Remembering and Uncertainty: Interdependencies of Experience as Individual and Collective Concerns in Team work'. *Journal of Language and Social Psychology*, 16/4: 389–410.

Miles, I., and Thomas, G. (1995). 'User Resistance to New Interactive Media: Participants, Processes and Paradigms', in M. Bauer (ed.), *Resistance to New Technology*. Cambridge: Cambridge University Press.

Miller, D. (1998). 'A Theory of Virtualism', in D. Miller and J. Carrier (eds.), *Virtualism: A New Political Economy*. Oxford: Berg.

——and Slater, D. (2000). *The Internet: An Ethnographic Approach*. Oxford: Berg.

Mitchell, W. (1995). *City of Bits: Space, Place and the Infobahn*. Cambridge, MA: MIT Press.

——(1999). 'The City of Bits Hypothesis', in D. Schön, B. Sanyal, and W. Mitchell (eds.), *High Technology and Low-Income Communities: Prospects for the Positive Use of Advanced Information Technology*. Cambridge, MA: MIT Press.

Moody, F. (1999). *The Visionary Position: Mapping the Virtual World*. London: Allen Lane.

Moss Kanter, R. (1972). *Commitment and Community: Communes and Utopias in Sociological Perspective*. Cambridge, MA: Harvard University Press.

Mousund, J. (1997). 'SANCTUARY: Social Support on the Internet', in J. Behar (ed.), *Mapping Cyberspace*. Binghampton, NY: Dowling College Press.

Muckersie, D. (1996). *'Continuous Assessment'. Managing Higher Education Series*. London: Hobson's Publishing plc.

Muncer, S., Burrows, R., Pleace, N., Loader, B., and Nettleton, S. (2000). 'Births, Deaths Sex and Marriage...But Very Few Presents? A Case Study of Social Support in Cyberspace'. *Critical Public Health*, 18/1: 1–18.

Musheno, M., Levine, J., and Palumbo, D. (1978). 'Television Surveillance and Crime Prevention: Evaluating an Attempt to Create Defensible Space in Public Housing' *Social Science Quarterly*, 58: 647–56.

Myers, G. (1991). 'Conflicting Perceptions of Plans for an Academic Research Centre' *Research Policy*, 20: 217–35.

—— (1993). 'The Rhetoric of Disciplines in Proposals for an Interdisciplinary Research Centre'. *Science, Technology and Human Values*, 18: 433–59.

Narayan, S. (1996). 'What's Happening?' *CCTV Today* (Nov.), 20–4.

National Strategy for Neighbourhood Renewal (2000). 'Policy Action Team Report Summaries: a compendium, PAT 2 Skills'; www.cabinet-office.gov.uk/ser/2000/coupendium/02.htm.

Neal, A. G., and Youngelson, H. L. (1988). 'The Folklore of Wall Street: Gamesmanship, Gurus and the Myth-Making Process'. *Journal of American Culture*, 11: 55–62.

Negroponte, N. (1995). *Being Digital*. London: Hodder & Stroughton.

Nelson, R., and Winter, S. (1982). *An Evolutionary Theory of Economic Change*. Cambridge, MA: Harvard University Press.

Newman, O. (1972). *Defensible Space*. New York: Macmillan.

Newstead, S. (1998). 'Individual Differences in Student Motivation', in S. Brown, S. Armstrong, and G. Thompson (eds.), *Motivating Students*. London: Kogan Page, 189–99.

Ngwenyama, O. K., and Lee, A. S. (1997). 'Communication Richness in Electronic Mail: Critical Social Theory and the Contextuality of Meaning'. *MIS Quarterly*, 21/2: 145–67.

Nie, N. H., and Erbring, L. (2000). 'Internet and Society: A Preliminary Report'; www.stanford.edu/group/sigss/press Release/Preliminary Report.pdf.

Nocera, J. (1996). 'Investing in a Fool's Paradise'. *Fortune*, 133: 86 *et passim*.

Nonaka, I., and Takeuchi, H. (1995). *The Knowledge-Creating Company: How Japanese Companies Create the Dynamics of Innovation*. New York: Oxford University Press.

NOP Research Group (1999). 'Internet User Profile Study, Wave 8 Core Data'; www.no-pres.co.uk.

Norris, C., Armstrong, G., and Moran, J. (1998). 'Algorithmic surveillance: The Future of Automated Visual Surveillance', in C. Norris, G. Armstrong, and J. Moran (eds.), *Surveillance, Closed Circuit Television and Social Control*. Aldershot: Ashgate.

NTIA (2002): National Telecommunications and Information Administration, 'A Nation Online: How Americans are Expanding their Use of the Internet'. US Department of Commerce, www.ntia.doc.gov/ntiahome/dn/Nation_Online.pdf.

Oblinger, D. O., and Rush, S. C. (1998). *The Future Compatible Campus: Planning, Designing, and Implementing Information Technology*. Boston: Anker.

OECD (1998): Organization for Economic Cooperation and Development, *Gateways to the Global Market: Consumers and Electronic Commerce*. Paris: OECD.

—— (1999). *The Economic and Social Impact of Electronic Commerce*. Paris: OECD.

Office of the e-Envoy (2001). Report from the e-Minister and e-Envoy, 2 July; http://www.citu.gov.uk/publications/reports/pmreports/rep2july.htm (accessed 11 July 2001).

Office of Science and Technology (1998). *Communications Technology: Visions Document*. London: HMSO.

Office of Telecommunications (2001). 'Consumers' Use of Internet: OFTEL Residential Survey'. OFTEL; www.oftel.gov.uk/publications/research/2001/q6intr1101.htm.

Oldenberg, R. (1991). *The Great Good Place: Cafes Coffee Shops Community Centres Beauty Parlors General Stores Bars Hangouts and How they Get you Through the Day*. New York: Paragon House.

Ong, W. J. (1988). *Orality and Literacy: The Technologizing of the Word*. London: Routledge.

Osborne, A. (1999). 'Sainsbury's Ends Home Shopping', *Daily Telegraph*, 18 May, 29.

Ottensmeyer, E. J., and McCarthy (1996). *Ethics in the Workplace*. New York: McGraw Hill.

Owen, D. E. (1983). *The Manchester Ship Canal.* Manchester: Manchester University Press.

Pakenham, T. (1991). *The Scramble for Africa.* London: Weidenfeld & Nicolson.

Peirce, C. S. (1991). *Peirce on Signs,* ed. J. Hoopes. Chapel Hill, NC: University of North Carolina Press.

Performance and Innovation Unit (1999). 'e-commerce@its.best.uk'.

Perri 6 (1997). *Escaping Poverty: From Safety Nets to Networks of Opportunity.* London: Demos.

Pew Internet Project (2001). 'Internet and American Life'; www.pewinternet.org/reports.

Pfaffenberger, B. (1995). 'Technical Ritual: Of Yams, Canoes, and the De-legitimation of Technology Studies in Social Anthropology'. ESRC Seminar on Technology as Skilled Practice, University of Manchester.

Phillips, D. J. (1996). 'Defending the Boundaries: Identifying and Countering Threats in a Usenet Newsgroup'. *Information Society* 12: 39–62.

Pimentel, K., and Teixeira, K. (1995). *Virtual Reality: Through the New Looking Glass.* 2nd edn. New York: Intel/McGraw-Hill.

Pleace, N., Burrows, R., Loader, B., Muncer, S., and Nettleton, S. (2000). 'On Line with the Friends of Bill W: Problem Drinkers, the Internet and Self Help' *Sociological Research On Line,* 5(2).

Pokras, S. (1997). *Working in Teams: A Team Member Guidebook.* Menlo Park, CA: Crisp Publications.

Policy Action Team 15 (2000). *Closing the Digital Divide: Information and Communication Technologies in Deprived Areas.* London: Department of Trade and Industry.

Pool, I. D. S. (1977) (ed.), *The Social Uses of the Telephone.* Cambridge, MA: MIT Press.

Postmes, T. (1997). 'Social Influence in Computer-Mediated Groups'. Unpublished Ph.D. thesis, University of Amsterdam.

——and Lea, M. (2000). 'Social Processes and Group Decision Making: Anonymity in Group Decision Support Systems'. *Ergonomics,* 43 (special issue on contemporary theory and methods in the analysis of team working), 1152–274.

——and Spears, R. (1998). 'Deindividuation and Antinormative Behaviour: A Meta-Analysis'. *Psychological Bulletin,* 123: 238–59.

————(1999). 'When Boys will be Boys, and it's all Girl's Talk: Status Differences in Computer-Mediated Group Discussions'. Unpublished typescript.

————and Lea, M. (1998). 'Breaching or Building Social Boundaries? SIDE-Effects of Computer Mediated Communication'. *Communication Research* 25 (special issue on (mis)communicating across boundaries), 689–715.

——————(2000a). 'The Formation of Group Norms in Computer-Mediated Communication'. *Human Communication Research,* 26: 341–71.

——————and Reicher, S. (2000b). SIDE Issues Centre-Stage: Recent Developments in Studies of Deindividuation in Groups. Amsterdam: KNAW.

————Sakhel, K., and de Groot, D. (2001). 'Social Influence in Computer-Mediated Groups: The Effects of Anonymity on Social Behaviour'. *Personality and Social Psychology Bulletin,* 27: 1243–54.

Potter, J. (1996). *Representing Reality: Discourse Rhetoric and Social Construction.* London Sage.

Powell, W. (1996). 'Interorganizational Collaboration in the Biotechnology Industry' *Journal of Institutional and Theoretical Economics,* 120: 197–215.

——Koput, K., Bowie, J., and Smith-Doerr, L. (2001). 'The Spatial Clustering of Science and Capital'. Paper presented at International Workshop, Socio-Economics of Space, University of Bonn.

Power, M. (1994). *The Audit Explosion*. London: Demos.

—— (1997). *The Audit Society: Rituals of Verification*. Oxford: Oxford University Press.

Premack, D., and Premack, J. (1996). 'Why Animals Lack Pedagogy and Some Cultures have More of it than Others', in D. Olson and N. Torrance (eds.), *The Handbook of Education and Human Development*. Oxford: Blackwell.

Price Waterhouse Coopers (2000). 'CBI Survey on e-Business', *Financial World* (Mar.).

Proust, M. (1981). *In Remembrance of Things Past*. iii. Harmondsworth: Penguin.

Putnam, R. (2000). *Bowling Alone: The Collapse and Revival of American Community*. New York: Simon & Schuster.

Radley, A. (1990). 'Artefacts, Memory and a Sense of the Past', in D. Middleton and D. Edwards (eds.), *Collective Remembering*. London: Sage.

Randall, D., and Hughes, J. A. (1994). 'Sociology, CSCW and Working with Customers', in P. Thomas (ed.), *Social and Interaction Dimensions of System Design*. Cambridge: Cambridge University Press.

——O'Brien, J., Rouncefield, M., and Hughes, J. (1996). 'Organisational Memory and CSCW: Supporting the "Mavis" Phenomenon'. Paper presented at OzCHI 96 conference, Hamilton, New Zealand.

——Hughes, J., O'Brien, J., Rodden, T., Rouncefield, M., Sommerville, I., and Tolmie, P. (1998*a*). 'Banking on the Old Technology: Understanding the Organizational Context of "Legacy" issues'. Paper presented at the Labour Process Conference, Manchester.

——O'Brien, J., Rouncefield, M., and Tolmie, P. (1998*b*). 'Customers and Cooperation'. Paper Presented at NCR Workshop in Financial Services, Lancaster University, May.

——Hughes, J., O'Brien, J., Rodden, T., Rouncefield, M., Sommerville, I., and Tolmie, P. (1999). 'Banking on the Old Technology: Understanding the Organizational Context of "Legacy" Issues'. *Communications of the Association for Information Systems*, 1: Article 21.

Redford, A., with the assistance of Russell, I. S. (1940). *The History of Local Government in Manchester*. London: Longmans.

Reeve, S. (1998). 'Net Loss'. *European*, 16–22 Feb., 26–7.

Reicher, S. D. (1984). 'Social Influence in the Crowd: Attitudinal and Behavioural Effects of Deindividuation in Conditions of High and Low Group Salience'. *British Journal of Social Psychology*, 23: 341–50.

—— (1987). 'Crowd Behaviour as Social Action', in J. C. Turner, M. A. Hogg, P. J. Oakes, S. D. Reicher, and M. S. Wetherell (eds.), *Rediscovering the Social Group: A Self-Categorization Theory*. Oxford: Blackwell.

——Spears, R., and Postmes, T. (1995). 'A Social Identity Model of Deindividuation Phenomena', in W. Stroebe and M. Hewstone (eds.), *European Review of Social Psychology*. Chichester: Wiley, vi. 161–98.

Rheingold, H. (1991). *Virtual Reality*. New York: Simon & Schuster and Touchstone.

—— (1993). *The Virtual Community: Homesteading on the Electronic Frontier*. New York: Addison-Wesley.

—— (1998). 'The Virtual Community'; www.rheingold.com/vc/book.

Rice, R. E. (1993). 'Media Appropriateness: Using Social Presence Theory to Compare Traditional and New Organizational Media'. *Human Communication Research*, 19: 451–84.

Rice, R. E. and Love, G. (1987). 'Electronic Emotion: Socioemotional Content in a Computer-Mediated Communication Network'. *Communication Research*, 14/1: 85–108.

Richardson, J. T. E. (2000). *Researching Student Learning: Approaches to Studying in Campus-Based and Distance Education*. Buckingham: SRHE and Open University Press.

Richter, I. A. (1952). *Notebooks of Leonardo da Vinci*. Oxford: Oxford University Press.

Riles, A. (1999). 'Seeing through Virtualism: Formalism and the Propertization of Time, for Panel "Temporal Horizons of Property" '. Paper presented at American Anthropological Association meetings.

—— (2000). *The Network Inside Out*. Ann Arbor: Michigan University Press.

Roberts, D., and Warwick, K. (1993). 'An Overview of Virtual Reality', in K. Warwick, J. Gray, and D. Roberts (eds.), *Virtual Reality in Engineering* (IEE computing series 20). London: Institution of Electrical Engineers.

Roberts, R. (1998). 'Time, Virtuality and the Goddess', in S. Lash, A. Quick, and R. Roberts (eds.), *Time and Value*. Oxford: Blackwell.

Romm, C. T., and Pliskin, N. (1999). 'The Office Tyrant: Social Control through E-Mail'. *Information Technology & People*, 12/1: 27–43.

Ronell, A. (1989). *The Telephone Book*. Lincoln, NE: University of Nebraska Press.

Rose, M. B. (1996). *The Lancashire Cotton Industry: A History Since 1700*. Preston: Lancashire County Books.

Rule, J. B. (1996). 'High-Tech Workplace Surveillance: What's Really New?', in D. Lyon and E. Zureik (eds.), *Computers, Surveillance and Privacy*. London: University of Minnesota Press.

Rutter, D. R. (1987). *Communicating by Telephone*. Oxford: Pergamon.

Sacks, H. (1992). 'A Single Instance of a Phone-Call Opening: Caller-Called, etc.', in G. Jefferson (ed.) *Lectures on Conversation*, Cambridge, MA: Blackwell, vol. II, pt. viii, lecture 3.

Sahal, D. (1985). 'Technology Guide-Posts and Innovation Avenues', *Research Policy*, 14/2: 61–82.

Saxenian, A.-L. (1994). *Regional Advantage: Culture and Competition in Silicon Valley and Route 128*. Cambridge, MA: Harvard University Press.

Schiller, D. (2000). *Digital Capitalism: Networking the Global Market System*. Cambridge, MA: MIT Press.

Schlecker, M., and Hirsch, E. (2001). 'Incomplete Knowledge: Ethnography and the Crisis of Context in Studies of Media, Science and Technology'. *History of the Human Sciences*, 14: 69–87.

Schuler, D. (1996). *New Community Networks: Wired for Change*. Reading, MA: Addison-Wesley.

Scott, P. (2000). 'The Impact of the Research Assessment Exercise on the Quality of British Science and Scholarship', *Anglistik*, 1: 129–43.

Segal, H. (1994). 'The Cultural Contradictions of High Tech', in E. Ezrahi, E. Mendelsohn, and H. P. Segal (eds.), *Technology, Pessimism, and Postmodernism*. Amherst, MA: University of Massachusetts Press.

Sewell, G., and Wilkinson, B. (1992). ' "Someone to watch over me": Surveillance, Discipline and the Just-in-Time Labour Process'. *Sociology*, 26/2: 271–89.

Shearman, C., and Communities on Line (1999). *Local Connections: Making the Net Work for Neighbourhood Renewal*. London: Communities on Line.

Sherman, W. R., and Craig, A. B. (1995). 'Literacy in Virtual Reality: A New Medium'. *Computer Graphics*, 29/4; http://archive.ncsa.edu/vrs/Publications/vrhit.html.

Sherwell, P. (2000). 'Magic is a Powerful Weapon in Sierra Leone'. *Sunday Telegraph*, 25 May.

Shields, R. (2000). 'Virtual Spaces?' *Space and Culture*, 4/5: 1–12.

Shiller, R. J. (2000). *Irrational Exuberance*. Princeton: Princeton University Press.

Shore, C., and Wright, S. (2000). 'Coercive Accountability: The New Audit Culture in Higher Education', in M. Strathern (ed.), *Audit Cultures: Anthropological Studies in Accountability, Ethics and the Academy*. London: Routledge.

Short, J., Williams, E., and Christie, B. (1976). *The Social Psychology of Telecommunications*. Chichester: Wiley & Son.

Siegel, D. (1999). *Futurise your Enterprise*. London: Wiley.

——Dubrovsky, V., Kiesler, S., and McGuire, T. (1986). 'Group Processes in Computer-Mediated Communication'. *Organizational Behaviour and Human Decision Processes*, 37: 157–87.

Silver, D. (2000). 'Looking Backwards, Looking Forwards: Cyberculture Studies 1990–2000', in D. Gauntlett (ed.), *Web.studies*. London: Arnold.

Silverstone, R., and Hirsch, E. (1992) (eds.). *Consuming Technologies: Media and Information in Domestic Spaces*. London: Routledge.

Simmel, G. (1997). 'The Metropolis and Mental Life', in D. Frisby and M. Featherstone (eds.), *Simmel on Culture*. London: Sage.

Simon, H. (1985). 'What do we Know about the Creative Process', in R. L. Kuhn (ed.), *Frontiers in Creative and Innovative Management*. Cambridge, MA: Ballinger.

Sinclair, D. (2001). 'Is "Big Brother" a Myth?' *Guardian*, 15 Mar.

Skilton, M. (1986). *Making an Entrance: Improving Living Conditions in Tower Blocks*. London: London Borough of Brent.

Slevin, J. (2000). *The Internet and Society*. Cambridge: Polity.

Slouka, M. Z. (1996). *War of the Worlds: Cyberspace and the High-Tech Assault on Reality*. London: Abacus.

Smith, C., and Agar, J. (1998). *Making Space for Science: Territorial Themes in the Shaping of Knowledge*. Basingstoke: Macmillan in association with the Centre for the History of Science, Technology and Medicine. University of Manchester.

Smith, C. W. (1981). *The Mind of the Market*. New York: Harper & Row.

Smith, M. A. (1999). 'Invisible Crowds in Cyberspace: Mapping the Social Structure of the Usenet', in M. A. Smith and P. Kollock (eds.), *Communities in Cyberspace*. London: Routledge.

——and Kollock, P. (1999) (eds.). *Communities in Cyberspace*. London: Routledge.

Soros, G. (1994). *The Alchemy of France*. New York: John Wiley & Sons.

——(1998). *The Crisis of Global Capitalism: Open Society Endangered*. New York: Public Affairs.

Spears, R., and Lea, M. (1992). 'Social Influence and the Influence of the "social" in Computer-Mediated Communication', in M. Lea (ed.), *Contexts of Computer-Mediated Communication*. Hemel-Hempstead: Harvester-Wheatsheaf.

————(1994). 'Panacea or Panopticon: The Hidden Power in Computer-Mediated Communication'. *Communication Research*, 21: 427–59.

————and Lee, S. (1990). 'De-Individuation and Group Polarization in Computer-Mediated Communication'. *British Journal of Social Psychology*, 29: 121–34.

Spears, R., Lea, M., and Postmes, T. (2001a). 'Social Psychological Theories of Computer-Mediated Communication: Social Pain or Social Gain?', in W. P. Robinson and H. Giles (eds.), *The New Handbook of Language and Social Psychology*. Chichester: Wiley, 601–23.

Spears, R., Postmes, T., Lea, M., and Watt, S. E. (2001b). 'A SIDE View of Social Influence', in J. P. Forgas and K. D. Williams (eds.), *Social Influence: Direct and Indirect Processes*. Philadelphia, PA: Psychology Press, 331–50.

Spector, R. (2000). *Amazon.com: Get Big Fast (Inside the Revolutionary Business Model that Changed the World)*. London: Random House.

Spinello, R. A. (1995). *Ethical Aspects of Information Technology*. Englewood Cliffs, NJ: Prentice-Hall.

Springer, C. (1996). *Electronic Eros: Bodies and Desire in the Postindustrial Age*. London: Athlone Press.

Sproull, L., and Kiesler, S. (1986). 'Reducing Social Context Cues: Electronic Mail in Organizational Communication'. *Management Science*, 32: 1492–512.

—— —— (1998). *Connections: New Ways of Working in the Networked Organization*. 6th edn. Cambridge, MA: MIT Press.

Stark, D. (1999). 'Heterarchy: Distributed Authority and Organizing of Diversity', in J. H. Clippinger (ed.), *The Biology of Business: Decoding the Natural Laws of Enterprise*. San Francisco: Jossey-Bass.

Stengers, I., and Gille, D. (1997). 'Time and Representation', in I. Stengers and P. Bains (eds.), *Power and Invention: Situating Science*. Minneapolis: University of Minnesota Press.

Stephenson, N. (1993). *Snow Crash*. London: Penguin.

Steuer, J. (1992). 'Defining Virtual Reality: Dimensions Determining Telepresence'. *Journal of Communication*, 42/4: 73–93.

Stevenson, A. (1997). 'Barclays Bank Information Strategy'. Quoted by Mike Gibson-Sharpe, Marketing Manager, International Business Division of BT.

Stoll, C. (1995). *Silicon Snake Oil: Second Thoughts on the Information Highway*. New York: Doubleday.

Stone, R. J. (1996). *A Study of the Virtual Reality Market*. London: Department of Trade and Industry.

—— and Swann, G. M. P. (2001). 'Virtually a Market? Selling Practice and the Diffusion of Virtual Reality', in K. M. Stanney (ed.), *Virtual Environments Handbook*. Mahwah, NJ: Lawrence Erlbaum Associates.

Storey, J. (1989). *New Perspectives on Human Resource Management*. London: Routledge.

Strathern, M. (1995). 'The Relation Issues in Complexity and Scale'. Prickly Pear Pamphlet 6, University of Cambridge.

—— (1997). ' "Improving Ratings": Audit in the British University System'. *European Review*, 5: 305–21.

—— (1999a). 'Bullet Proofing'. Seminar in Political Thought and Intellectual History, Faculty of Philosophy, University of Cambridge.

—— (1999b). 'The Ethnographic Effect', in C. Essays (ed.), *Property, Substance and Effect: Anthropological Essays on Persons and Things*. London: Athlone Press.

—— (2000). 'The Tyranny of Transparency'. *British Education Research Journal*, 26: 309–21.

Suchman, L. (1987). *Plans and Situated Action: The Problem of Human–Machine Communication*. Cambridge: Cambridge University Press.

Sudweeks, F., McLaughlin, M., and Rafaeli, S. (1998). *Networks and Netplay: Virtual Groups on the Internet*. Cambridge, MA: MIT Press.

Sullivan, C. D. (1983). *Standards and Standardization: Basic Principles and Applications*. New York: Marcel Dekker.

Summerton, J. (1994). *Changing Large Technical Systems*. Boulder, CO: Westview Press.

Swann, G. M. P. (1999). 'The Internet and the Distribution of Economic Activity', in S. Macdonald, J. Nightingale, and D. Allen (eds.), *Information and Organization: A Tribute to the Work of Don Lamberton*. Amsterdam: Elsevier.

——and Gill, J. (1993). *Corporate Vision and Rapid Technological Change*. London: Routledge.

——and Watts, T. P. (2001). 'Visualization, Narrative and Market: The Economics of Virtual Reality'. Unpublished typescript.

——Temple, P., and Shurmer, M. (1996). 'Standards and Trade Performance: The British Experience'. *Economic Journal*, 106: 1297–313.

Tajfel, H., and Turner, J. C. (1979). 'An Integrative Theory of Intergroup Conflict', in W. G. Austin and S. Worchel (eds.), *The Social Psychology of Intergroup Relations*. Monterey, CA: Brooks/Cole.

Terranova, T. (2000). 'Free Labor: Producing Culture for the Digital Economy'. *Social Text*, 18/2: 33–58.

Thoits, P. A. (1995). 'Stress, Coping and Social Support Processes: Where are we? What Next?' *Journal of Health and Social Behaviour*, Extra Issue: 53–79.

Thomas, G., and Wyatt, S. (1999). 'Shaping Cyberspace: Interpreting and Transforming the Internet'. *Research Policy*, 28/7: 681–98.

—— —— (2000). 'Access is not the Only Problem: Using and Controlling the Internet', in S. Wyatt (ed.), *Technology and In/equality: Questioning the Information Society*. London: Routledge.

Thomas, R. R., Jr. (1991). 'Beyond Race and Gender: Unleashing the Power of your Total Workforce by Managing Diversity'. New York: AMACOM American Management Association.

Thompson, P., and Ackroyd, S. (1995). 'All Quiet on the Workplace Front? A Critique of Recent Trends in British Industrial Sociology'. *Sociology*, 29/4: 615–33.

Toffler, A. (1971). *Future Shock*. London: Pan.

Tolmie, A., and Boyle, J. (2000). 'Factors Influencing the Success of Computer Mediated Communication (CMC) Environments in University Teaching: A Review and Case Study'. *Computers and Education*, 34: 119–40.

——Hughes, J. A., O'Brien, J., and Rouncefield, M. (1998a). 'The Importance of Being Earnest: Everyday Managerial Work in Financial Services', Paper presented at NCR Workshop in Financial Services, Lancaster University.

—— ——Rouncefield, M., and Sharrock, W. (1998b). 'Managing Relationships: Where the "Virtual" meets the "Real"'. Paper presented at the European Association for the Study of Science and Technology Conference, Lisbon, 1–3 Oct.

—— —— —— —— (1998c). 'The "virtual" Manager?: Change and Continuity in Managerial Work'. Work, Employment, and Society Conference, Cambridge.

—— —— —— —— (1999a). 'Real Work in the "Virtual" Organization'. Paper presented at the Society for Social Studies of Science (4S) Conference, San Diego.

—— —— —— —— (1999b). 'Working with the Work: Process Modelling in Financial Services'. Paper presented at the BSA Workplace Studies Symposium, Manchester.

—— ——Rodden, T., and Rouncefield, M. (2000). 'Representing Knowledge'. Paper presented at KMAC 2000 Knowledge Management Beyond the Hype Conference, Birmingham.

Toulouse, C., and Luke, T. W. (1998) (eds.). *The Politics of Cyberspace*. London: Routledge.

Townsend, A. (2001). 'Mobile Communications in the 21st Century City', in B. Brown, N. Green, and R. Harper (eds.), *Wireless World: Social and Interactional Aspects of the Mobile Age*. London: Springer-Verlag.

Traweek, S. (1988). *Beamtimes and Lifetimes: The World of High Energy Physicists*. Cambridge, MA: Harvard University Press.

Tsagarousianou, R., Tambini, D., and Bryan, C. (1998). *Cyberdemocracy: Technology, Cities and Civic Networks*, London: Routledge.

Tsoukas, H. (1994). 'Introduction: From Social Engineering to Reflective Action', in H. Tsoukas (ed.), *New Thinking in Organizational Behaviour: From Social Engineering to Reflective Action in Organizational Behaviour*. Oxford: Butterworth/Heinemann.

Turkle, S. (1996). 'Virtuality and its Discontents: Searching for Community in Cyberspace'. *American Prospect*, 24: 50–7.

Turner, J. C., Hogg, M. A., Oakes, P. J., Reicher, S. D., and Wetherell, M. S. (1987). *Rediscovering the Social Group: A Self-Categorization Theory*. New York: Blackwell.

Turner, M. J. (1994). 'Gas, Police and the Struggle for Mastery in Manchester in the Eighteen-Twenties'. *Historical Research*, 67: 301–17.

Unit, S. S. N. (1985). *After Entryphones: Improving Management and Security in Multi-Storey Blocks*. London: HMSO.

—— (1994). *High Expectations: A Guide to the Development of Concierge Schemes and Controlled Access in High Rise Social Housing*. London: HMSO.

—— (1997). *High Hopes: Concierge Controlled Entry and Similar Schemes for High Rise Blocks*. London: HMSO.

UNDP (1999): United Nation's Development Programme, *Human Development Report*; www.undp.org/hdro/report.html.

Urry, J. (2000). 'Mobile Sociology'. *British Journal of Sociology*, 51/1: 185–203.

Valsiner, J. (2000). *Culture and Human Development: An Introduction*. London: Sage.

Velody, I. (1999). 'Knowledge for what? The Intellectual Consequences of the Research Assesment Exercise'. *History of Human Sciences*, 12 (Symposium), 111–46.

Virilio, P. (2000). *Polar Inertia*. London: Sage.

Virnoche, M. (1998). 'The Seamless Web and Communications Equity: The Shaping of a Community Network'. *Science, Technology and Human Values*, 23/2: 199–220.

Voyle, S. (2000*a*). 'Tesco Planning to Create 20,000 Jobs'. *Financial Times*, 3 Apr.

—— (2000*b*). 'Tesco Plans to put e-Commerce in own Basket'. *Financial Times*, 12 Apr.

Wakeford, N. (2000). 'New Media, New Methodologies: Studying the Web', in D. Gauntlett (ed.), Web.studies. London: Arnold.

Walter, T. (1999). *On Bereavement: The Culture of Grief*. Buckingham: Open University Press.

Walther, J. B. (1992). 'Interpersonal Effects in Computer-Mediated Interaction: A Relational Perspective'. *Communication Research*, 19: 52–90.

—— (1994). 'Anticipated Ongoing Interaction Versus Channel Effects on Relational Communication in Computer-Mediated Interaction'. *Human Communication Research*, 20: 473–501.

—— (1997). 'Group and Interpersonal Effects in International Computer-Mediated Collaboration'. *Human Communication Research*, 24: 186–203.

—— and Burgoon, J. K. (1992). 'Relational Communication in Computer-Mediated Interaction'. *Human Communication Research*, 19: 50–88.

Ward, K. (2000). 'The Emergence of the Hybrid Community: Rethinking the Physical Virtual Dichotomy'. *Space and Culture*, 4/5: 71–86.

Ward, M. (2000). 'Some Britons Still Refuse to Surf'. *BBC News Online*, 7 July.

Watson, N. (1997). 'Why we Argue about the Virtual Community: A Case Study of phish.net Fan Community', in S. G. Jones (ed.), *Virtual Culture: Identity and Communication in Cybersociety*. London: Sage.

Watts, T. P., Swann, G. M., and Pandit, N. R. (1998). 'Virtual Reality and Innovation Potential'. *Business Strategy Review*, 9/3: 45–54.

Webb, M., and Palmer, G. (1998). 'Evading Surveillance and Making Time: An Ethnographic View of the Japanese Factory Floor in Britain'. *Work, Employment and Society*, 10/2: 251–71.

Weber, M. (1954). 'Herrschaft durch Organisation'. In Weber, *Wirtschaft und Gesellschaft*. 4th edn. Tübinger: Mohr.

Weber, S. (1996). *Mass Mediauras: Form, Technics, Media*. Stanford, CA: Stanford University Press.

Webster, F. (1995). *Theories of the Information Society*. London: Routledge.

——and Robins, K. (1993). '"I'll be watching you": Comment on Sewell and Wilkinson'. *Sociology*, 27/2: 243–52.

Weick, K. (1977). 'Enactment Processes in Organizations', in B. M. Shaw and G. R. Salacnik (eds.), *New Directions in Organizational Behavior*. Chicago: St Clair Press.

——(1979). *The Social Psychology of Organizing*. Reading, MA: Addison-Wesley.

Weimer, D. M. (1994). 'Brave New Virtual Worlds', in C. A. Pickover and S. K. Tewksbury (eds.), *Frontiers of Scientific Visualization*. New York: John Wiley & Son.

Weinberg, N., Schmale, J., Uken, J., and Wessel, K. (1996). 'Online Help: Cancer Patients Participate in a Computer Mediated Support Group'. *Health and Social Work*. 21/1: 24–9.

Weintraub, J., and Kumar, K. (1997) (eds.). *Public and Private in Thought and Practice*. Chicago: University of Chicago Press.

Weintraut, J., and Davis, J. (1999). 'Building the Bulletproof Net Startup'. *Business* 2.0 (July), 62–8.

Weisband, S. P., Scheider, S. K., and Connolly, T. (1995). 'Computer-Mediated Communication and Social Information: Status Salience and Status Differences'. *Academy of Management Journal*, 38: 1124–51.

Wellman, B. (1998). 'The Network Community', in B. Wellman (ed.), *Networks in the Global Village*; www.chass.utoronto.ca/~wellmann/publications/globalvillage/in.htm.

——and Gulia, M. (1999). 'Virtual Communities as Communities: Net Surfers Don't Ride Alone', in M. A. Smith and P. Kollock (eds.), *Communities in Cyberspace*. London: Routledge.

——Carrington, P., and Hall, A. (1998). 'Networks as Personal Communities', in B. Wellman and S. Berkowitz (eds.), *Social Structures: A Network Approach*. Cambridge: Cambridge University Press.

——Salaff, J., Dimitrova, D., Garton, L., Gulia, M., and Haythornwaite, C. (1988). 'Computer Networks as Social Networks'. *Annual Review of Sociology*, 22: 211–38.

Wells, H. G. (1898/1971). *The War of the Worlds*. Harmondsworth: Penguin.

Wenger, E. (1998). *Communities of Practice*. Cambridge: Cambridge University Press.

Westin, A. (1992). 'Two Key Factors that Belong in a Macroergonomic Analysis of Electronic Monitoring: Employee Perceptions of Fairness and the Climate of Organisational Trust or Distrust'. *Applied Ergonomics*, 23/1: 35–42.

Which? (1998). 'Controversy, Conspiracy or Control: Are we Ready for the e-Nation?' London: *Which? Online.*

White, K. W., and Weight, B. H. (2000). *The Online Teaching Guide: A Handbook of Attitudes, Strategies and Techniques for the Virtual Classroom.* Boston: Allyn & Bacon.

Wieners, B. (1999). 'Pass it on'. *Wired* (July), 60.

Wilbur, S. (2000). 'An Archaeology of Cyberspaces: Virtuality, Community, Identity', in D. Bell and B. Kennedy (eds.), *The Cybercultures Reader.* London: Routledge.

Wilkinson, R. (1996). *Unhealthy Societies: The Afflictions of Inequality.* London: Routledge.

Williams, Raymond (1974). *Television: Technology and Cultural Form.* London: Fontana.

Williams, Robin (1997). 'The Social Shaping of Information and Communications Technologies', in H. Kubicek, W. H. Dutton, and R. Williams (eds.), *The Social Shaping of Information Superhighways.* New York: St Martin's Press.

Williams, S. (1998). 'Capitalizing on Emotions? Rethinking the Inequalities in Health Debate'. *Sociology*, 32/1: 121–40.

——(2000). 'Chronic Illness as Biographical Disruption or Biographical Disruption as Chronic Illness? Reflections on a Core Concept'. *Sociology of Health and Illness*, 22/1: 40–67.

Wills, T. A. (1985). 'Supportive Functions of Interpersonal Relationships', in S. Cohen and S. L. Syme (eds.), *Social Support and Health.* New York: Academic Press.

Wingham, R. (1999). *Net Benefit.* London: Macmillan Business Press.

Winner, L. (2000). 'Enthusiasm and Concern: Results of a New Technology Poll'. *Tech Knowledge Revue*, 29/13.

Winston, B. (1998). *Media Technology and Society.* London: Routledge.

Wired (2001). 'The Wired Index' (June), 93–135.

Wood, D. (1988). *How Children Think and Learn.* Oxford: Blackwell.

Woolgar, S. (1991). 'Configuring the User', in J. Law (ed.), *A Sociology of Monsters: Essays on Power, Technology, and Domination.* London: Routledge.

——(1997). 'Accountability and Identity in the Age of UABs', Discussion paper 60, CRICT, Brunel University.

——(1998). 'A New Theory of Innovation?' *Prometheus*, 16/4: 441–53.

——(1999). 'Analytic Scepticism', in W. D. Dutton (ed.) *Society on the Line: Information Politics in the Digital Age.* Oxford: Oxford University Press.

——(2000a). 'The Social Basis of Interactive Social Science'. *Science and Public Policy*, 27/3: 165–73.

——(2000b). 'Virtual Technologies and Social Theory: A Technographic Approach', in R. Rogers (ed.), *Preferred Placement: Knowlege Politics on the Web.* Maastricht: Jan van Eyck Editions.

——and Cooper, G. (1999). 'Do Artefacts have Ambivalence? Moses' Bridges, Winner's Bridges and other Urban Legends'. *Social Studies of Science*, 29/3: 433–49.

Wyatt, S. (2000). 'Talking about the Future: Metaphors of the Internet', in N. Brown, B. Rappert, and A. Webster (eds.), *Contested Futures.* Aldershot: Ashgate.

Wynn, E., and Katz, J. E. (1997). 'Hyperbole over Cyberspace: Self-presentation and Social Boundaries in Internet Home Pages and Discourse'. *Information Society*, 13: 297–328.

Zimbardo, P. G. (1970). 'The Human Choice: Individuation, Reason, and Order vs. Deindividuation, Impulse and Chaos', in W. J. Arnold and D. Levine (eds.), *Nebraska Symposium on Motivation, 1969.* Lincoln, Neb.: University of Nebraska Press.

Zimmerman, F. O. (1997). 'Structural and managerial aspects of virtual Enterprises'. Paper presented at European Conference on Virtual Enterprises and Networked Solutions, Paderborn, Germany, 7–10 Apr.

INDEX